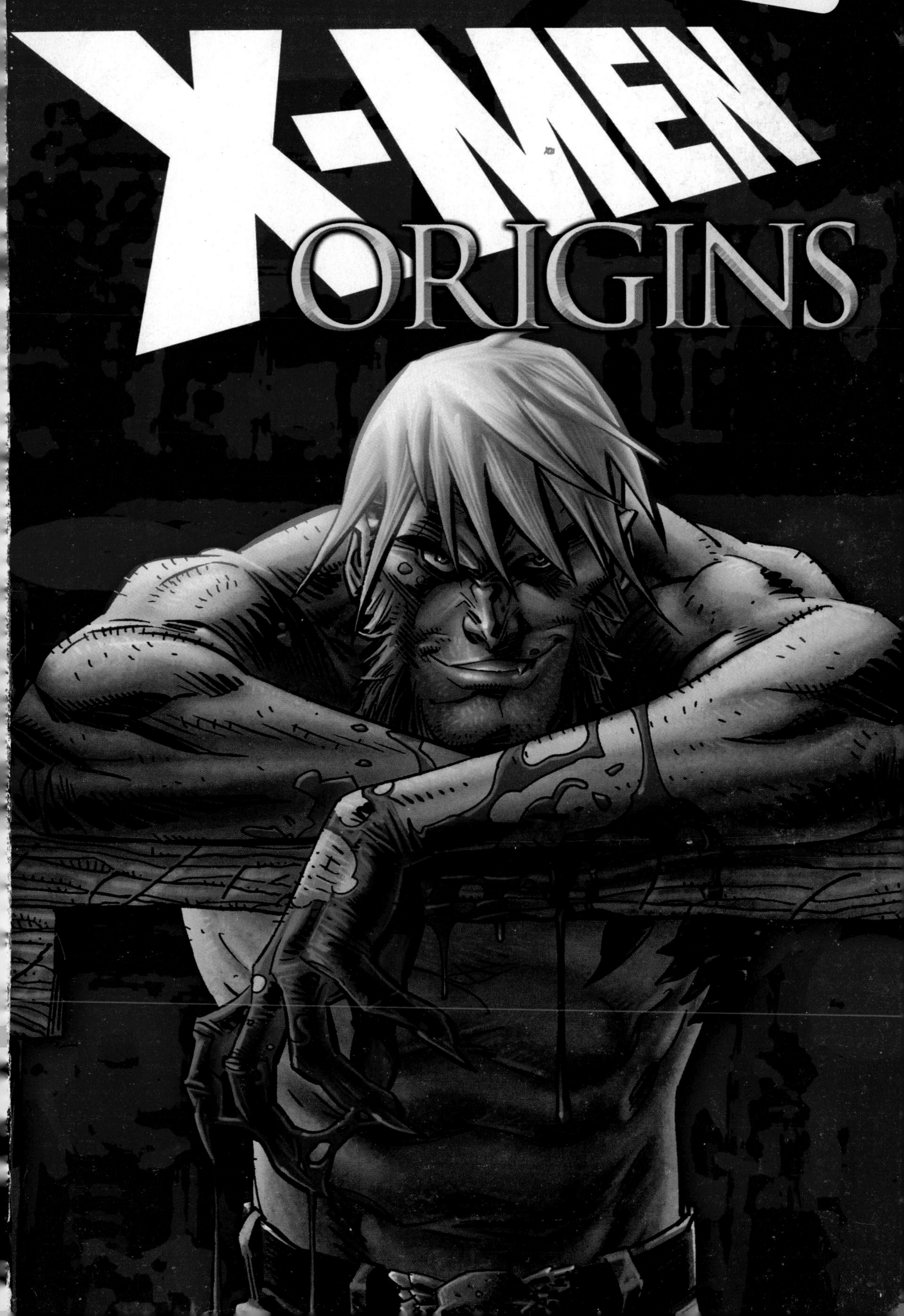
X-MEN
ORIGINS

# X-MEN ORIGINS

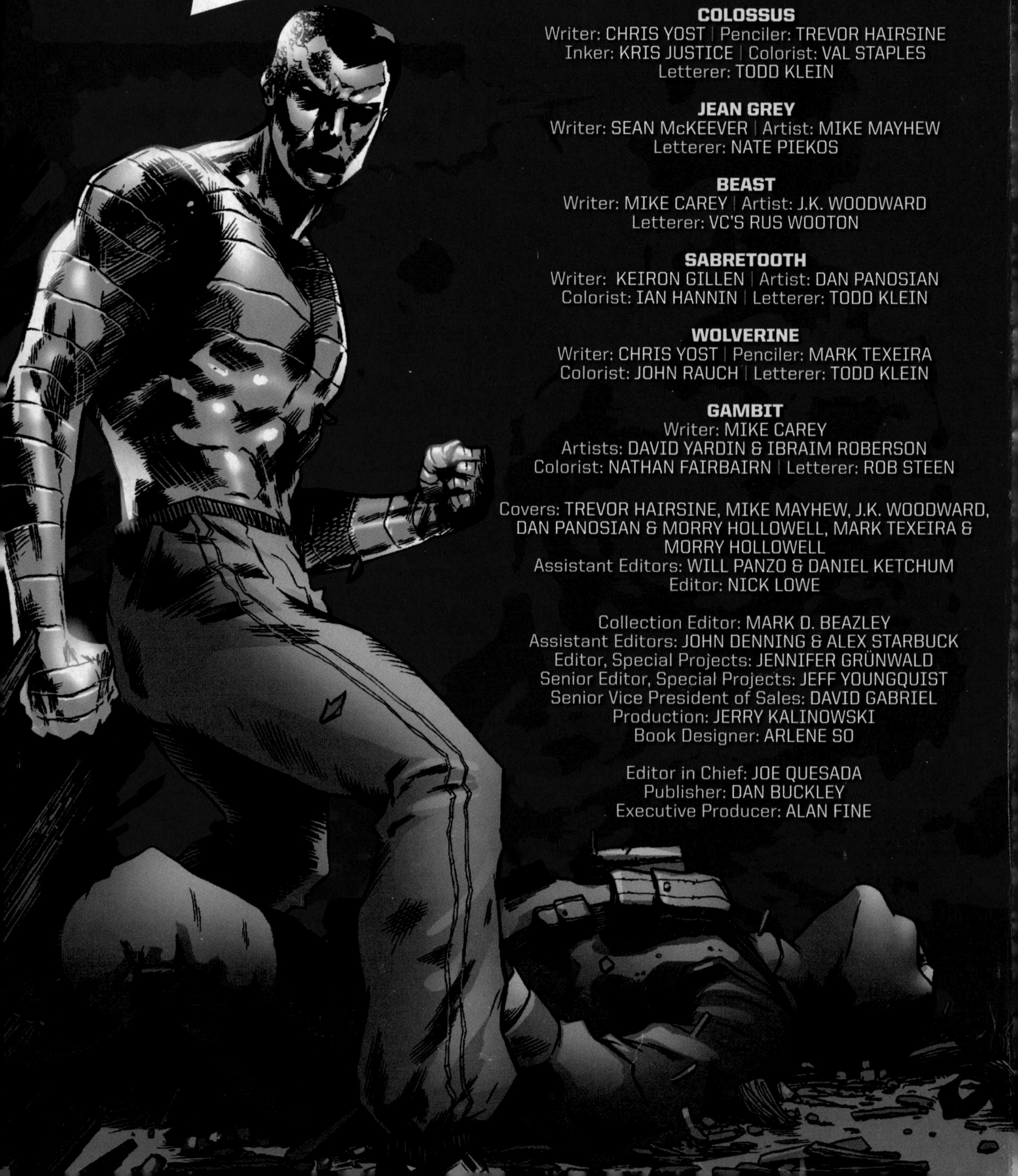

**COLOSSUS**
Writer: CHRIS YOST | Penciler: TREVOR HAIRSINE
Inker: KRIS JUSTICE | Colorist: VAL STAPLES
Letterer: TODD KLEIN

**JEAN GREY**
Writer: SEAN McKEEVER | Artist: MIKE MAYHEW
Letterer: NATE PIEKOS

**BEAST**
Writer: MIKE CAREY | Artist: J.K. WOODWARD
Letterer: VC'S RUS WOOTON

**SABRETOOTH**
Writer: KEIRON GILLEN | Artist: DAN PANOSIAN
Colorist: IAN HANNIN | Letterer: TODD KLEIN

**WOLVERINE**
Writer: CHRIS YOST | Penciler: MARK TEXEIRA
Colorist: JOHN RAUCH | Letterer: TODD KLEIN

**GAMBIT**
Writer: MIKE CAREY
Artists: DAVID YARDIN & IBRAIM ROBERSON
Colorist: NATHAN FAIRBAIRN | Letterer: ROB STEEN

Covers: TREVOR HAIRSINE, MIKE MAYHEW, J.K. WOODWARD, DAN PANOSIAN & MORRY HOLLOWELL, MARK TEXEIRA & MORRY HOLLOWELL
Assistant Editors: WILL PANZO & DANIEL KETCHUM
Editor: NICK LOWE

Collection Editor: MARK D. BEAZLEY
Assistant Editors: JOHN DENNING & ALEX STARBUCK
Editor, Special Projects: JENNIFER GRÜNWALD
Senior Editor, Special Projects: JEFF YOUNGQUIST
Senior Vice President of Sales: DAVID GABRIEL
Production: JERRY KALINOWSKI
Book Designer: ARLENE SO

Editor in Chief: JOE QUESADA
Publisher: DAN BUCKLEY
Executive Producer: ALAN FINE

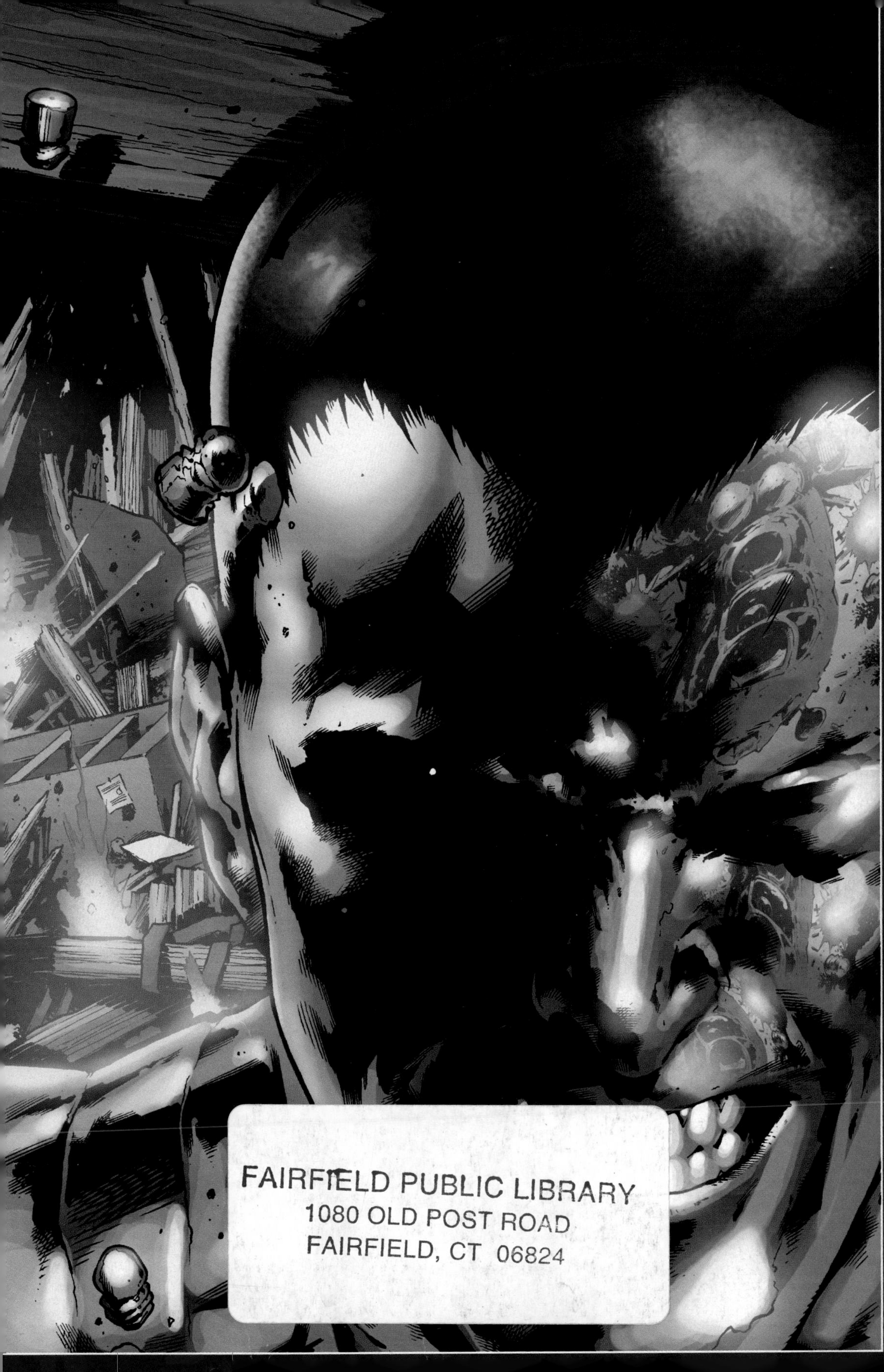

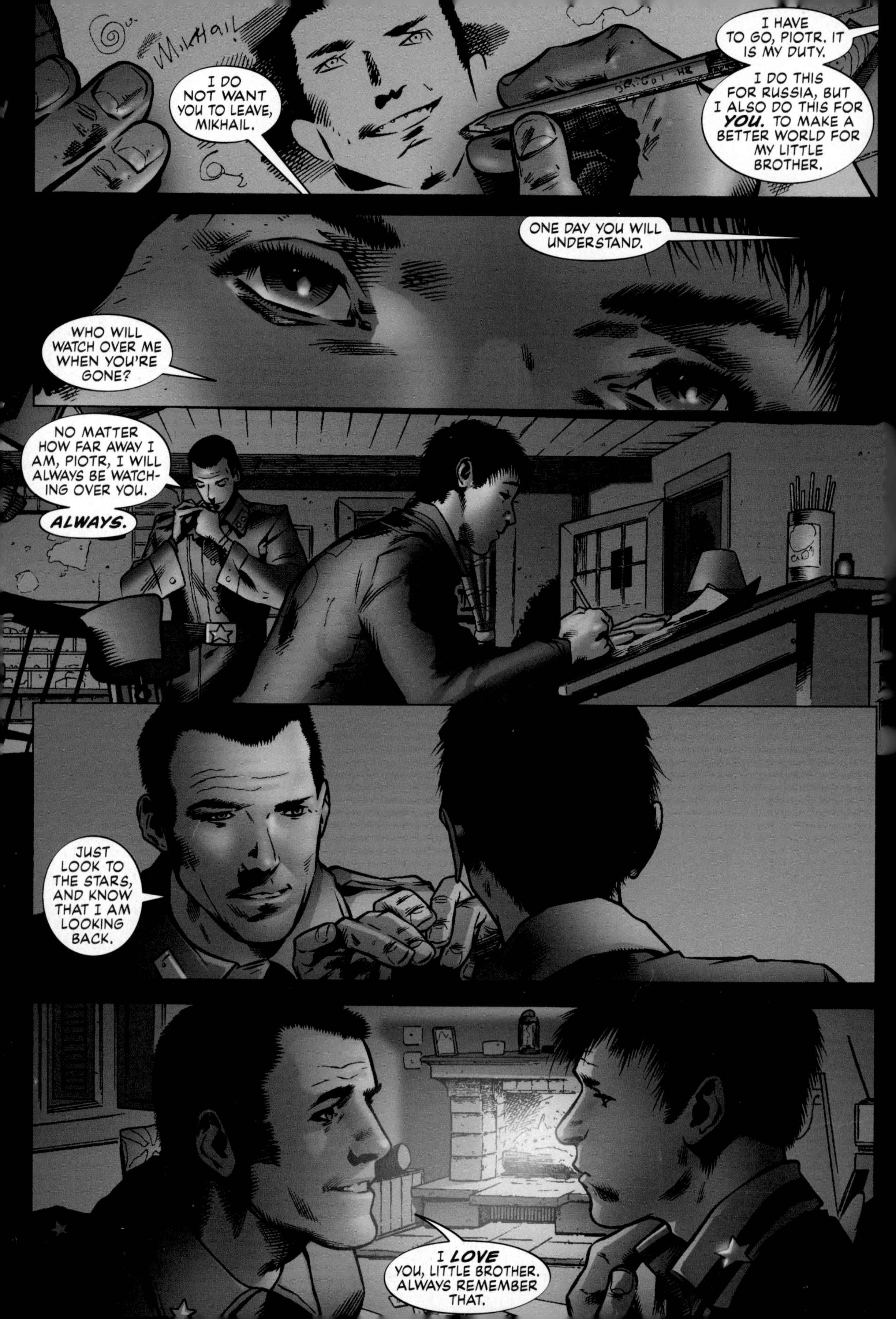
MIKHAIL!
I DO NOT WANT YOU TO LEAVE, MIKHAIL.
I HAVE TO GO, PIOTR. IT IS MY DUTY.
I DO THIS FOR RUSSIA, BUT I ALSO DO THIS FOR YOU. TO MAKE A BETTER WORLD FOR MY LITTLE BROTHER.
ONE DAY YOU WILL UNDERSTAND.
WHO WILL WATCH OVER ME WHEN YOU'RE GONE?
NO MATTER HOW FAR AWAY I AM, PIOTR, I WILL ALWAYS BE WATCHING OVER YOU.
ALWAYS.
JUST LOOK TO THE STARS, AND KNOW THAT I AM LOOKING BACK.
I LOVE YOU, LITTLE BROTHER. ALWAYS REMEMBER THAT.

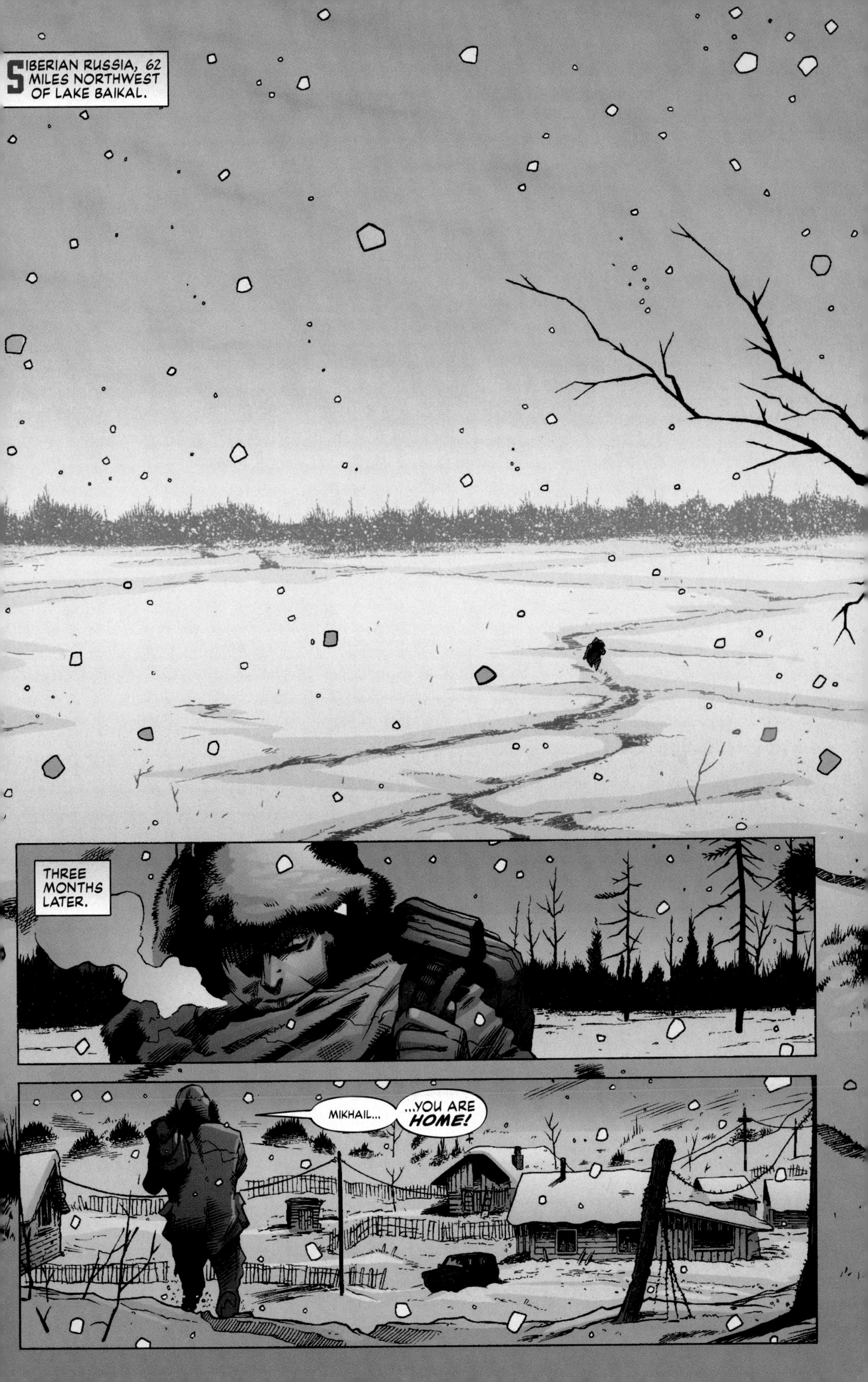

SIBERIAN RUSSIA, 62 MILES NORTHWEST OF LAKE BAIKAL.
THREE MONTHS LATER.
MIKHAIL...
...YOU ARE *HOME!*

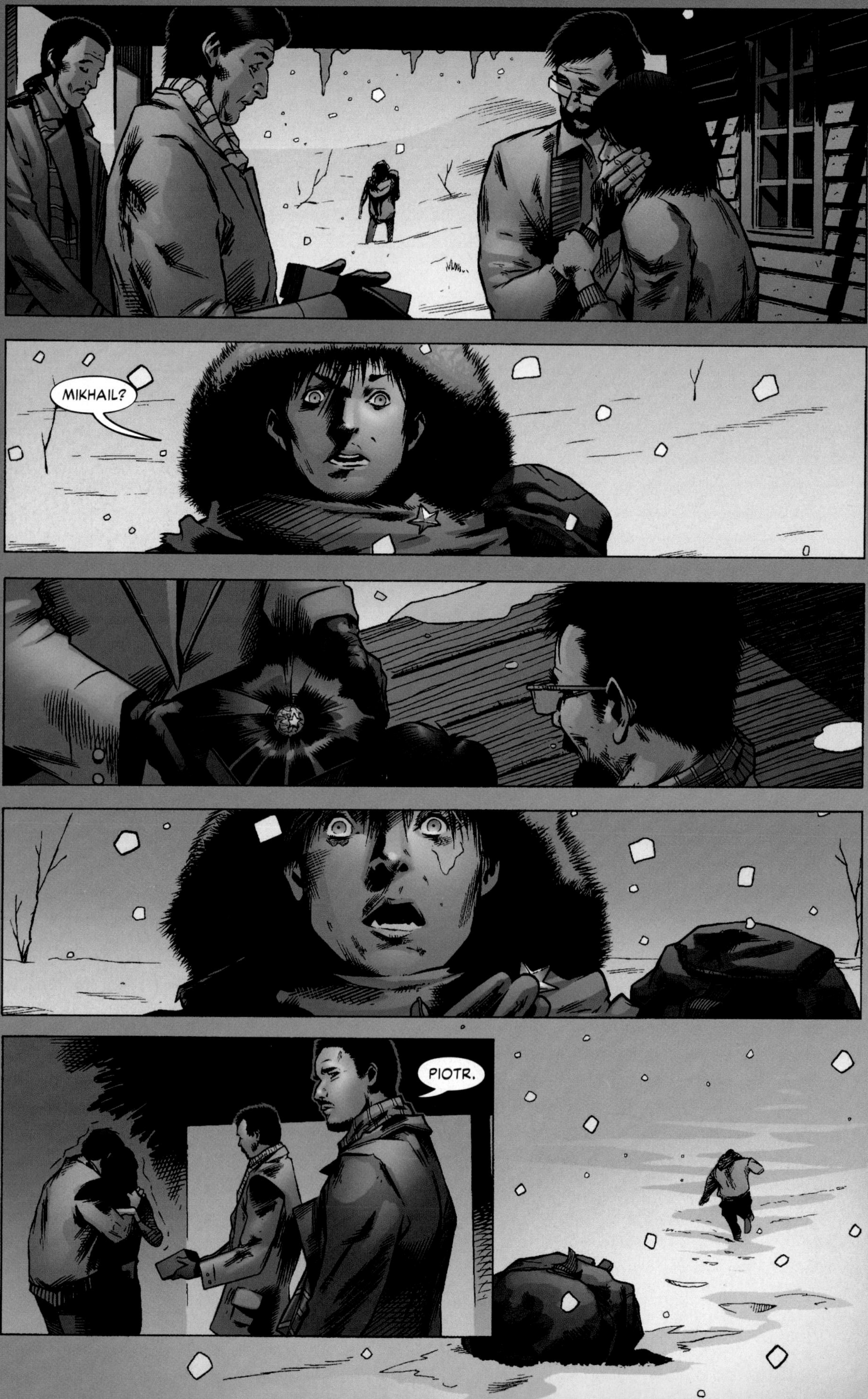
MIKHAIL?
PIOTR.

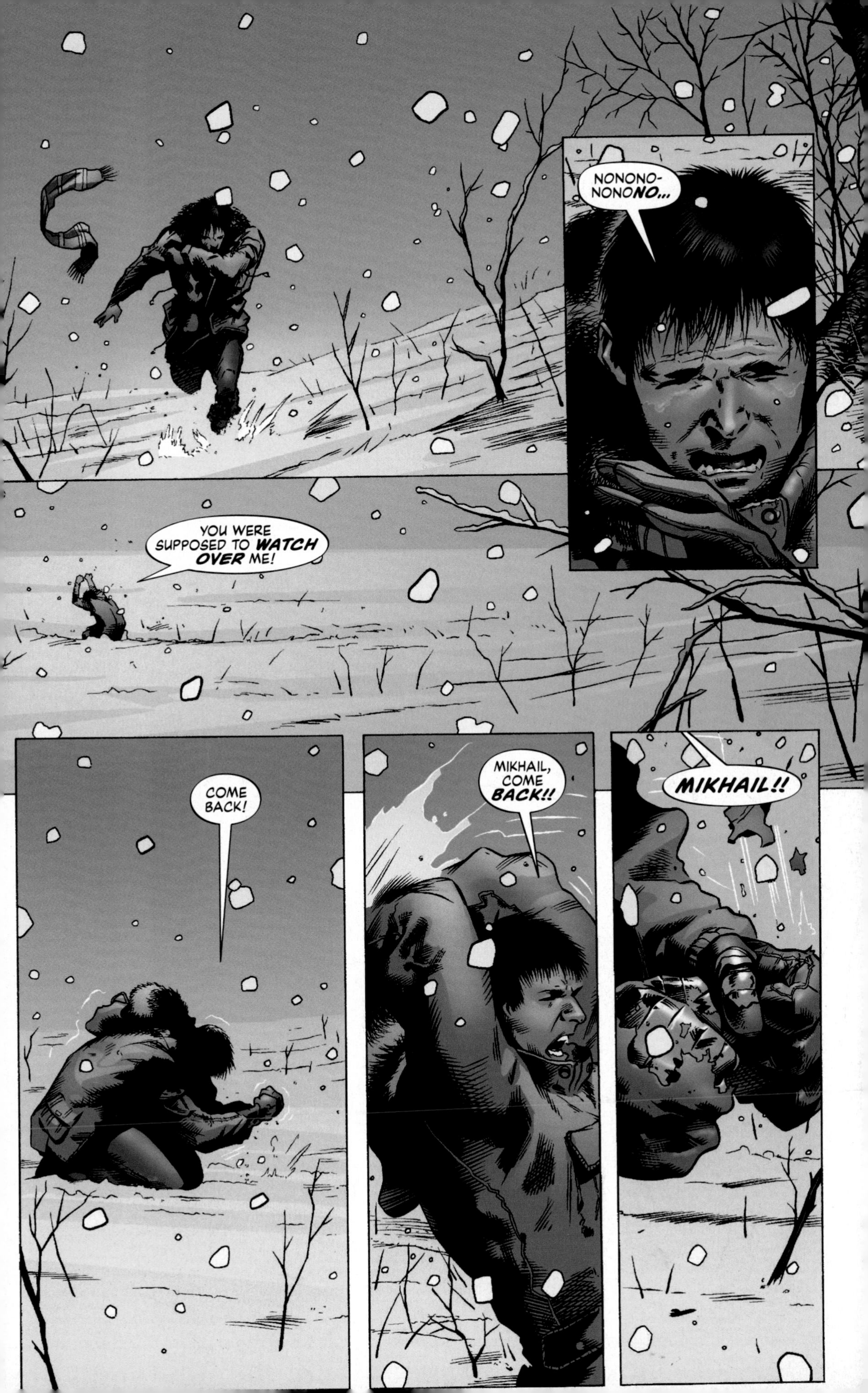
NONONO-NONONO...
YOU WERE SUPPOSED TO WATCH OVER ME!
COME BACK!
MIKHAIL, COME BACK!!
MIKHAIL!!

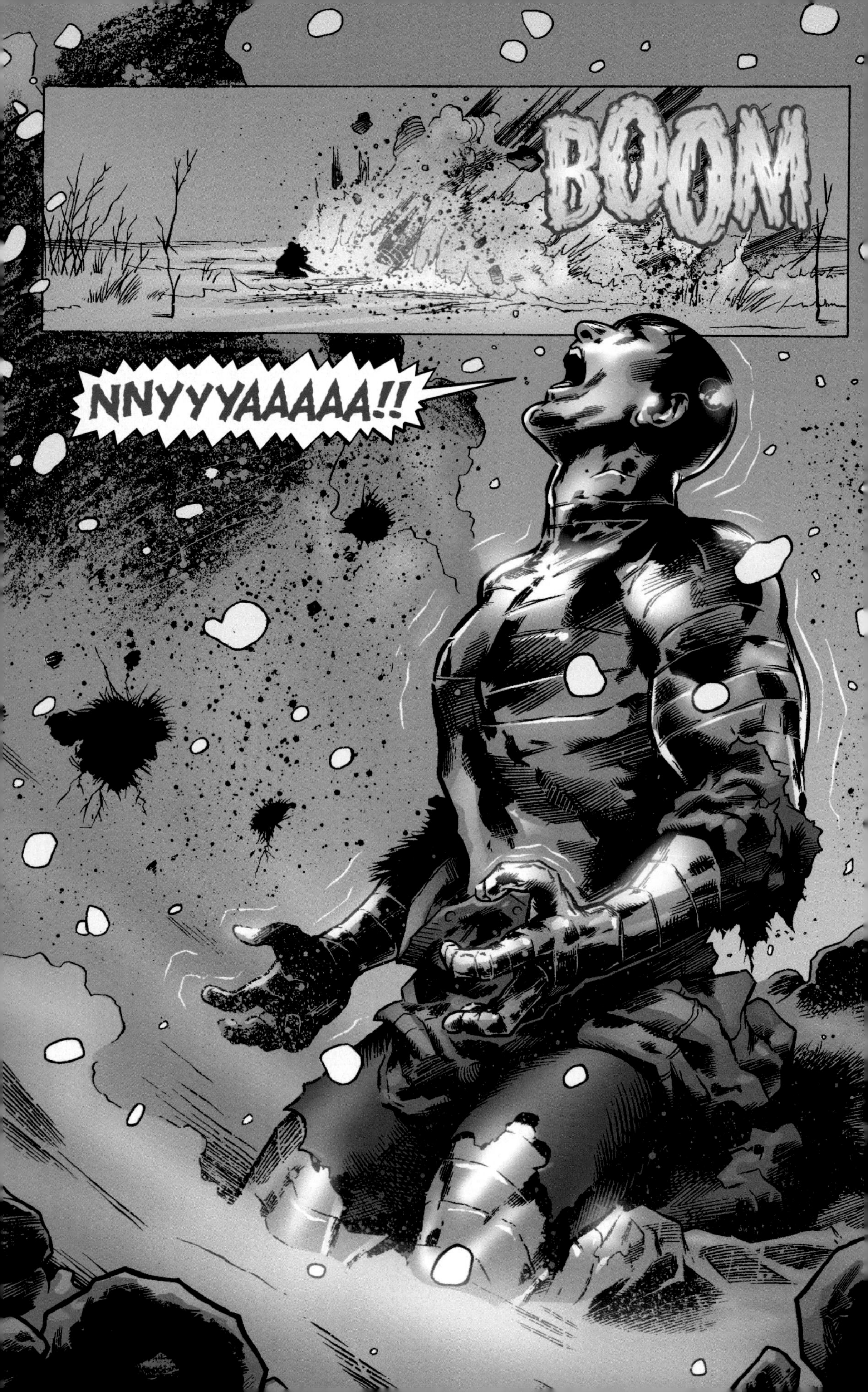
BOOM
NNYYYAAAAA!!

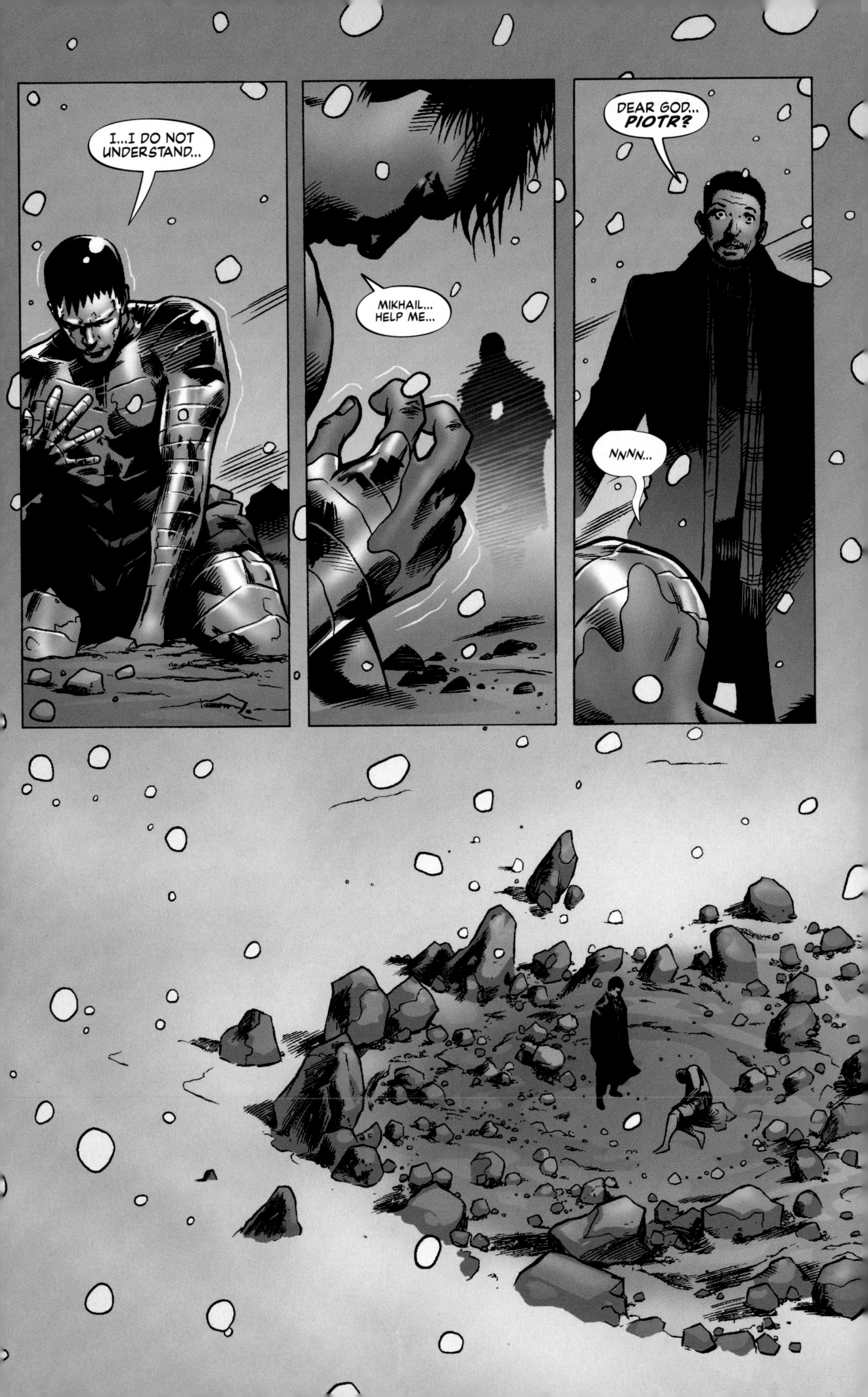
I...I DO NOT UNDERSTAND...
MIKHAIL... HELP ME...
DEAR GOD... PIOTR?
NNNN...

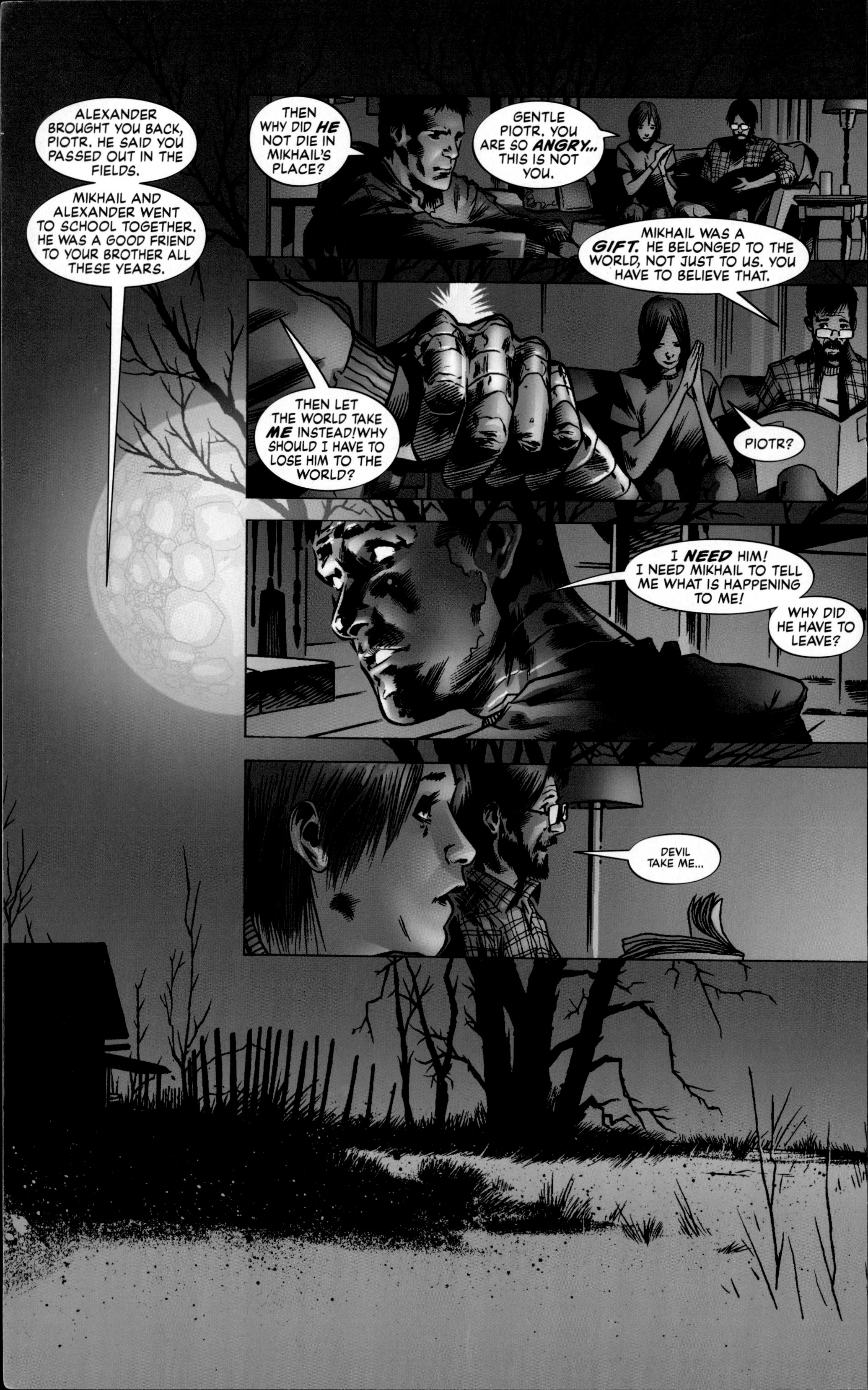
ALEXANDER BROUGHT YOU BACK, PIOTR. HE SAID YOU PASSED OUT IN THE FIELDS.
MIKHAIL AND ALEXANDER WENT TO SCHOOL TOGETHER. HE WAS A GOOD FRIEND TO YOUR BROTHER ALL THESE YEARS.
THEN WHY DID HE NOT DIE IN MIKHAIL'S PLACE?
GENTLE PIOTR. YOU ARE SO ANGRY... THIS IS NOT YOU.
MIKHAIL WAS A GIFT. HE BELONGED TO THE WORLD, NOT JUST TO US. YOU HAVE TO BELIEVE THAT.
THEN LET THE WORLD TAKE ME INSTEAD! WHY SHOULD I HAVE TO LOSE HIM TO THE WORLD?
PIOTR?
I NEED HIM! I NEED MIKHAIL TO TELL ME WHAT IS HAPPENING TO ME!
WHY DID HE HAVE TO LEAVE?
DEVIL TAKE ME...

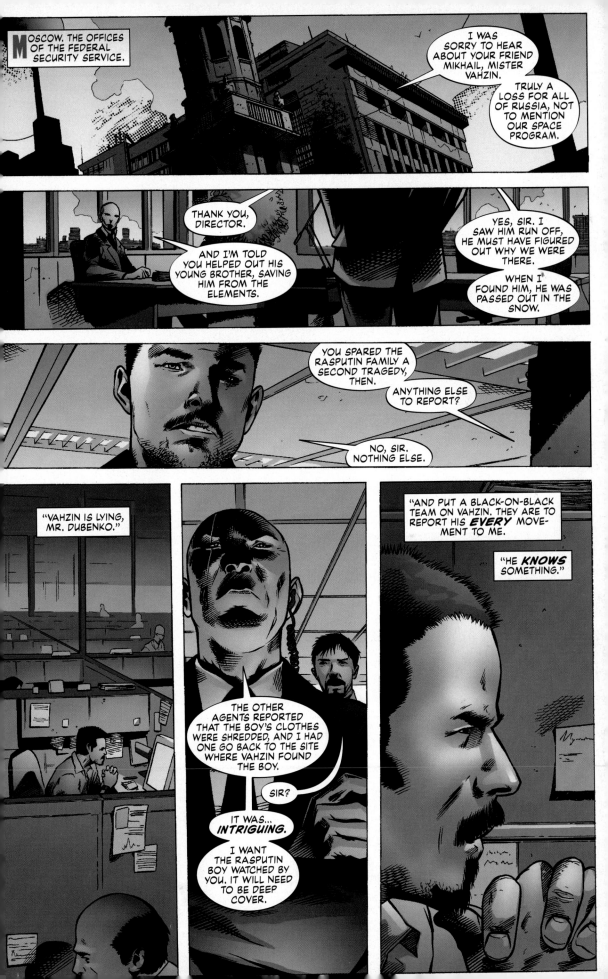

**MOSCOW. THE OFFICES OF THE FEDERAL SECURITY SERVICE.**

I WAS SORRY TO HEAR ABOUT YOUR FRIEND MIKHAIL, MISTER VAHZIN.

TRULY A LOSS FOR ALL OF RUSSIA, NOT TO MENTION OUR SPACE PROGRAM.

THANK YOU, DIRECTOR.

AND I'M TOLD YOU HELPED OUT HIS YOUNG BROTHER, SAVING HIM FROM THE ELEMENTS.

YES, SIR. I SAW HIM RUN OFF, HE MUST HAVE FIGURED OUT WHY WE WERE THERE.

WHEN I FOUND HIM, HE WAS PASSED OUT IN THE SNOW.

YOU SPARED THE RASPUTIN FAMILY A SECOND TRAGEDY, THEN.

ANYTHING ELSE TO REPORT?

NO, SIR. NOTHING ELSE.

"VAHZIN IS LYING, MR. DUBENKO."

"AND PUT A BLACK-ON-BLACK TEAM ON VAHZIN. THEY ARE TO REPORT HIS *EVERY* MOVEMENT TO ME.

"HE *KNOWS* SOMETHING."

THE OTHER AGENTS REPORTED THAT THE BOY'S CLOTHES WERE SHREDDED, AND I HAD ONE GO BACK TO THE SITE WHERE VAHZIN FOUND THE BOY.

SIR?

IT WAS... *INTRIGUING.*

I WANT THE RASPUTIN BOY WATCHED BY YOU. IT WILL NEED TO BE DEEP COVER.

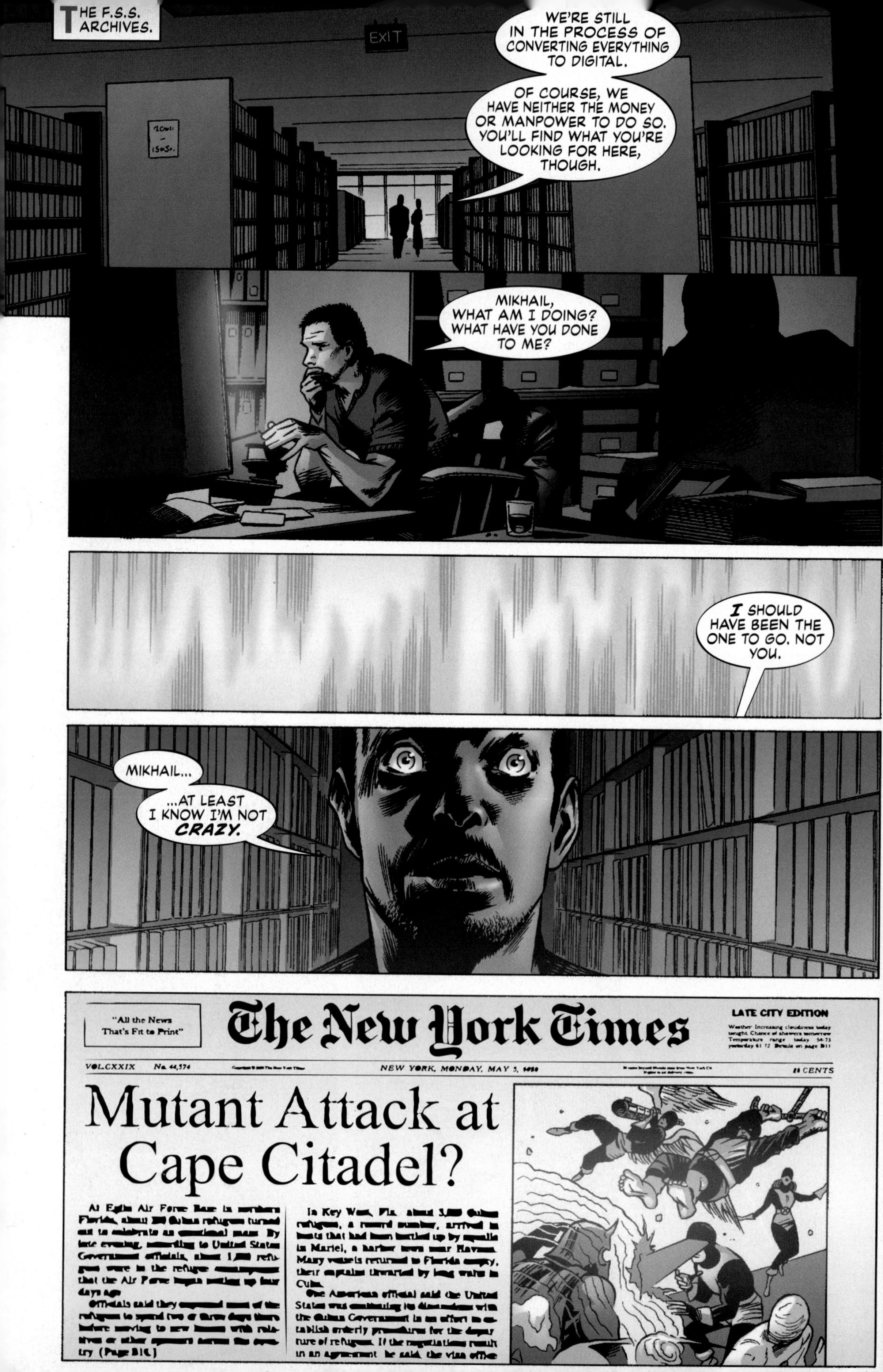
THE F.S.S. ARCHIVES.
EXIT
WE'RE STILL IN THE PROCESS OF CONVERTING EVERYTHING TO DIGITAL.
OF COURSE, WE HAVE NEITHER THE MONEY OR MANPOWER TO DO SO. YOU'LL FIND WHAT YOU'RE LOOKING FOR HERE, THOUGH.
MIKHAIL, WHAT AM I DOING? WHAT HAVE YOU DONE TO ME?
I SHOULD HAVE BEEN THE ONE TO GO. NOT YOU.
MIKHAIL...
...AT LEAST I KNOW I'M NOT CRAZY.
"All the News That's Fit to Print"
The New York Times
LATE CITY EDITION
NEW YORK, MONDAY, MAY 5,
CENTS
Mutant Attack at Cape Citadel?

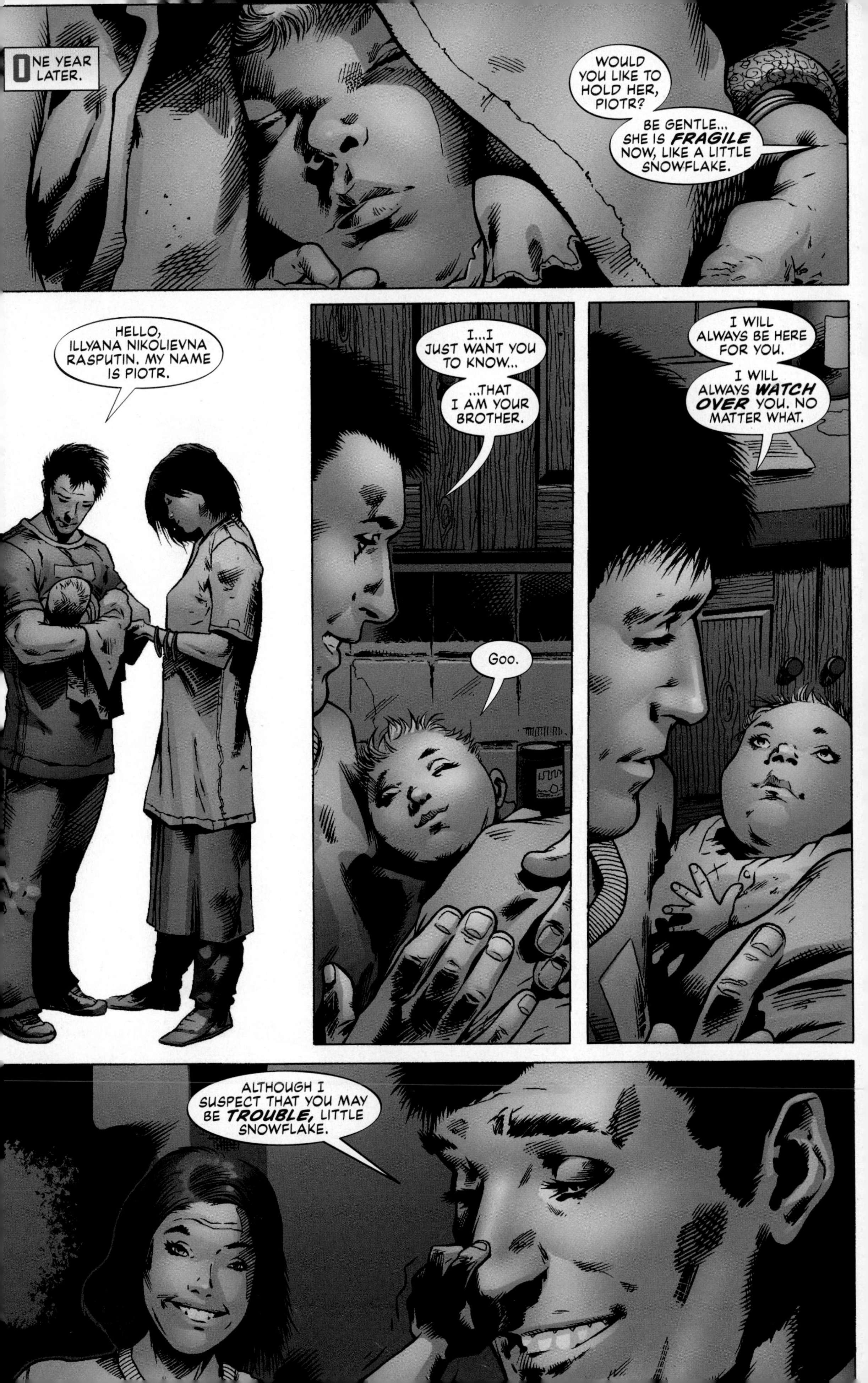
ONE YEAR LATER.
WOULD YOU LIKE TO HOLD HER, PIOTR?
BE GENTLE... SHE IS ***FRAGILE*** NOW, LIKE A LITTLE SNOWFLAKE.
HELLO, ILLYANA NIKOLIEVNA RASPUTIN. MY NAME IS PIOTR.
I...I JUST WANT YOU TO KNOW...
...THAT I AM YOUR BROTHER.
Goo.
I WILL ALWAYS BE HERE FOR YOU.
I WILL ALWAYS ***WATCH OVER*** YOU. NO MATTER WHAT.
ALTHOUGH I SUSPECT THAT YOU MAY BE ***TROUBLE,*** LITTLE SNOWFLAKE.

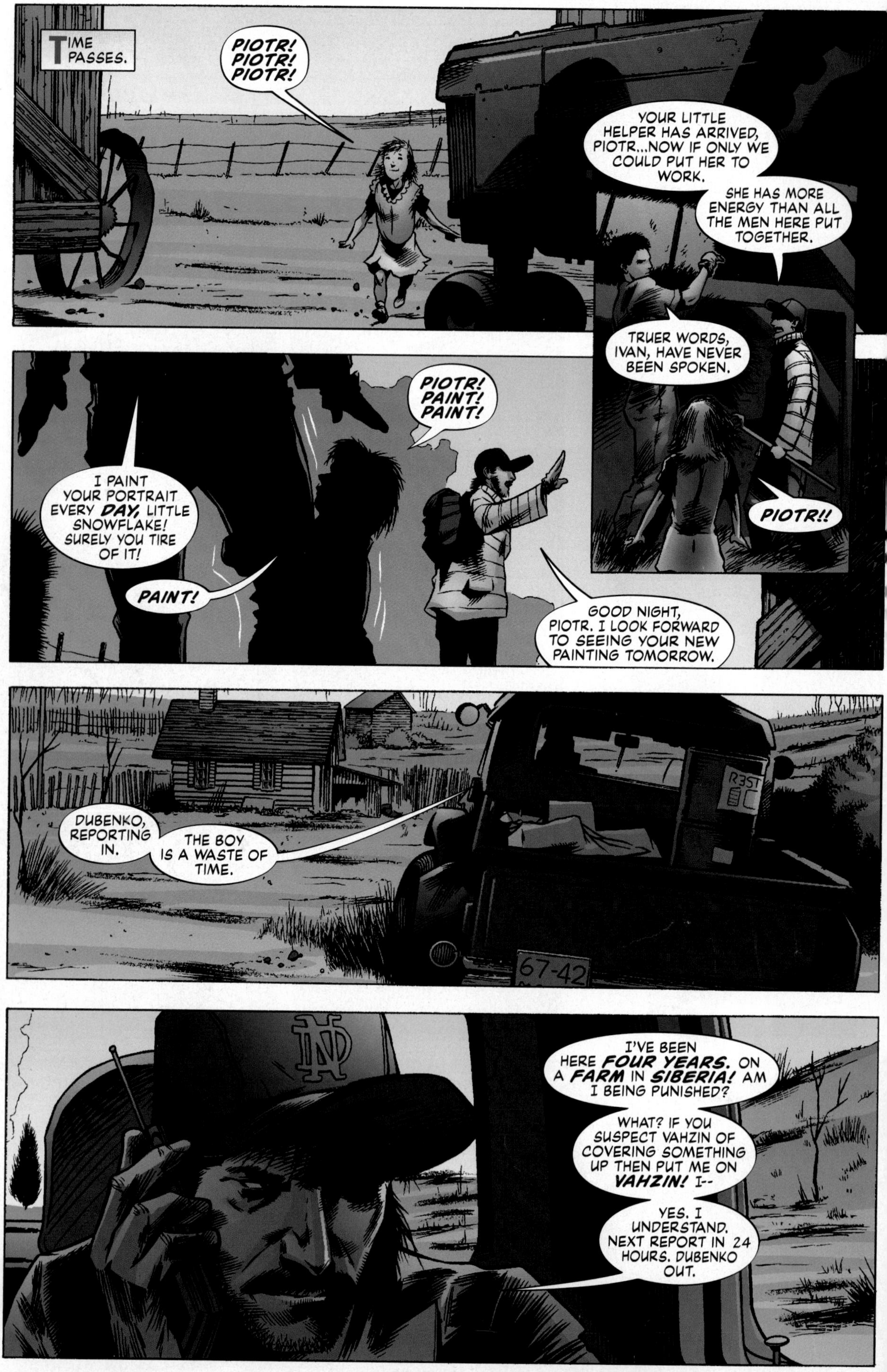
TIME PASSES.
PIOTR! PIOTR! PIOTR!
YOUR LITTLE HELPER HAS ARRIVED, PIOTR...NOW IF ONLY WE COULD PUT HER TO WORK.
SHE HAS MORE ENERGY THAN ALL THE MEN HERE PUT TOGETHER.
TRUER WORDS, IVAN, HAVE NEVER BEEN SPOKEN.
PIOTR!!
PIOTR! PAINT! PAINT!
I PAINT YOUR PORTRAIT EVERY DAY, LITTLE SNOWFLAKE! SURELY YOU TIRE OF IT!
PAINT!
GOOD NIGHT, PIOTR. I LOOK FORWARD TO SEEING YOUR NEW PAINTING TOMORROW.
DUBENKO, REPORTING IN.
THE BOY IS A WASTE OF TIME.
67-42
I'VE BEEN HERE FOUR YEARS. ON A FARM IN SIBERIA! AM I BEING PUNISHED?
WHAT? IF YOU SUSPECT VAHZIN OF COVERING SOMETHING UP THEN PUT ME ON VAHZIN! I--
YES. I UNDERSTAND. NEXT REPORT IN 24 HOURS. DUBENKO OUT.

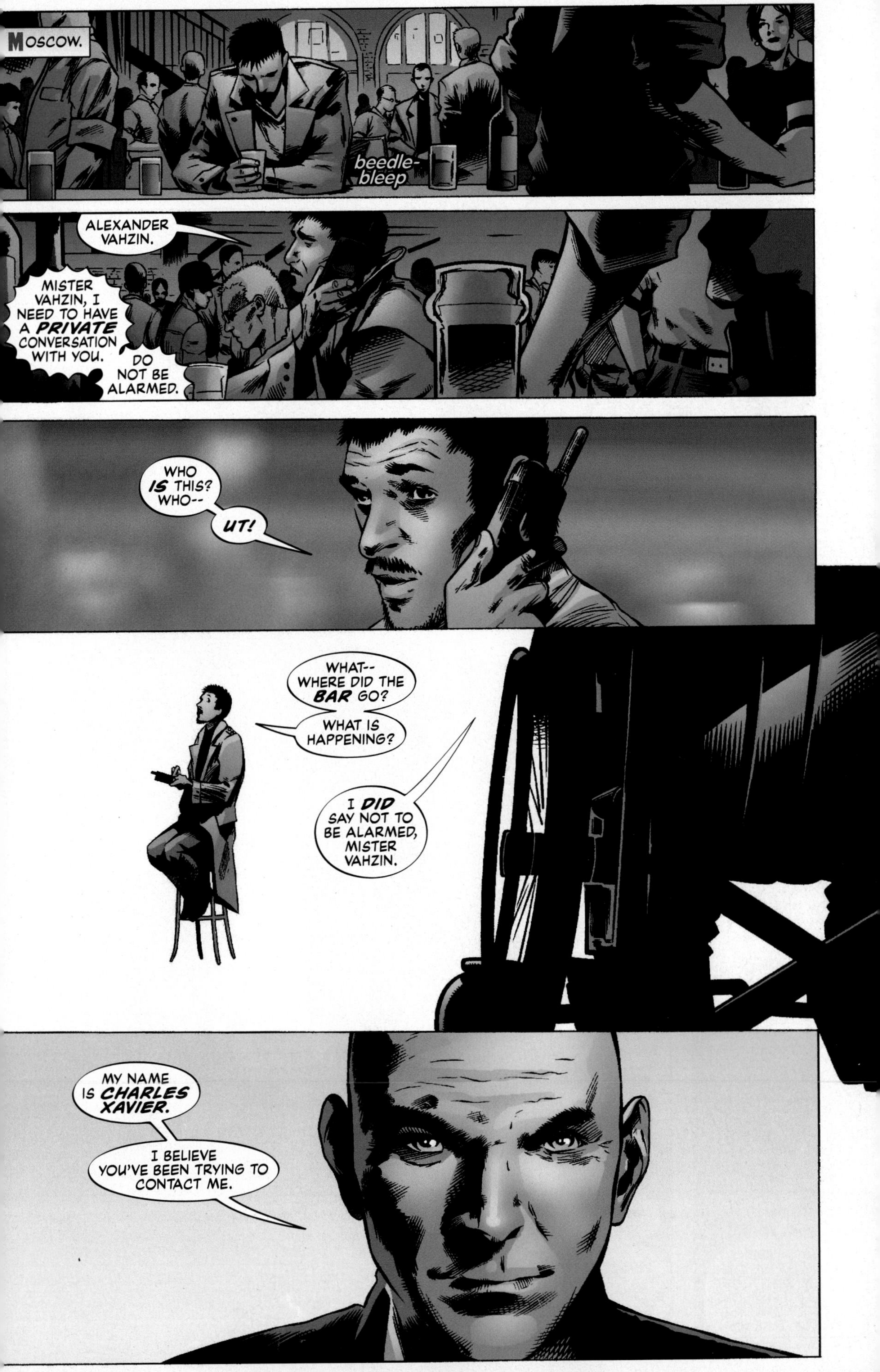
MOSCOW.
beedle-bleep
ALEXANDER VAHZIN.
MISTER VAHZIN, I NEED TO HAVE A PRIVATE CONVERSATION WITH YOU.
DO NOT BE ALARMED.
WHO IS THIS? WHO--
UT!
WHAT-- WHERE DID THE BAR GO?
WHAT IS HAPPENING?
I DID SAY NOT TO BE ALARMED, MISTER VAHZIN.
MY NAME IS CHARLES XAVIER.
I BELIEVE YOU'VE BEEN TRYING TO CONTACT ME.

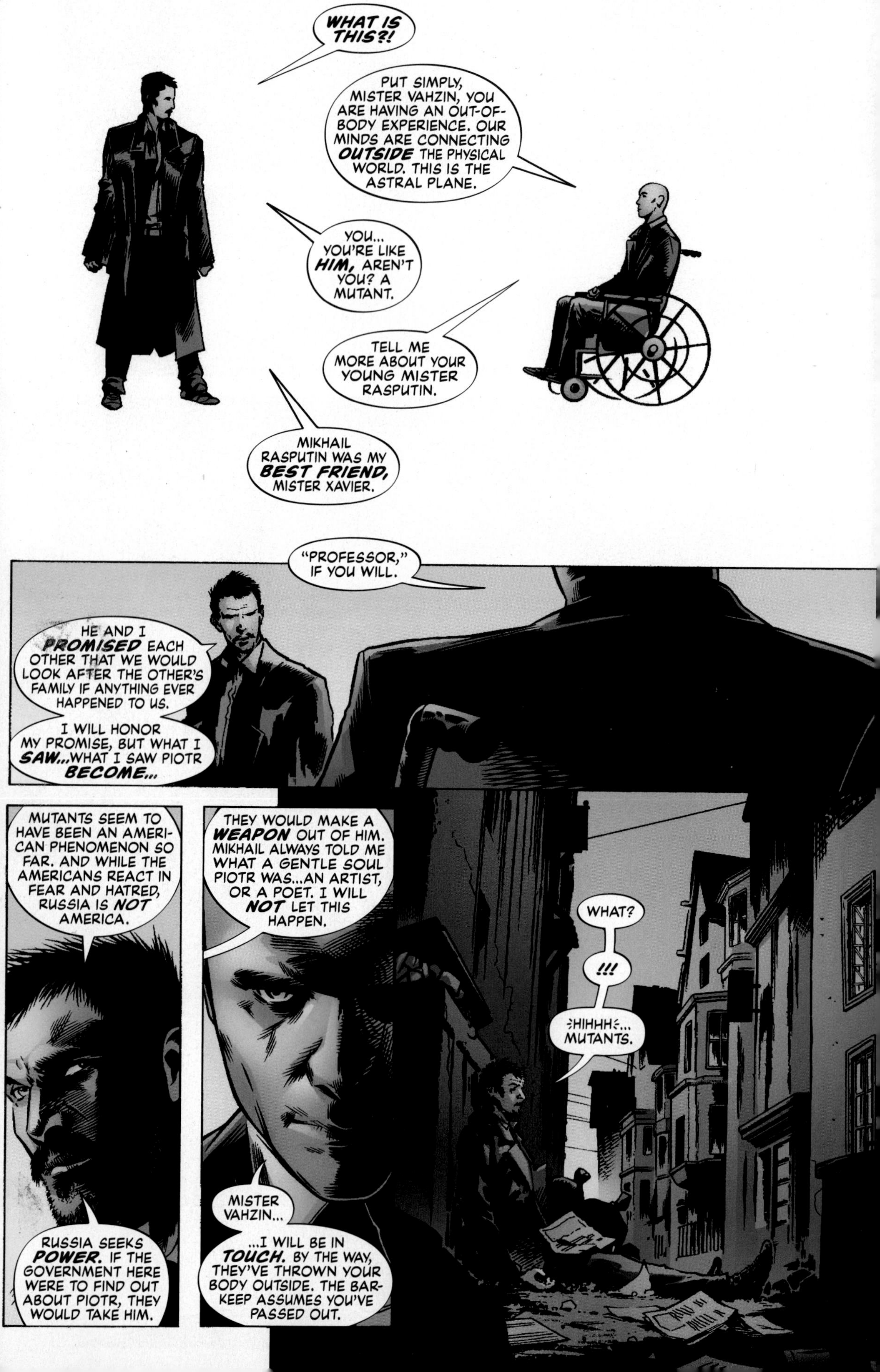

WHAT IS THIS?!
PUT SIMPLY, MISTER VAHZIN, YOU ARE HAVING AN OUT-OF-BODY EXPERIENCE. OUR MINDS ARE CONNECTING OUTSIDE THE PHYSICAL WORLD. THIS IS THE ASTRAL PLANE.
YOU... YOU'RE LIKE HIM, AREN'T YOU? A MUTANT.
TELL ME MORE ABOUT YOUR YOUNG MISTER RASPUTIN.
MIKHAIL RASPUTIN WAS MY BEST FRIEND, MISTER XAVIER.
"PROFESSOR," IF YOU WILL.
HE AND I PROMISED EACH OTHER THAT WE WOULD LOOK AFTER THE OTHER'S FAMILY IF ANYTHING EVER HAPPENED TO US.
I WILL HONOR MY PROMISE, BUT WHAT I SAW...WHAT I SAW PIOTR BECOME...
MUTANTS SEEM TO HAVE BEEN AN AMERICAN PHENOMENON SO FAR. AND WHILE THE AMERICANS REACT IN FEAR AND HATRED, RUSSIA IS NOT AMERICA.
RUSSIA SEEKS POWER. IF THE GOVERNMENT HERE WERE TO FIND OUT ABOUT PIOTR, THEY WOULD TAKE HIM.
THEY WOULD MAKE A WEAPON OUT OF HIM. MIKHAIL ALWAYS TOLD ME WHAT A GENTLE SOUL PIOTR WAS...AN ARTIST, OR A POET. I WILL NOT LET THIS HAPPEN.
MISTER VAHZIN...
...I WILL BE IN TOUCH. BY THE WAY, THEY'VE THROWN YOUR BODY OUTSIDE. THE BARKEEP ASSUMES YOU'VE PASSED OUT.
WHAT?
!!!
HIHHH... MUTANTS.

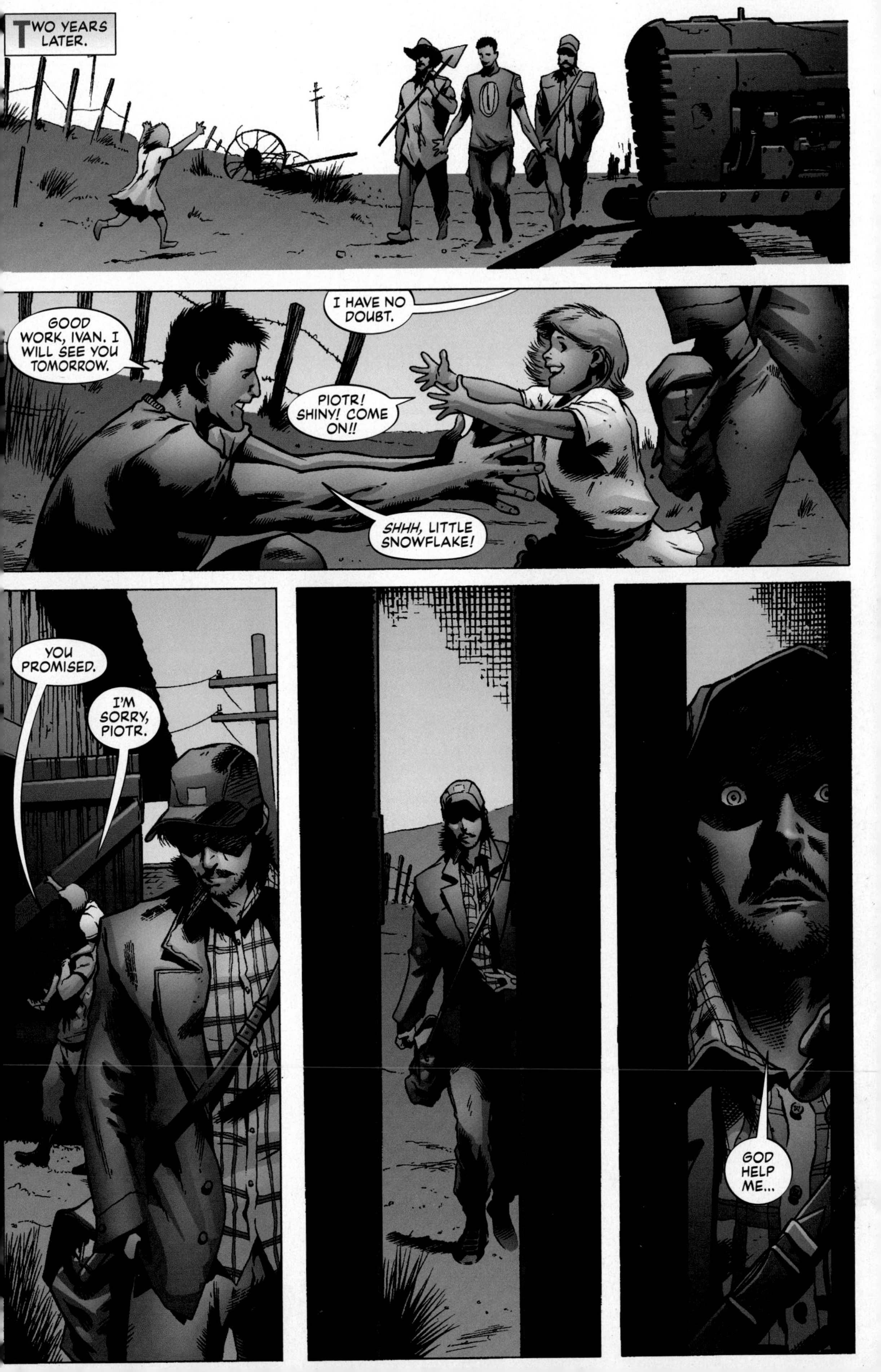
TWO YEARS LATER.
GOOD WORK, IVAN. I WILL SEE YOU TOMORROW.
I HAVE NO DOUBT.
PIOTR! SHINY! COME ON!!
SHHH, LITTLE SNOWFLAKE!
YOU PROMISED.
I'M SORRY, PIOTR.
GOD HELP ME...

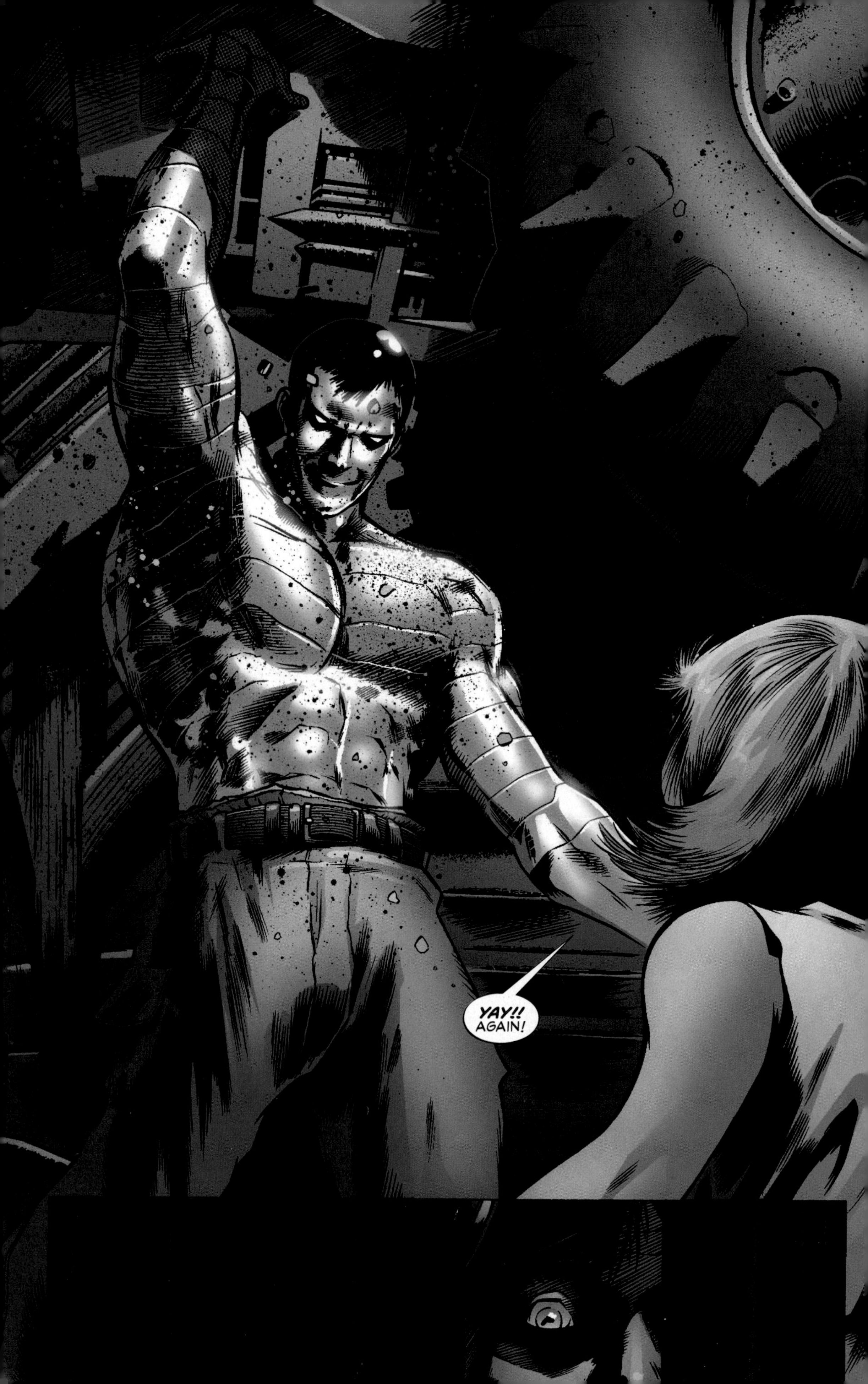
YAY!! AGAIN!

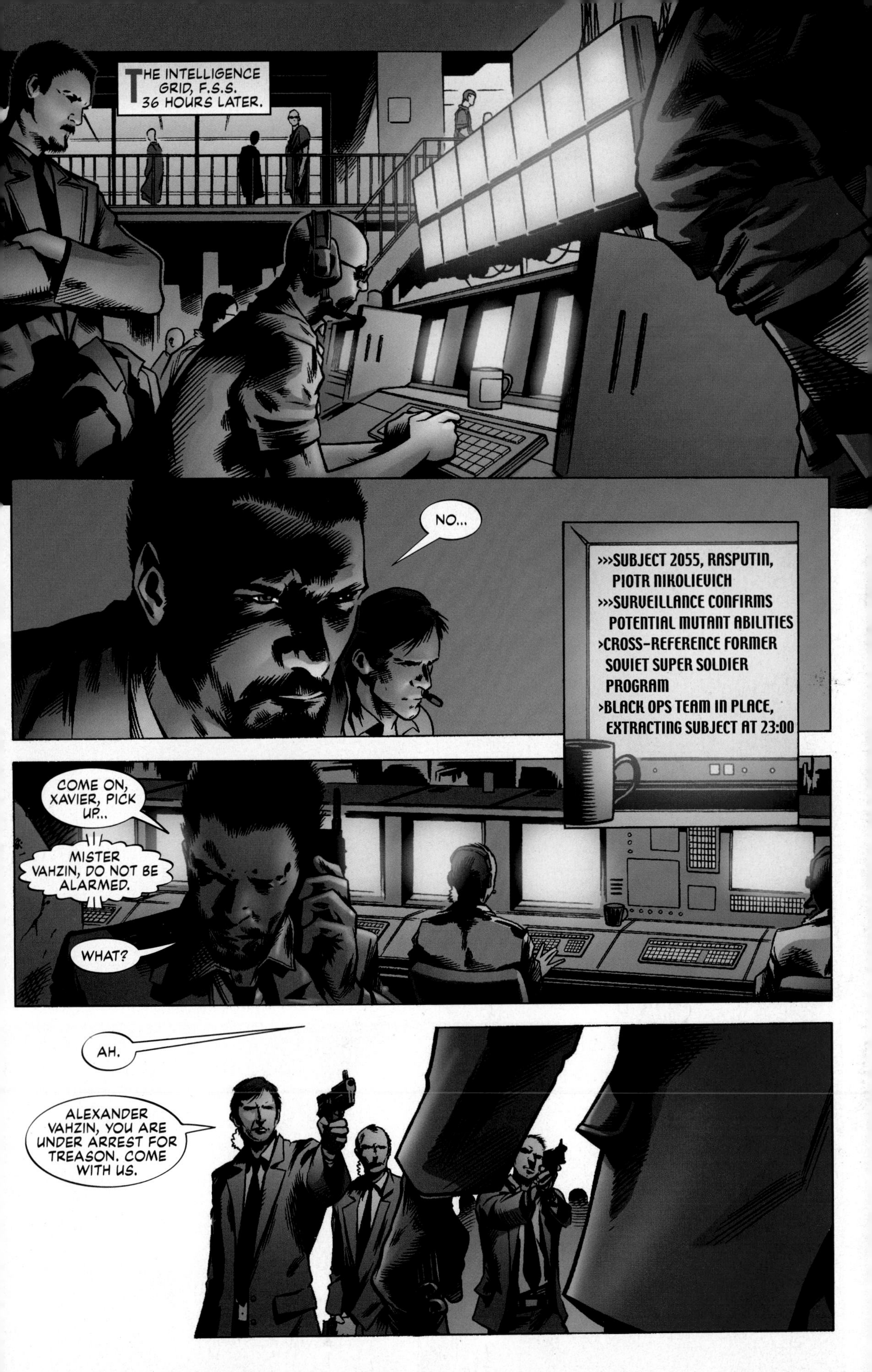
THE INTELLIGENCE GRID, F.S.S. 36 HOURS LATER.
NO...
>>>SUBJECT 2055, RASPUTIN, PIOTR NIKOLIEVICH
>>>SURVEILLANCE CONFIRMS POTENTIAL MUTANT ABILITIES
>CROSS-REFERENCE FORMER SOVIET SUPER SOLDIER PROGRAM
>BLACK OPS TEAM IN PLACE, EXTRACTING SUBJECT AT 23:00
COME ON, XAVIER, PICK UP...
MISTER VAHZIN, DO NOT BE ALARMED.
WHAT?
AH.
ALEXANDER VAHZIN, YOU ARE UNDER ARREST FOR TREASON. COME WITH US.

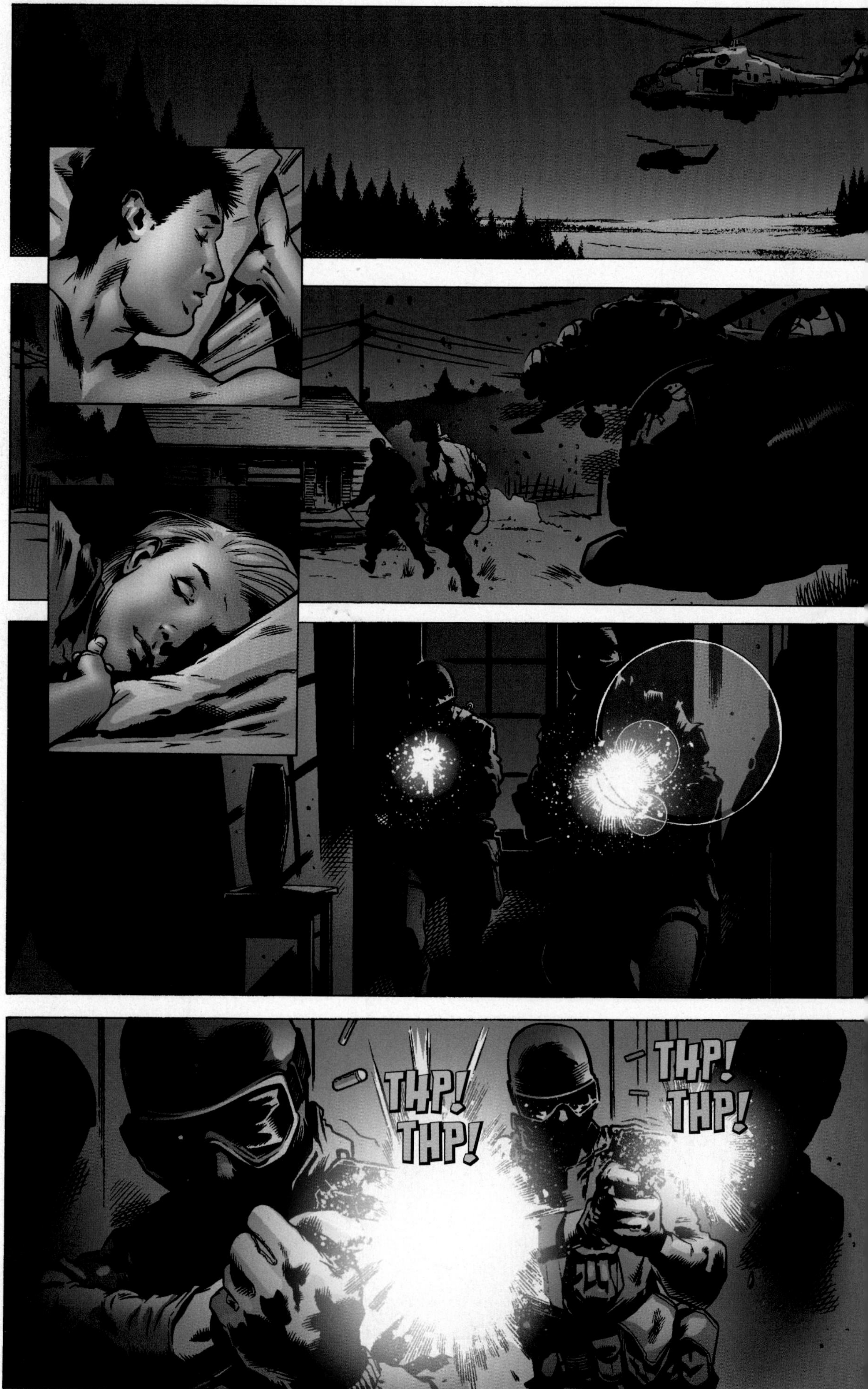
THP!
THP!
THP!
THP!

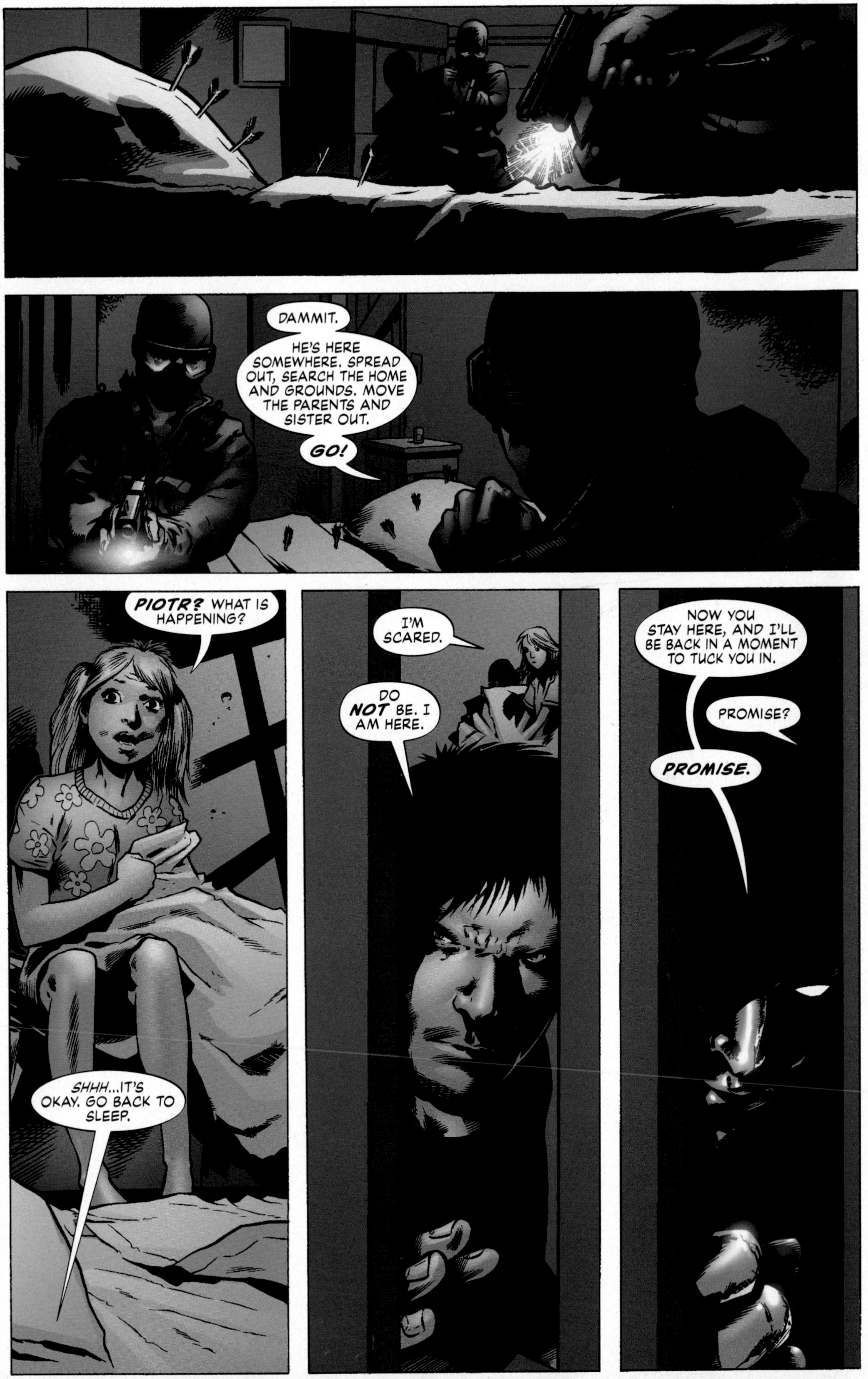
DAMMIT.
HE'S HERE SOMEWHERE. SPREAD OUT, SEARCH THE HOME AND GROUNDS. MOVE THE PARENTS AND SISTER OUT.
GO!
PIOTR? WHAT IS HAPPENING?
SHHH...IT'S OKAY. GO BACK TO SLEEP.
I'M SCARED.
DO NOT BE. I AM HERE.
NOW YOU STAY HERE, AND I'LL BE BACK IN A MOMENT TO TUCK YOU IN.
PROMISE?
PROMISE.

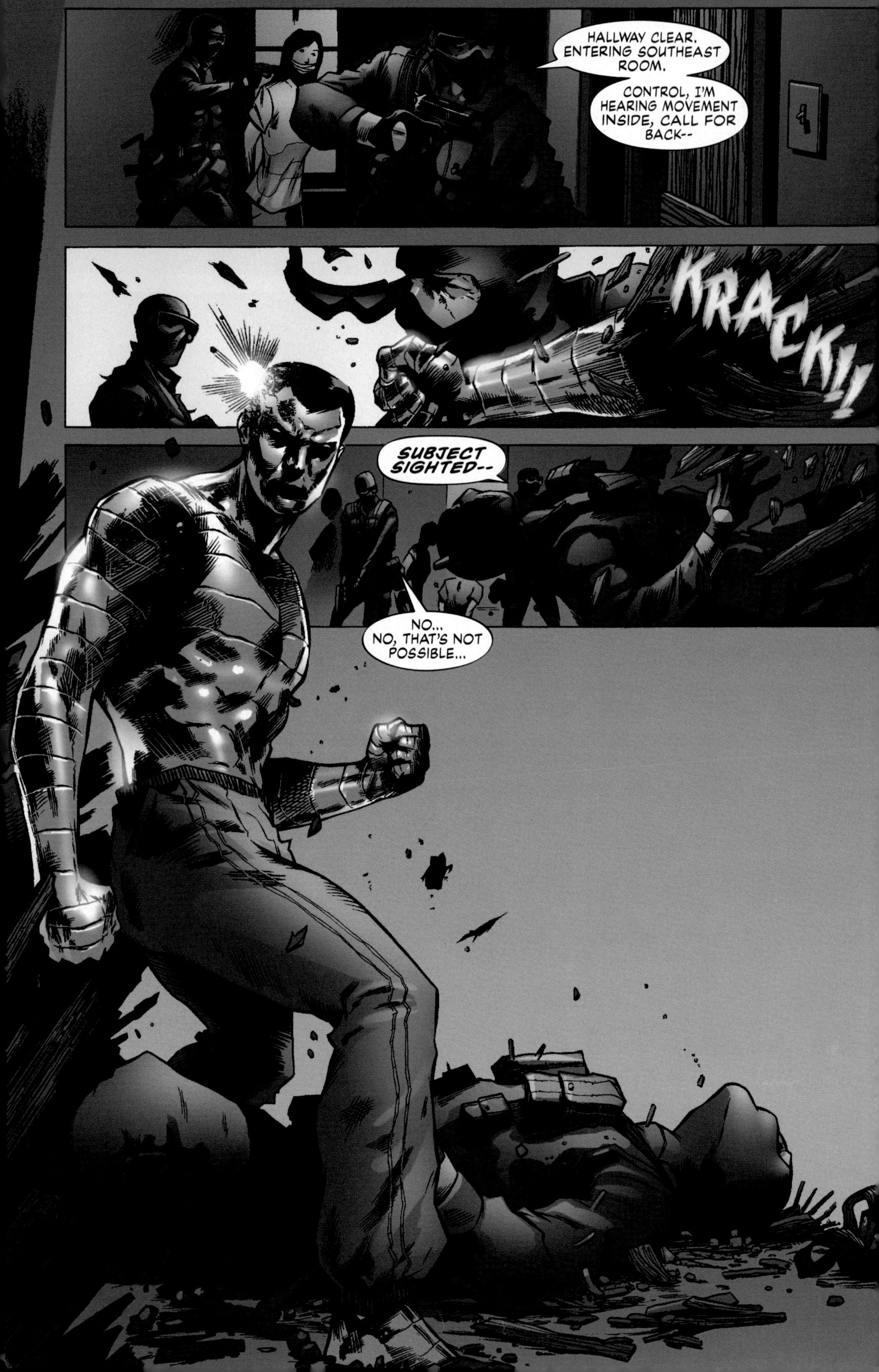
HALLWAY CLEAR. ENTERING SOUTHEAST ROOM.
CONTROL, I'M HEARING MOVEMENT INSIDE, CALL FOR BACK--
KRACK!!
SUBJECT SIGHTED--
NO... NO, THAT'S NOT POSSIBLE...

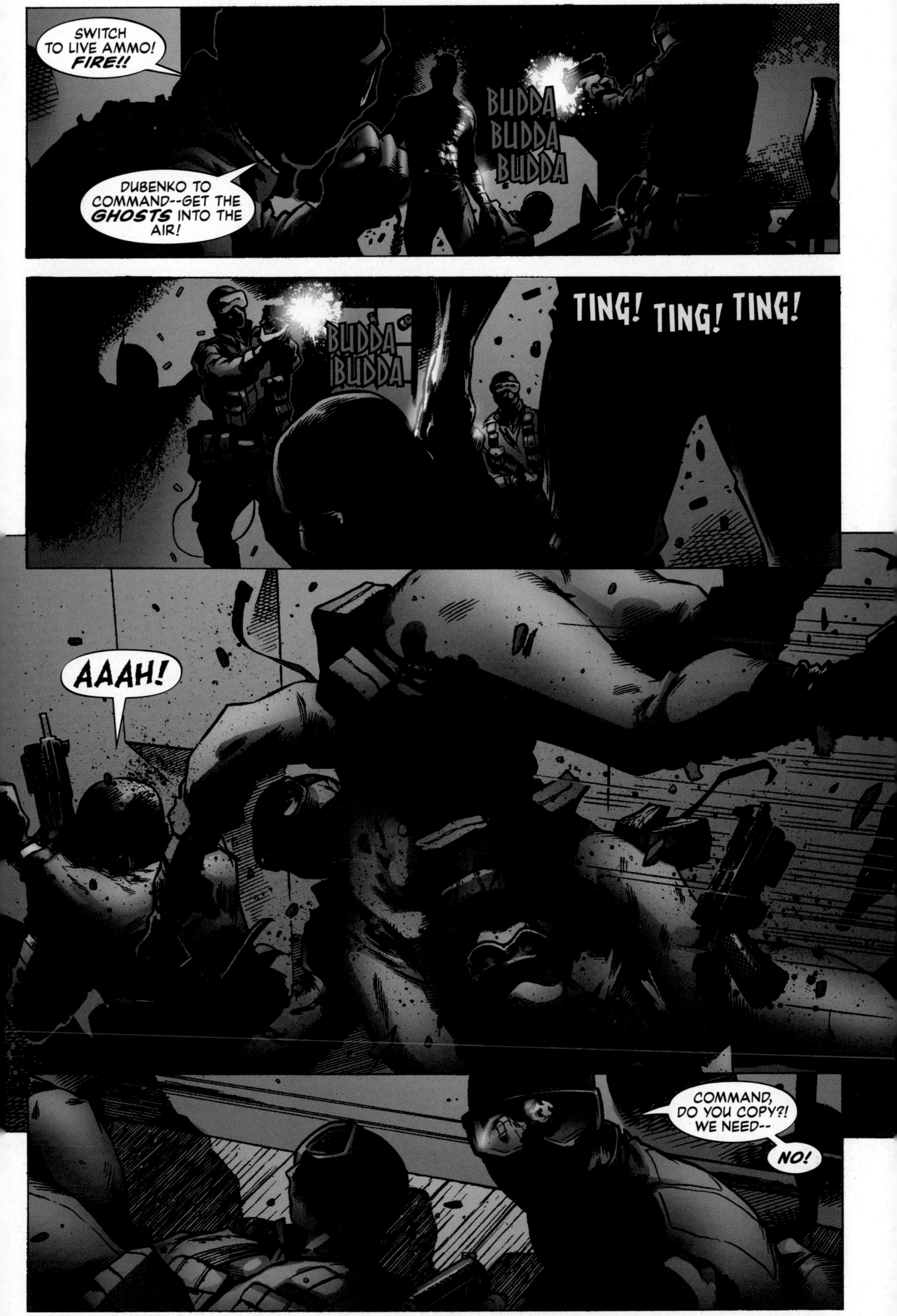
SWITCH TO LIVE AMMO! FIRE!!
BUDDA BUDDA BUDDA
DUBENKO TO COMMAND--GET THE GHOSTS INTO THE AIR!
BUDDA BUDDA
TING! TING! TING!
AAAH!
COMMAND, DO YOU COPY?! WE NEED--
NO!

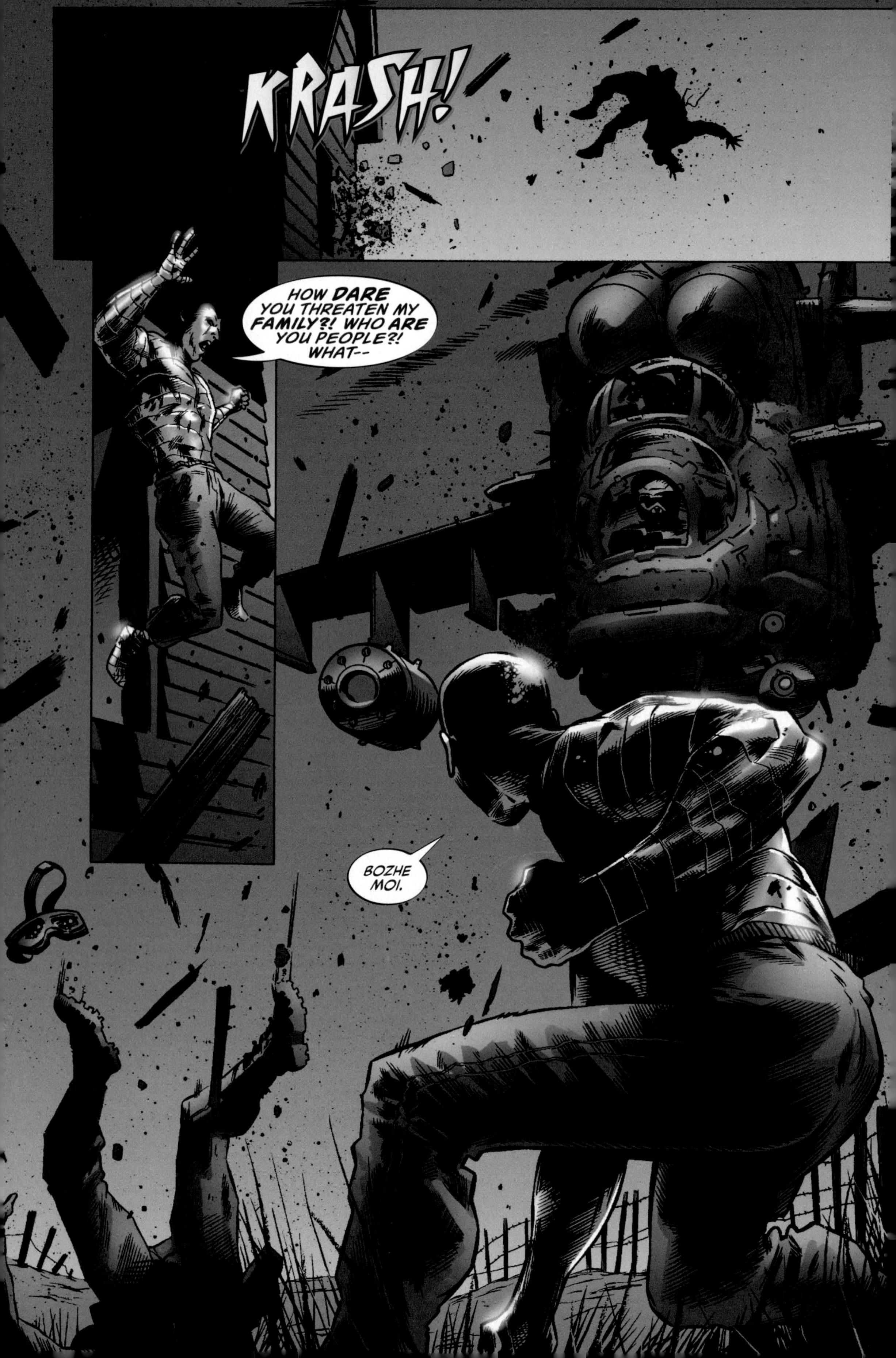
KRASH!
HOW DARE YOU THREATEN MY FAMILY?! WHO ARE YOU PEOPLE?! WHAT--
BOZHE MOI.

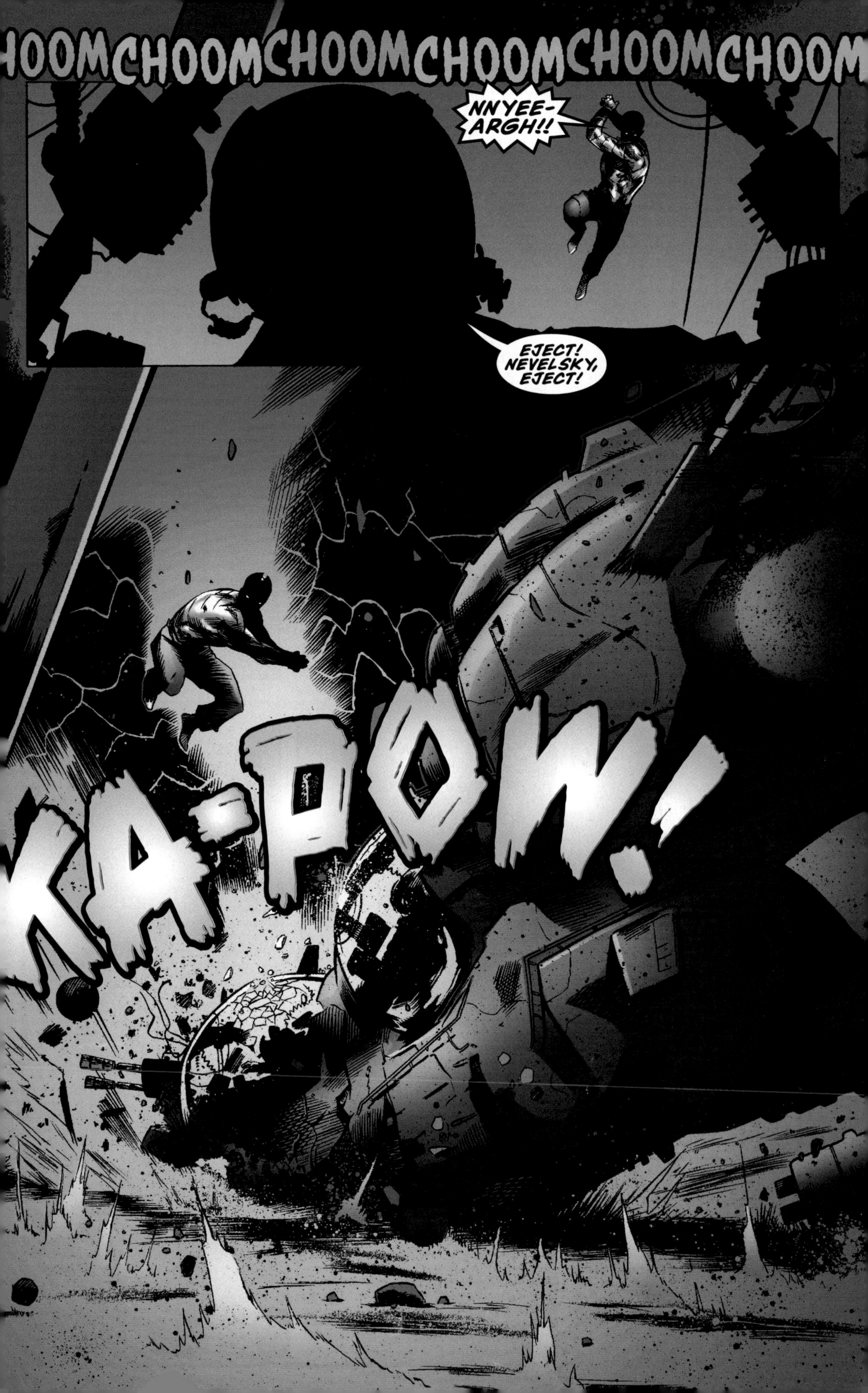
HOOMCHOOMCHOOMCHOOMCHOOM
NNYEE-ARGH!!
EJECT! NEVELSKY, EJECT!
KA-POW!

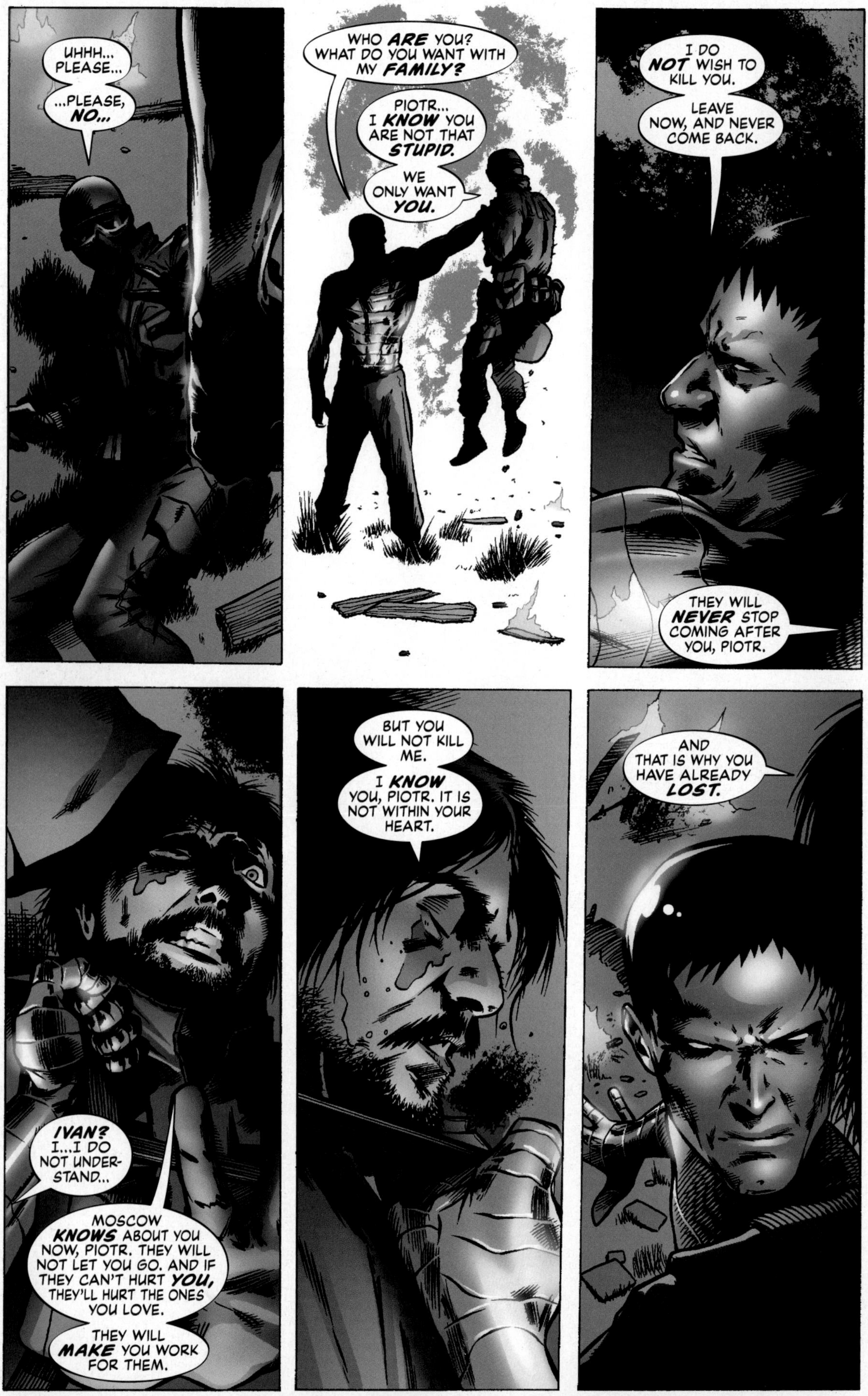
UHHH... PLEASE...
...PLEASE, NO...
WHO ARE YOU? WHAT DO YOU WANT WITH MY FAMILY?
PIOTR... I KNOW YOU ARE NOT THAT STUPID.
WE ONLY WANT YOU.
I DO NOT WISH TO KILL YOU.
LEAVE NOW, AND NEVER COME BACK.
THEY WILL NEVER STOP COMING AFTER YOU, PIOTR.
IVAN? I...I DO NOT UNDER-STAND...
MOSCOW KNOWS ABOUT YOU NOW, PIOTR. THEY WILL NOT LET YOU GO. AND IF THEY CAN'T HURT YOU, THEY'LL HURT THE ONES YOU LOVE.
THEY WILL MAKE YOU WORK FOR THEM.
BUT YOU WILL NOT KILL ME.
I KNOW YOU, PIOTR. IT IS NOT WITHIN YOUR HEART.
AND THAT IS WHY YOU HAVE ALREADY LOST.

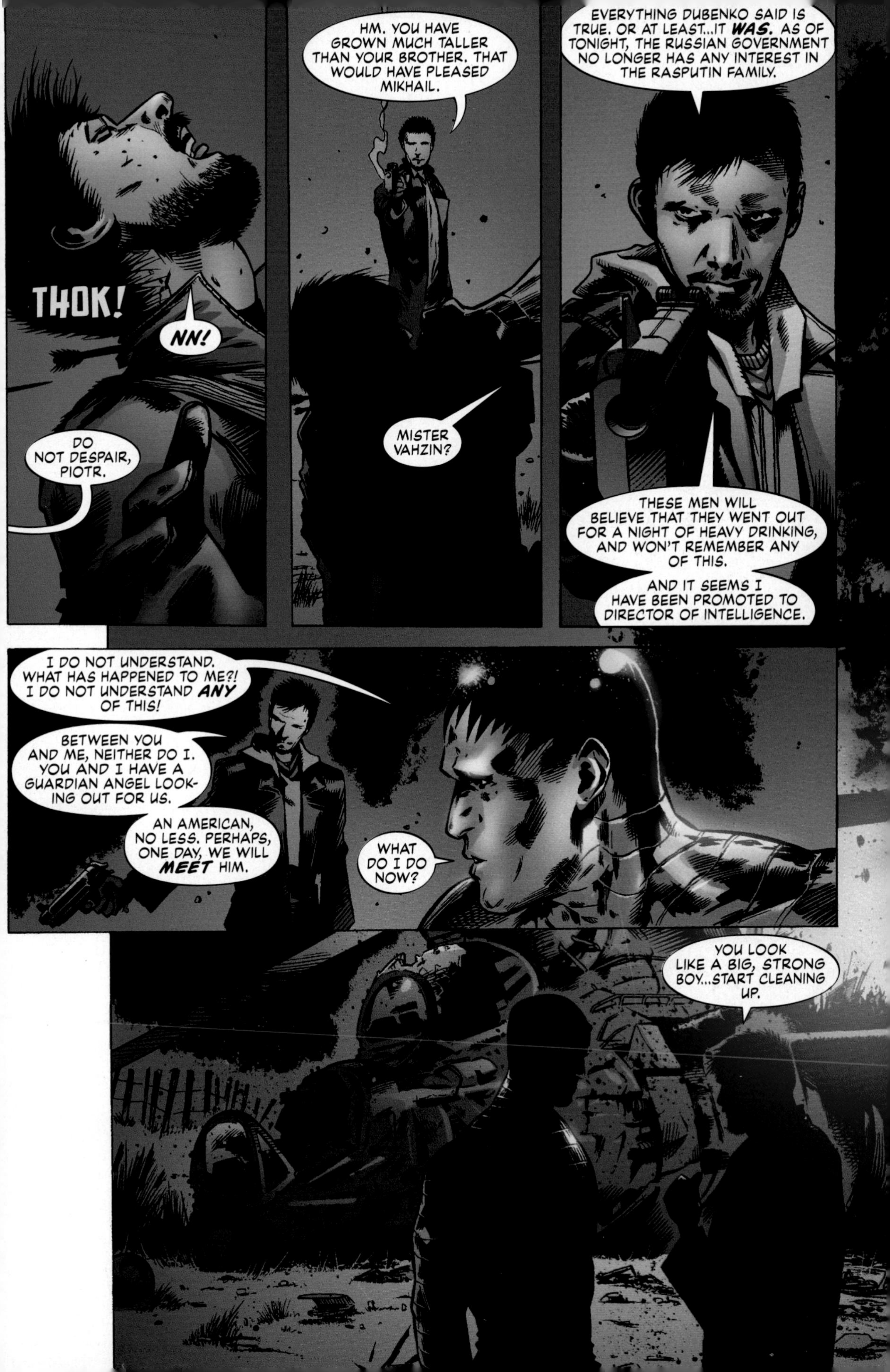
THOK!
NN!
DO NOT DESPAIR, PIOTR.
HM. YOU HAVE GROWN MUCH TALLER THAN YOUR BROTHER. THAT WOULD HAVE PLEASED MIKHAIL.
MISTER VAHZIN?
EVERYTHING DUBENKO SAID IS TRUE. OR AT LEAST...IT WAS. AS OF TONIGHT, THE RUSSIAN GOVERNMENT NO LONGER HAS ANY INTEREST IN THE RASPUTIN FAMILY.
THESE MEN WILL BELIEVE THAT THEY WENT OUT FOR A NIGHT OF HEAVY DRINKING, AND WON'T REMEMBER ANY OF THIS.
AND IT SEEMS I HAVE BEEN PROMOTED TO DIRECTOR OF INTELLIGENCE.
I DO NOT UNDERSTAND. WHAT HAS HAPPENED TO ME?! I DO NOT UNDERSTAND ANY OF THIS!
BETWEEN YOU AND ME, NEITHER DO I. YOU AND I HAVE A GUARDIAN ANGEL LOOKING OUT FOR US.
AN AMERICAN, NO LESS. PERHAPS, ONE DAY, WE WILL MEET HIM.
WHAT DO I DO NOW?
YOU LOOK LIKE A BIG, STRONG BOY...START CLEANING UP.

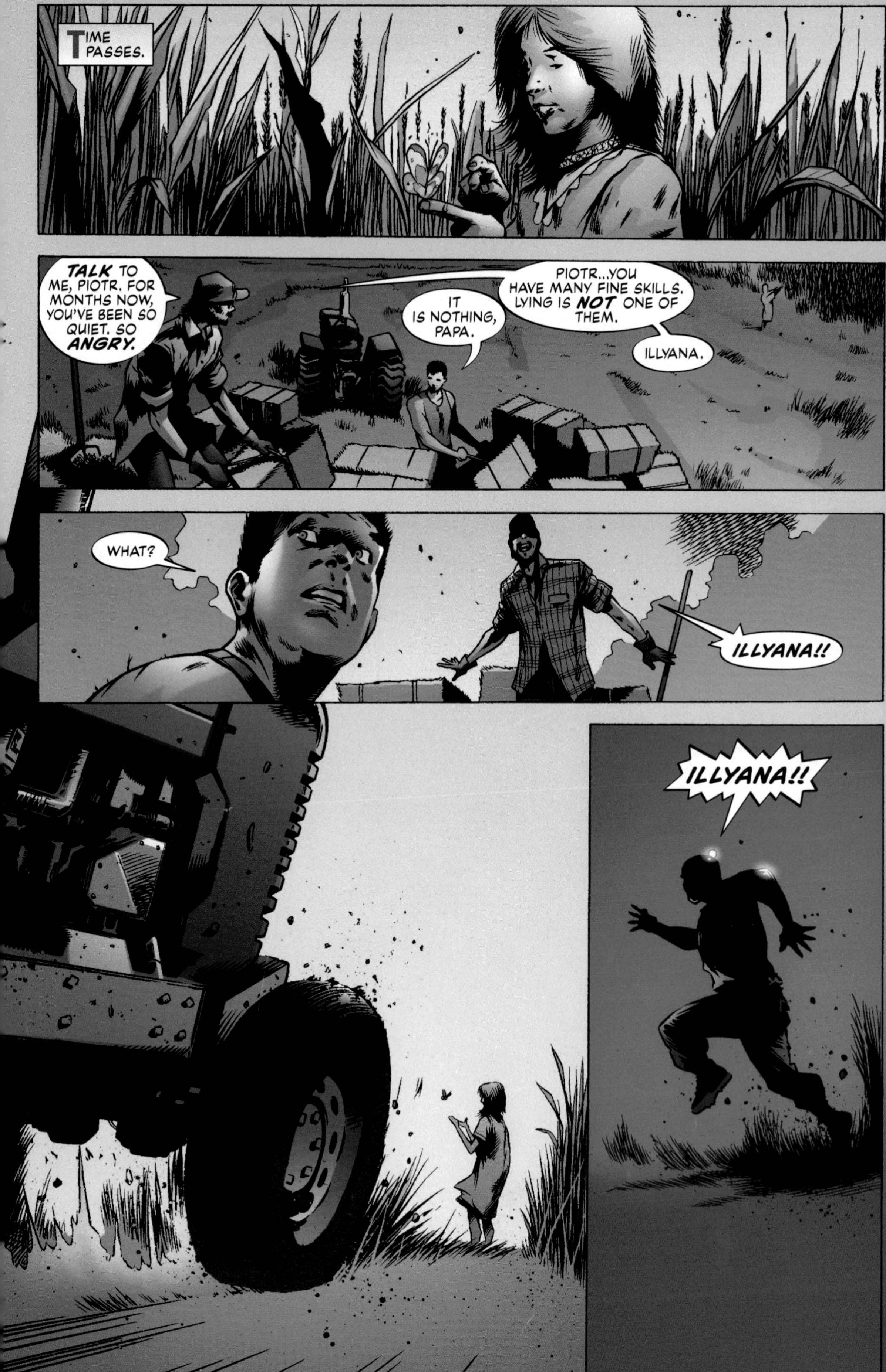
TIME PASSES.
TALK TO ME, PIOTR. FOR MONTHS NOW, YOU'VE BEEN SO QUIET. SO ANGRY.
IT IS NOTHING, PAPA.
PIOTR...YOU HAVE MANY FINE SKILLS. LYING IS NOT ONE OF THEM.
ILLYANA.
WHAT?
ILLYANA!!
ILLYANA!!

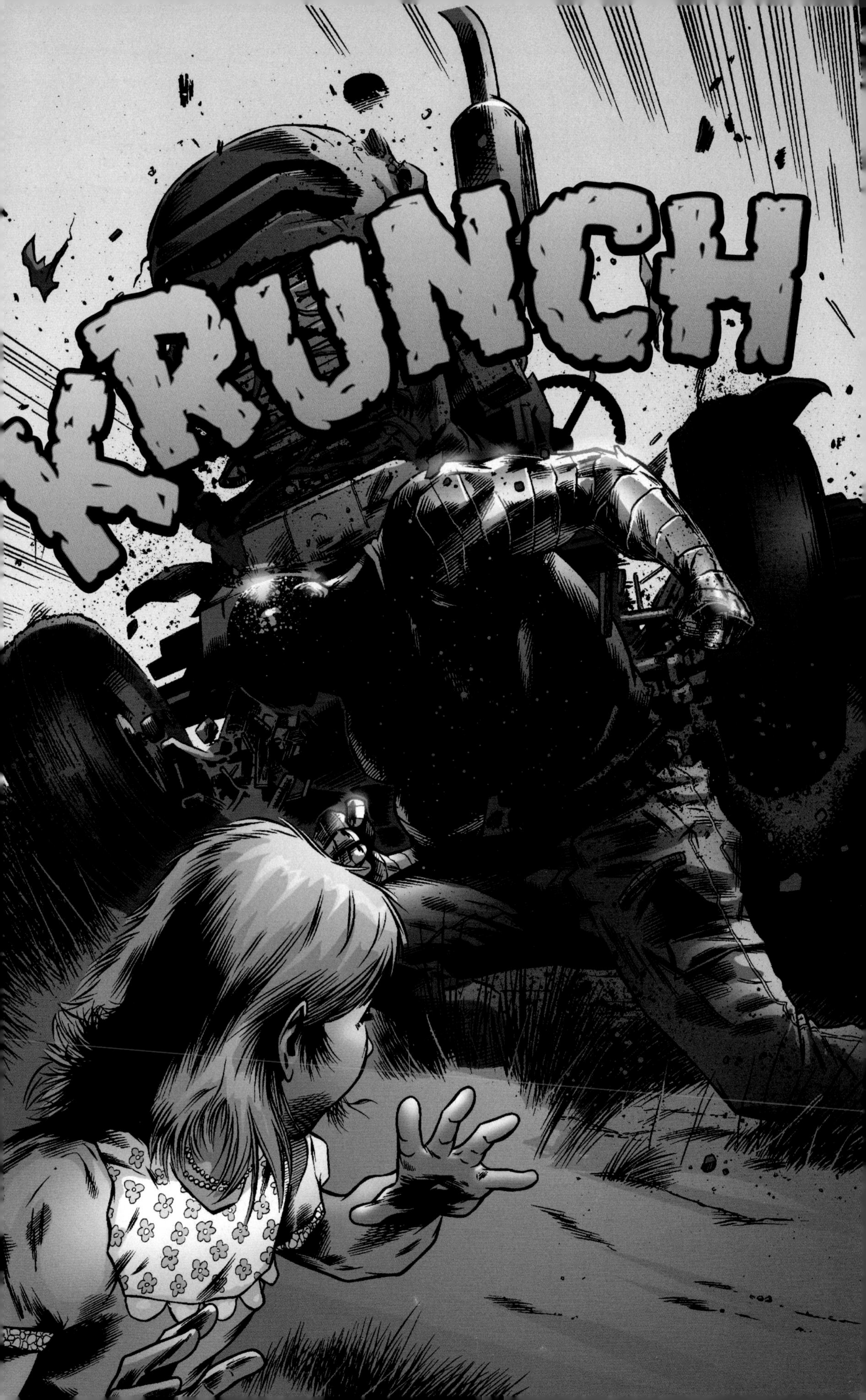
KRUNCH

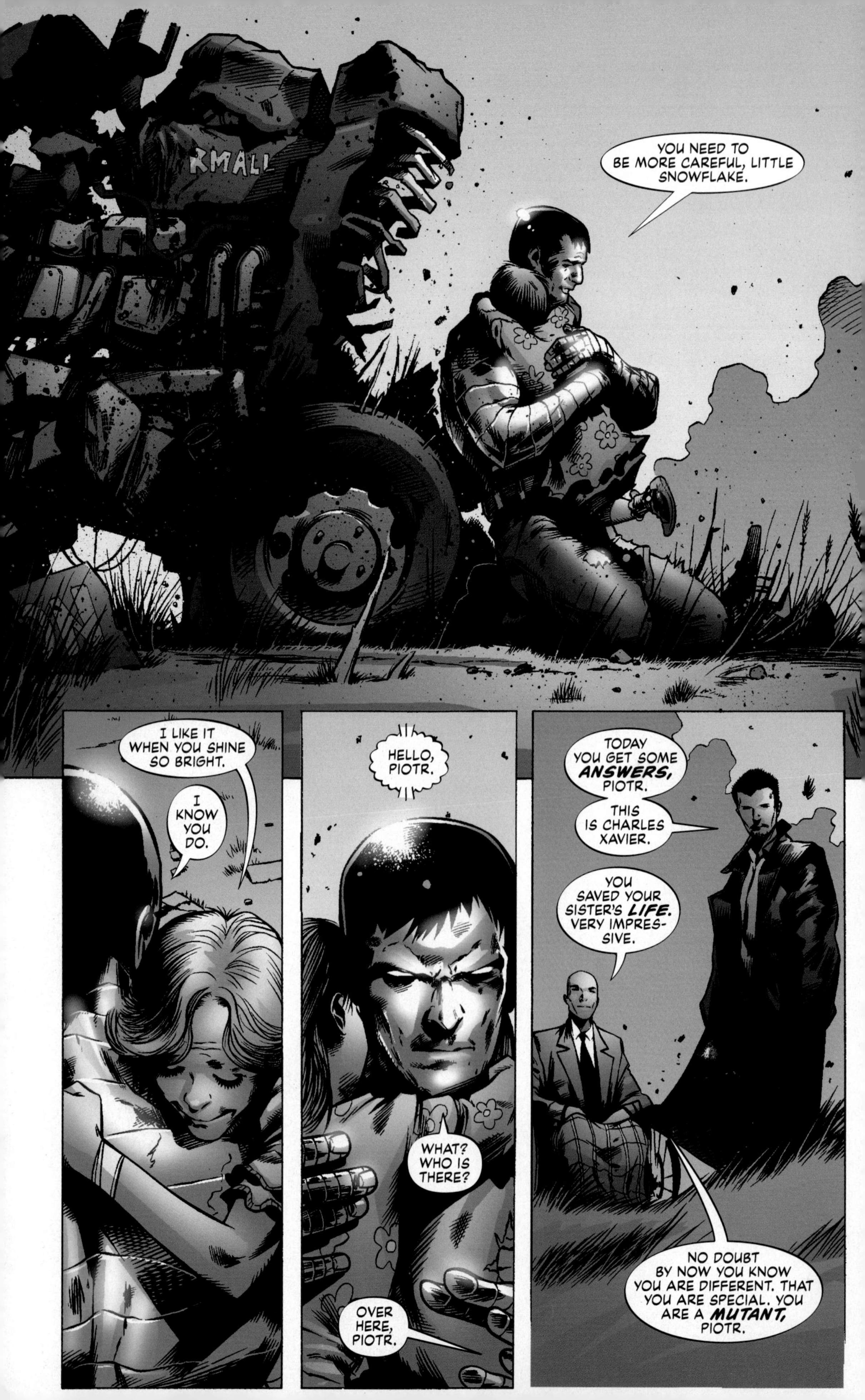
RMALL
YOU NEED TO BE MORE CAREFUL, LITTLE SNOWFLAKE.
I LIKE IT WHEN YOU SHINE SO BRIGHT.
I KNOW YOU DO.
HELLO, PIOTR.
WHAT? WHO IS THERE?
OVER HERE, PIOTR.
TODAY YOU GET SOME ANSWERS, PIOTR.
THIS IS CHARLES XAVIER.
YOU SAVED YOUR SISTER'S LIFE. VERY IMPRES-SIVE.
NO DOUBT BY NOW YOU KNOW YOU ARE DIFFERENT. THAT YOU ARE SPECIAL. YOU ARE A MUTANT, PIOTR.

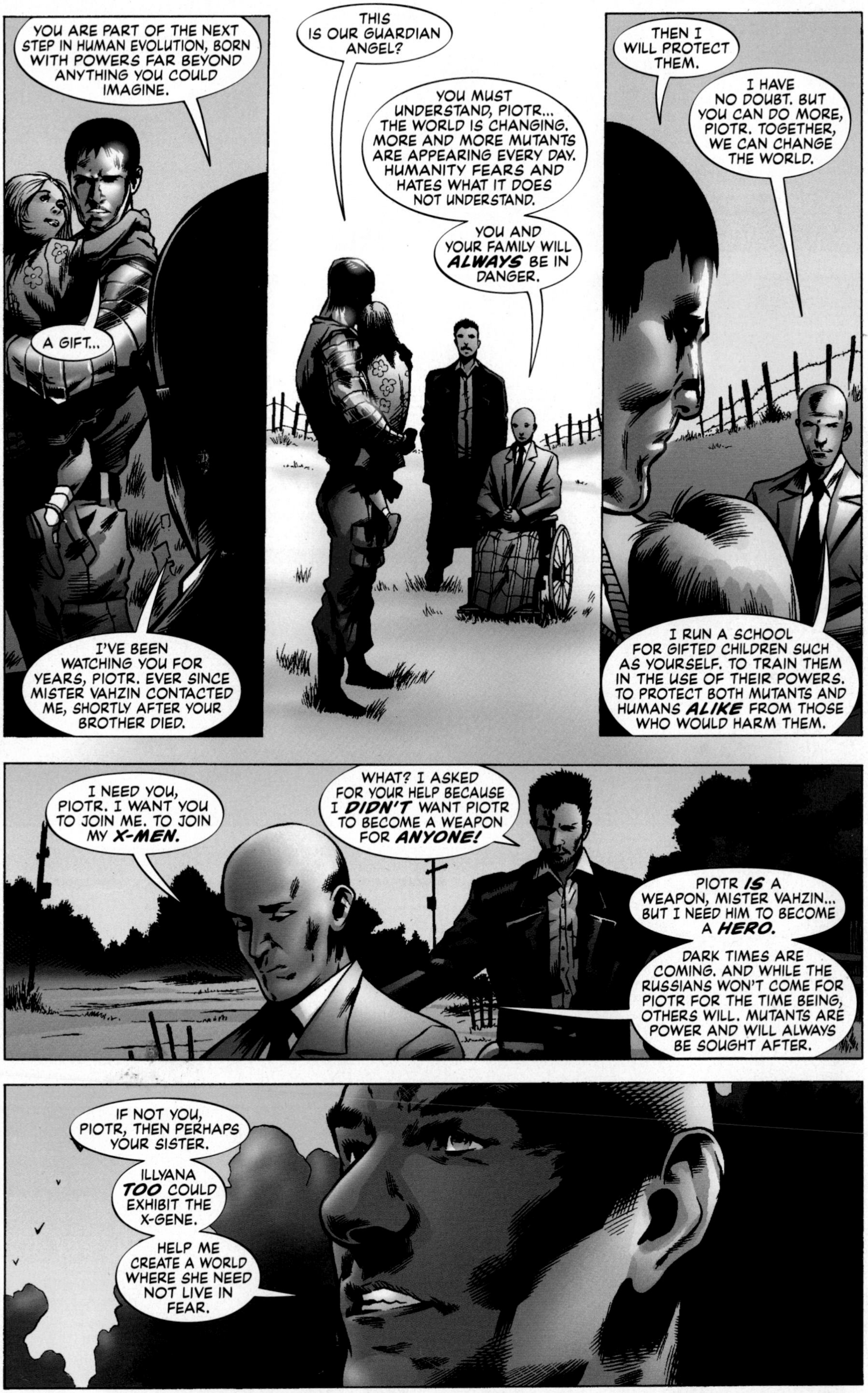
YOU ARE PART OF THE NEXT STEP IN HUMAN EVOLUTION, BORN WITH POWERS FAR BEYOND ANYTHING YOU COULD IMAGINE.
A GIFT...
I'VE BEEN WATCHING YOU FOR YEARS, PIOTR. EVER SINCE MISTER VAHZIN CONTACTED ME, SHORTLY AFTER YOUR BROTHER DIED.
THIS IS OUR GUARDIAN ANGEL?
YOU MUST UNDERSTAND, PIOTR... THE WORLD IS CHANGING. MORE AND MORE MUTANTS ARE APPEARING EVERY DAY. HUMANITY FEARS AND HATES WHAT IT DOES NOT UNDERSTAND.
YOU AND YOUR FAMILY WILL ALWAYS BE IN DANGER.
THEN I WILL PROTECT THEM.
I HAVE NO DOUBT. BUT YOU CAN DO MORE, PIOTR. TOGETHER, WE CAN CHANGE THE WORLD.
I RUN A SCHOOL FOR GIFTED CHILDREN SUCH AS YOURSELF. TO TRAIN THEM IN THE USE OF THEIR POWERS. TO PROTECT BOTH MUTANTS AND HUMANS ALIKE FROM THOSE WHO WOULD HARM THEM.
I NEED YOU, PIOTR. I WANT YOU TO JOIN ME. TO JOIN MY X-MEN.
WHAT? I ASKED FOR YOUR HELP BECAUSE I DIDN'T WANT PIOTR TO BECOME A WEAPON FOR ANYONE!
PIOTR IS A WEAPON, MISTER VAHZIN... BUT I NEED HIM TO BECOME A HERO.
DARK TIMES ARE COMING. AND WHILE THE RUSSIANS WON'T COME FOR PIOTR FOR THE TIME BEING, OTHERS WILL. MUTANTS ARE POWER AND WILL ALWAYS BE SOUGHT AFTER.
IF NOT YOU, PIOTR, THEN PERHAPS YOUR SISTER.
ILLYANA TOO COULD EXHIBIT THE X-GENE.
HELP ME CREATE A WORLD WHERE SHE NEED NOT LIVE IN FEAR.

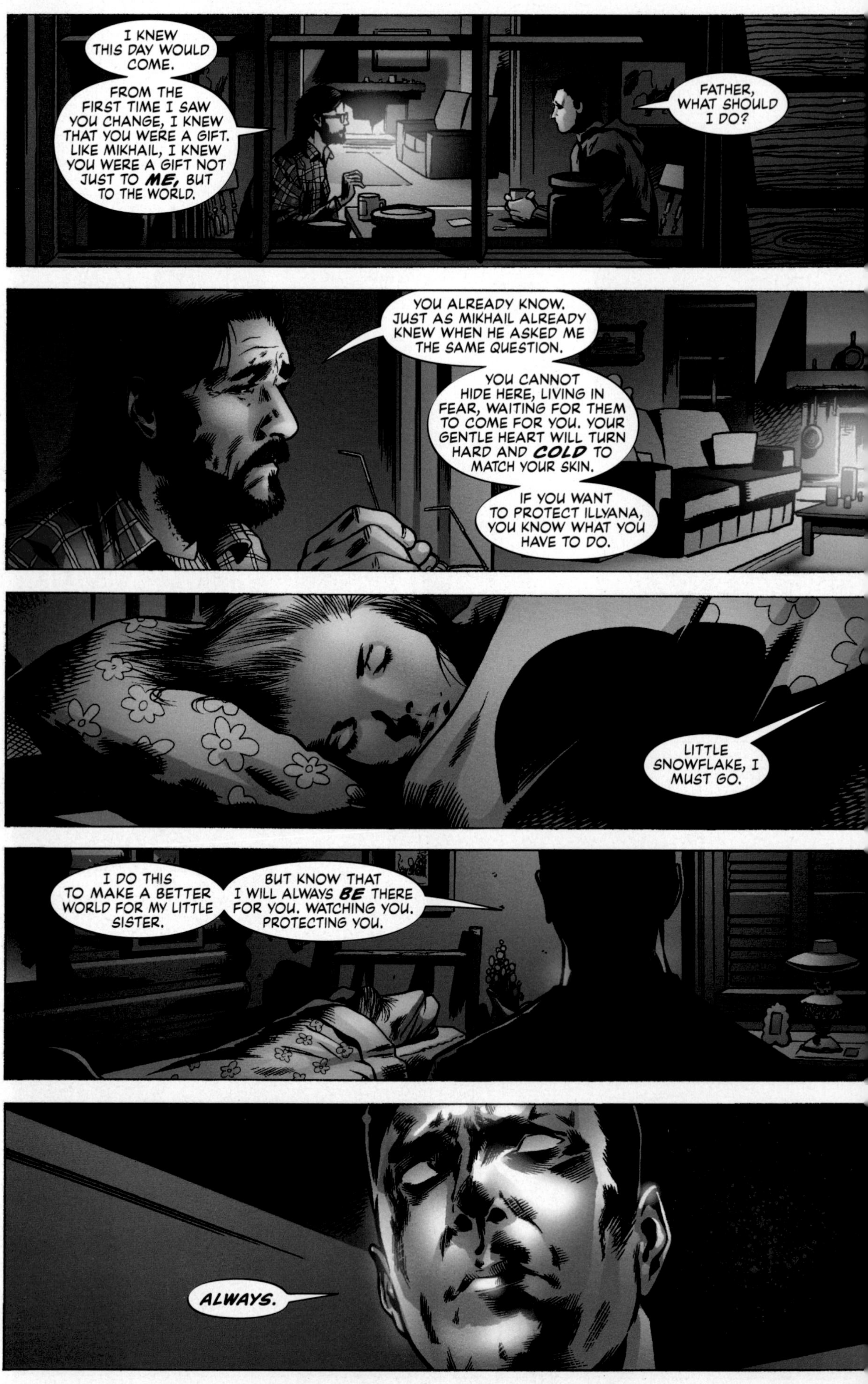
I KNEW THIS DAY WOULD COME.
FROM THE FIRST TIME I SAW YOU CHANGE, I KNEW THAT YOU WERE A GIFT. LIKE MIKHAIL, I KNEW YOU WERE A GIFT NOT JUST TO *ME,* BUT TO THE WORLD.
FATHER, WHAT SHOULD I DO?
YOU ALREADY KNOW. JUST AS MIKHAIL ALREADY KNEW WHEN HE ASKED ME THE SAME QUESTION.
YOU CANNOT HIDE HERE, LIVING IN FEAR, WAITING FOR THEM TO COME FOR YOU. YOUR GENTLE HEART WILL TURN HARD AND *COLD* TO MATCH YOUR SKIN.
IF YOU WANT TO PROTECT ILLYANA, YOU KNOW WHAT YOU HAVE TO DO.
LITTLE SNOWFLAKE, I MUST GO.
I DO THIS TO MAKE A BETTER WORLD FOR MY LITTLE SISTER.
BUT KNOW THAT I WILL ALWAYS *BE* THERE FOR YOU. WATCHING YOU. PROTECTING YOU.
*ALWAYS.*

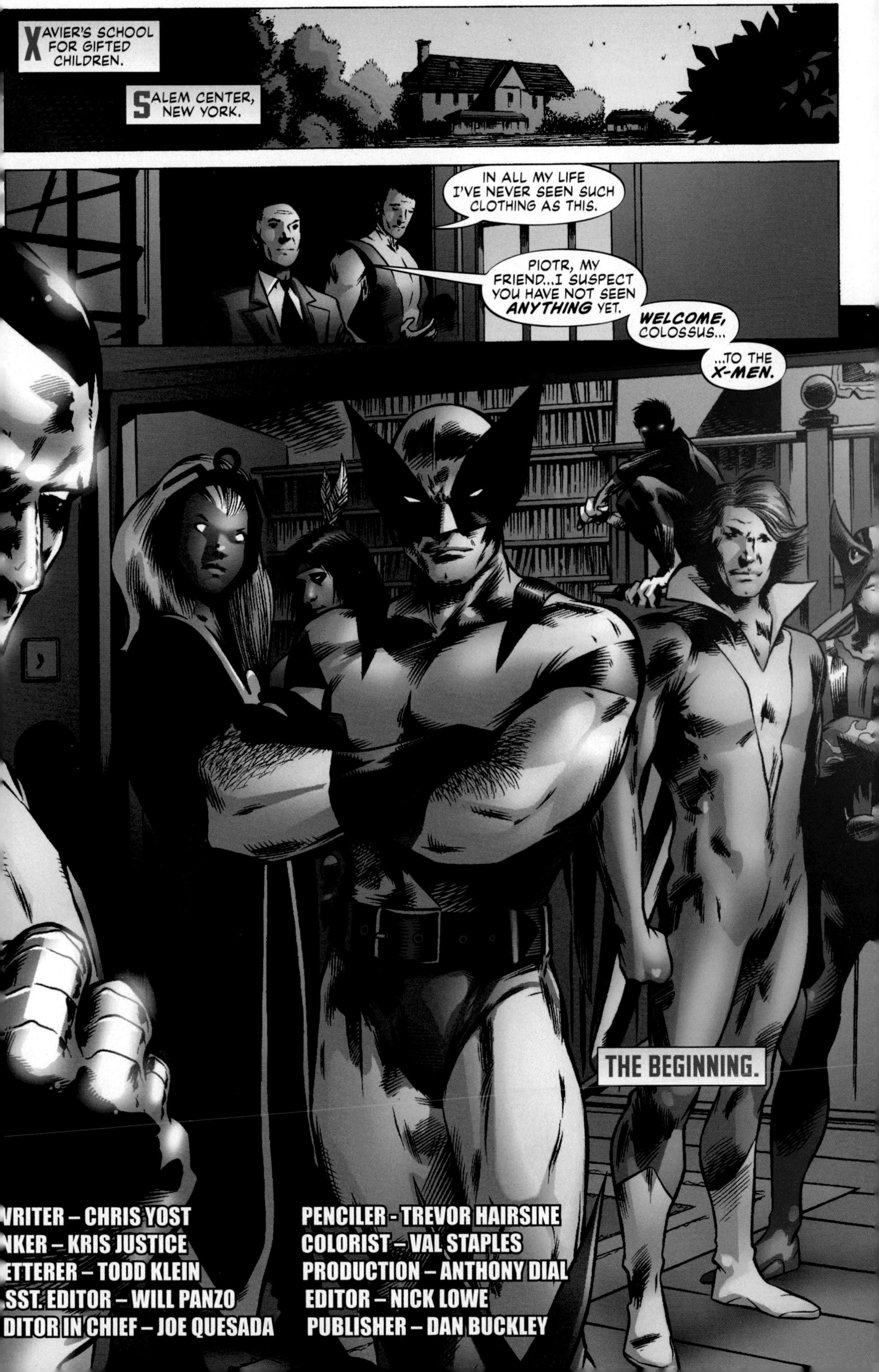
XAVIER'S SCHOOL FOR GIFTED CHILDREN.
SALEM CENTER, NEW YORK.
IN ALL MY LIFE I'VE NEVER SEEN SUCH CLOTHING AS THIS.
PIOTR, MY FRIEND...I SUSPECT YOU HAVE NOT SEEN ANYTHING YET.
WELCOME, COLOSSUS...
...TO THE X-MEN.
THE BEGINNING.

VRITER – CHRIS YOST
NKER – KRIS JUSTICE
ETTERER – TODD KLEIN
SST. EDITOR – WILL PANZO
DITOR IN CHIEF – JOE QUESADA
PENCILER - TREVOR HAIRSINE
COLORIST – VAL STAPLES
PRODUCTION – ANTHONY DIAL
EDITOR – NICK LOWE
PUBLISHER – DAN BUCKLEY

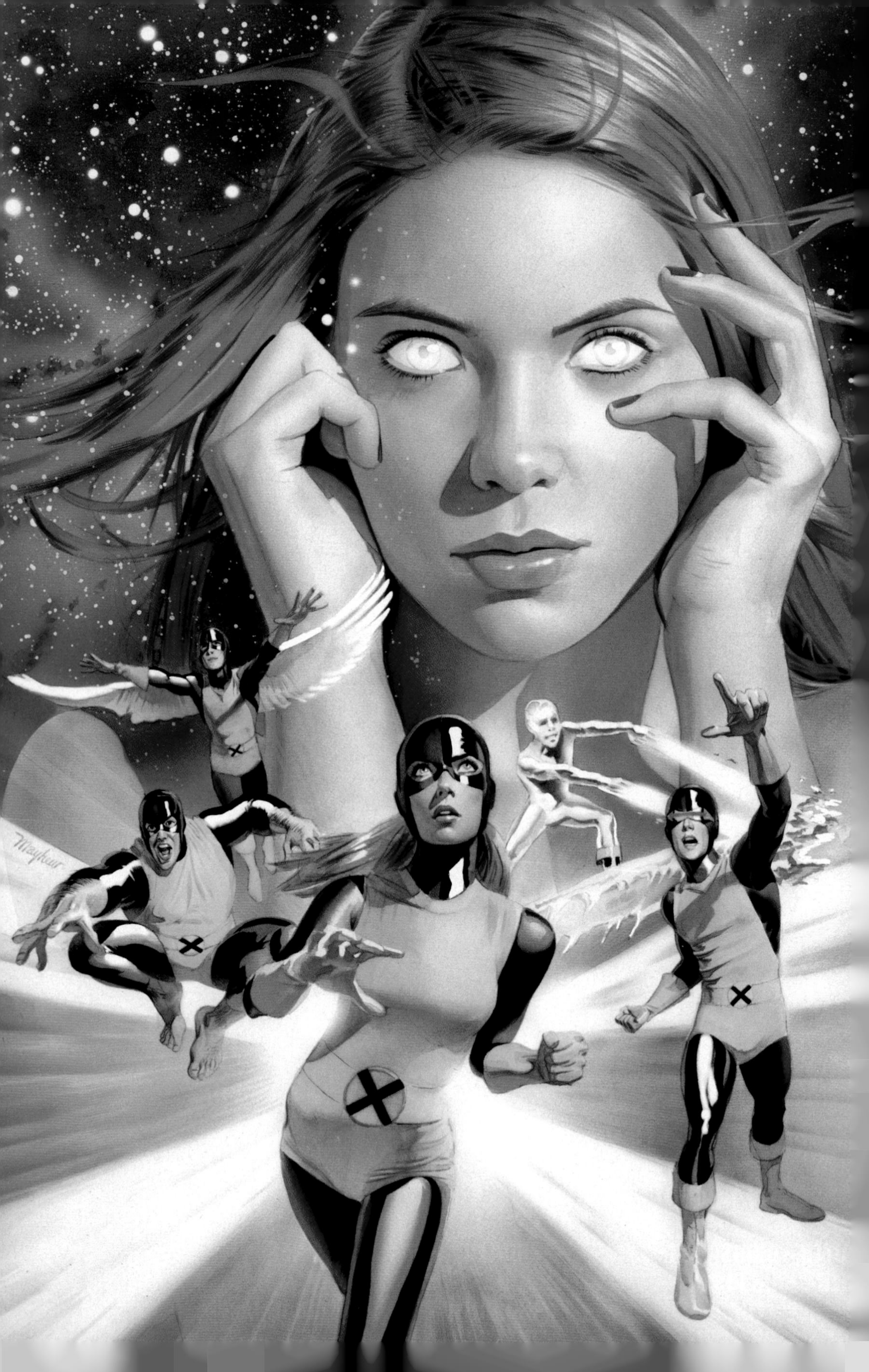

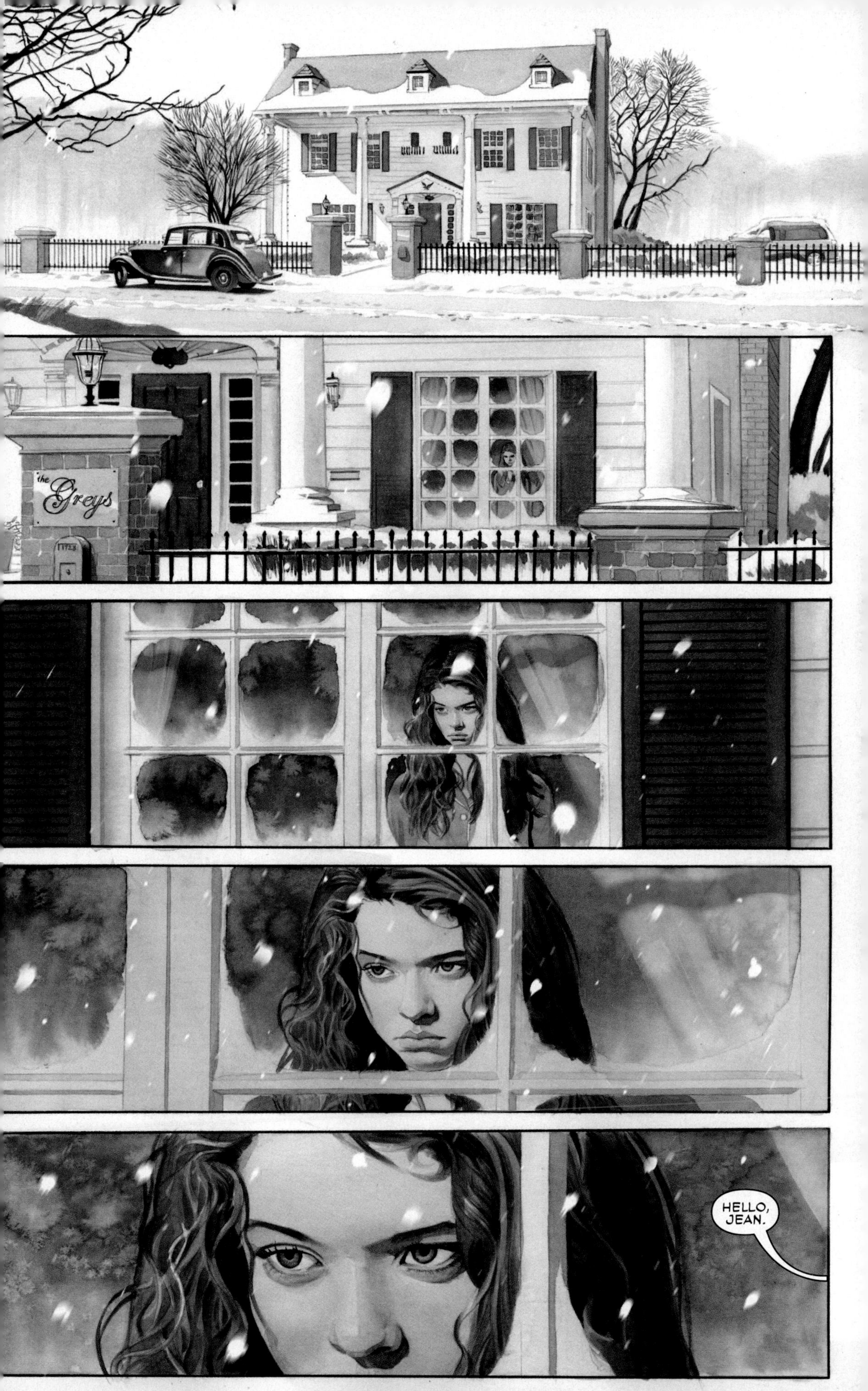
the Greys
HELLO, JEAN.

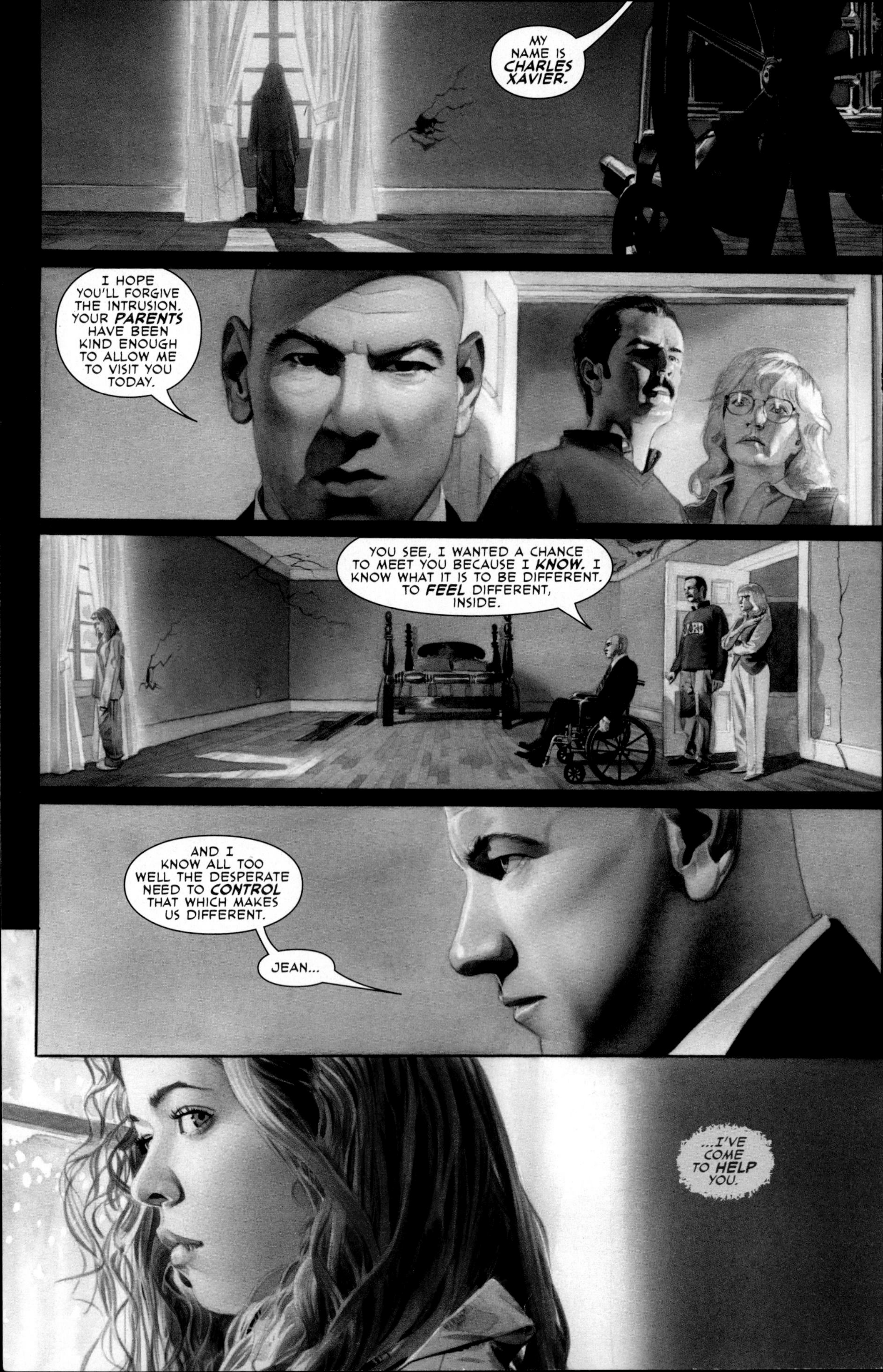
MY NAME IS CHARLES XAVIER.
I HOPE YOU'LL FORGIVE THE INTRUSION. YOUR PARENTS HAVE BEEN KIND ENOUGH TO ALLOW ME TO VISIT YOU TODAY.
YOU SEE, I WANTED A CHANCE TO MEET YOU BECAUSE I KNOW. I KNOW WHAT IT IS TO BE DIFFERENT. TO FEEL DIFFERENT, INSIDE.
AND I KNOW ALL TOO WELL THE DESPERATE NEED TO CONTROL THAT WHICH MAKES US DIFFERENT.
JEAN...
...I'VE COME TO HELP YOU.

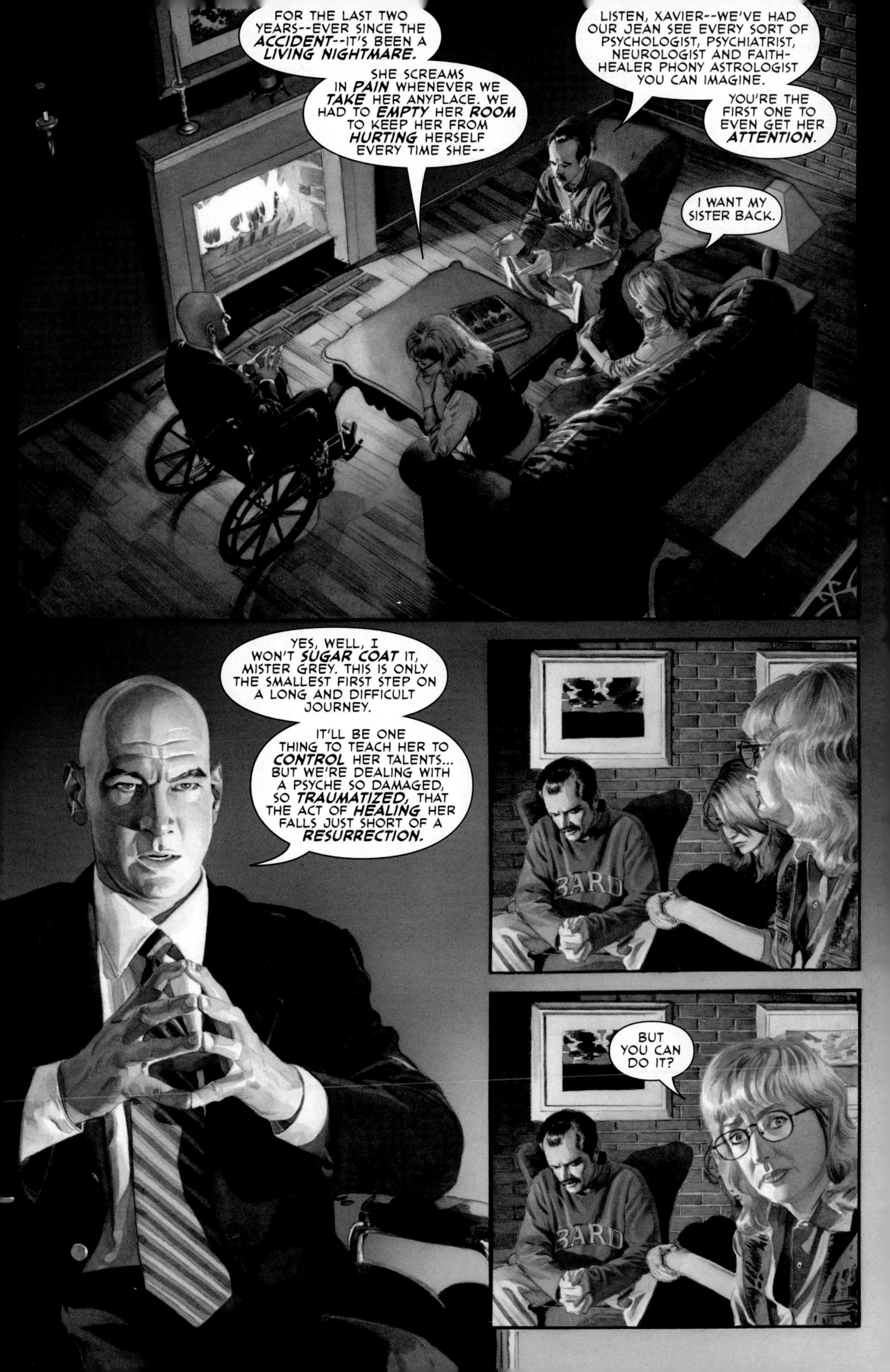
FOR THE LAST TWO YEARS--EVER SINCE THE ACCIDENT--IT'S BEEN A LIVING NIGHTMARE.
SHE SCREAMS IN PAIN WHENEVER WE TAKE HER ANYPLACE. WE HAD TO EMPTY HER ROOM TO KEEP HER FROM HURTING HERSELF EVERY TIME SHE--
LISTEN, XAVIER--WE'VE HAD OUR JEAN SEE EVERY SORT OF PSYCHOLOGIST, PSYCHIATRIST, NEUROLOGIST AND FAITH-HEALER PHONY ASTROLOGIST YOU CAN IMAGINE.
YOU'RE THE FIRST ONE TO EVEN GET HER ATTENTION.
I WANT MY SISTER BACK.
YES, WELL, I WON'T SUGAR COAT IT, MISTER GREY. THIS IS ONLY THE SMALLEST FIRST STEP ON A LONG AND DIFFICULT JOURNEY.
IT'LL BE ONE THING TO TEACH HER TO CONTROL HER TALENTS... BUT WE'RE DEALING WITH A PSYCHE SO DAMAGED, SO TRAUMATIZED, THAT THE ACT OF HEALING HER FALLS JUST SHORT OF A RESURRECTION.
BUT YOU CAN DO IT?

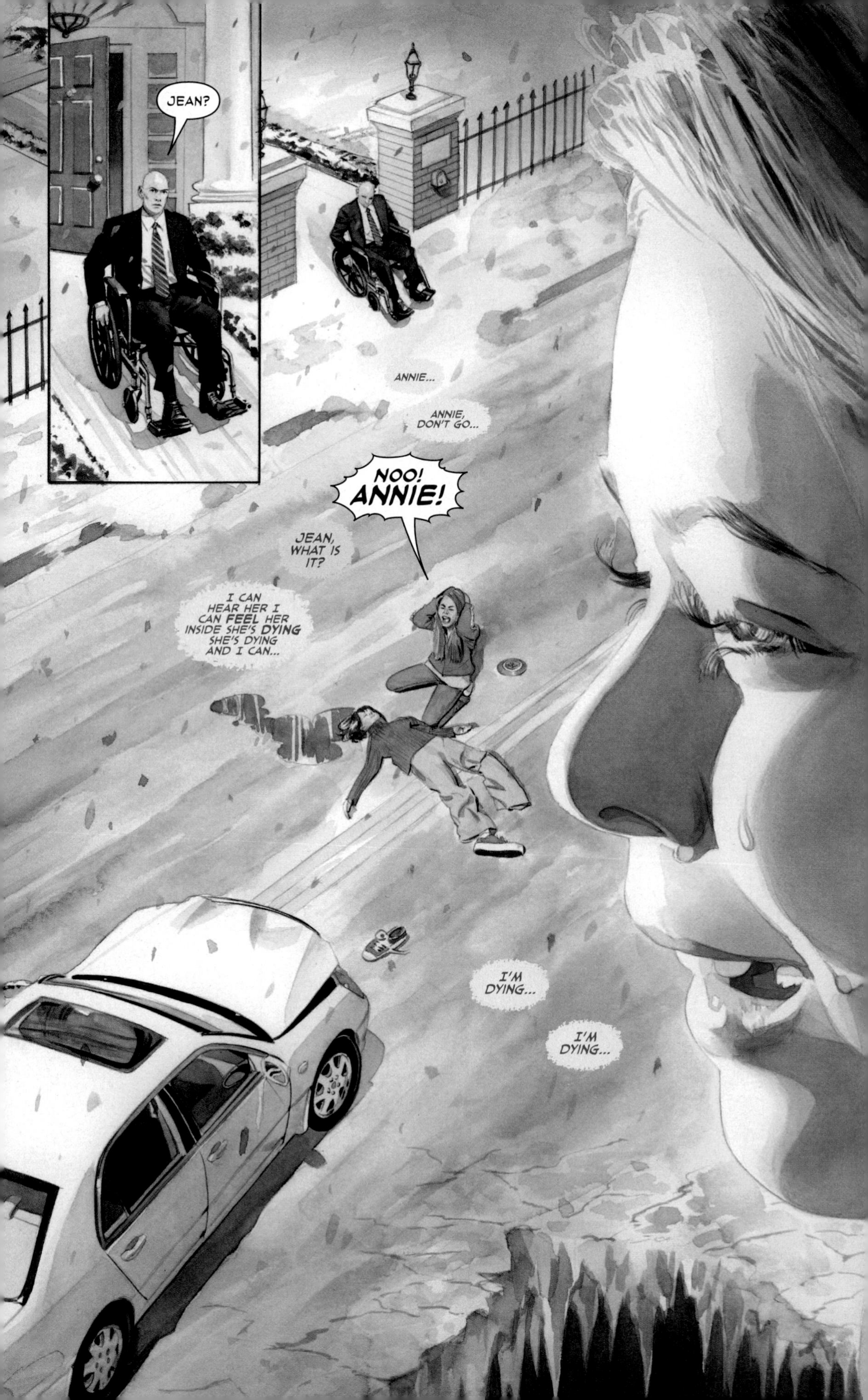
JEAN?
ANNIE...
ANNIE, DON'T GO...
NOO! ANNIE!
JEAN, WHAT IS IT?
I CAN HEAR HER I CAN FEEL HER INSIDE SHE'S DYING SHE'S DYING AND I CAN...
I'M DYING...
I'M DYING...

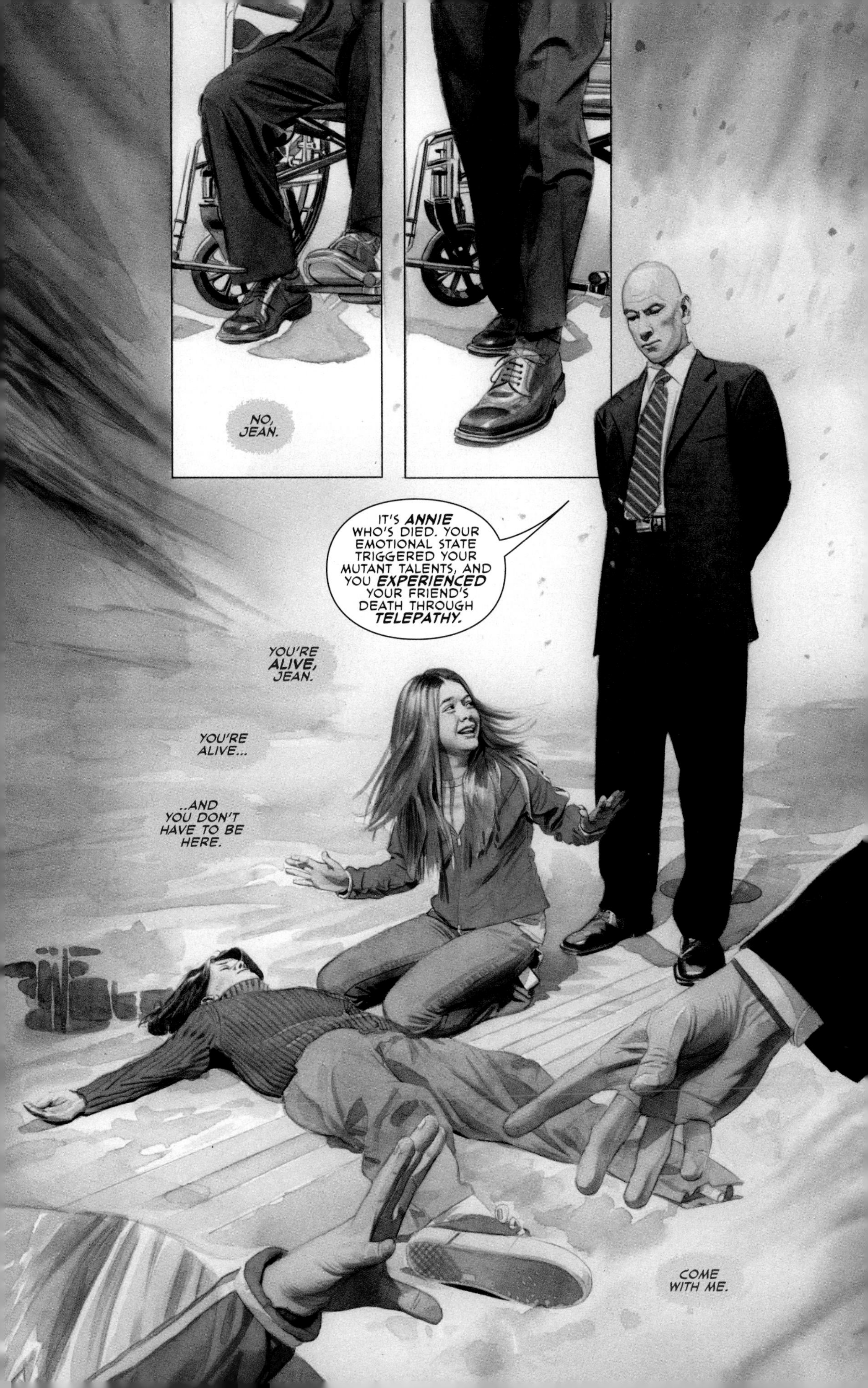
NO, JEAN.
IT'S ANNIE WHO'S DIED. YOUR EMOTIONAL STATE TRIGGERED YOUR MUTANT TALENTS, AND YOU EXPERIENCED YOUR FRIEND'S DEATH THROUGH TELEPATHY.
YOU'RE ALIVE, JEAN.
YOU'RE ALIVE...
..AND YOU DON'T HAVE TO BE HERE.
COME WITH ME.

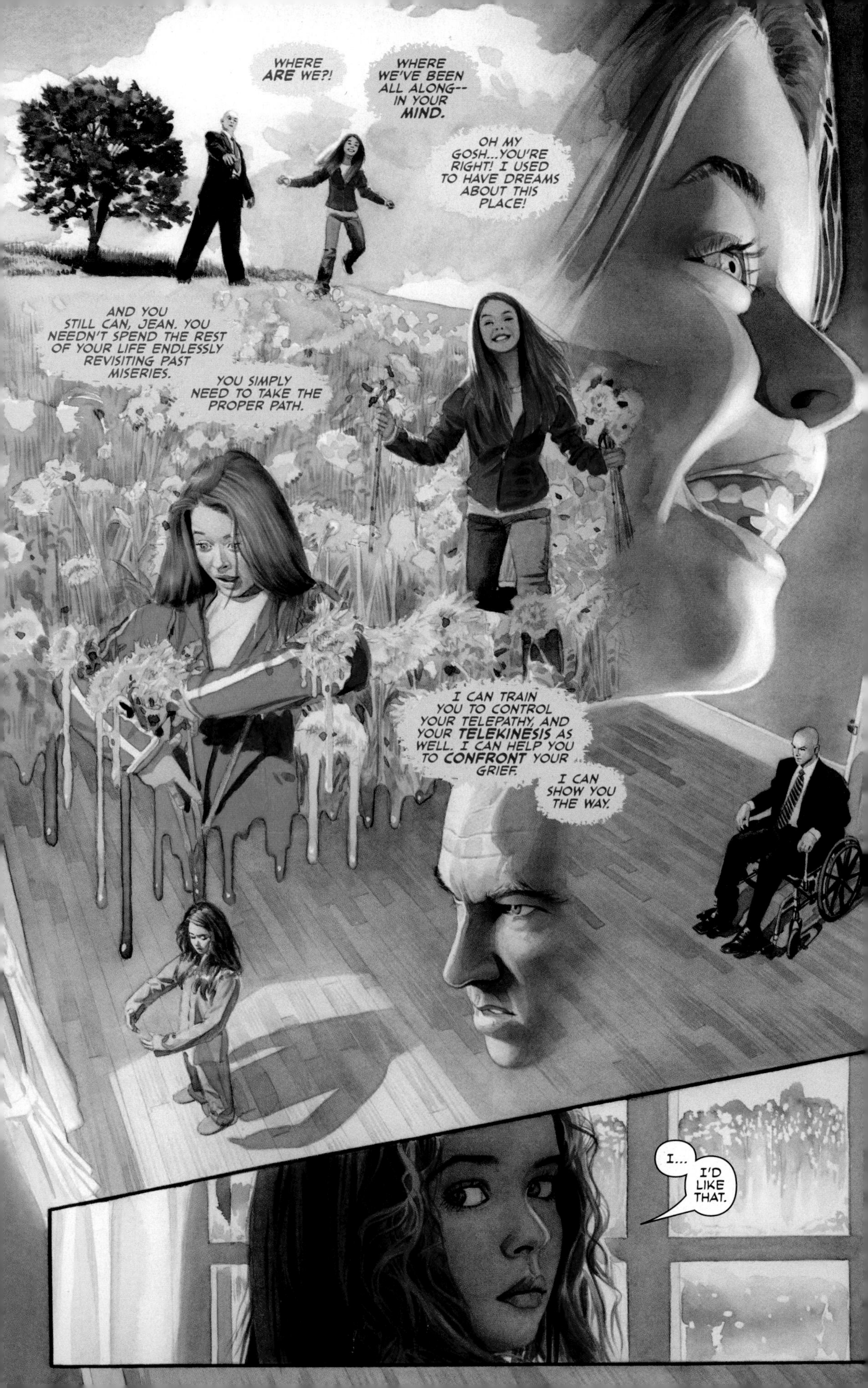
WHERE ARE WE?!
WHERE WE'VE BEEN ALL ALONG-- IN YOUR MIND.
OH MY GOSH...YOU'RE RIGHT! I USED TO HAVE DREAMS ABOUT THIS PLACE!
AND YOU STILL CAN, JEAN. YOU NEEDN'T SPEND THE REST OF YOUR LIFE ENDLESSLY REVISITING PAST MISERIES.
YOU SIMPLY NEED TO TAKE THE PROPER PATH.
I CAN TRAIN YOU TO CONTROL YOUR TELEPATHY, AND YOUR TELEKINESIS AS WELL. I CAN HELP YOU TO CONFRONT YOUR GRIEF.
I CAN SHOW YOU THE WAY.
I... I'D LIKE THAT.

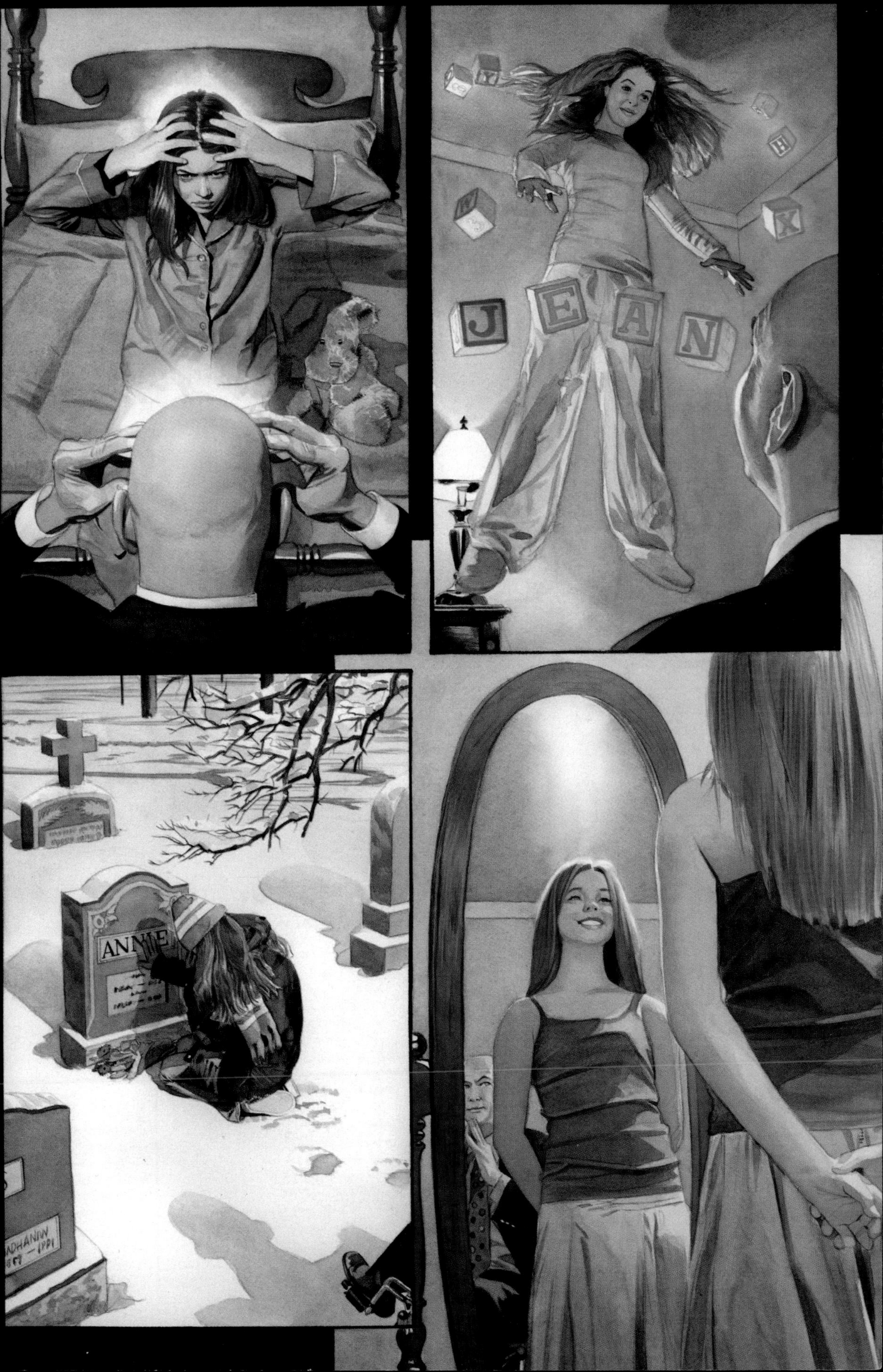
JEAN
X

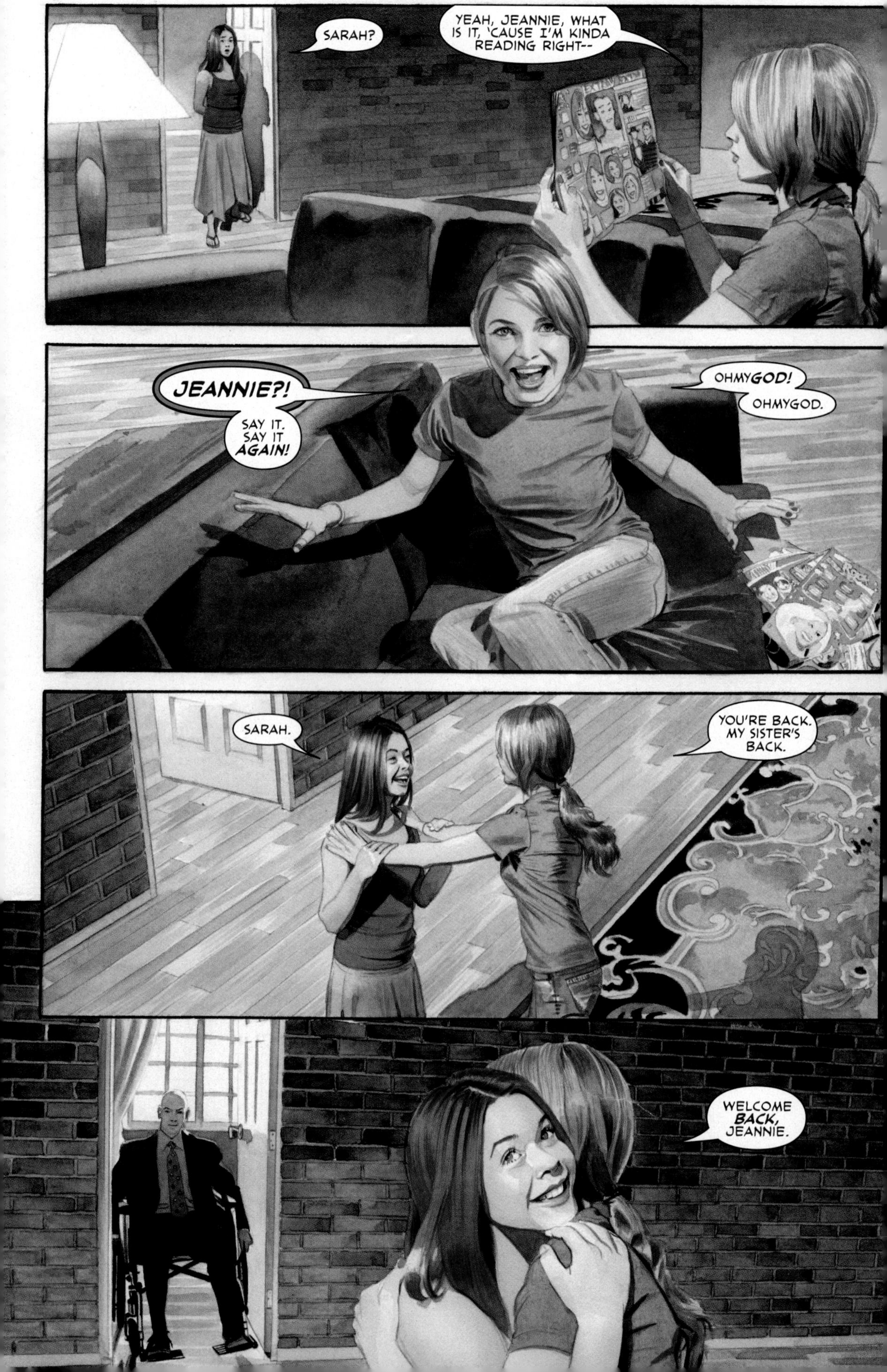
SARAH?
YEAH, JEANNIE, WHAT IS IT, 'CAUSE I'M KINDA READING RIGHT--
JEANNIE?!
SAY IT. SAY IT AGAIN!
OHMYGOD!
OHMYGOD.
SARAH.
YOU'RE BACK. MY SISTER'S BACK.
WELCOME BACK, JEANNIE.

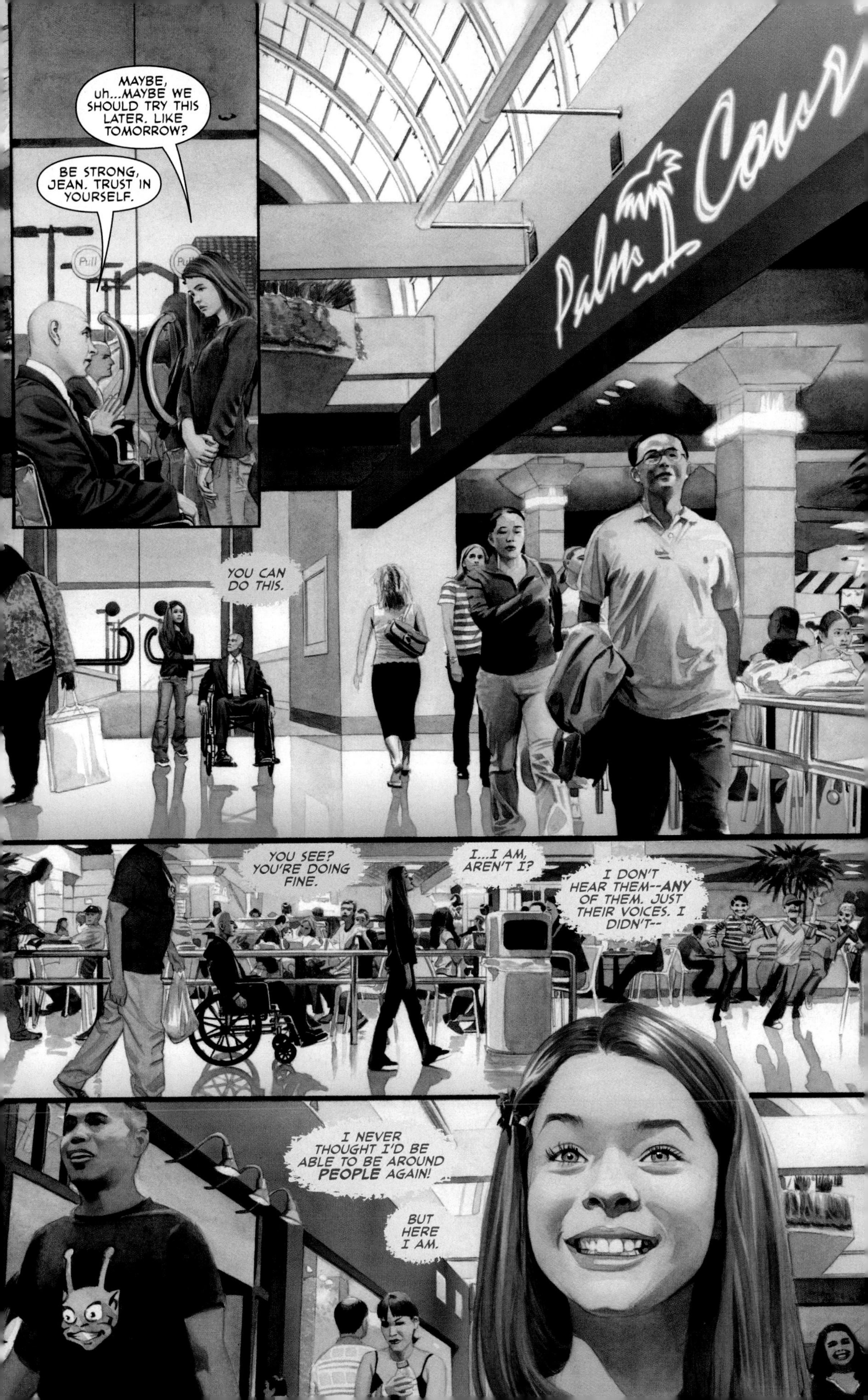
MAYBE, uh...MAYBE WE SHOULD TRY THIS LATER. LIKE TOMORROW?
BE STRONG, JEAN. TRUST IN YOURSELF.
Palm Cour
YOU CAN DO THIS.
YOU SEE? YOU'RE DOING FINE.
I...I AM, AREN'T I?
I DON'T HEAR THEM--ANY OF THEM. JUST THEIR VOICES. I DIDN'T--
I NEVER THOUGHT I'D BE ABLE TO BE AROUND PEOPLE AGAIN!
BUT HERE I AM.

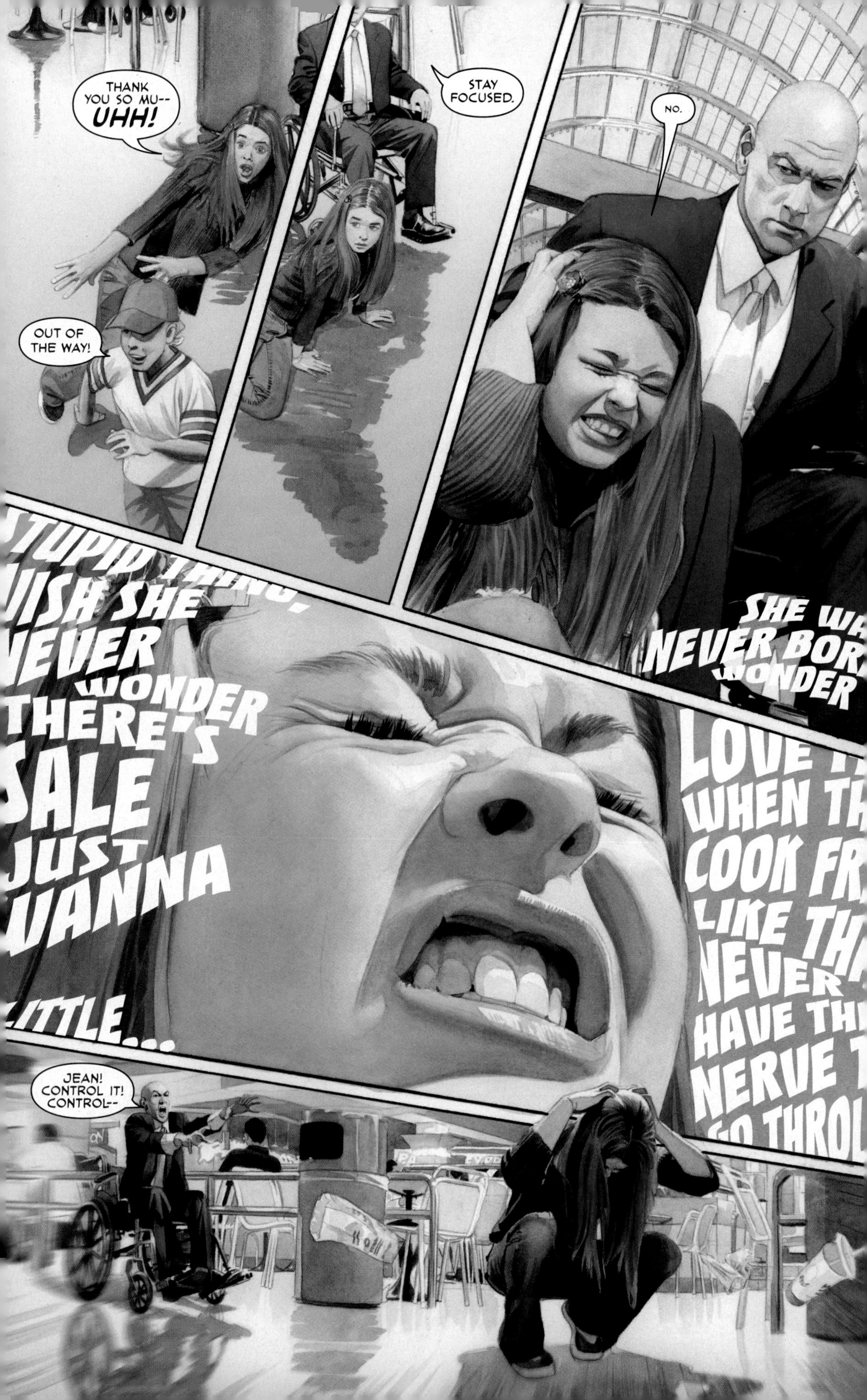
THANK YOU SO MU-- UHH!
OUT OF THE WAY!
STAY FOCUSED.
NO.
SHE
NEVER
WONDER
THERE'S
SALE
JUST
LITTLE...
NEVER
WONDER
WHEN
COOK
NEVER
HAVE
NERVE
JEAN! CONTROL IT! CONTROL--

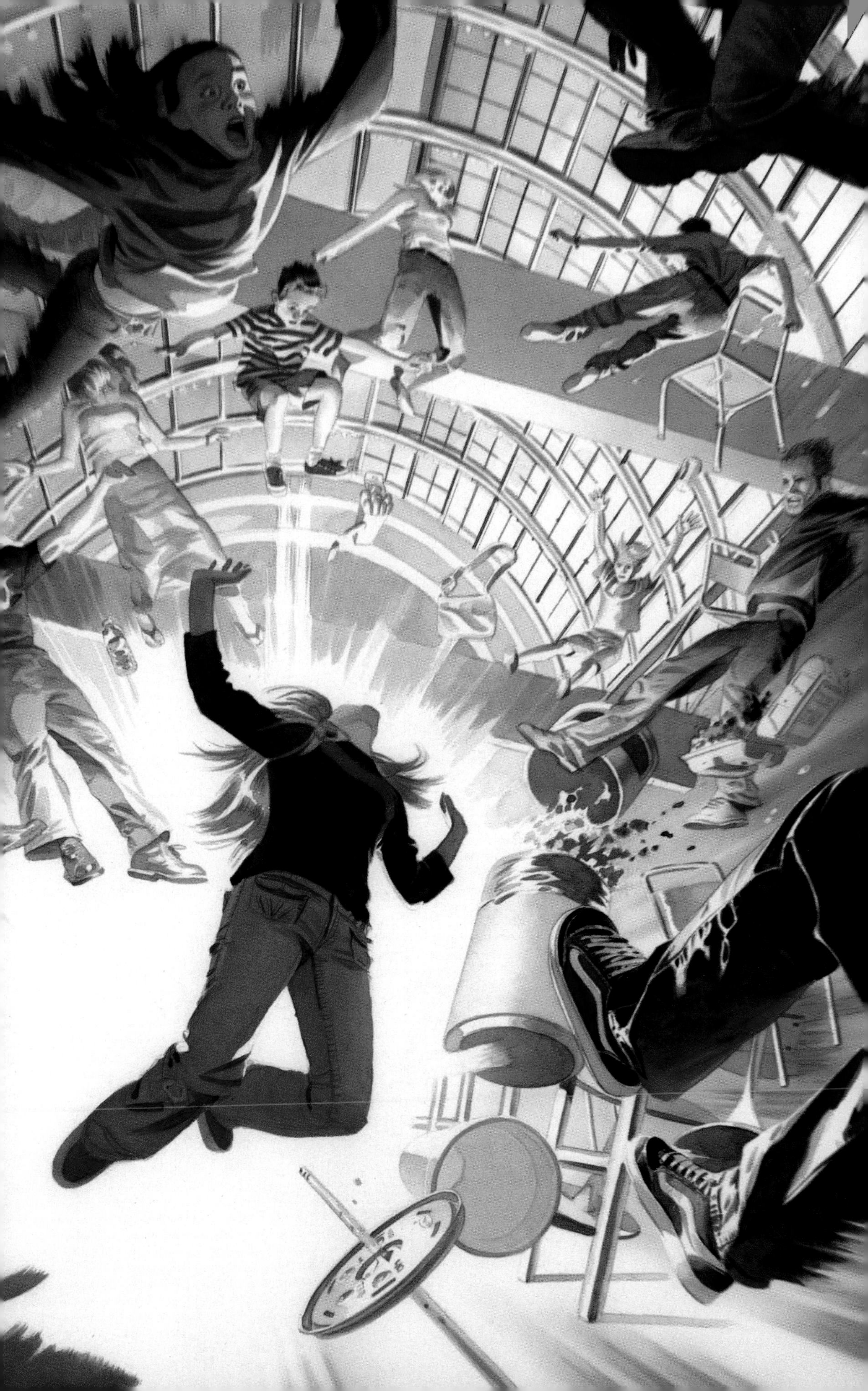

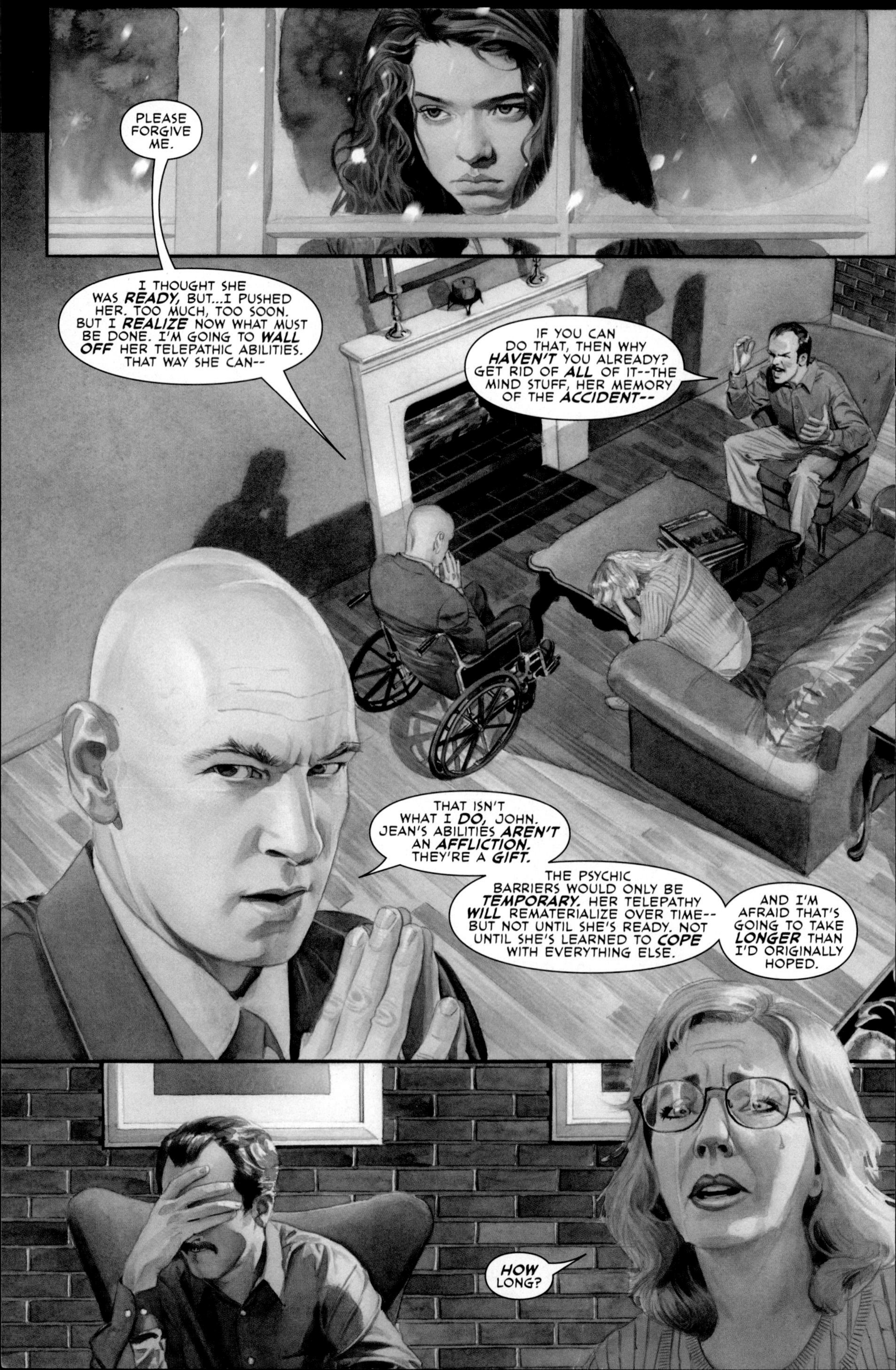
PLEASE FORGIVE ME.
I THOUGHT SHE WAS READY, BUT...I PUSHED HER. TOO MUCH, TOO SOON. BUT I REALIZE NOW WHAT MUST BE DONE. I'M GOING TO WALL OFF HER TELEPATHIC ABILITIES. THAT WAY SHE CAN--
IF YOU CAN DO THAT, THEN WHY HAVEN'T YOU ALREADY? GET RID OF ALL OF IT--THE MIND STUFF, HER MEMORY OF THE ACCIDENT--
THAT ISN'T WHAT I DO, JOHN. JEAN'S ABILITIES AREN'T AN AFFLICTION. THEY'RE A GIFT.
THE PSYCHIC BARRIERS WOULD ONLY BE TEMPORARY. HER TELEPATHY WILL REMATERIALIZE OVER TIME-- BUT NOT UNTIL SHE'S READY. NOT UNTIL SHE'S LEARNED TO COPE WITH EVERYTHING ELSE.
AND I'M AFRAID THAT'S GOING TO TAKE LONGER THAN I'D ORIGINALLY HOPED.
HOW LONG?

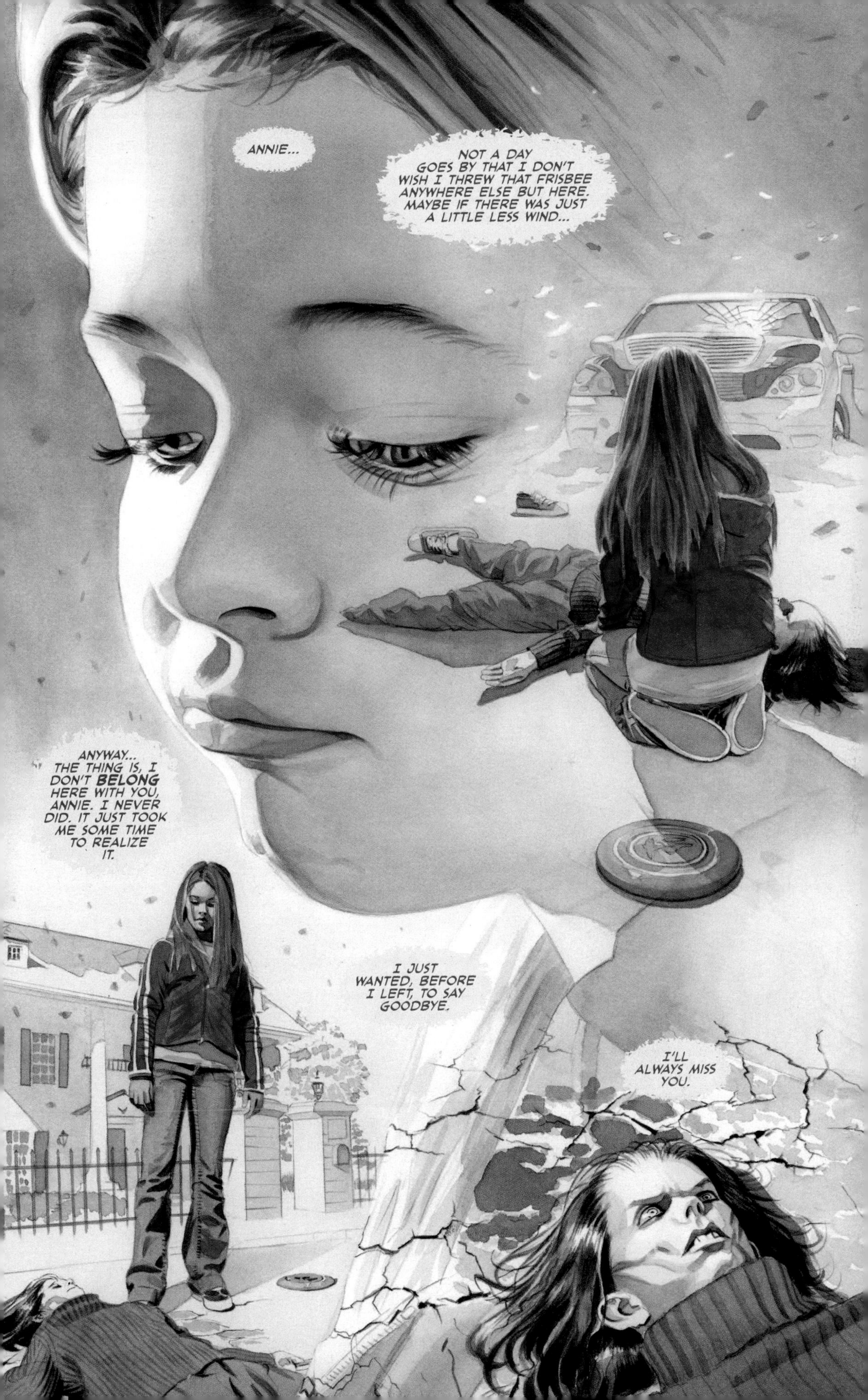
ANNIE...
NOT A DAY GOES BY THAT I DON'T WISH I THREW THAT FRISBEE ANYWHERE ELSE BUT HERE. MAYBE IF THERE WAS JUST A LITTLE LESS WIND...
ANYWAY... THE THING IS, I DON'T **BELONG** HERE WITH YOU, ANNIE. I NEVER DID. IT JUST TOOK ME SOME TIME TO REALIZE IT.
I JUST WANTED, BEFORE I LEFT, TO SAY GOODBYE.
I'LL ALWAYS MISS YOU.

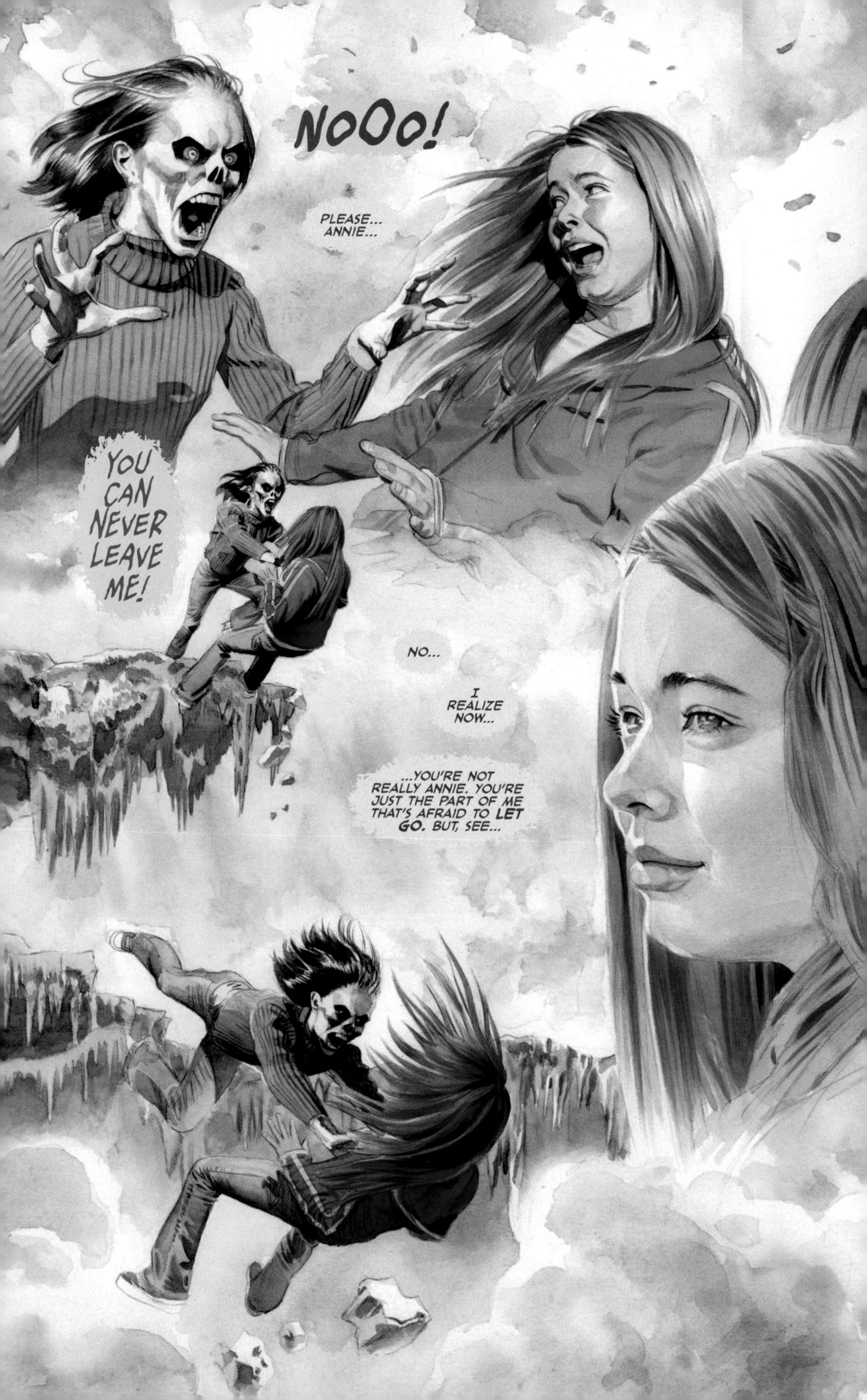
NOOO!
PLEASE... ANNIE...
YOU CAN NEVER LEAVE ME!
NO...
I REALIZE NOW...
...YOU'RE NOT REALLY ANNIE. YOU'RE JUST THE PART OF ME THAT'S AFRAID TO LET GO. BUT, SEE...

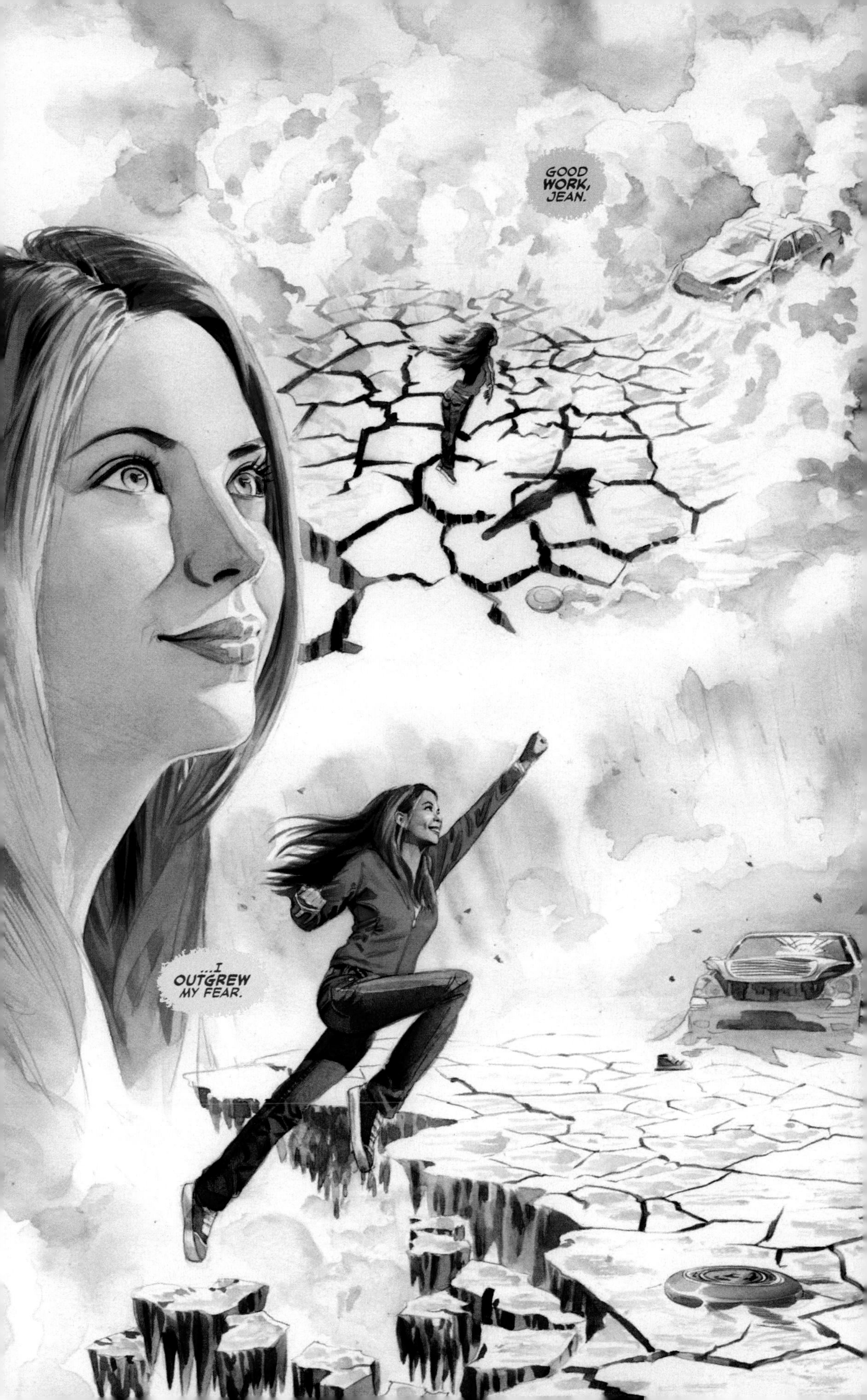
GOOD WORK, JEAN.
...I OUTGREW MY FEAR.

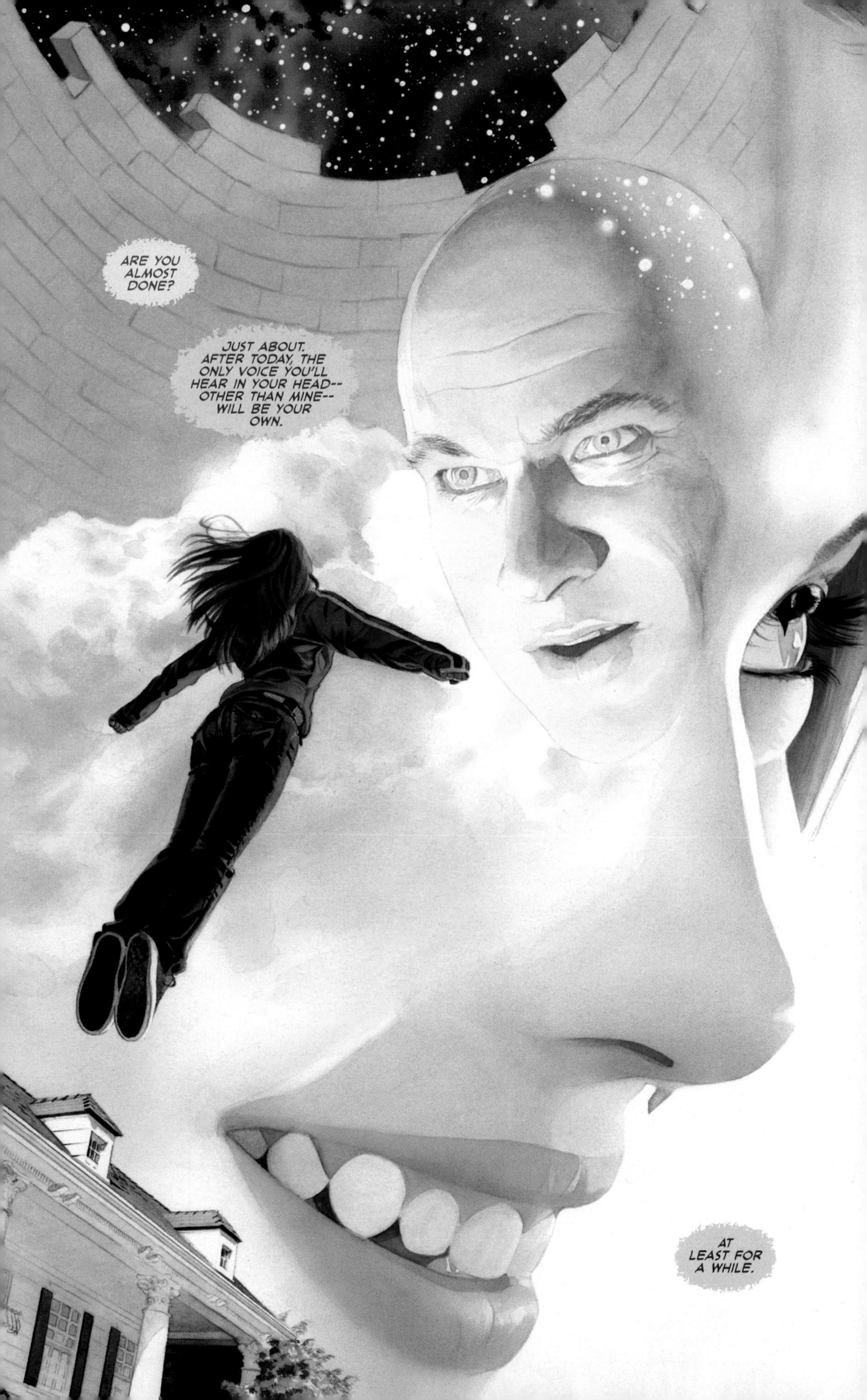
ARE YOU ALMOST DONE?
JUST ABOUT. AFTER TODAY, THE ONLY VOICE YOU'LL HEAR IN YOUR HEAD-- OTHER THAN MINE-- WILL BE YOUR OWN.
AT LEAST FOR A WHILE.

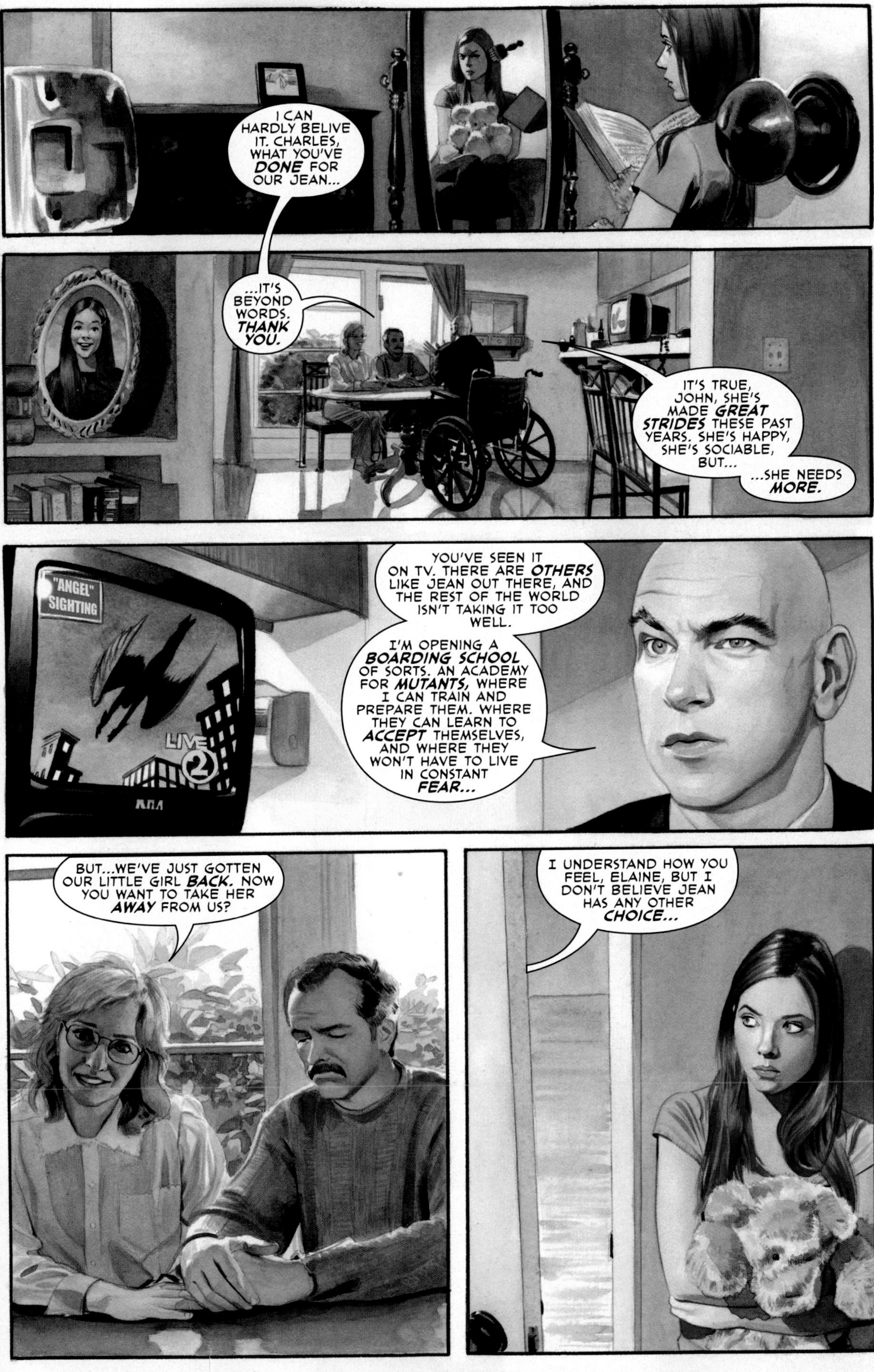
I CAN HARDLY BELIVE IT. CHARLES, WHAT YOU'VE DONE FOR OUR JEAN...
...IT'S BEYOND WORDS. THANK YOU.
IT'S TRUE, JOHN, SHE'S MADE GREAT STRIDES THESE PAST YEARS. SHE'S HAPPY, SHE'S SOCIABLE, BUT...
...SHE NEEDS MORE.
"ANGEL" SIGHTING
LIVE 2
YOU'VE SEEN IT ON TV. THERE ARE OTHERS LIKE JEAN OUT THERE, AND THE REST OF THE WORLD ISN'T TAKING IT TOO WELL.
I'M OPENING A BOARDING SCHOOL OF SORTS. AN ACADEMY FOR MUTANTS, WHERE I CAN TRAIN AND PREPARE THEM. WHERE THEY CAN LEARN TO ACCEPT THEMSELVES, AND WHERE THEY WON'T HAVE TO LIVE IN CONSTANT FEAR...
BUT...WE'VE JUST GOTTEN OUR LITTLE GIRL BACK. NOW YOU WANT TO TAKE HER AWAY FROM US?
I UNDERSTAND HOW YOU FEEL, ELAINE, BUT I DON'T BELIEVE JEAN HAS ANY OTHER CHOICE...

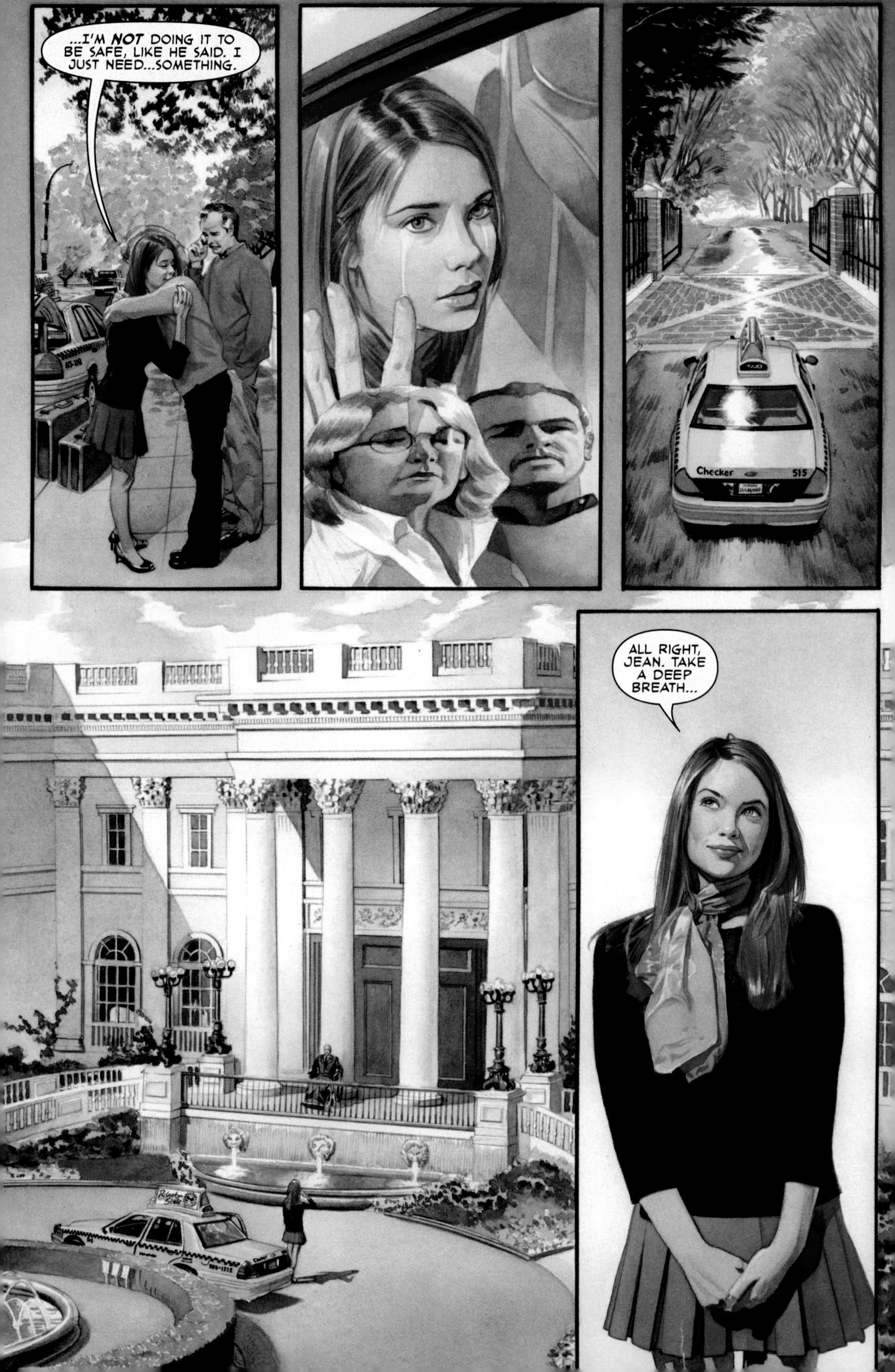
...I'M **NOT** DOING IT TO BE SAFE, LIKE HE SAID. I JUST NEED...SOMETHING.
Checker
515
ALL RIGHT, JEAN. TAKE A DEEP BREATH...

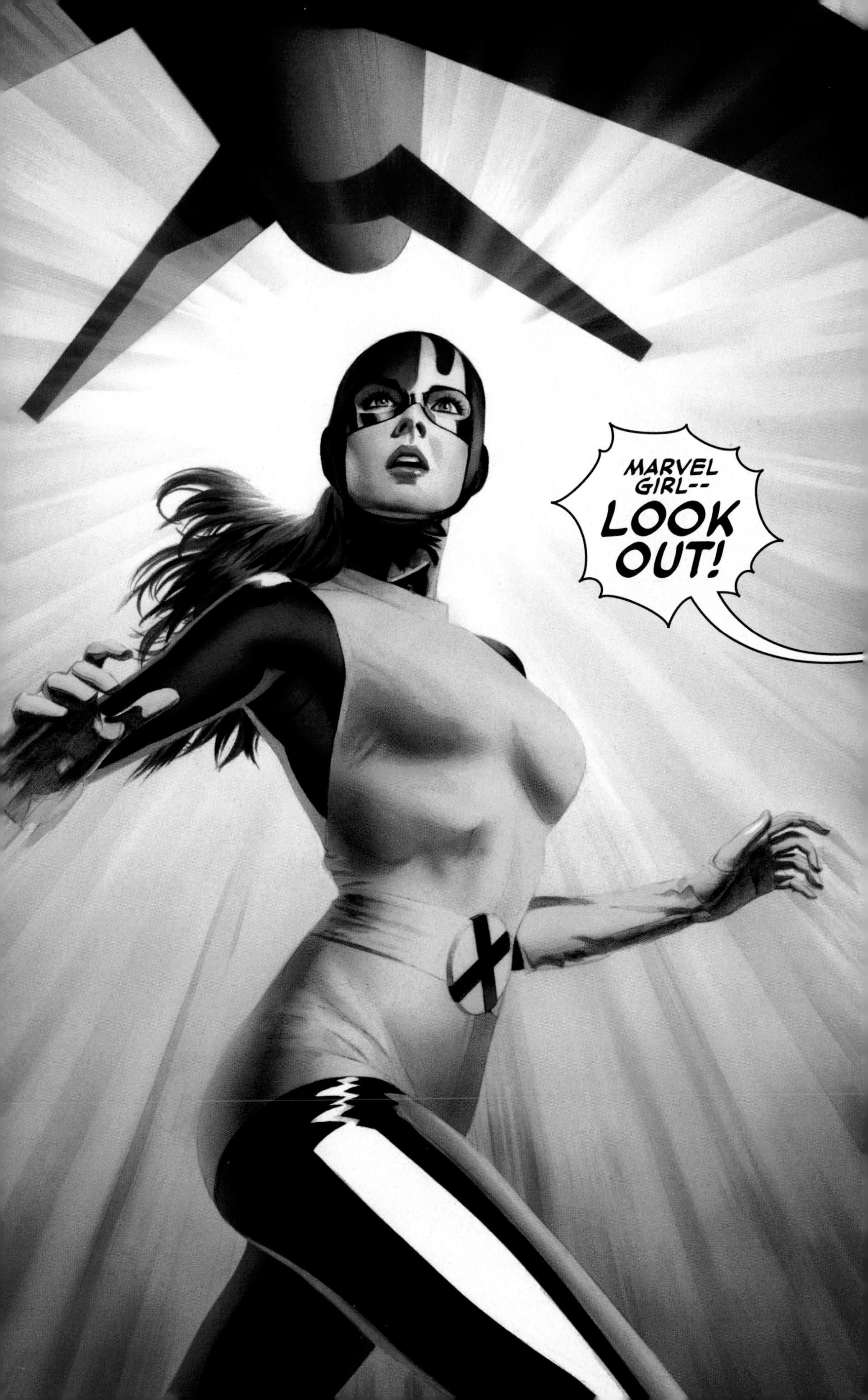
MARVEL GIRL-- LOOK OUT!

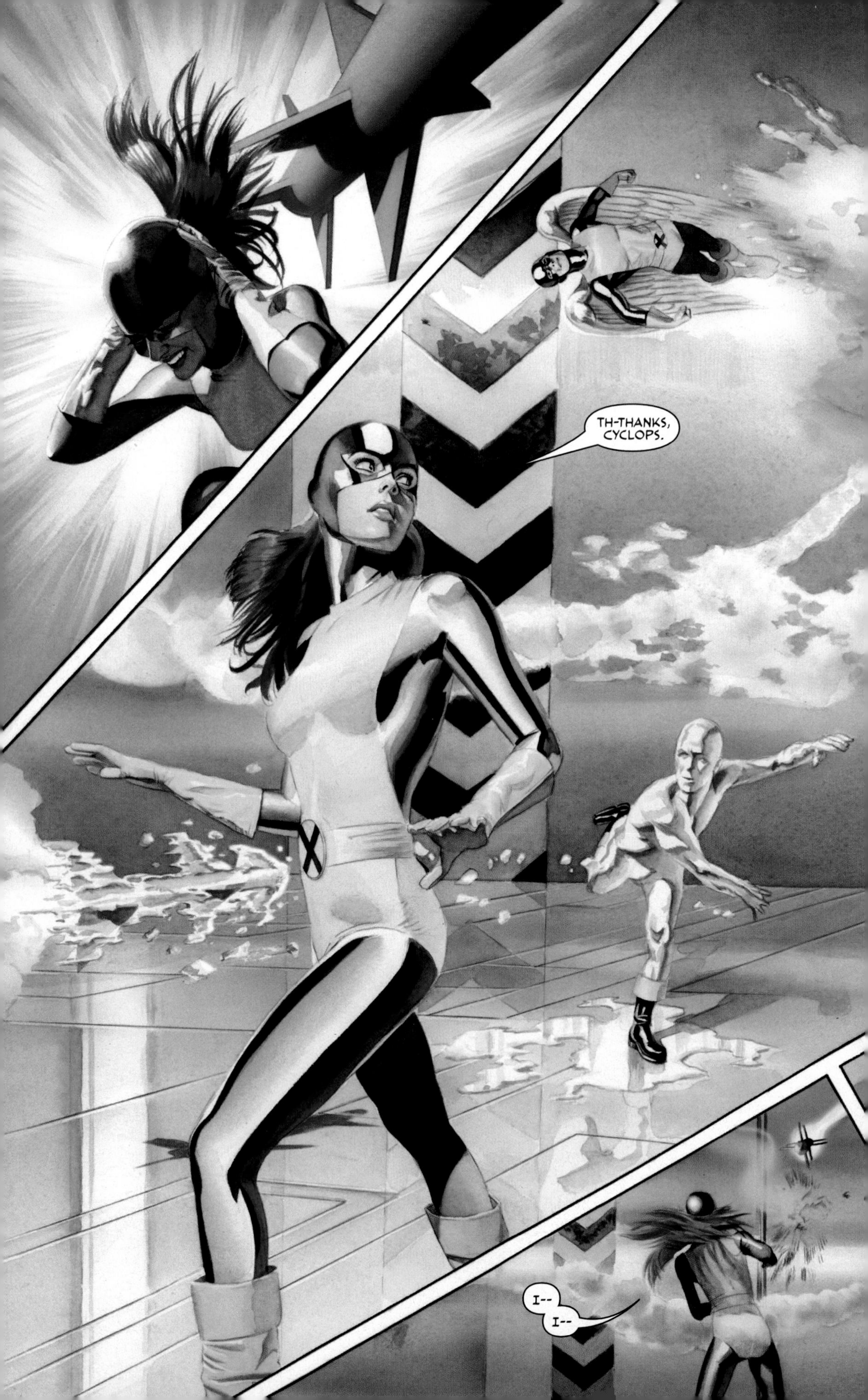
TH-THANKS, CYCLOPS.
I--
I--

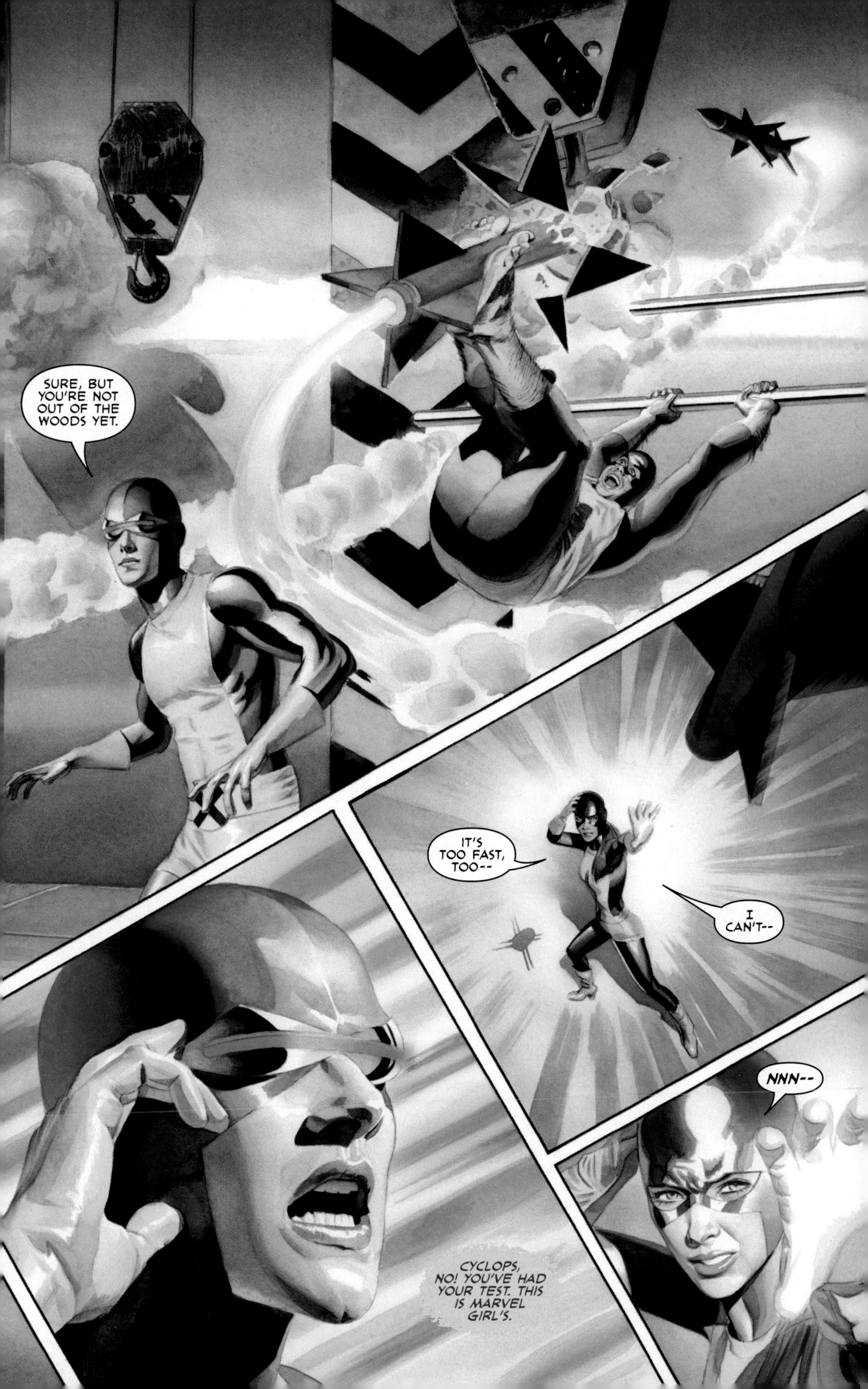
SURE, BUT YOU'RE NOT OUT OF THE WOODS YET.
IT'S TOO FAST, TOO--
I CAN'T--
CYCLOPS, NO! YOU'VE HAD YOUR TEST. THIS IS MARVEL GIRL'S.
NNN--

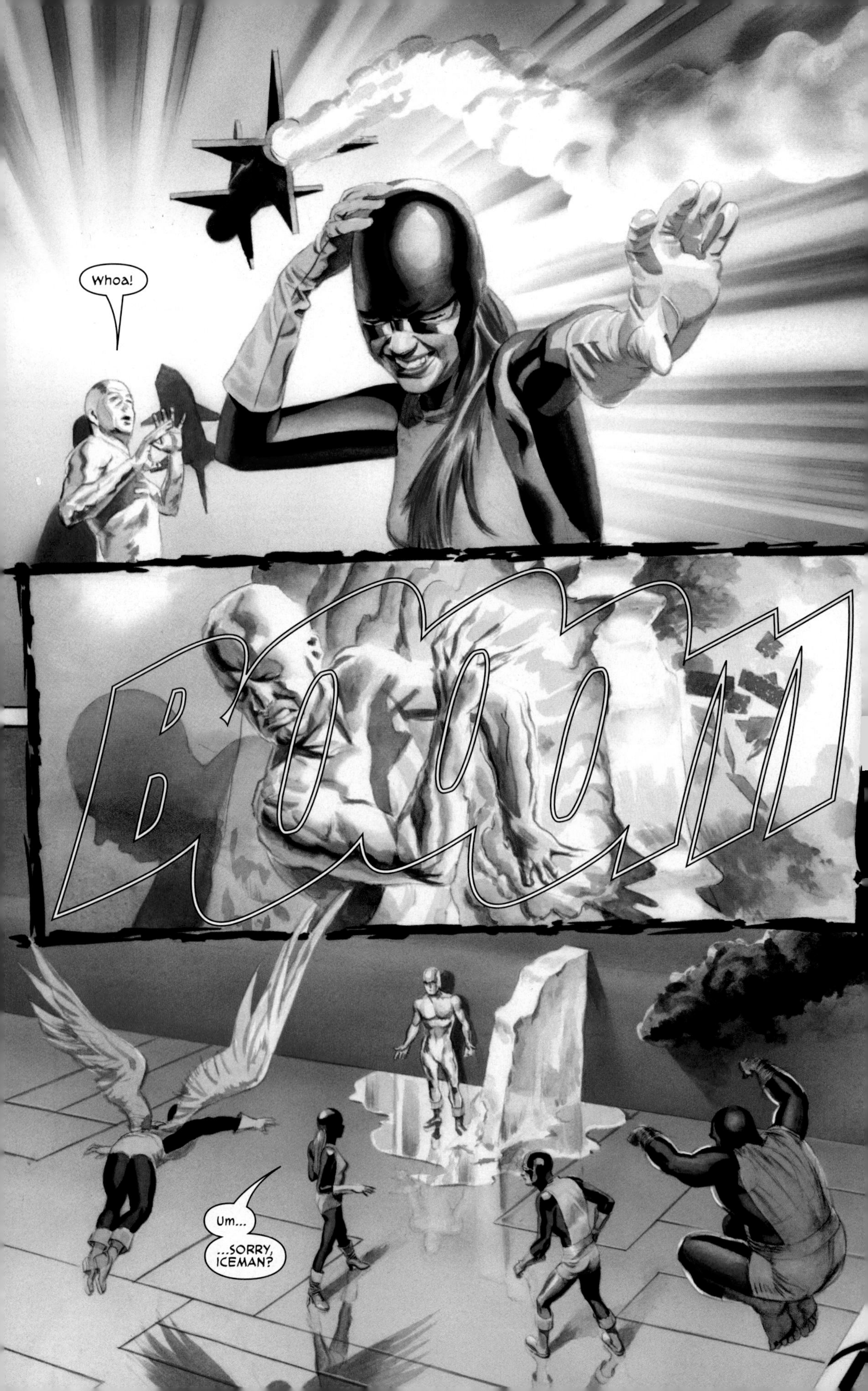
Whoa!
BOOOM
Um...
...SORRY, ICEMAN?

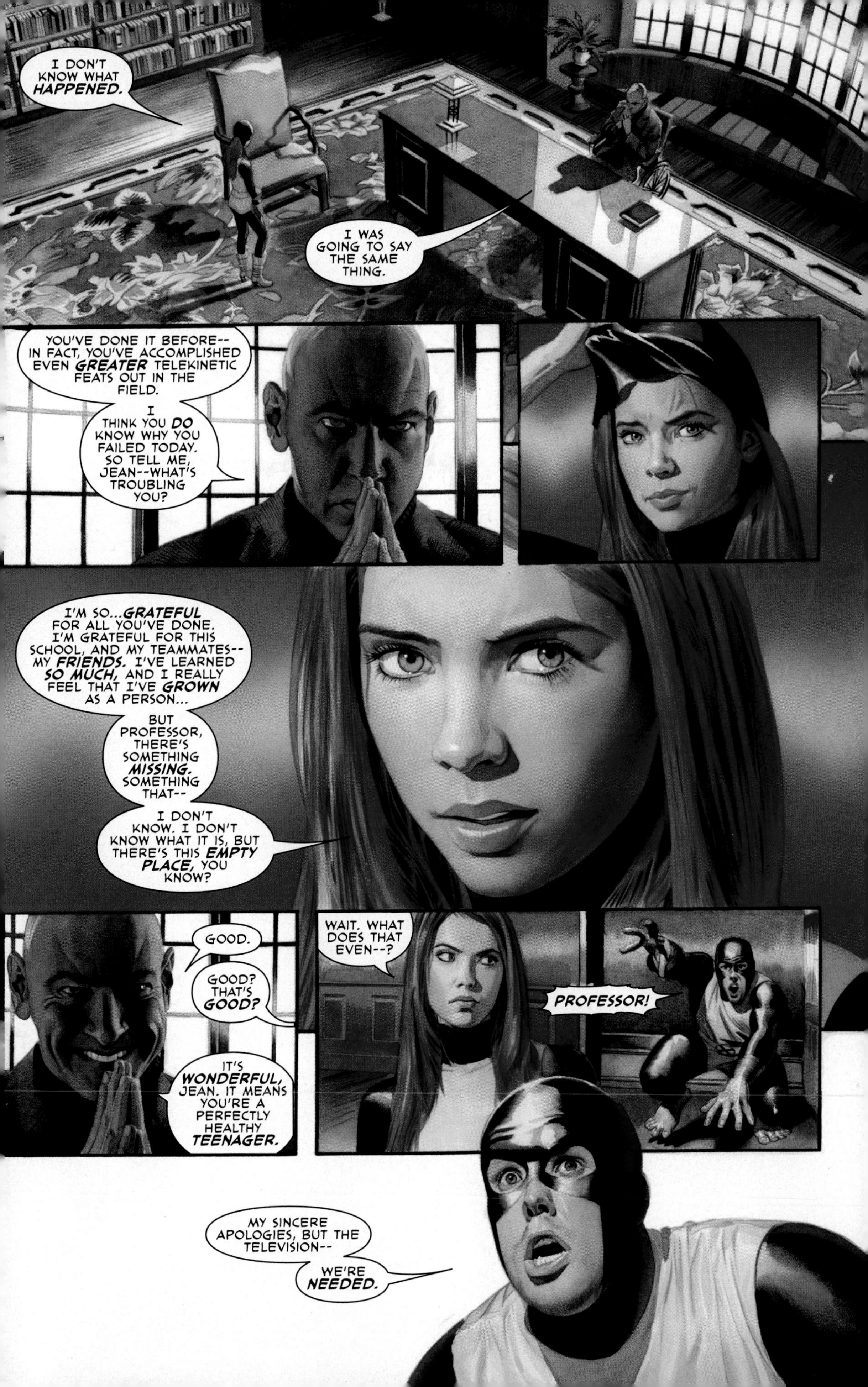

I DON'T KNOW WHAT HAPPENED.
I WAS GOING TO SAY THE SAME THING.
YOU'VE DONE IT BEFORE-- IN FACT, YOU'VE ACCOMPLISHED EVEN GREATER TELEKINETIC FEATS OUT IN THE FIELD.
I THINK YOU DO KNOW WHY YOU FAILED TODAY. SO TELL ME, JEAN--WHAT'S TROUBLING YOU?
I'M SO...GRATEFUL FOR ALL YOU'VE DONE. I'M GRATEFUL FOR THIS SCHOOL, AND MY TEAMMATES-- MY FRIENDS. I'VE LEARNED SO MUCH, AND I REALLY FEEL THAT I'VE GROWN AS A PERSON...
BUT PROFESSOR, THERE'S SOMETHING MISSING. SOMETHING THAT--
I DON'T KNOW. I DON'T KNOW WHAT IT IS, BUT THERE'S THIS EMPTY PLACE, YOU KNOW?
GOOD.
GOOD? THAT'S GOOD?
IT'S WONDERFUL, JEAN. IT MEANS YOU'RE A PERFECTLY HEALTHY TEENAGER.
WAIT. WHAT DOES THAT EVEN--?
PROFESSOR!
MY SINCERE APOLOGIES, BUT THE TELEVISION--
WE'RE NEEDED.

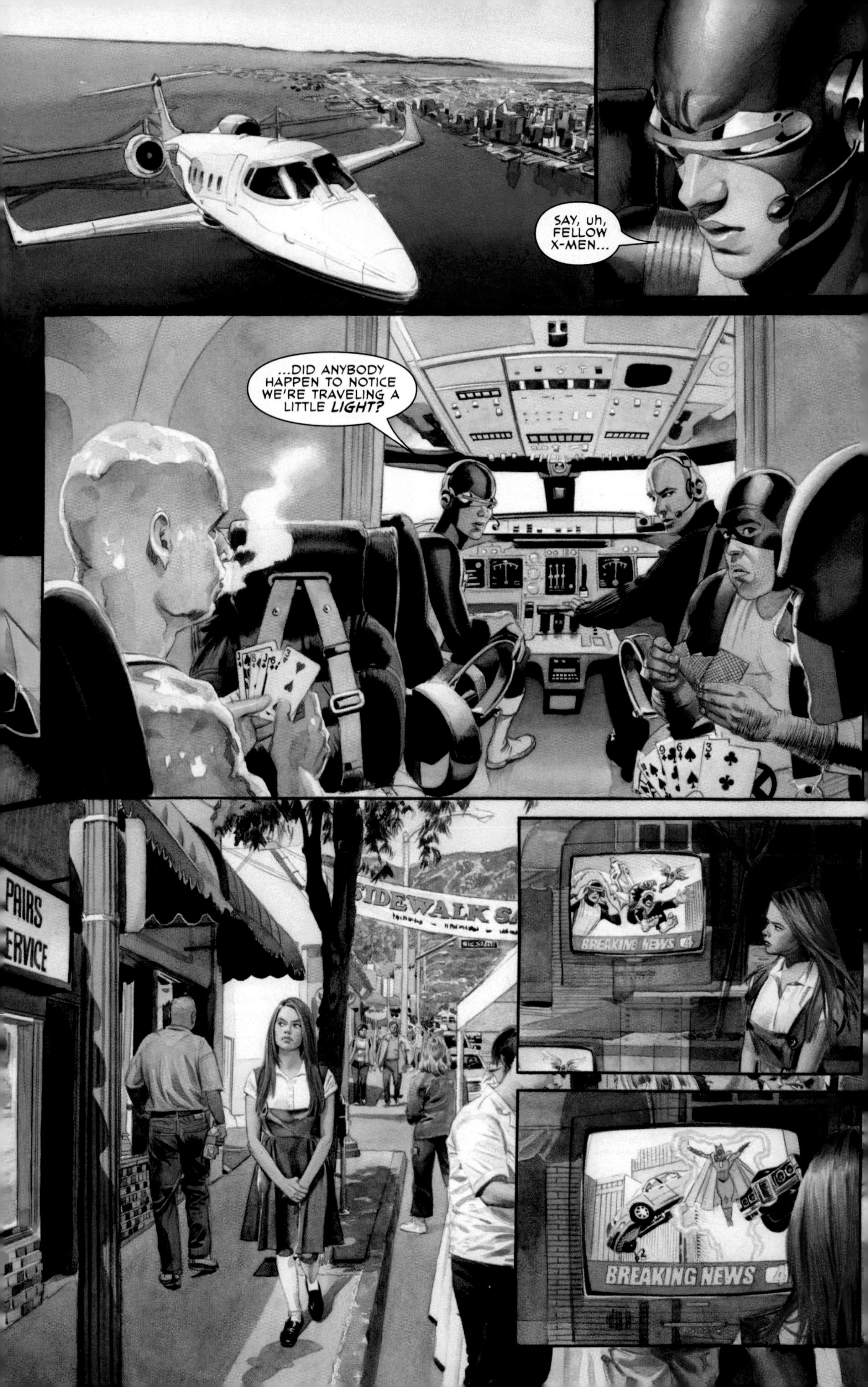
SAY, uh, FELLOW X-MEN...
...DID ANYBODY HAPPEN TO NOTICE WE'RE TRAVELING A LITTLE *LIGHT?*
PAIRS
ERVICE
SIDEWALK SA
BREAKING NEWS 4
BREAKING NEWS 4

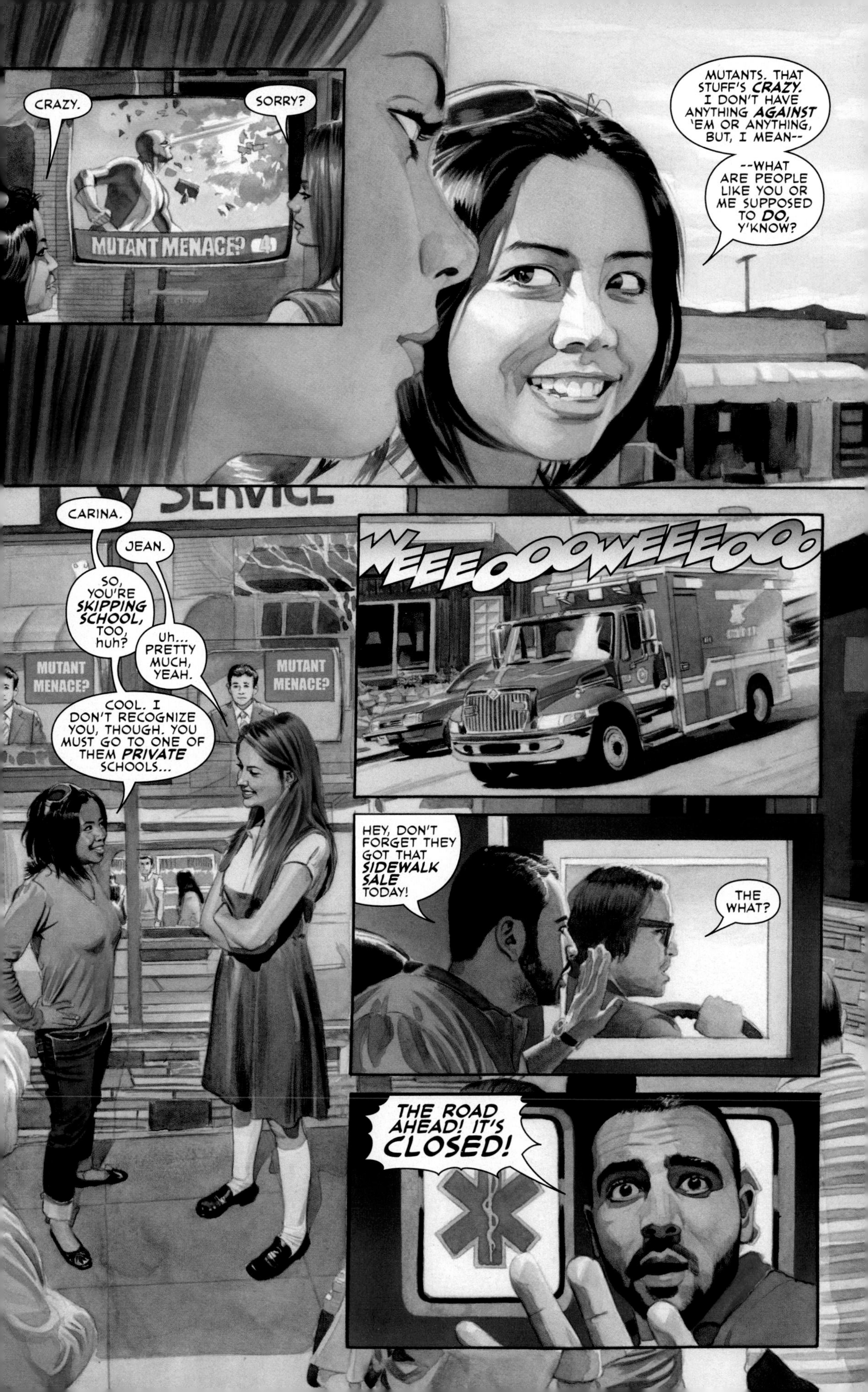
CRAZY.
SORRY?
MUTANT MENACE?
MUTANTS. THAT STUFF'S CRAZY. I DON'T HAVE ANYTHING AGAINST 'EM OR ANYTHING, BUT, I MEAN--
--WHAT ARE PEOPLE LIKE YOU OR ME SUPPOSED TO DO, Y'KNOW?
SERVICE
CARINA.
JEAN.
SO, YOU'RE SKIPPING SCHOOL, TOO, huh?
Uh... PRETTY MUCH, YEAH.
MUTANT MENACE?
MUTANT MENACE?
COOL. I DON'T RECOGNIZE YOU, THOUGH. YOU MUST GO TO ONE OF THEM PRIVATE SCHOOLS...
WEEEOOOWEEEOOO
HEY, DON'T FORGET THEY GOT THAT SIDEWALK SALE TODAY!
THE WHAT?
THE ROAD AHEAD! IT'S CLOSED!

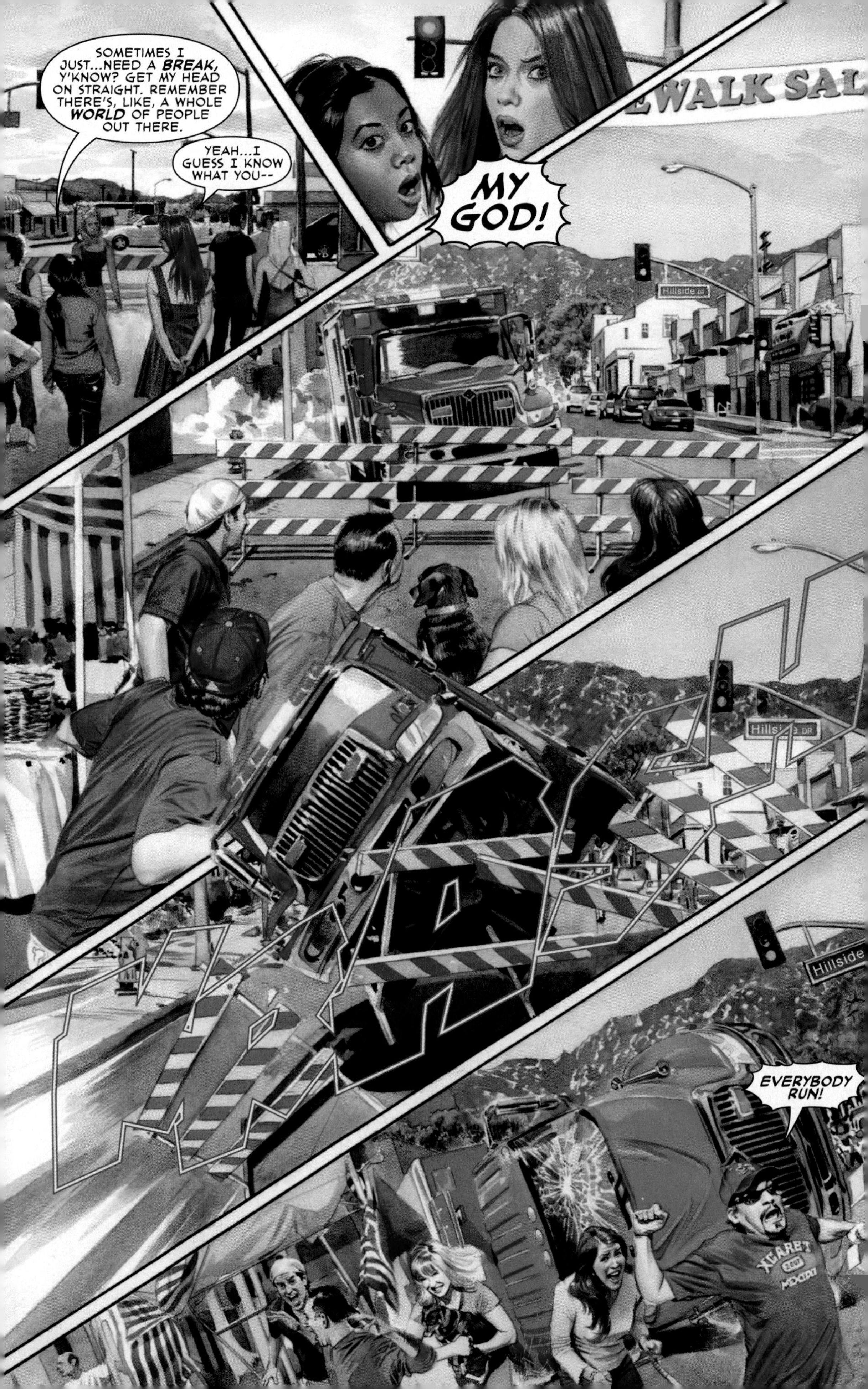
SOMETIMES I JUST...NEED A BREAK, Y'KNOW? GET MY HEAD ON STRAIGHT. REMEMBER THERE'S, LIKE, A WHOLE WORLD OF PEOPLE OUT THERE.
YEAH...I GUESS I KNOW WHAT YOU--
EWALK SAL
MY GOD!
Hillside DR
Hillside DR
Hillside
EVERYBODY RUN!

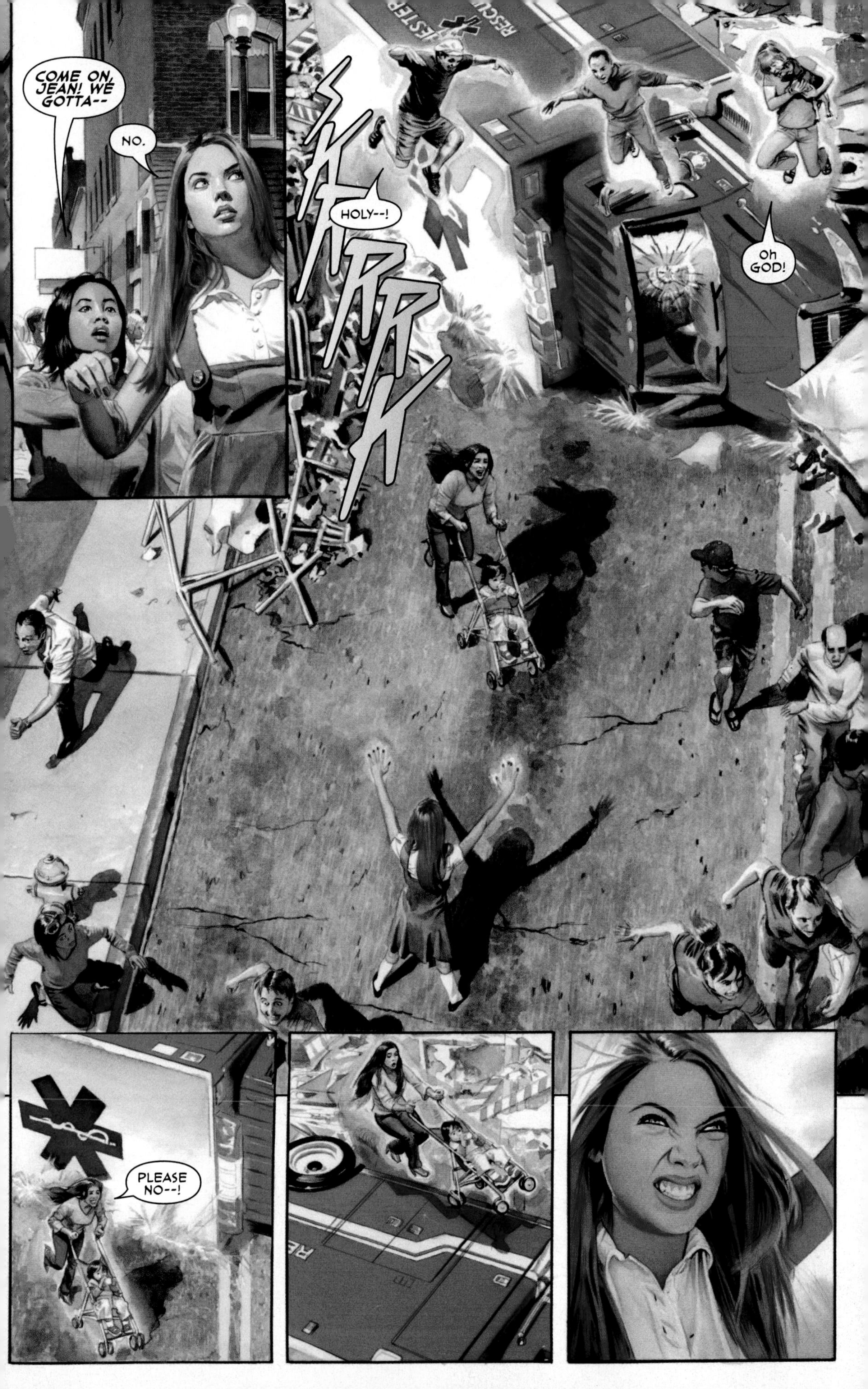
COME ON, JEAN! WE GOTTA--
NO.
SKRRRK
HOLY--!
Oh GOD!
PLEASE NO--!

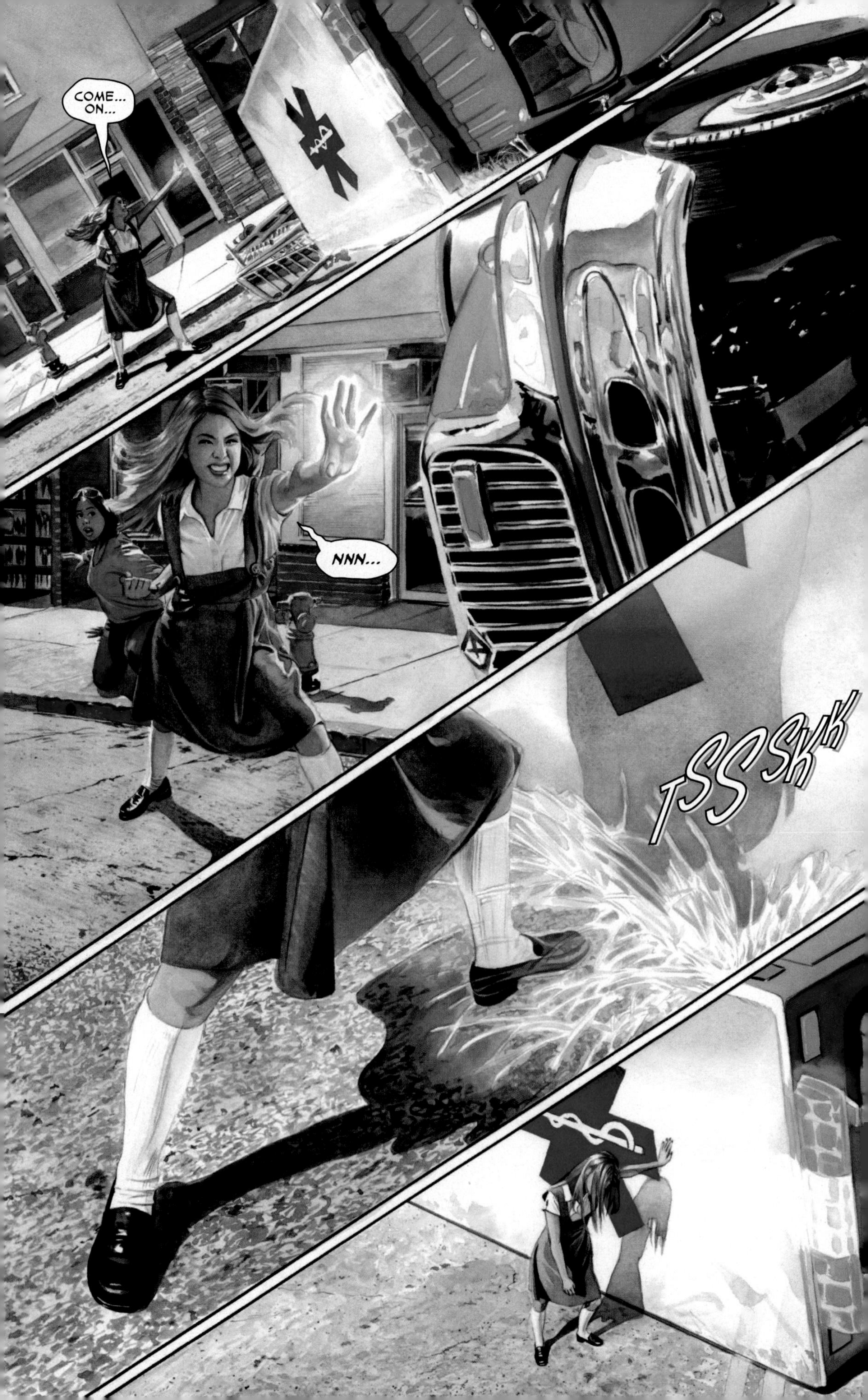
COME... ON...
NNN...
TSSSKK

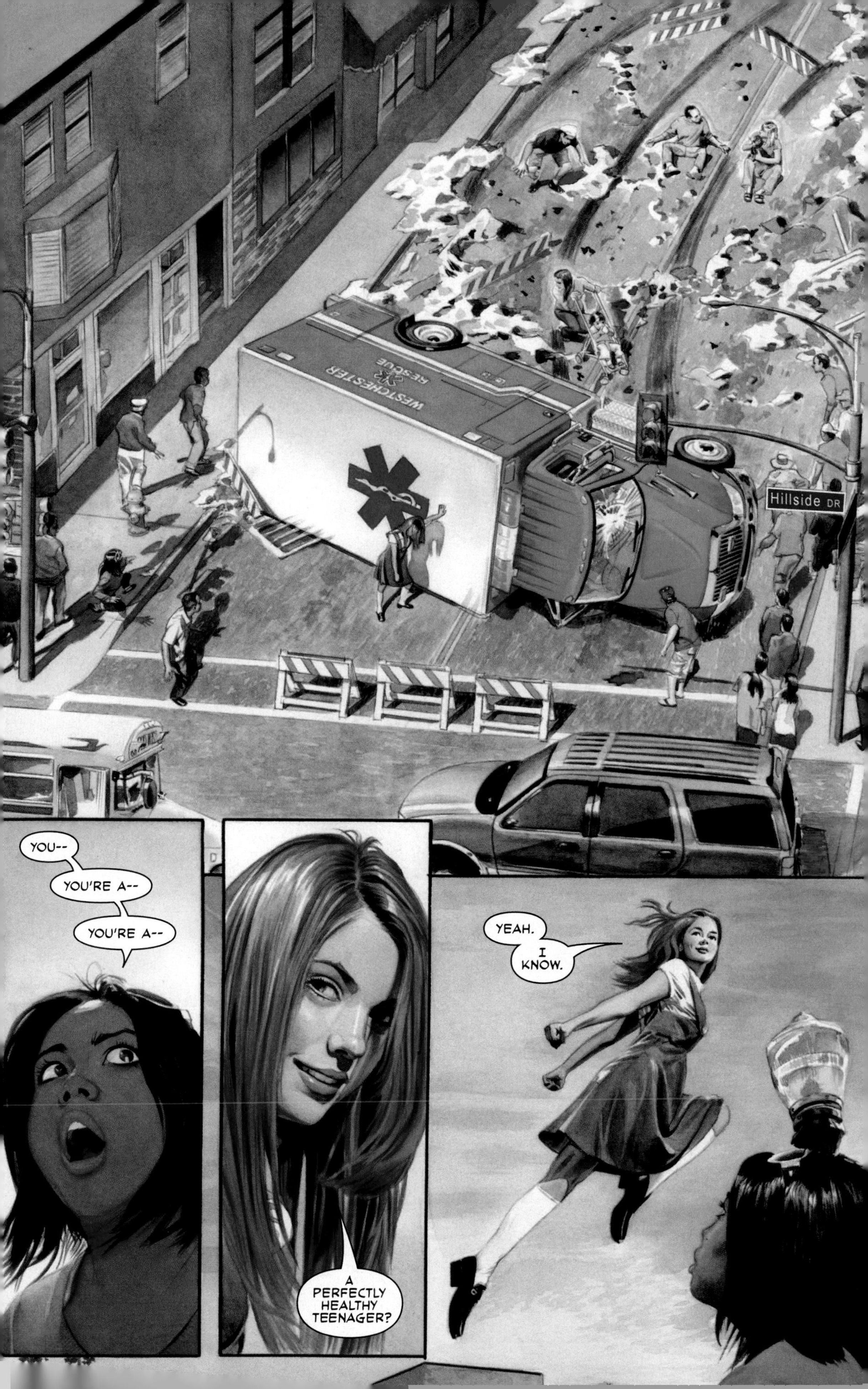
WESTCHESTER
RESCUE
Hillside DR
YOU--
YOU'RE A--
YOU'RE A--
A PERFECTLY HEALTHY TEENAGER?
YEAH.
I KNOW.

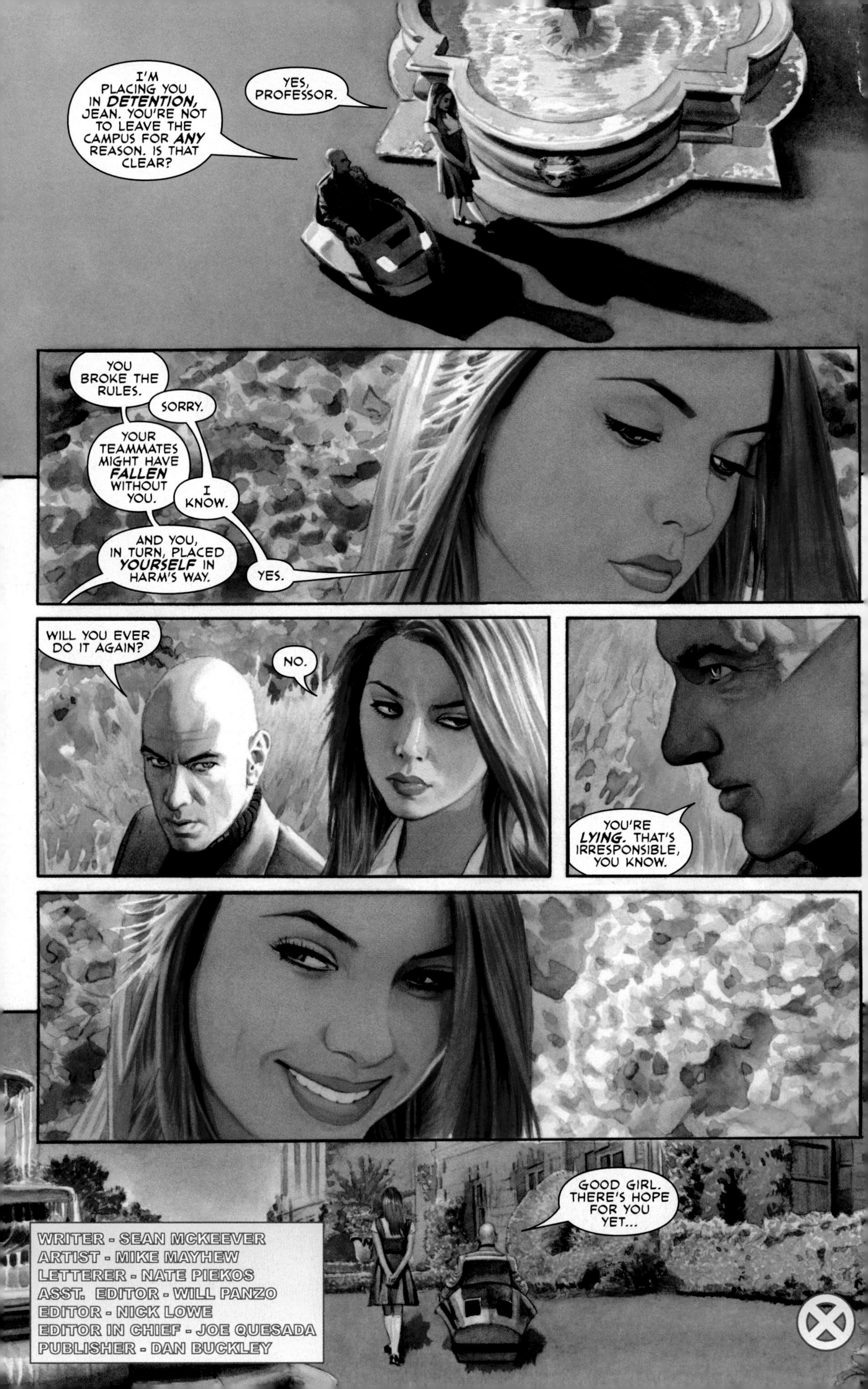
I'M PLACING YOU IN DETENTION, JEAN. YOU'RE NOT TO LEAVE THE CAMPUS FOR ANY REASON. IS THAT CLEAR?
YES, PROFESSOR.
YOU BROKE THE RULES.
SORRY.
YOUR TEAMMATES MIGHT HAVE FALLEN WITHOUT YOU.
I KNOW.
AND YOU, IN TURN, PLACED YOURSELF IN HARM'S WAY.
YES.
WILL YOU EVER DO IT AGAIN?
NO.
YOU'RE LYING. THAT'S IRRESPONSIBLE, YOU KNOW.
GOOD GIRL. THERE'S HOPE FOR YOU YET...
WRITER - SEAN MCKEEVER
ARTIST - MIKE MAYHEW
LETTERER - NATE PIEKOS
ASST. EDITOR - WILL PANZO
EDITOR - NICK LOWE
EDITOR IN CHIEF - JOE QUESADA
PUBLISHER - DAN BUCKLEY

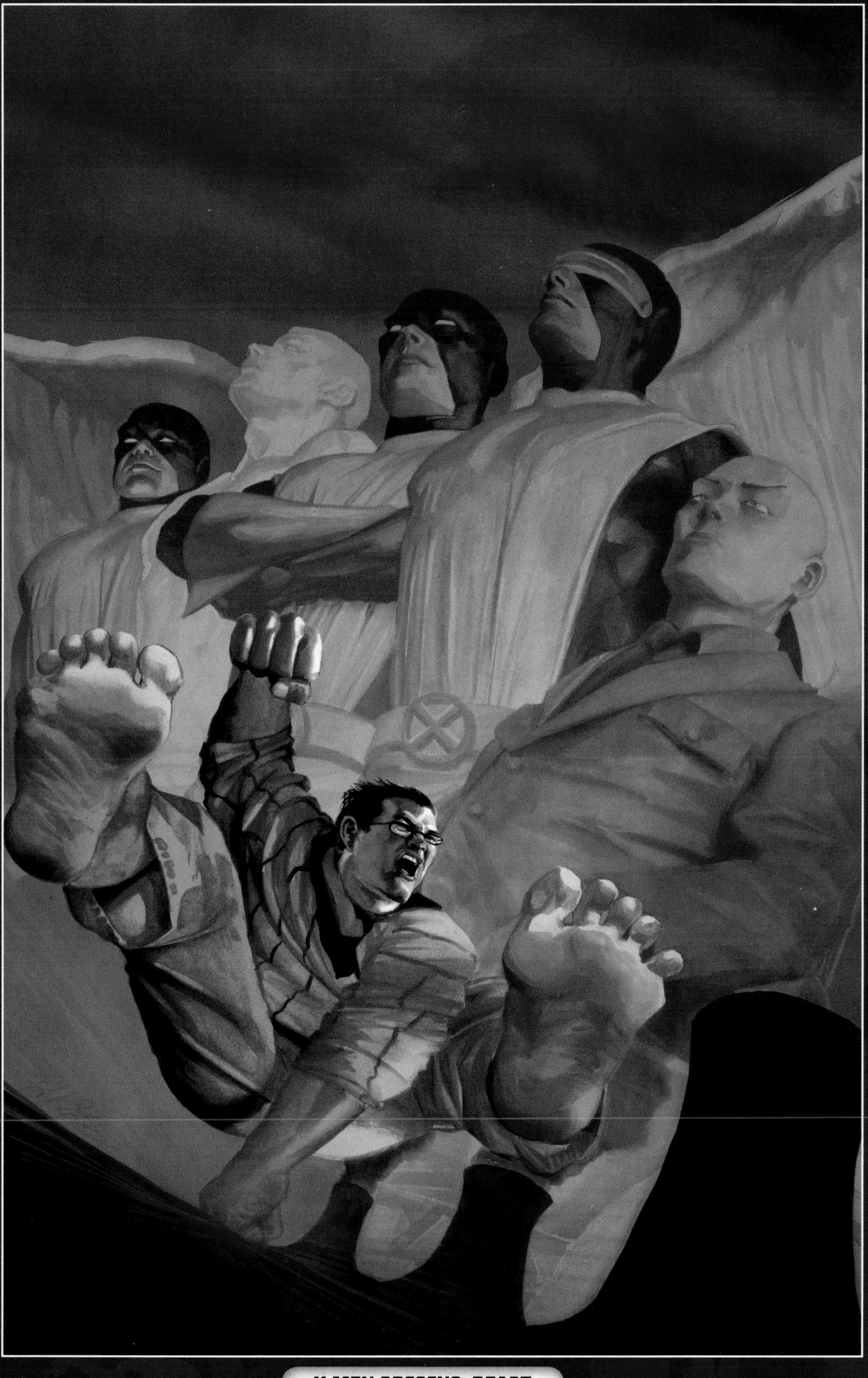

X-MEN ORIGINS: BEAST

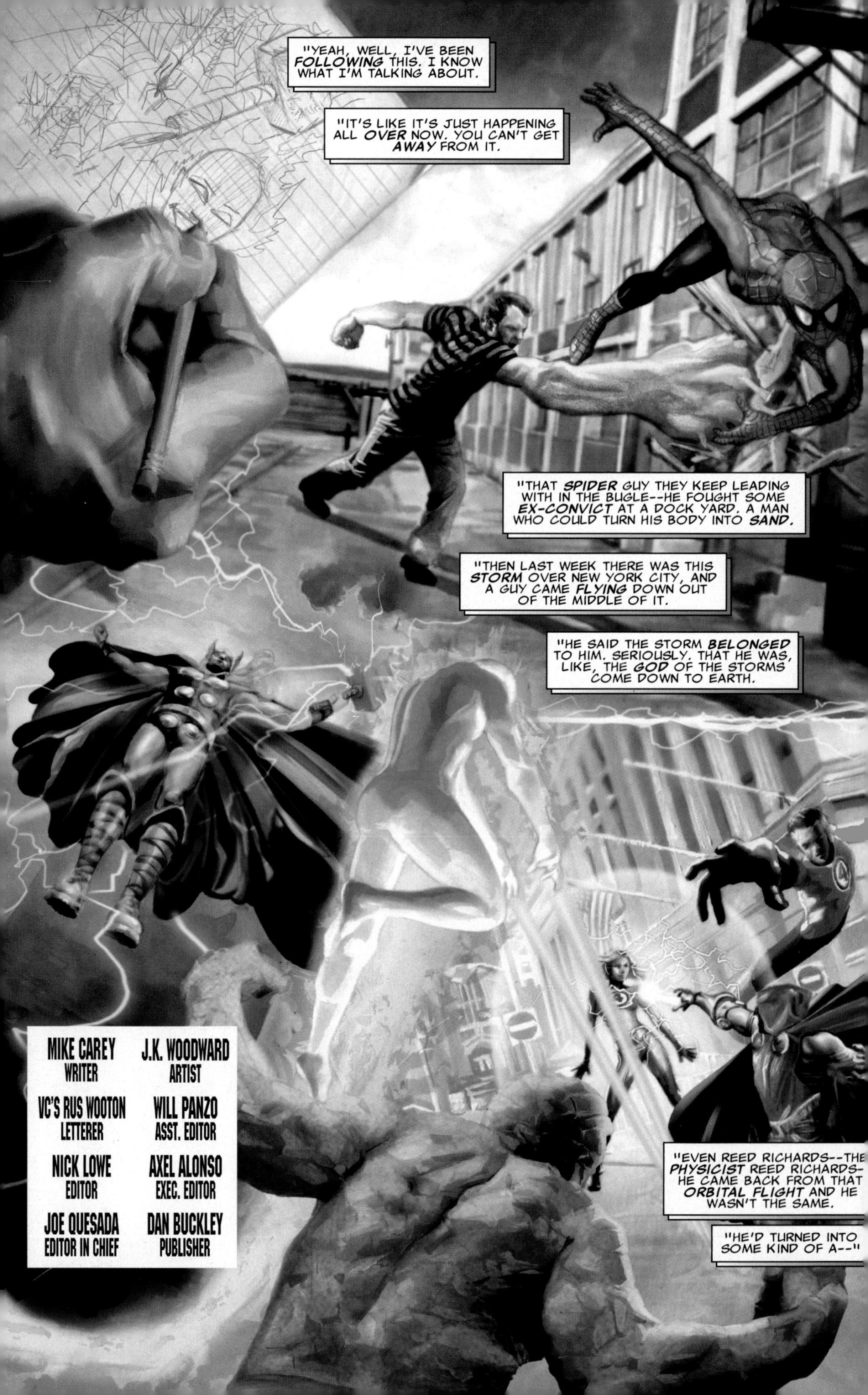
"YEAH, WELL, I'VE BEEN FOLLOWING THIS. I KNOW WHAT I'M TALKING ABOUT.
"IT'S LIKE IT'S JUST HAPPENING ALL OVER NOW. YOU CAN'T GET AWAY FROM IT.
"THAT SPIDER GUY THEY KEEP LEADING WITH IN THE BUGLE--HE FOUGHT SOME EX-CONVICT AT A DOCK YARD. A MAN WHO COULD TURN HIS BODY INTO SAND.
"THEN LAST WEEK THERE WAS THIS STORM OVER NEW YORK CITY, AND A GUY CAME FLYING DOWN OUT OF THE MIDDLE OF IT.
"HE SAID THE STORM BELONGED TO HIM. SERIOUSLY. THAT HE WAS, LIKE, THE GOD OF THE STORMS COME DOWN TO EARTH.
"EVEN REED RICHARDS--THE PHYSICIST REED RICHARDS--HE CAME BACK FROM THAT ORBITAL FLIGHT AND HE WASN'T THE SAME.
"HE'D TURNED INTO SOME KIND OF A--"
MIKE CAREY WRITER
J.K. WOODWARD ARTIST
VC'S RUS WOOTON LETTERER
WILL PANZO ASST. EDITOR
NICK LOWE EDITOR
AXEL ALONSO EXEC. EDITOR
JOE QUESADA EDITOR IN CHIEF
DAN BUCKLEY PUBLISHER

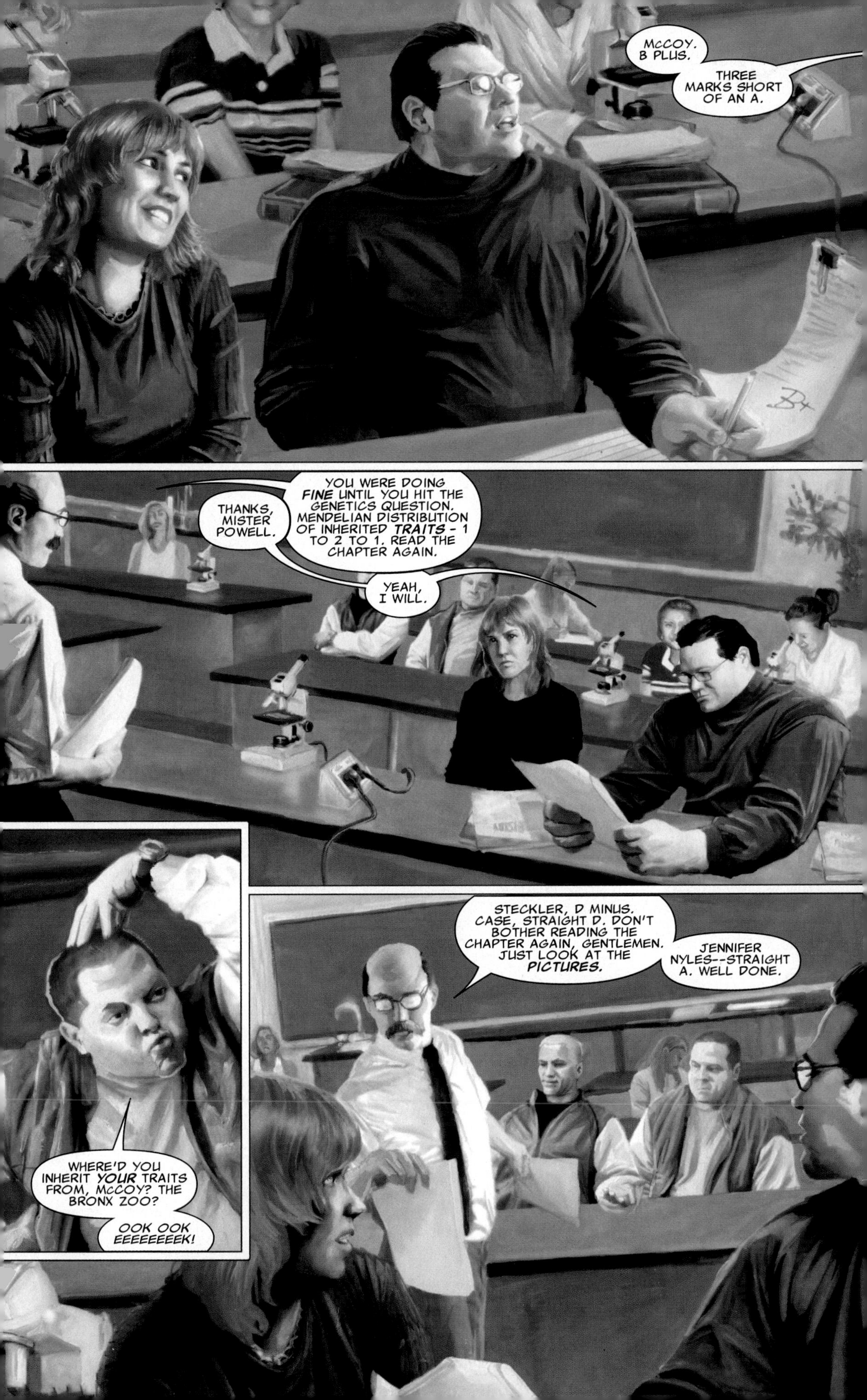
McCOY. B PLUS.
THREE MARKS SHORT OF AN A.
YOU WERE DOING FINE UNTIL YOU HIT THE GENETICS QUESTION. MENDELIAN DISTRIBUTION OF INHERITED TRAITS - 1 TO 2 TO 1. READ THE CHAPTER AGAIN.
THANKS, MISTER POWELL.
YEAH, I WILL.
WHERE'D YOU INHERIT YOUR TRAITS FROM, McCOY? THE BRONX ZOO?
OOK OOK EEEEEEEEK!
STECKLER, D MINUS. CASE, STRAIGHT D. DON'T BOTHER READING THE CHAPTER AGAIN, GENTLEMEN. JUST LOOK AT THE PICTURES.
JENNIFER NYLES--STRAIGHT A. WELL DONE.

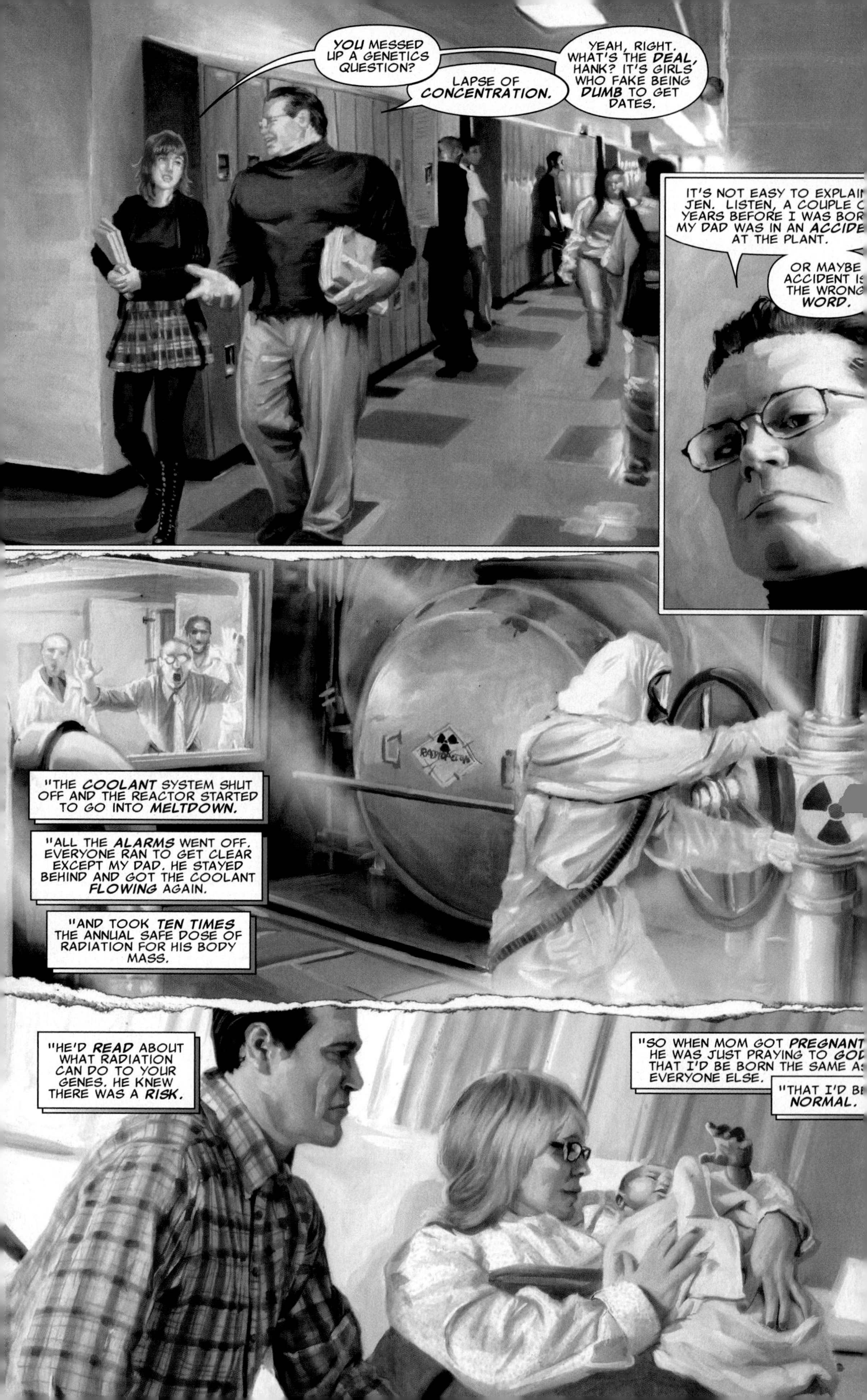
YOU MESSED UP A GENETICS QUESTION?
LAPSE OF CONCENTRATION.
YEAH, RIGHT. WHAT'S THE DEAL, HANK? IT'S GIRLS WHO FAKE BEING DUMB TO GET DATES.
IT'S NOT EASY TO EXPLAIN JEN. LISTEN, A COUPLE OF YEARS BEFORE I WAS BORN MY DAD WAS IN AN ACCIDENT AT THE PLANT.
OR MAYBE ACCIDENT IS THE WRONG WORD.
"THE COOLANT SYSTEM SHUT OFF AND THE REACTOR STARTED TO GO INTO MELTDOWN.
"ALL THE ALARMS WENT OFF. EVERYONE RAN TO GET CLEAR EXCEPT MY DAD. HE STAYED BEHIND AND GOT THE COOLANT FLOWING AGAIN.
"AND TOOK TEN TIMES THE ANNUAL SAFE DOSE OF RADIATION FOR HIS BODY MASS.
"HE'D READ ABOUT WHAT RADIATION CAN DO TO YOUR GENES. HE KNEW THERE WAS A RISK.
"SO WHEN MOM GOT PREGNANT HE WAS JUST PRAYING TO GOD THAT I'D BE BORN THE SAME AS EVERYONE ELSE.
"THAT I'D BE NORMAL.

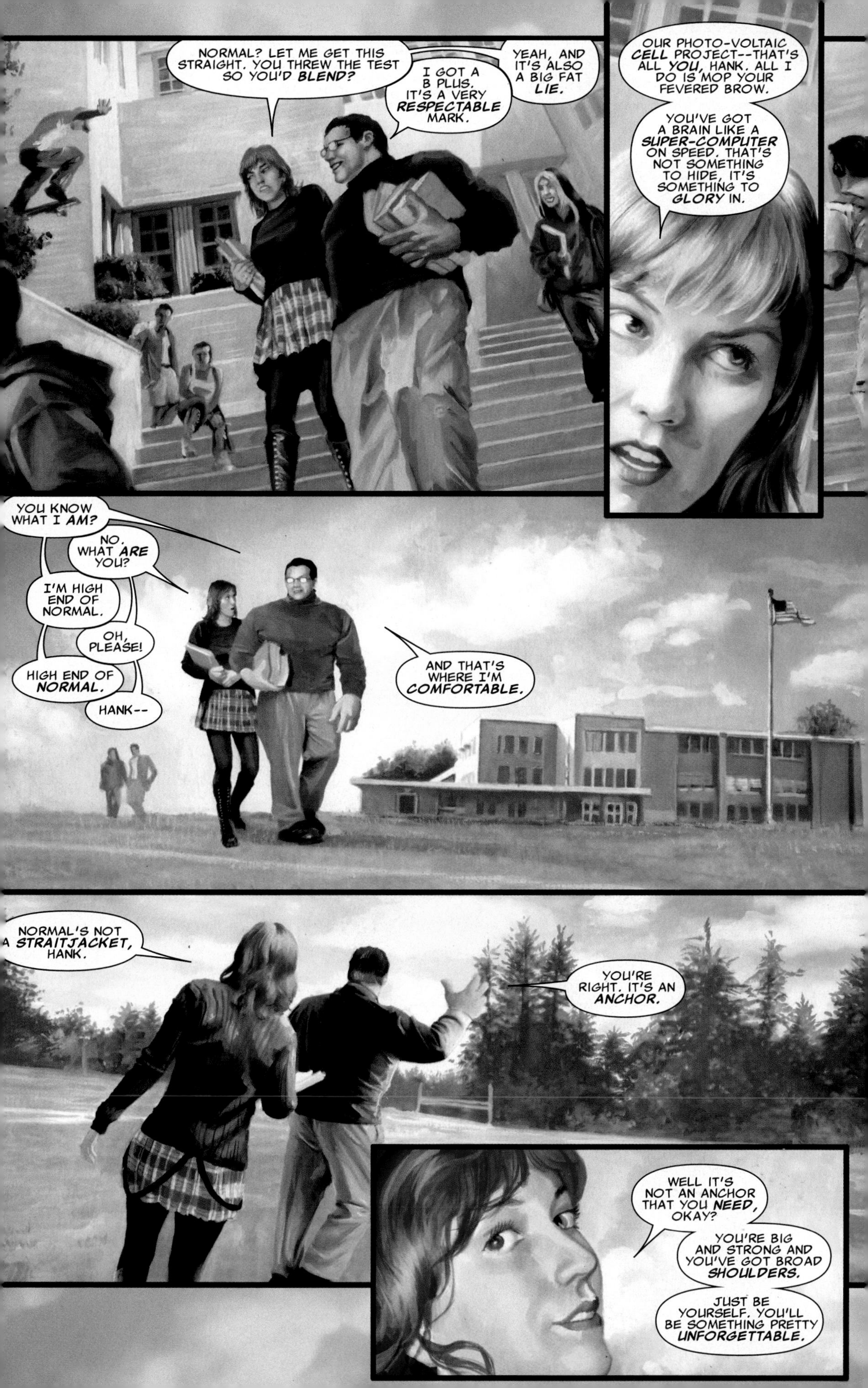
NORMAL? LET ME GET THIS STRAIGHT. YOU THREW THE TEST SO YOU'D BLEND?
I GOT A B PLUS. IT'S A VERY RESPECTABLE MARK.
YEAH, AND IT'S ALSO A BIG FAT LIE.
OUR PHOTO-VOLTAIC CELL PROJECT--THAT'S ALL YOU, HANK. ALL I DO IS MOP YOUR FEVERED BROW.
YOU'VE GOT A BRAIN LIKE A SUPER-COMPUTER ON SPEED. THAT'S NOT SOMETHING TO HIDE, IT'S SOMETHING TO GLORY IN.
YOU KNOW WHAT I AM?
NO. WHAT ARE YOU?
I'M HIGH END OF NORMAL.
OH, PLEASE!
HIGH END OF NORMAL.
HANK--
AND THAT'S WHERE I'M COMFORTABLE.
NORMAL'S NOT A STRAITJACKET, HANK.
YOU'RE RIGHT. IT'S AN ANCHOR.
WELL IT'S NOT AN ANCHOR THAT YOU NEED, OKAY?
YOU'RE BIG AND STRONG AND YOU'VE GOT BROAD SHOULDERS.
JUST BE YOURSELF. YOU'LL BE SOMETHING PRETTY UNFORGETTABLE.

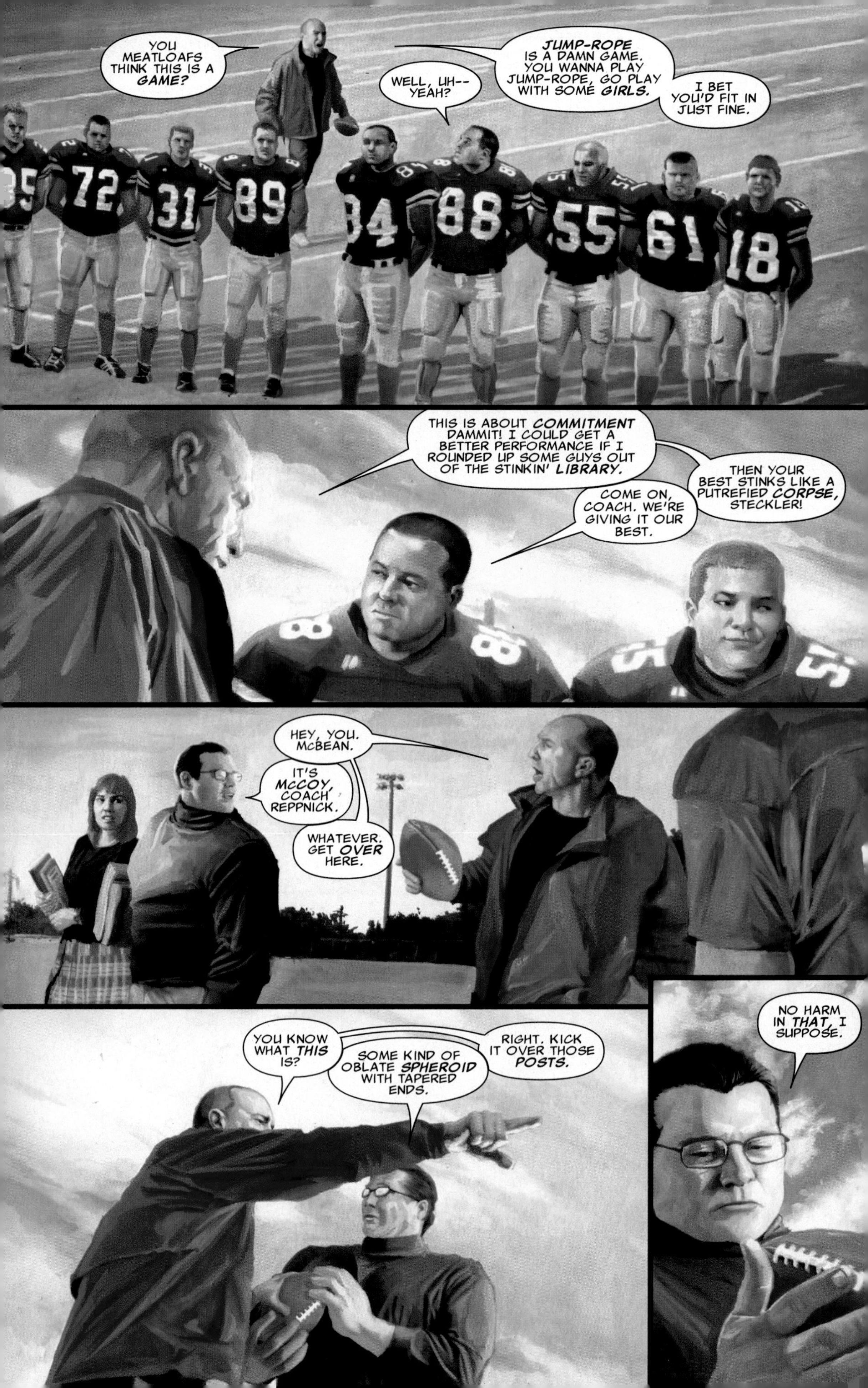
YOU MEATLOAFS THINK THIS IS A GAME?
WELL, UH-- YEAH?
JUMP-ROPE IS A DAMN GAME. YOU WANNA PLAY JUMP-ROPE, GO PLAY WITH SOME GIRLS.
I BET YOU'D FIT IN JUST FINE.
THIS IS ABOUT COMMITMENT DAMMIT! I COULD GET A BETTER PERFORMANCE IF I ROUNDED UP SOME GUYS OUT OF THE STINKIN' LIBRARY.
COME ON, COACH. WE'RE GIVING IT OUR BEST.
THEN YOUR BEST STINKS LIKE A PUTREFIED CORPSE, STECKLER!
HEY, YOU. McBEAN.
IT'S McCOY, COACH REPPNICK.
WHATEVER. GET OVER HERE.
YOU KNOW WHAT THIS IS?
SOME KIND OF OBLATE SPHEROID WITH TAPERED ENDS.
RIGHT. KICK IT OVER THOSE POSTS.
NO HARM IN THAT, I SUPPOSE.

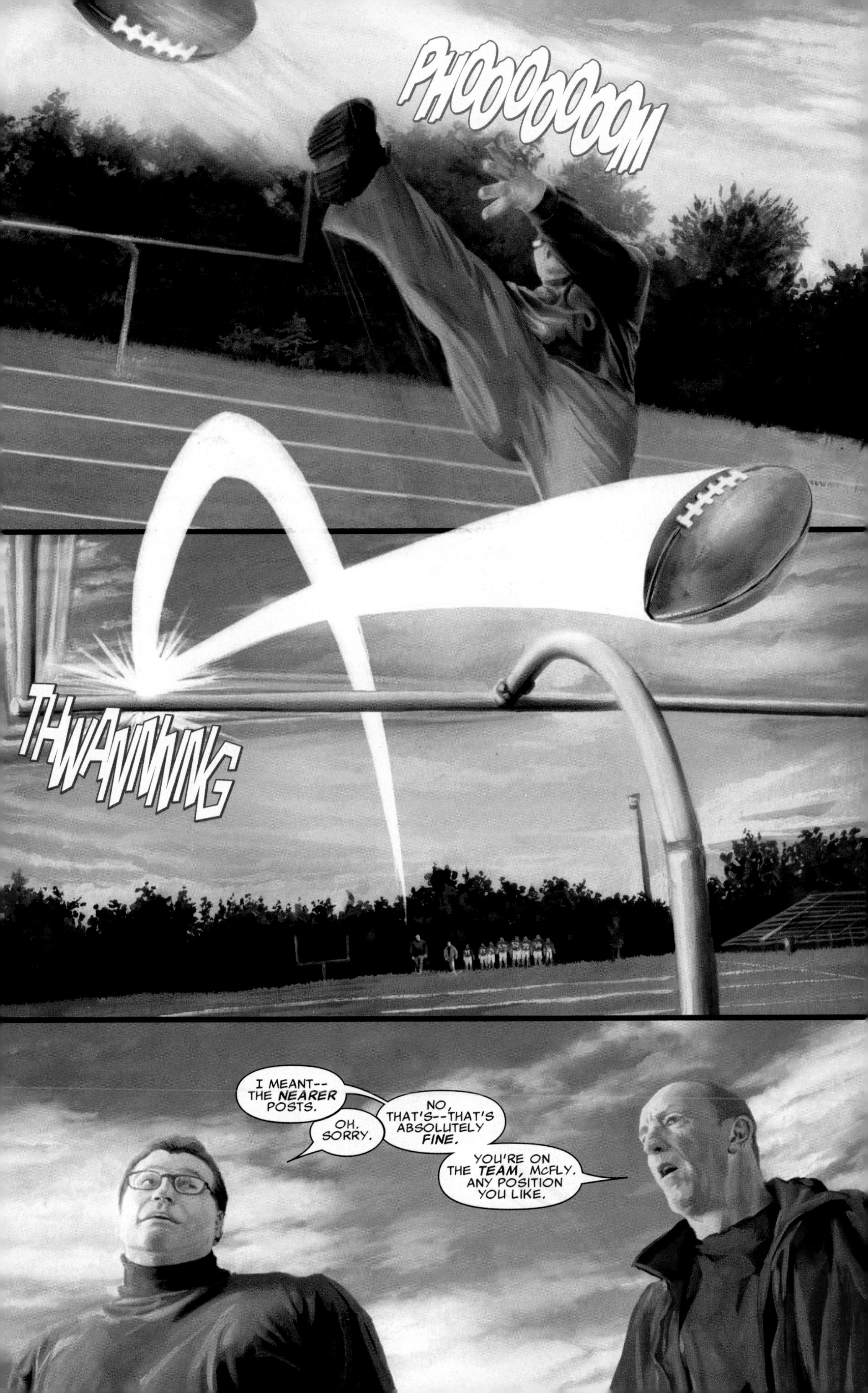
PHOOOOOOOOM
THWANNNNG
I MEANT-- THE NEARER POSTS.
OH. SORRY.
NO, THAT'S--THAT'S ABSOLUTELY FINE.
YOU'RE ON THE TEAM, McFLY. ANY POSITION YOU LIKE.

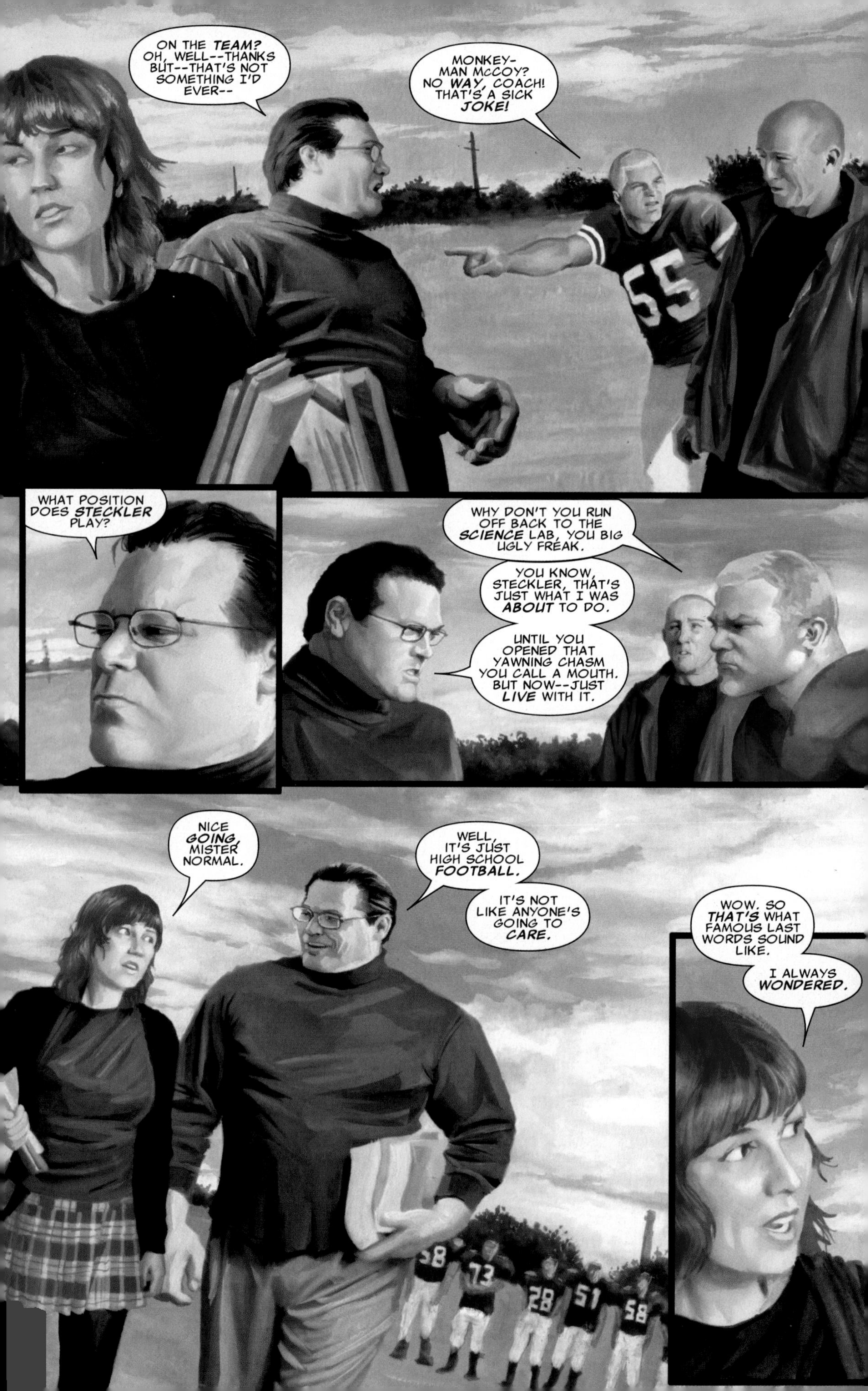
ON THE TEAM? OH, WELL--THANKS BUT--THAT'S NOT SOMETHING I'D EVER--
MONKEY-MAN McCOY? NO WAY, COACH! THAT'S A SICK JOKE!
WHAT POSITION DOES STECKLER PLAY?
WHY DON'T YOU RUN OFF BACK TO THE SCIENCE LAB, YOU BIG UGLY FREAK.
YOU KNOW, STECKLER, THAT'S JUST WHAT I WAS ABOUT TO DO.
UNTIL YOU OPENED THAT YAWNING CHASM YOU CALL A MOUTH. BUT NOW--JUST LIVE WITH IT.
NICE GOING, MISTER NORMAL.
WELL, IT'S JUST HIGH SCHOOL FOOTBALL.
IT'S NOT LIKE ANYONE'S GOING TO CARE.
WOW. SO THAT'S WHAT FAMOUS LAST WORDS SOUND LIKE.
I ALWAYS WONDERED.

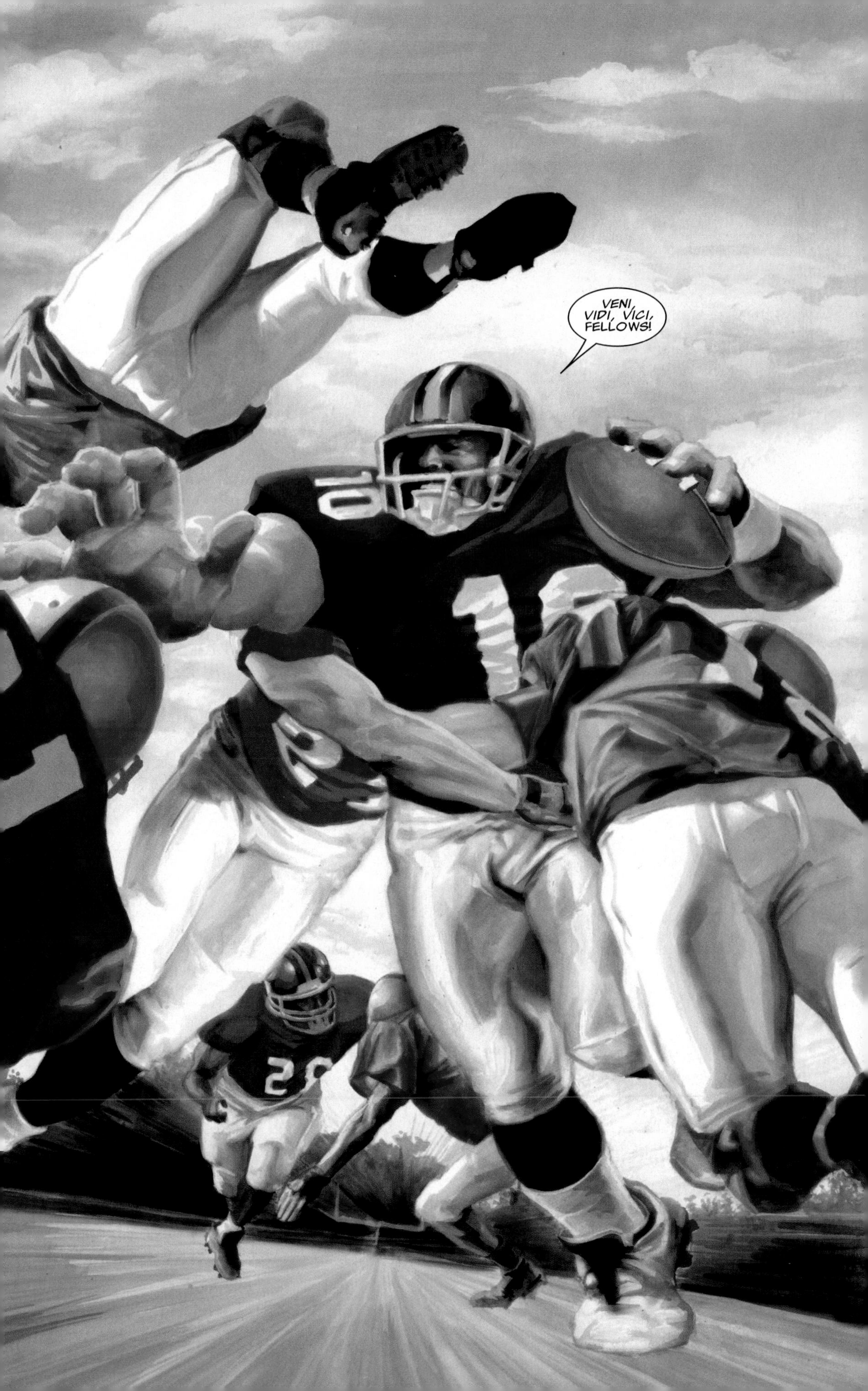
VENI, VIDI, VICI, FELLOWS!

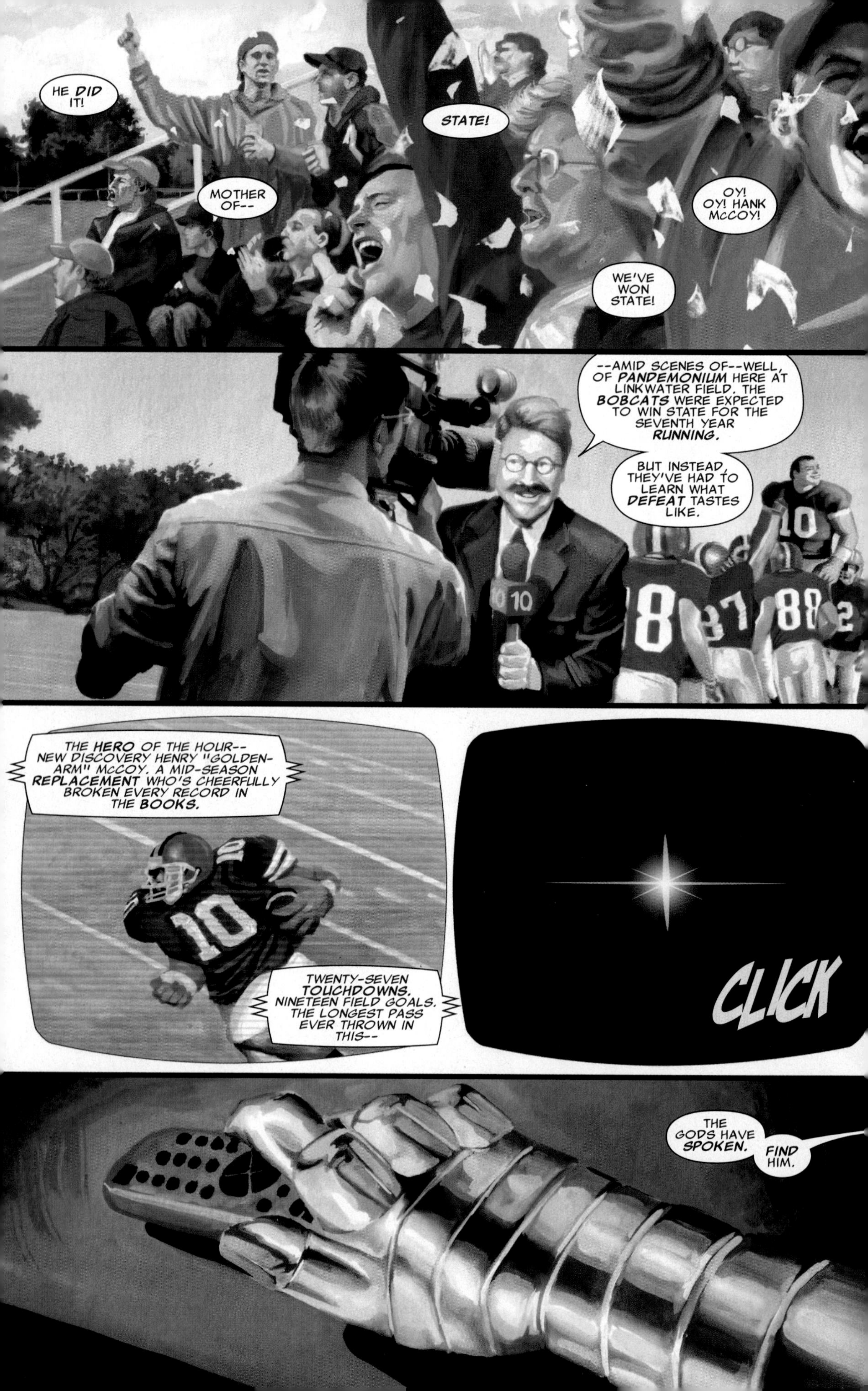
HE DID IT!
STATE!
MOTHER OF--
OY! OY! HANK McCOY!
WE'VE WON STATE!
--AMID SCENES OF--WELL, OF PANDEMONIUM HERE AT LINKWATER FIELD. THE BOBCATS WERE EXPECTED TO WIN STATE FOR THE SEVENTH YEAR RUNNING.
BUT INSTEAD, THEY'VE HAD TO LEARN WHAT DEFEAT TASTES LIKE.
THE HERO OF THE HOUR-- NEW DISCOVERY HENRY "GOLDEN-ARM" McCOY. A MID-SEASON REPLACEMENT WHO'S CHEERFULLY BROKEN EVERY RECORD IN THE BOOKS.
TWENTY-SEVEN TOUCHDOWNS. NINETEEN FIELD GOALS. THE LONGEST PASS EVER THROWN IN THIS--
CLICK
THE GODS HAVE SPOKEN.
FIND HIM.

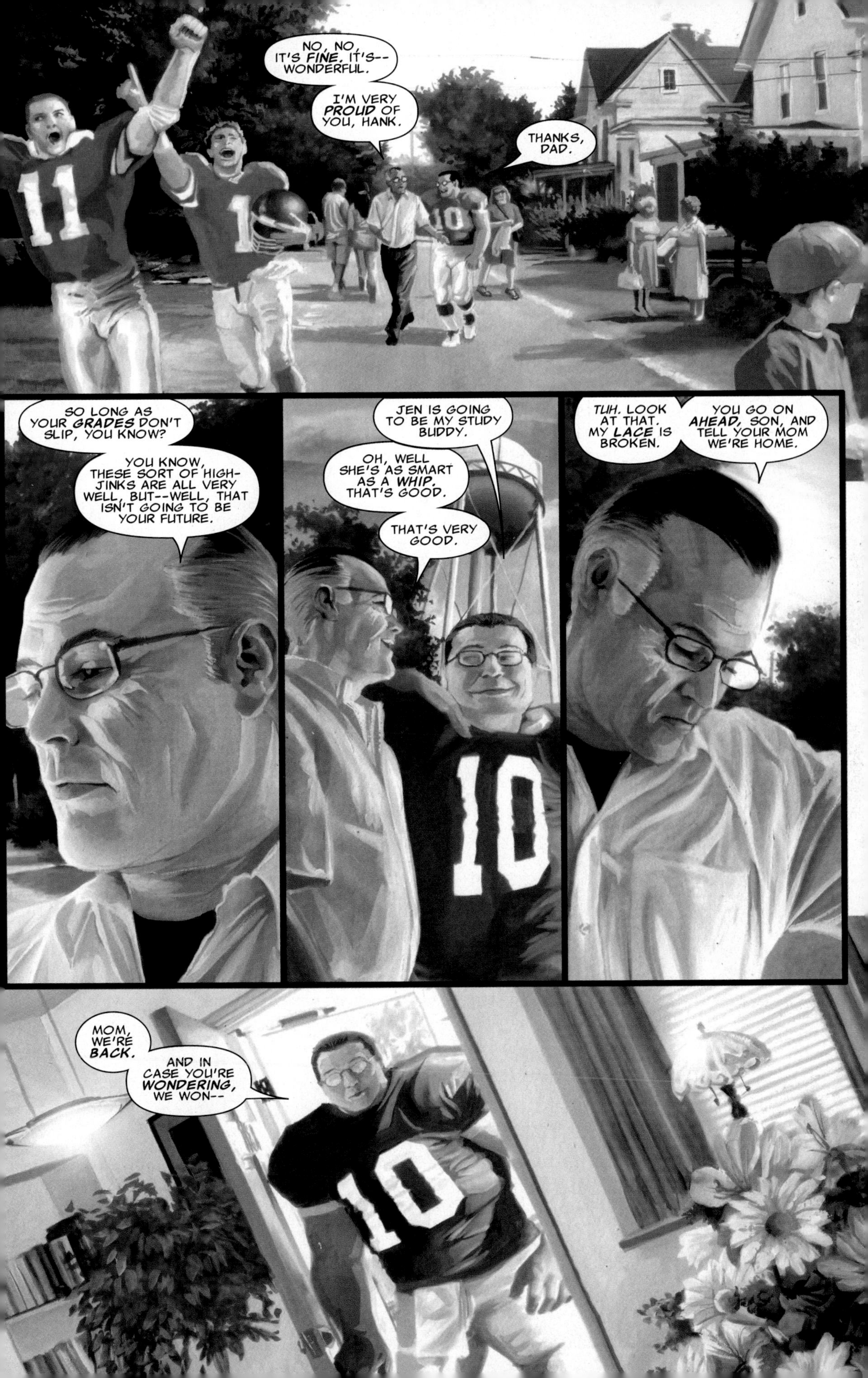
NO, NO, IT'S FINE. IT'S--WONDERFUL.
I'M VERY PROUD OF YOU, HANK.
THANKS, DAD.
SO LONG AS YOUR GRADES DON'T SLIP, YOU KNOW?
YOU KNOW, THESE SORT OF HIGH-JINKS ARE ALL VERY WELL, BUT--WELL, THAT ISN'T GOING TO BE YOUR FUTURE.
JEN IS GOING TO BE MY STUDY BUDDY.
OH, WELL SHE'S AS SMART AS A WHIP. THAT'S GOOD.
THAT'S VERY GOOD.
TUH. LOOK AT THAT. MY LACE IS BROKEN.
YOU GO ON AHEAD, SON, AND TELL YOUR MOM WE'RE HOME.
MOM, WE'RE BACK.
AND IN CASE YOU'RE WONDERING, WE WON--

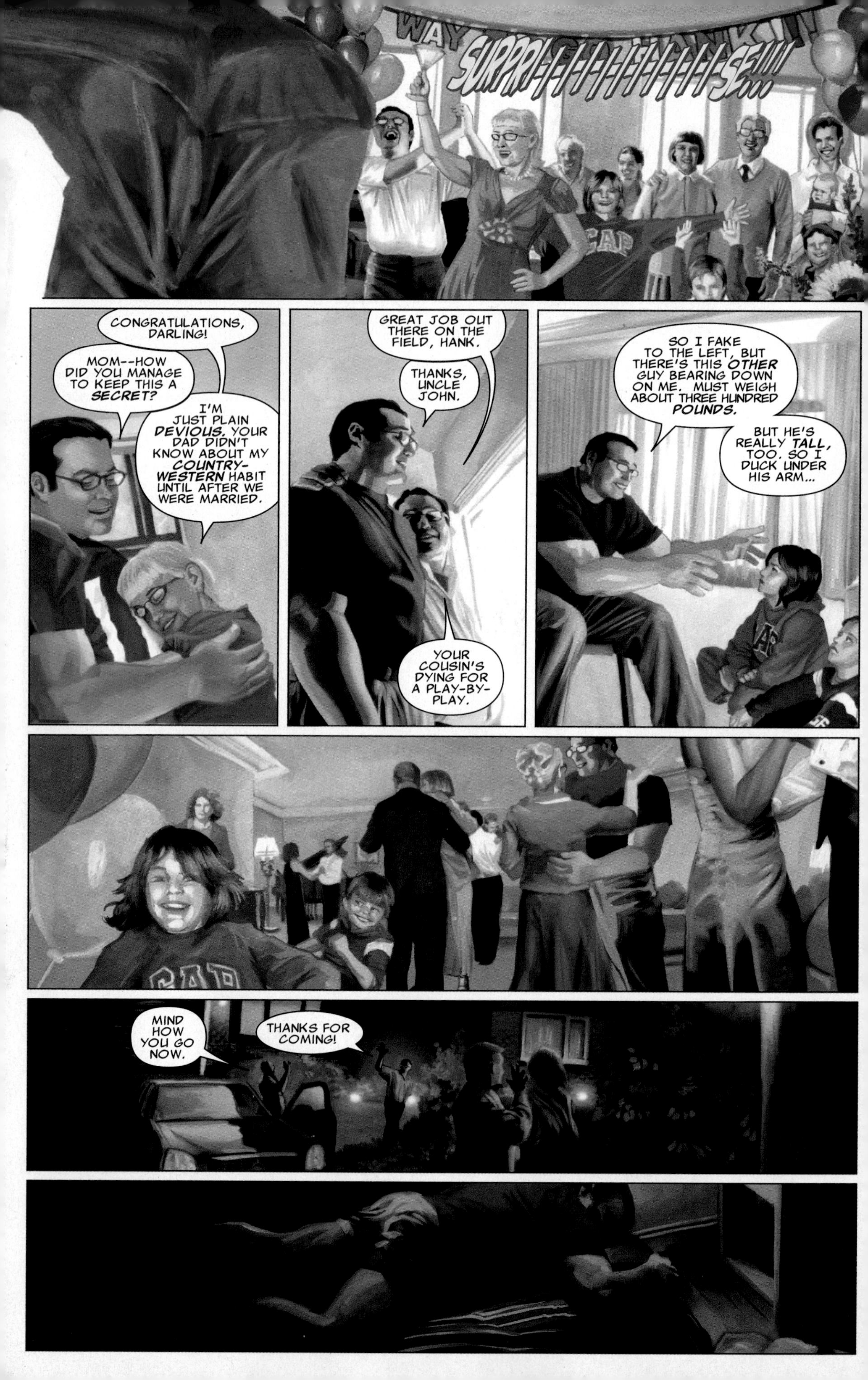
WAY
SURPRI-I-I-I-I-I-I-I-I-I-I-I-SE!!!
CONGRATULATIONS, DARLING!
MOM--HOW DID YOU MANAGE TO KEEP THIS A SECRET?
I'M JUST PLAIN DEVIOUS. YOUR DAD DIDN'T KNOW ABOUT MY COUNTRY-WESTERN HABIT UNTIL AFTER WE WERE MARRIED.
GREAT JOB OUT THERE ON THE FIELD, HANK.
THANKS, UNCLE JOHN.
YOUR COUSIN'S DYING FOR A PLAY-BY-PLAY.
SO I FAKE TO THE LEFT, BUT THERE'S THIS OTHER GUY BEARING DOWN ON ME. MUST WEIGH ABOUT THREE HUNDRED POUNDS.
BUT HE'S REALLY TALL, TOO. SO I DUCK UNDER HIS ARM...
MIND HOW YOU GO NOW.
THANKS FOR COMING!

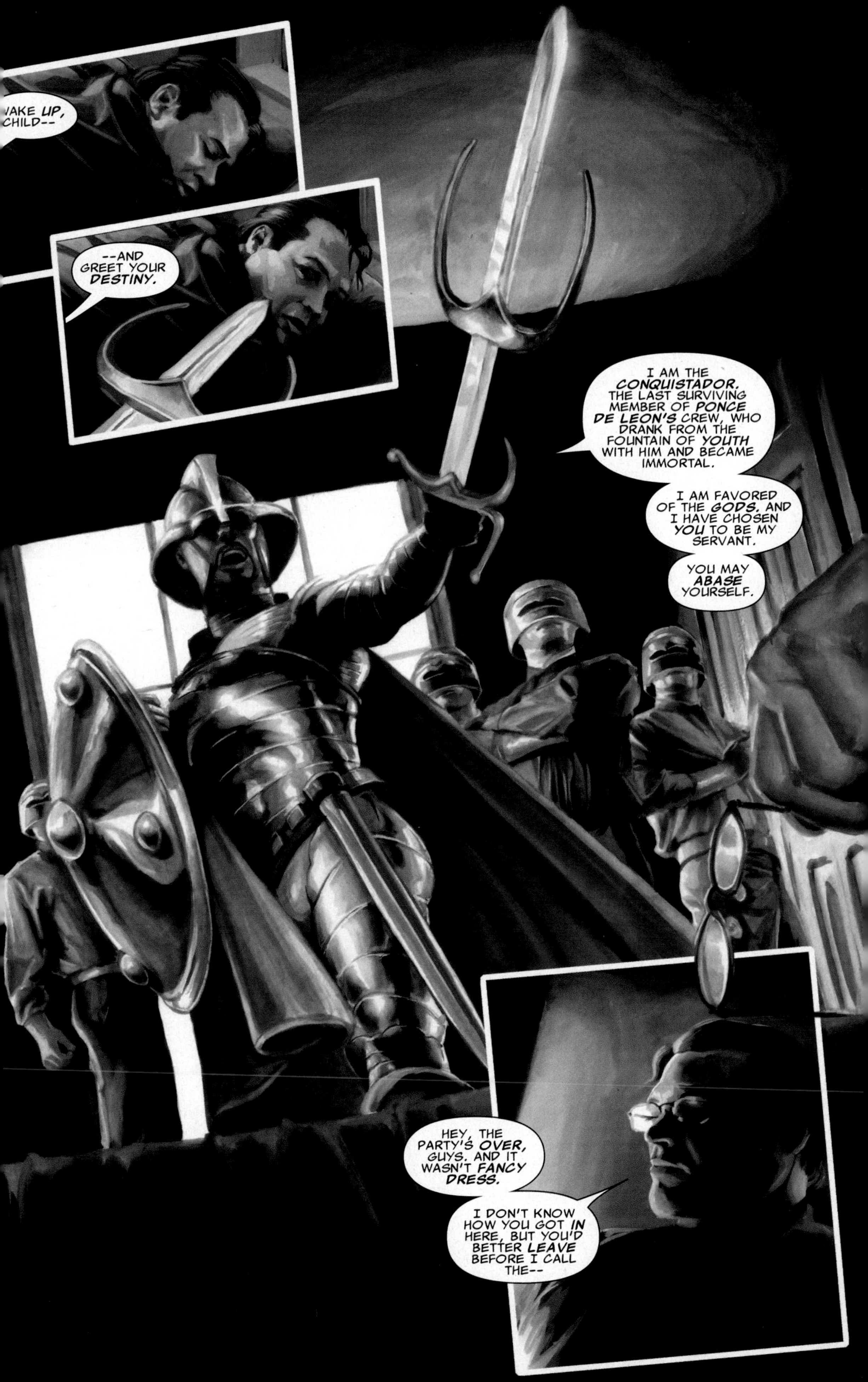
WAKE UP, CHILD--
--AND GREET YOUR DESTINY.
I AM THE CONQUISTADOR. THE LAST SURVIVING MEMBER OF PONCE DE LEON'S CREW, WHO DRANK FROM THE FOUNTAIN OF YOUTH WITH HIM AND BECAME IMMORTAL.
I AM FAVORED OF THE GODS. AND I HAVE CHOSEN YOU TO BE MY SERVANT.
YOU MAY ABASE YOURSELF.
HEY, THE PARTY'S OVER, GUYS. AND IT WASN'T FANCY DRESS.
I DON'T KNOW HOW YOU GOT IN HERE, BUT YOU'D BETTER LEAVE BEFORE I CALL THE--

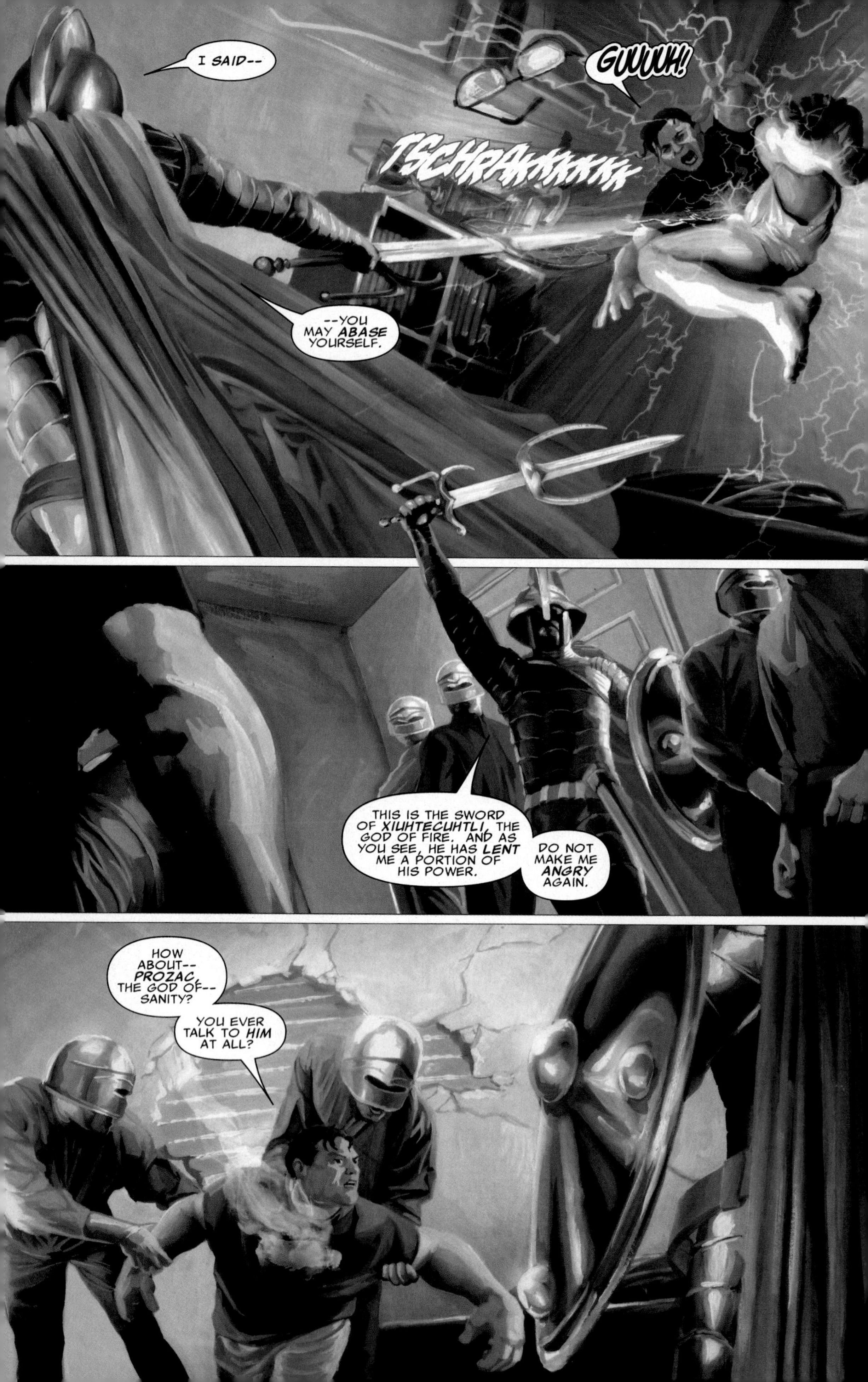
I SAID--
GUUUUH!
TSCHRAKKKKKK
--YOU MAY ABASE YOURSELF.
THIS IS THE SWORD OF XIUHTECUHTLI, THE GOD OF FIRE. AND AS YOU SEE, HE HAS LENT ME A PORTION OF HIS POWER.
DO NOT MAKE ME ANGRY AGAIN.
HOW ABOUT-- PROZAC, THE GOD OF-- SANITY?
YOU EVER TALK TO HIM AT ALL?

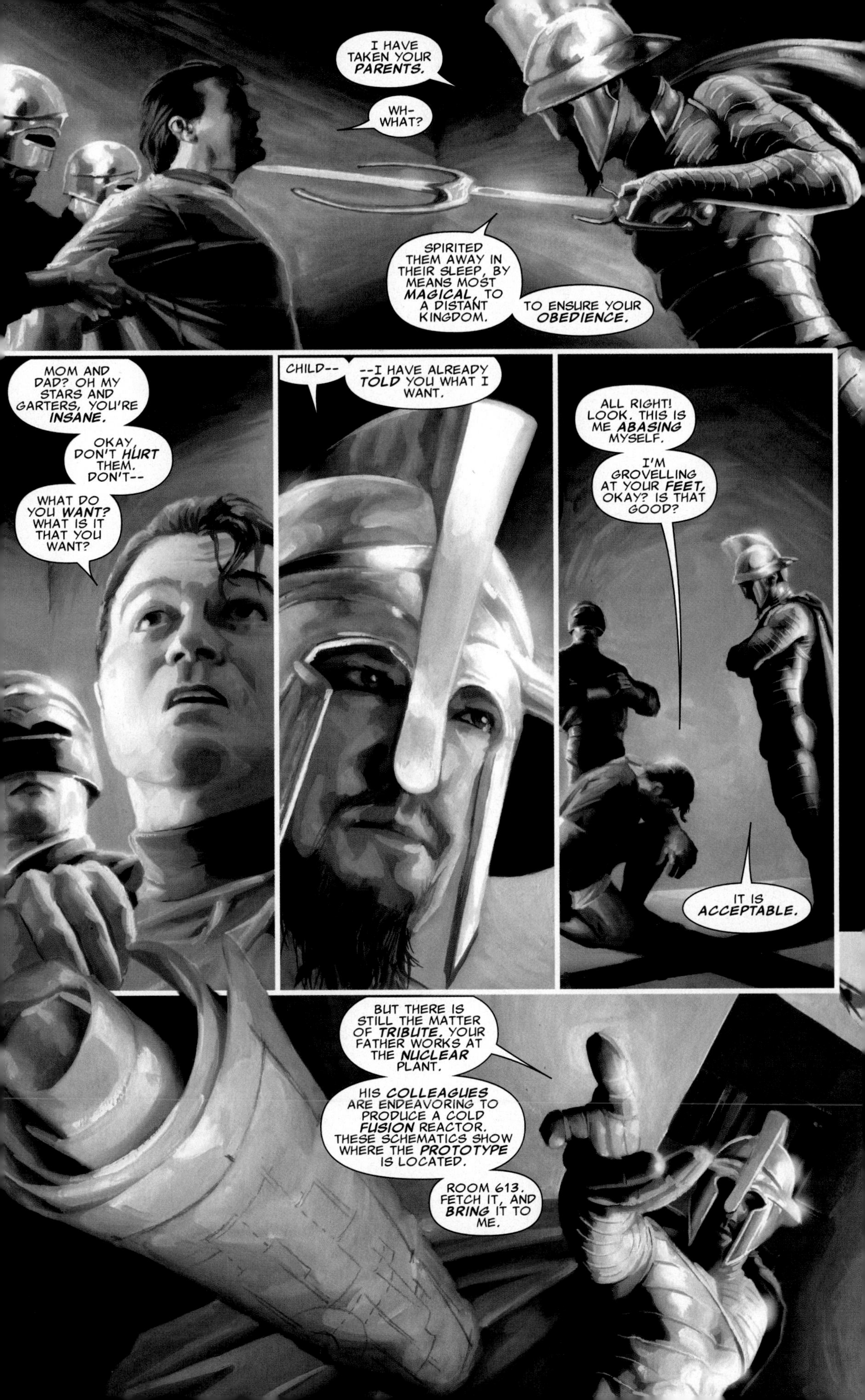

I HAVE TAKEN YOUR PARENTS.
WH-WHAT?
SPIRITED THEM AWAY IN THEIR SLEEP, BY MEANS MOST MAGICAL, TO A DISTANT KINGDOM.
TO ENSURE YOUR OBEDIENCE.
MOM AND DAD? OH MY STARS AND GARTERS, YOU'RE INSANE.
OKAY, DON'T HURT THEM. DON'T--
WHAT DO YOU WANT? WHAT IS IT THAT YOU WANT?
CHILD--
--I HAVE ALREADY TOLD YOU WHAT I WANT.
ALL RIGHT! LOOK. THIS IS ME ABASING MYSELF.
I'M GROVELLING AT YOUR FEET, OKAY? IS THAT GOOD?
IT IS ACCEPTABLE.
BUT THERE IS STILL THE MATTER OF TRIBUTE. YOUR FATHER WORKS AT THE NUCLEAR PLANT.
HIS COLLEAGUES ARE ENDEAVORING TO PRODUCE A COLD FUSION REACTOR. THESE SCHEMATICS SHOW WHERE THE PROTOTYPE IS LOCATED.
ROOM 613. FETCH IT, AND BRING IT TO ME.

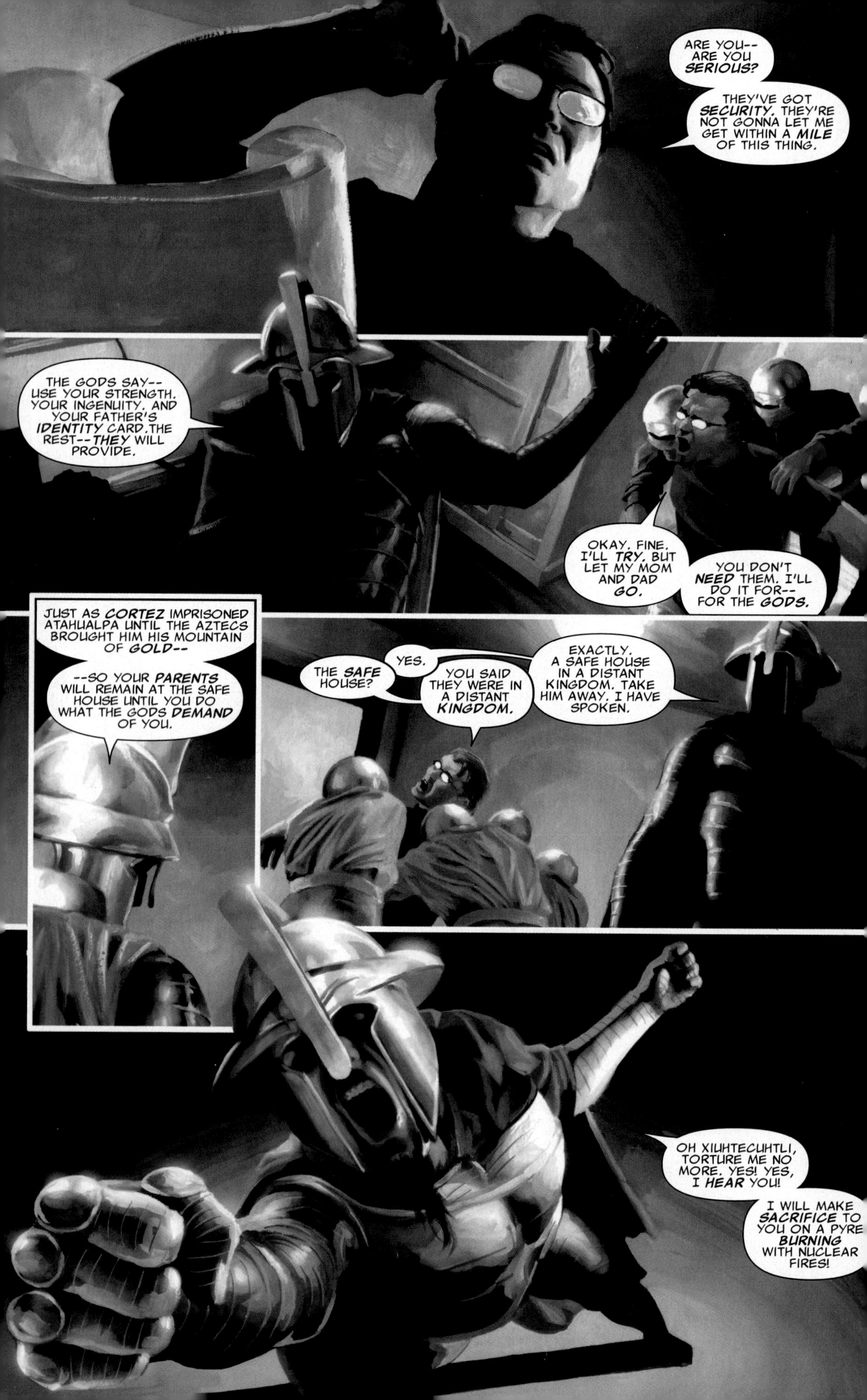
ARE YOU-- ARE YOU SERIOUS?
THEY'VE GOT SECURITY. THEY'RE NOT GONNA LET ME GET WITHIN A MILE OF THIS THING.
THE GODS SAY-- USE YOUR STRENGTH. YOUR INGENUITY. AND YOUR FATHER'S IDENTITY CARD. THE REST--THEY WILL PROVIDE.
OKAY. FINE. I'LL TRY. BUT LET MY MOM AND DAD GO.
YOU DON'T NEED THEM. I'LL DO IT FOR-- FOR THE GODS.
JUST AS CORTEZ IMPRISONED ATAHUALPA UNTIL THE AZTECS BROUGHT HIM HIS MOUNTAIN OF GOLD--
--SO YOUR PARENTS WILL REMAIN AT THE SAFE HOUSE UNTIL YOU DO WHAT THE GODS DEMAND OF YOU.
THE SAFE HOUSE?
YES.
YOU SAID THEY WERE IN A DISTANT KINGDOM.
EXACTLY. A SAFE HOUSE IN A DISTANT KINGDOM. TAKE HIM AWAY. I HAVE SPOKEN.
OH XIUHTECUHTLI, TORTURE ME NO MORE. YES! YES, I HEAR YOU!
I WILL MAKE SACRIFICE TO YOU ON A PYRE BURNING WITH NUCLEAR FIRES!

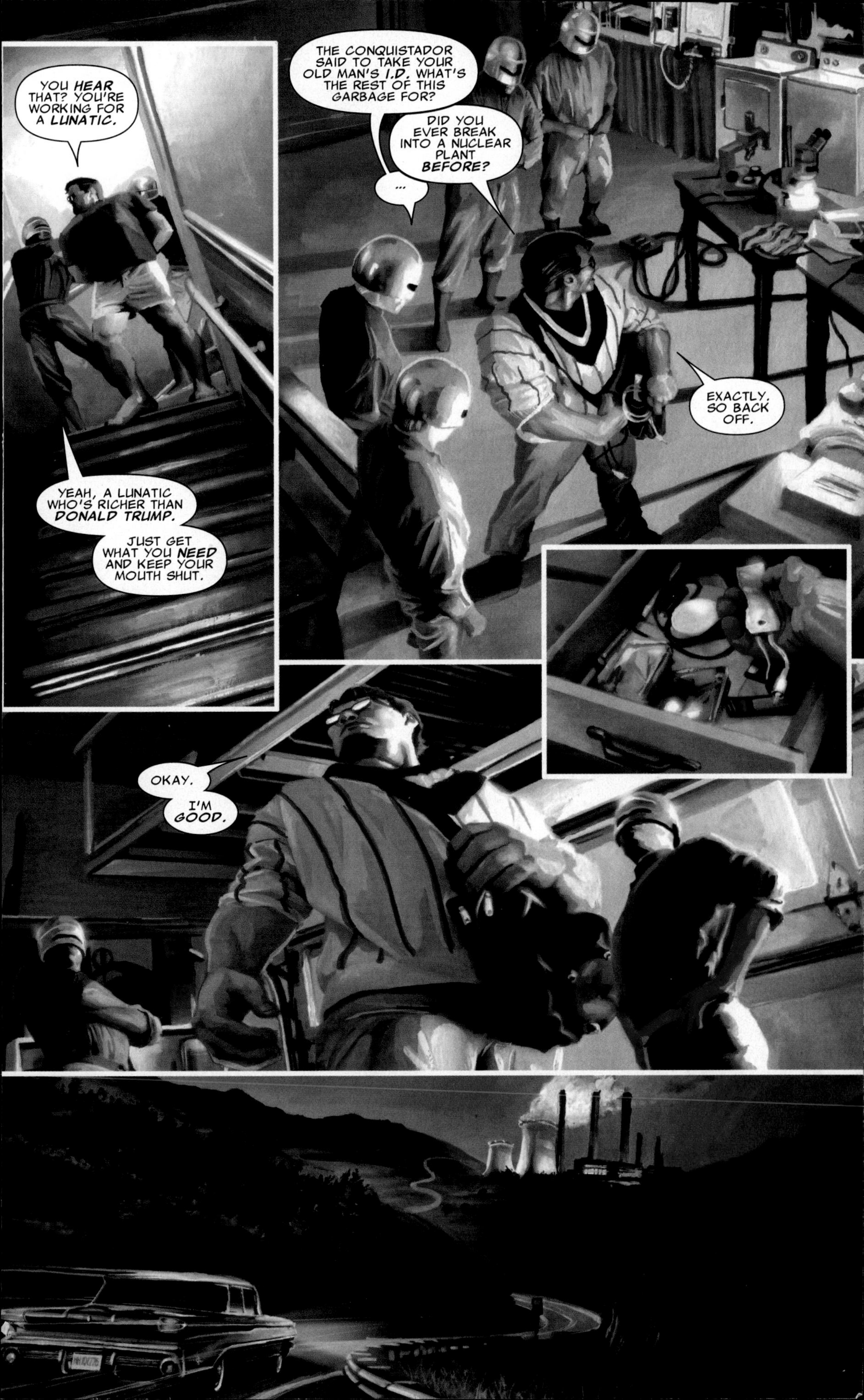
YOU **HEAR** THAT? YOU'RE WORKING FOR A ***LUNATIC.***
YEAH, A LUNATIC WHO'S RICHER THAN ***DONALD TRUMP.***
JUST GET WHAT YOU ***NEED*** AND KEEP YOUR MOUTH SHUT.
THE CONQUISTADOR SAID TO TAKE YOUR OLD MAN'S ***I.D.*** WHAT'S THE REST OF THIS GARBAGE FOR?
...
DID YOU EVER BREAK INTO A NUCLEAR PLANT ***BEFORE?***
EXACTLY. SO BACK OFF.
OKAY.
I'M ***GOOD.***

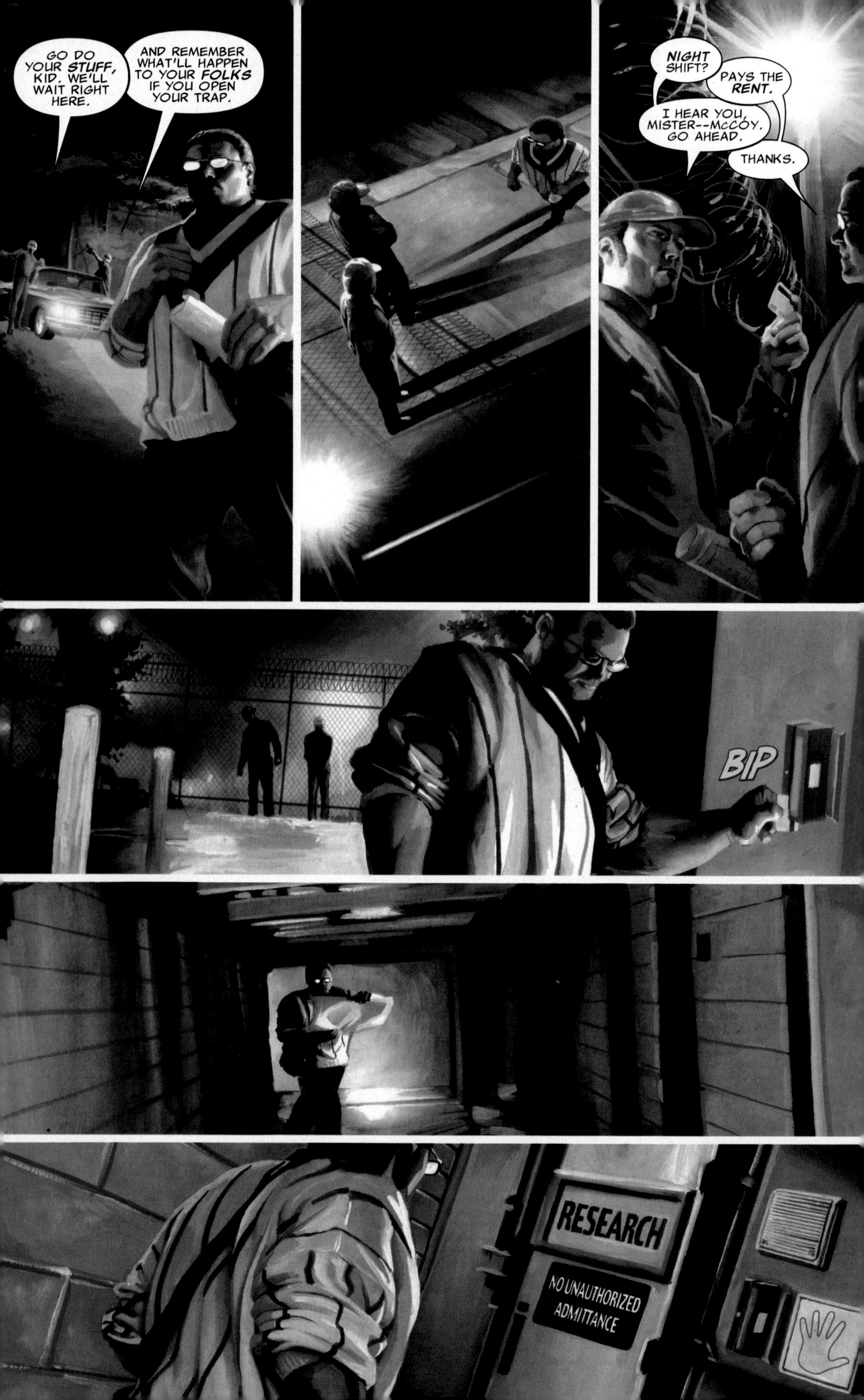
GO DO YOUR STUFF, KID. WE'LL WAIT RIGHT HERE.
AND REMEMBER WHAT'LL HAPPEN TO YOUR FOLKS IF YOU OPEN YOUR TRAP.
NIGHT SHIFT?
PAYS THE RENT.
I HEAR YOU, MISTER--McCOY. GO AHEAD.
THANKS.
BIP
RESEARCH
NO UNAUTHORIZED ADMITTANCE

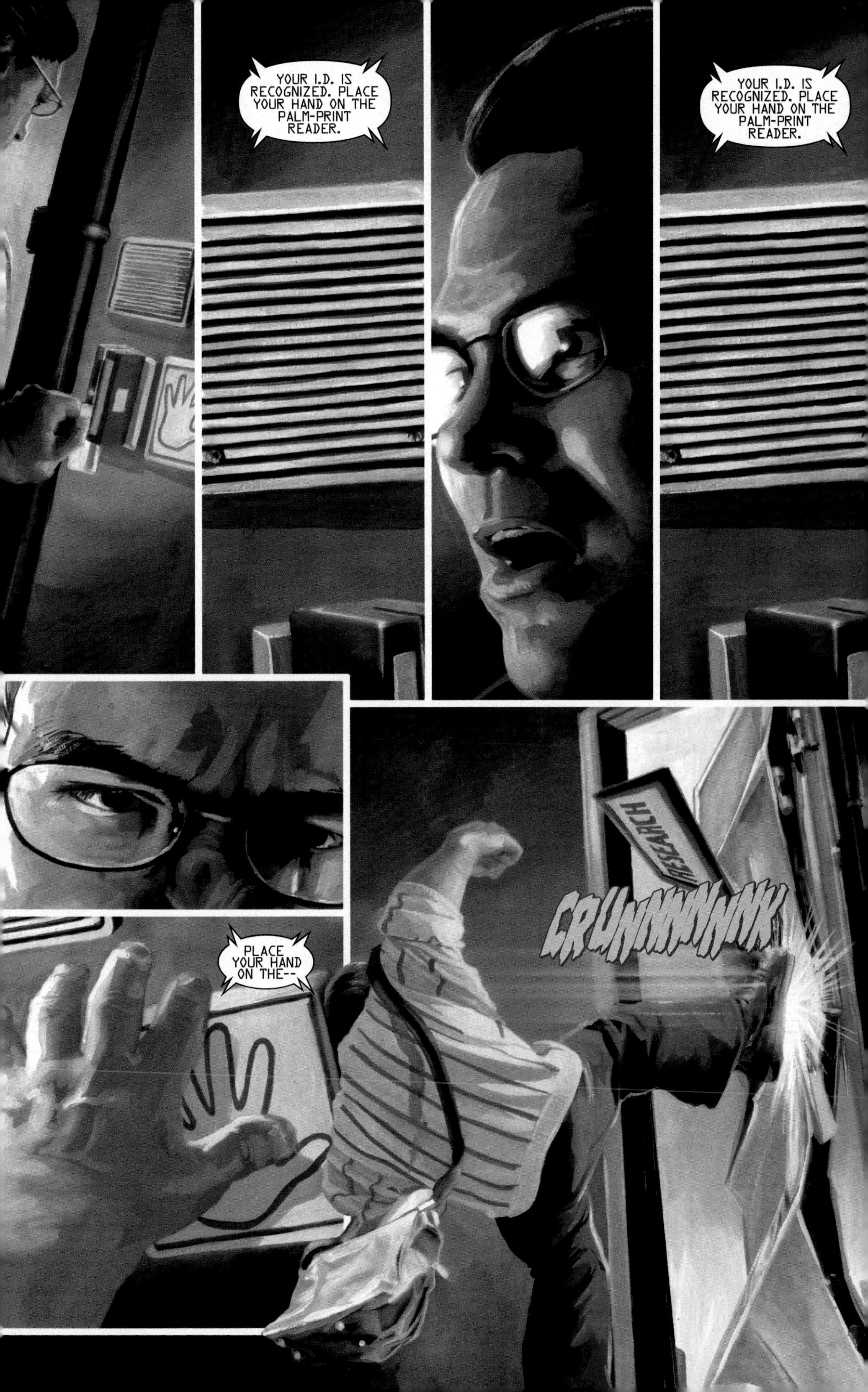
YOUR I.D. IS RECOGNIZED. PLACE YOUR HAND ON THE PALM-PRINT READER.
YOUR I.D. IS RECOGNIZED. PLACE YOUR HAND ON THE PALM-PRINT READER.
PLACE YOUR HAND ON THE--
RESEARCH
CRUNNNNNNK

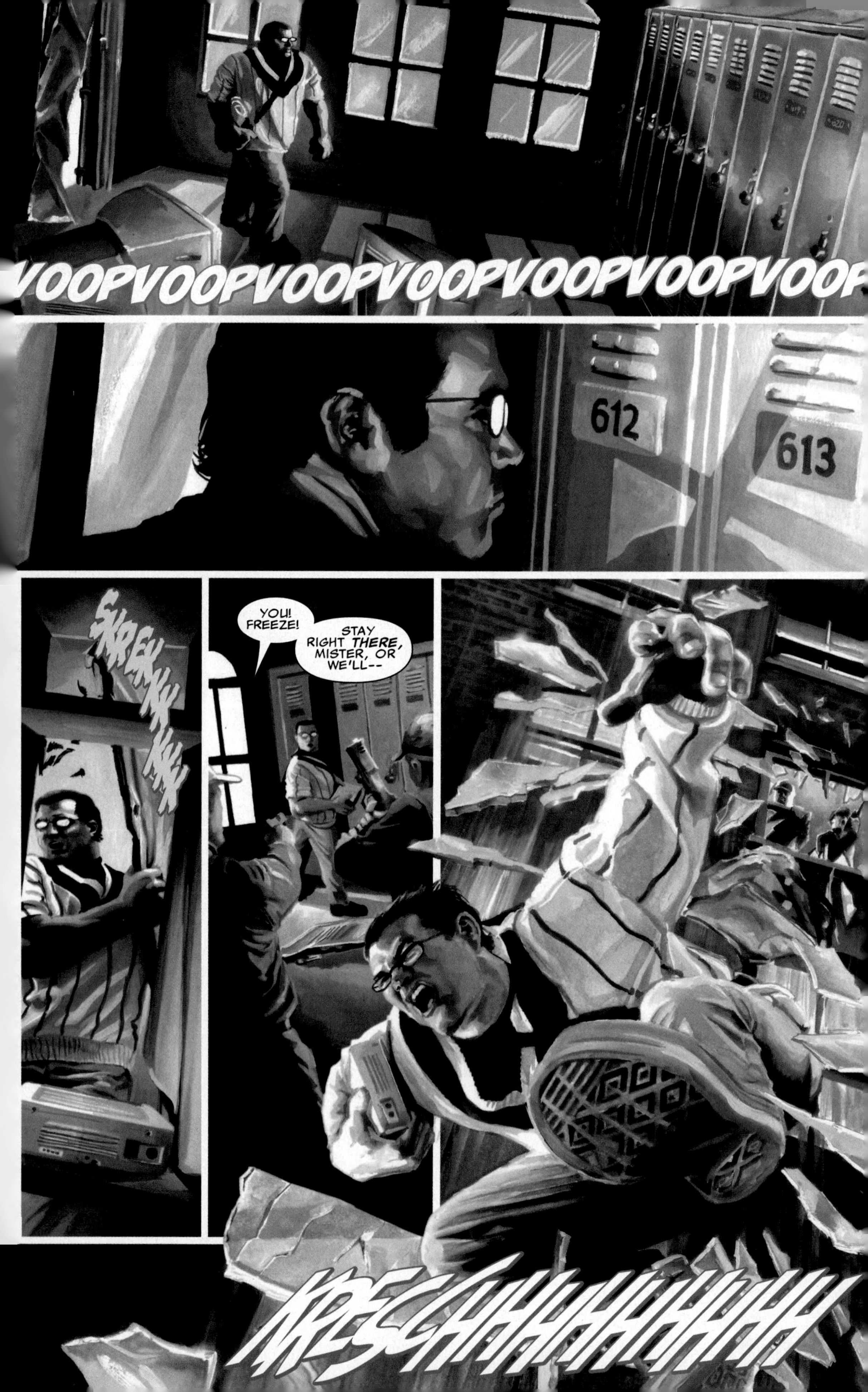
VOOPVOOPVOOPVOOPVOOPVOOPVOOP
612
613
YOU! FREEZE!
STAY RIGHT THERE, MISTER, OR WE'LL--

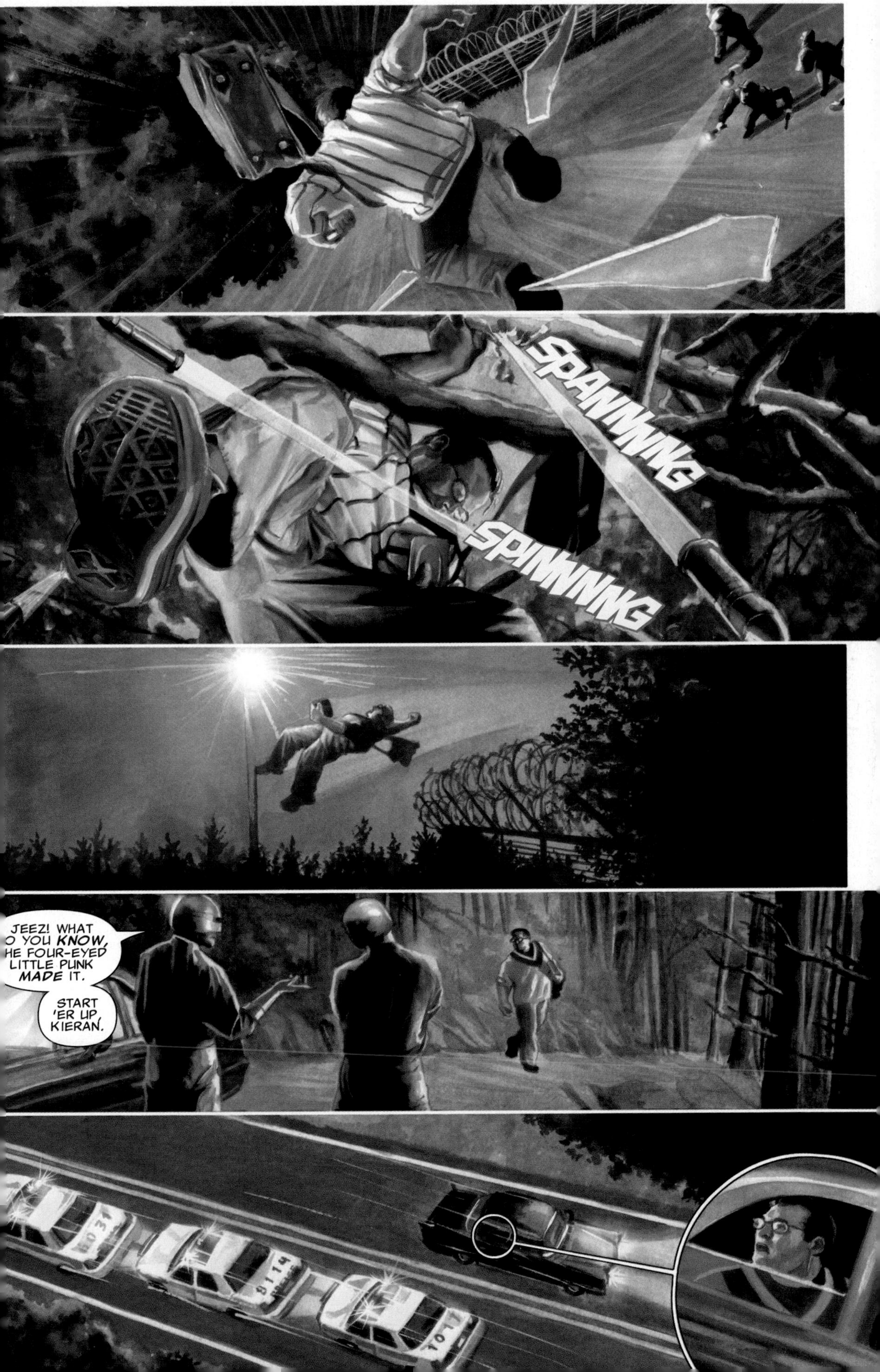
SPANNNNG
SPINNNNG
JEEZ! WHAT O YOU KNOW, HE FOUR-EYED LITTLE PUNK MADE IT.
START 'ER UP, KIERAN.

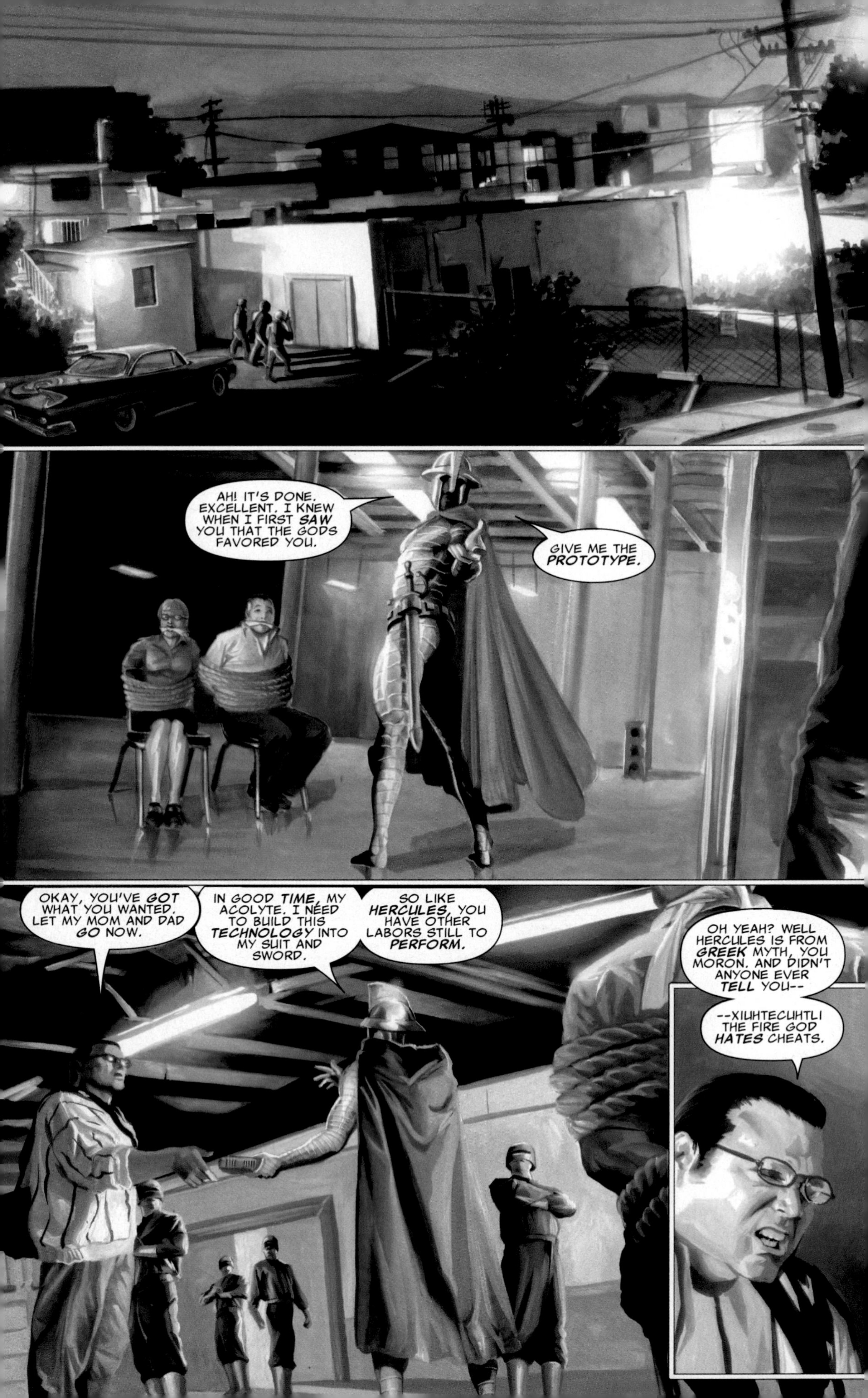
AH! IT'S DONE. EXCELLENT. I KNEW WHEN I FIRST SAW YOU THAT THE GODS FAVORED YOU.
GIVE ME THE PROTOTYPE.
OKAY, YOU'VE GOT WHAT YOU WANTED. LET MY MOM AND DAD GO NOW.
IN GOOD TIME, MY ACOLYTE. I NEED TO BUILD THIS TECHNOLOGY INTO MY SUIT AND SWORD.
SO LIKE HERCULES, YOU HAVE OTHER LABORS STILL TO PERFORM.
OH YEAH? WELL HERCULES IS FROM GREEK MYTH, YOU MORON. AND DIDN'T ANYONE EVER TELL YOU--
--XIUHTECUHTLI THE FIRE GOD HATES CHEATS.

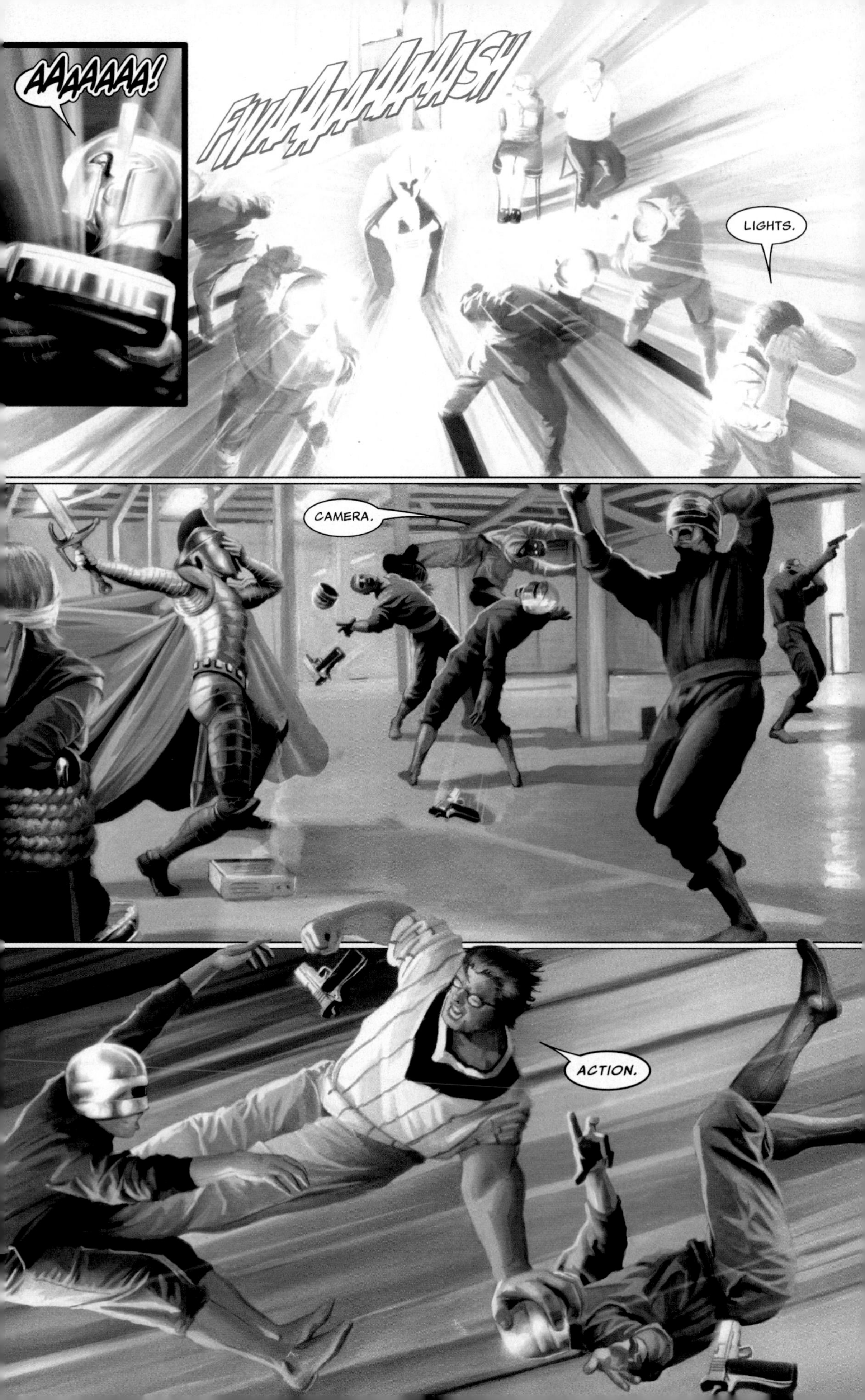
AAAAAAA!
FWAAAAAAAAASH
LIGHTS.
CAMERA.
ACTION.

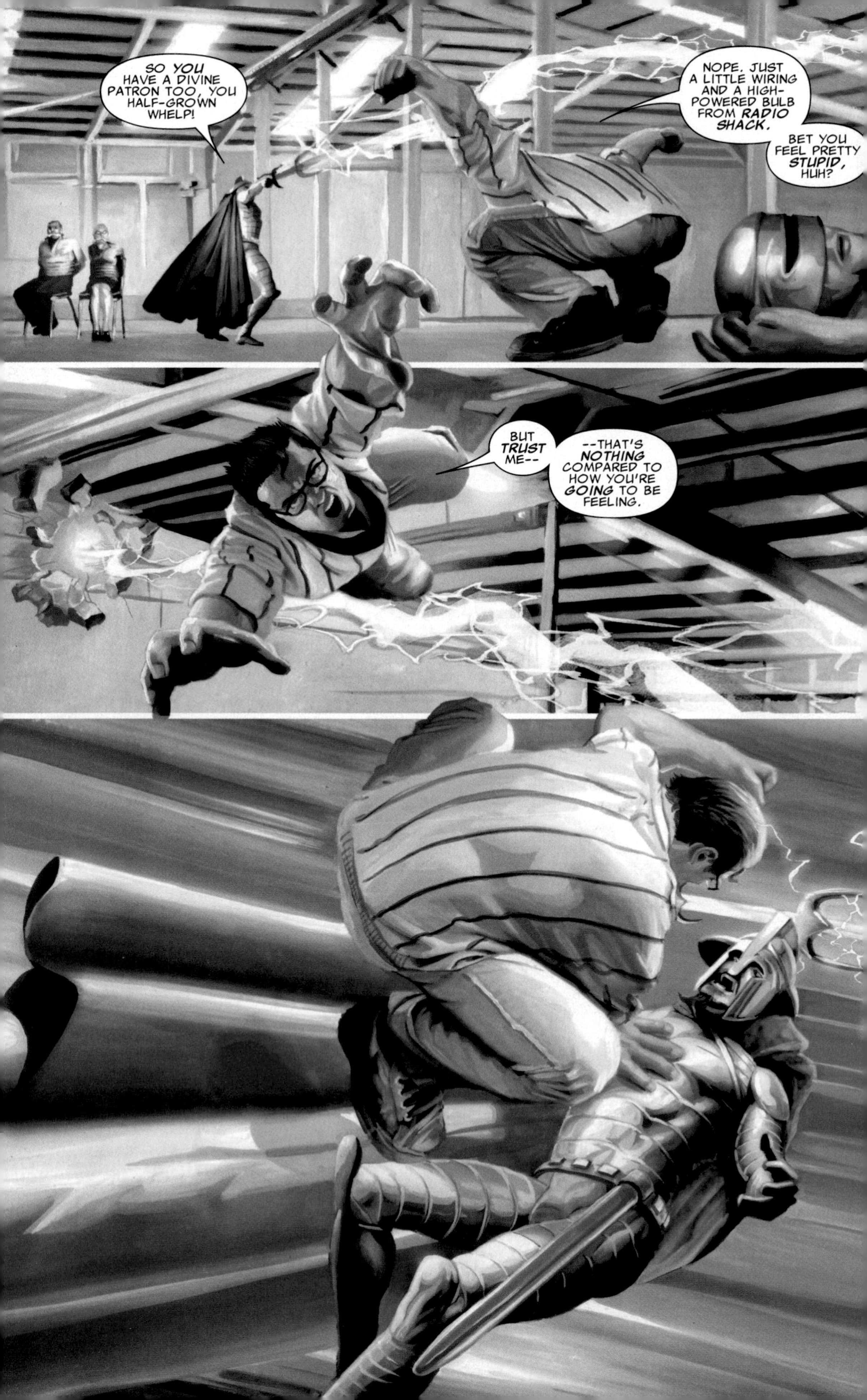
SO YOU HAVE A DIVINE PATRON TOO, YOU HALF-GROWN WHELP!
NOPE. JUST A LITTLE WIRING AND A HIGH-POWERED BULB FROM RADIO SHACK.
BET YOU FEEL PRETTY STUPID, HUH?
BUT TRUST ME--
--THAT'S NOTHING COMPARED TO HOW YOU'RE GOING TO BE FEELING.

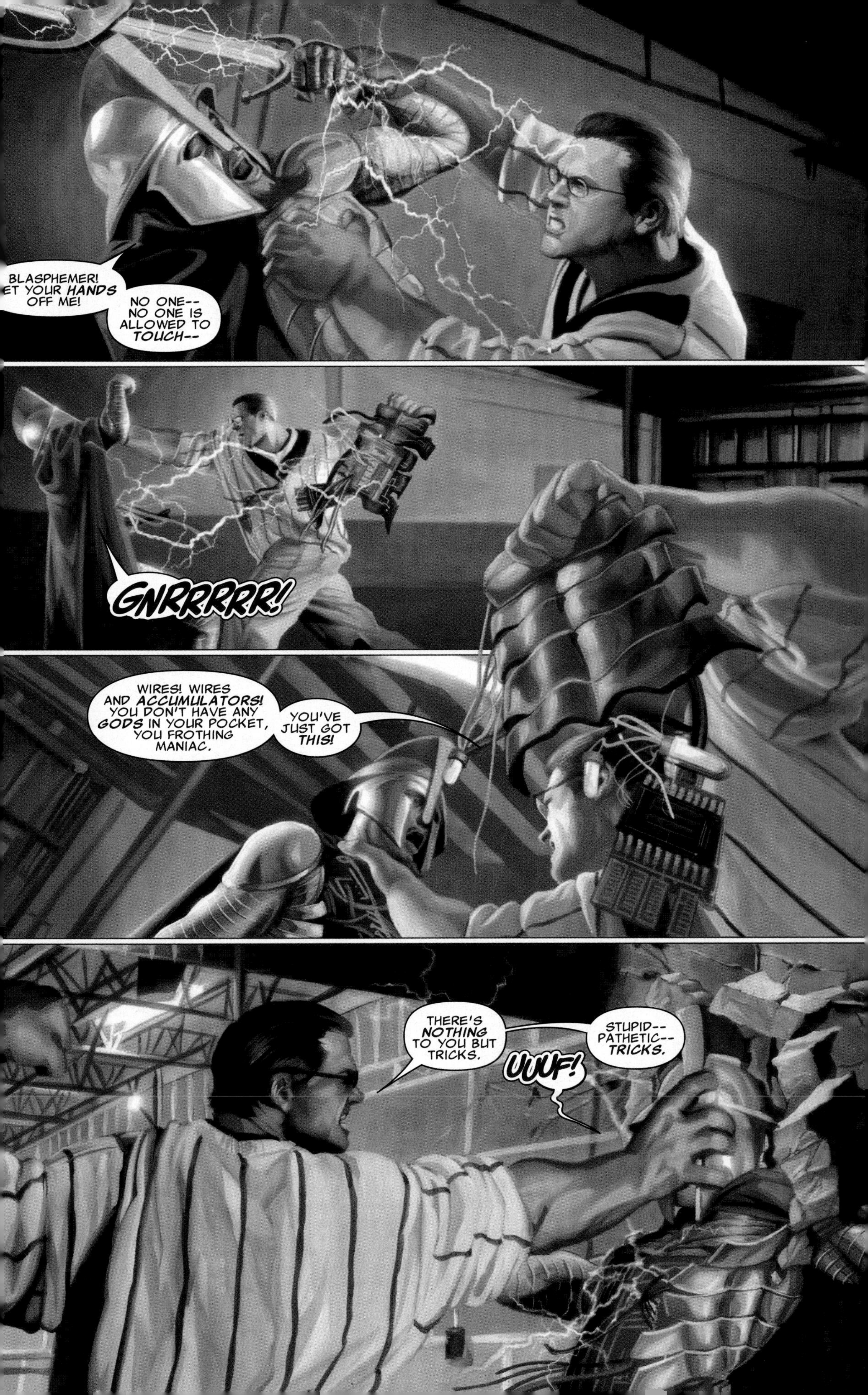

BLASPHEMER! ET YOUR HANDS OFF ME!
NO ONE-- NO ONE IS ALLOWED TO TOUCH--
GNRRRRR!
WIRES! WIRES AND ACCUMULATORS! YOU DON'T HAVE ANY GODS IN YOUR POCKET, YOU FROTHING MANIAC.
YOU'VE JUST GOT THIS!
THERE'S NOTHING TO YOU BUT TRICKS.
STUPID-- PATHETIC-- TRICKS.
UUUF!

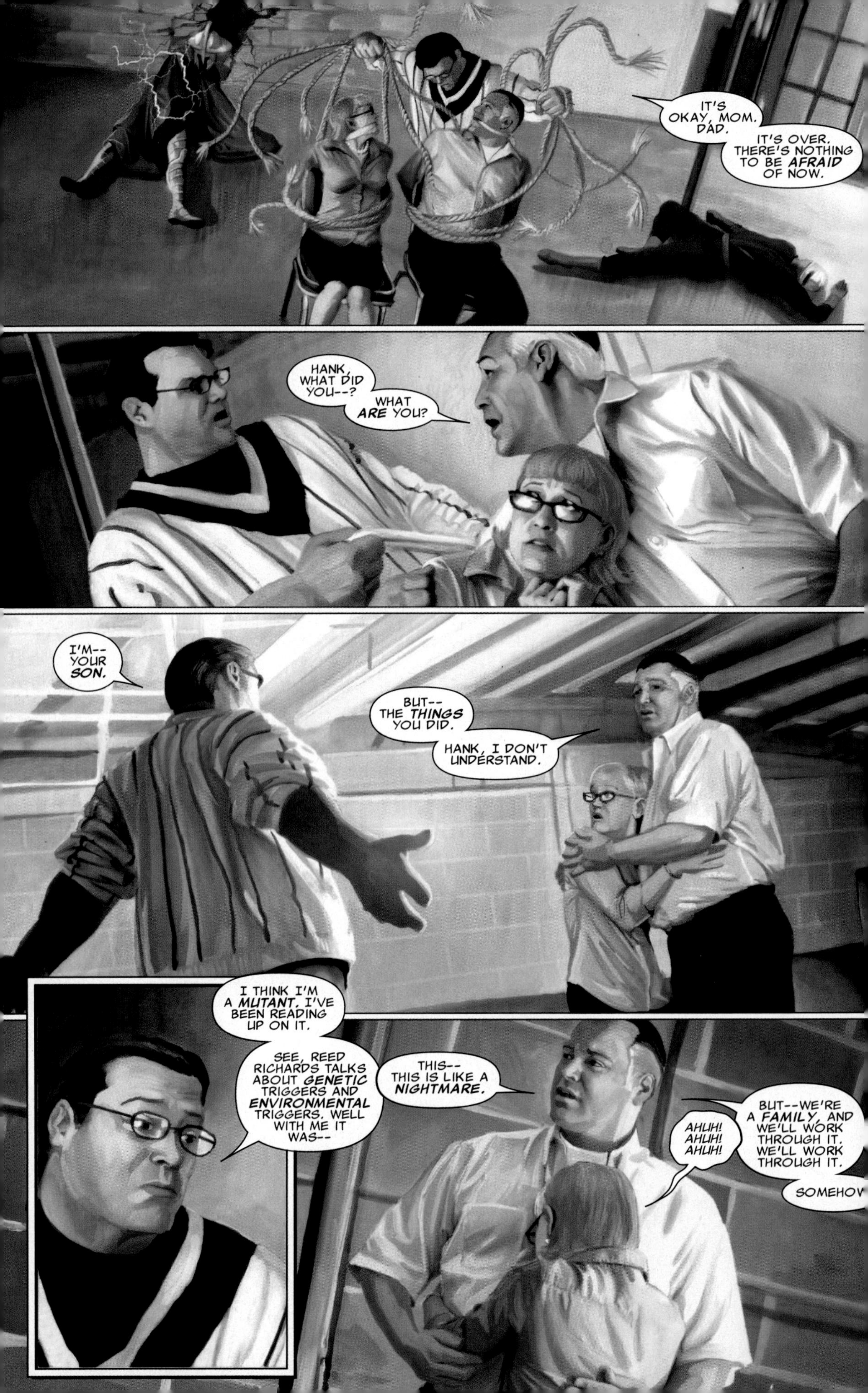

IT'S OKAY, MOM. DAD.
IT'S OVER. THERE'S NOTHING TO BE AFRAID OF NOW.
HANK, WHAT DID YOU--?
WHAT ARE YOU?
I'M-- YOUR SON.
BUT-- THE THINGS YOU DID.
HANK, I DON'T UNDERSTAND.
I THINK I'M A MUTANT. I'VE BEEN READING UP ON IT.
SEE, REED RICHARDS TALKS ABOUT GENETIC TRIGGERS AND ENVIRONMENTAL TRIGGERS. WELL WITH ME IT WAS--
THIS-- THIS IS LIKE A NIGHTMARE.
AHUH! AHUH! AHUH!
BUT--WE'RE A FAMILY, AND WE'LL WORK THROUGH IT. WE'LL WORK THROUGH IT.
SOMEHOV

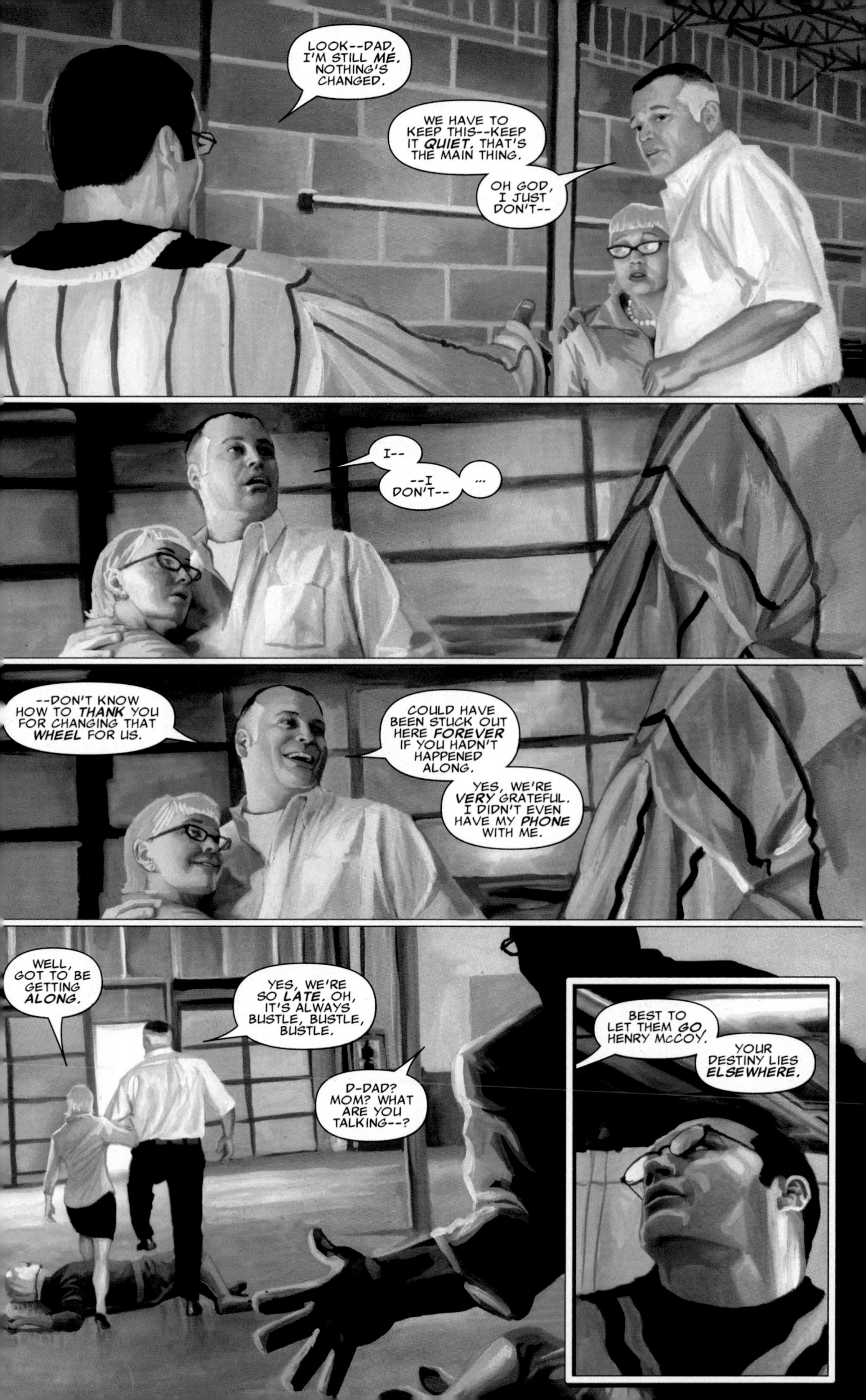
LOOK--DAD, I'M STILL ME. NOTHING'S CHANGED.
WE HAVE TO KEEP THIS--KEEP IT QUIET. THAT'S THE MAIN THING.
OH GOD, I JUST DON'T--
I--
--I DON'T--
...
--DON'T KNOW HOW TO THANK YOU FOR CHANGING THAT WHEEL FOR US.
COULD HAVE BEEN STUCK OUT HERE FOREVER IF YOU HADN'T HAPPENED ALONG.
YES, WE'RE VERY GRATEFUL. I DIDN'T EVEN HAVE MY PHONE WITH ME.
WELL, GOT TO BE GETTING ALONG.
YES, WE'RE SO LATE. OH, IT'S ALWAYS BUSTLE, BUSTLE, BUSTLE.
D-DAD? MOM? WHAT ARE YOU TALKING--?
BEST TO LET THEM GO, HENRY McCOY.
YOUR DESTINY LIES ELSEWHERE.

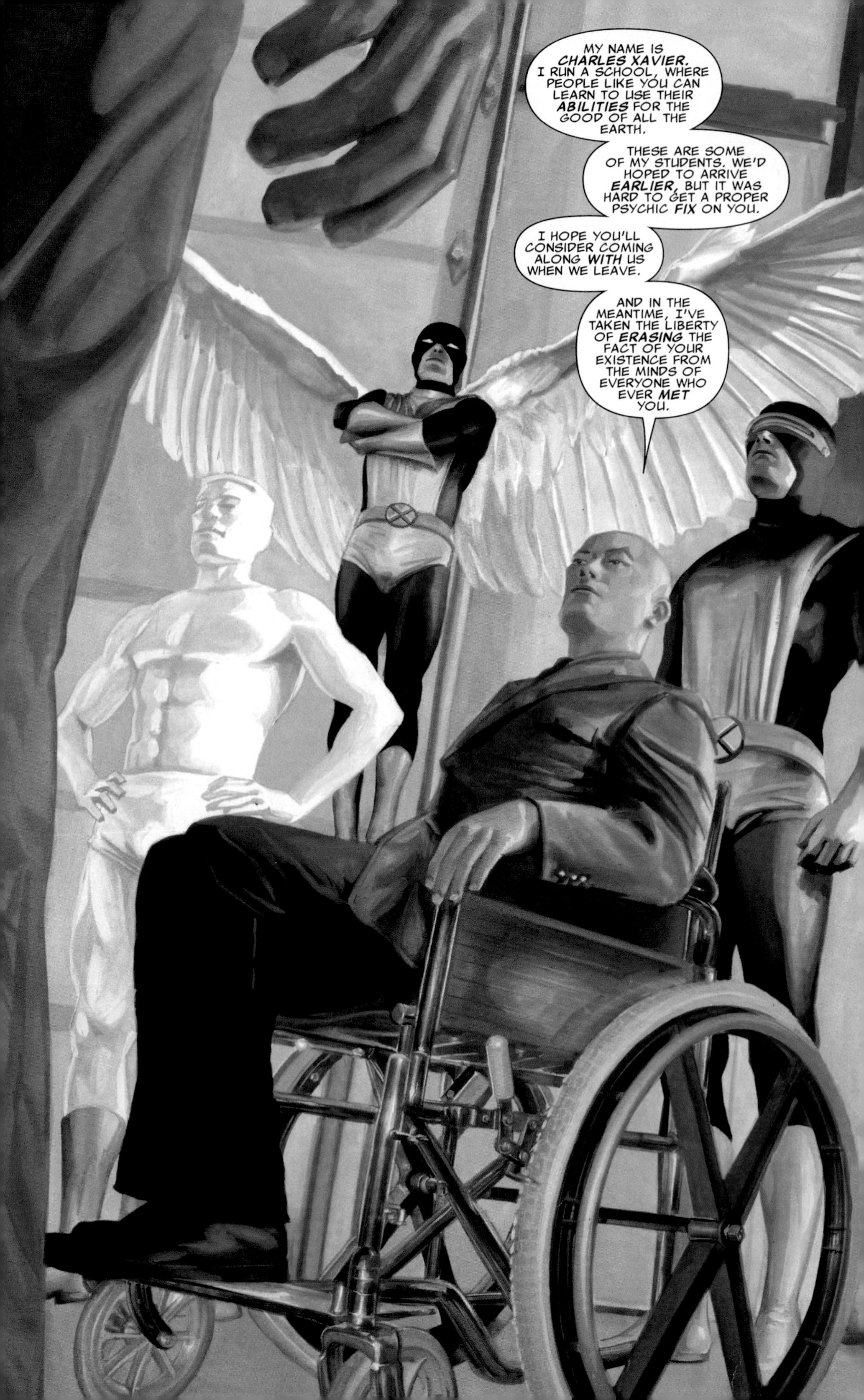
MY NAME IS CHARLES XAVIER. I RUN A SCHOOL, WHERE PEOPLE LIKE YOU CAN LEARN TO USE THEIR ABILITIES FOR THE GOOD OF ALL THE EARTH.
THESE ARE SOME OF MY STUDENTS. WE'D HOPED TO ARRIVE EARLIER, BUT IT WAS HARD TO GET A PROPER PSYCHIC FIX ON YOU.
I HOPE YOU'LL CONSIDER COMING ALONG WITH US WHEN WE LEAVE.
AND IN THE MEANTIME, I'VE TAKEN THE LIBERTY OF ERASING THE FACT OF YOUR EXISTENCE FROM THE MINDS OF EVERYONE WHO EVER MET YOU.

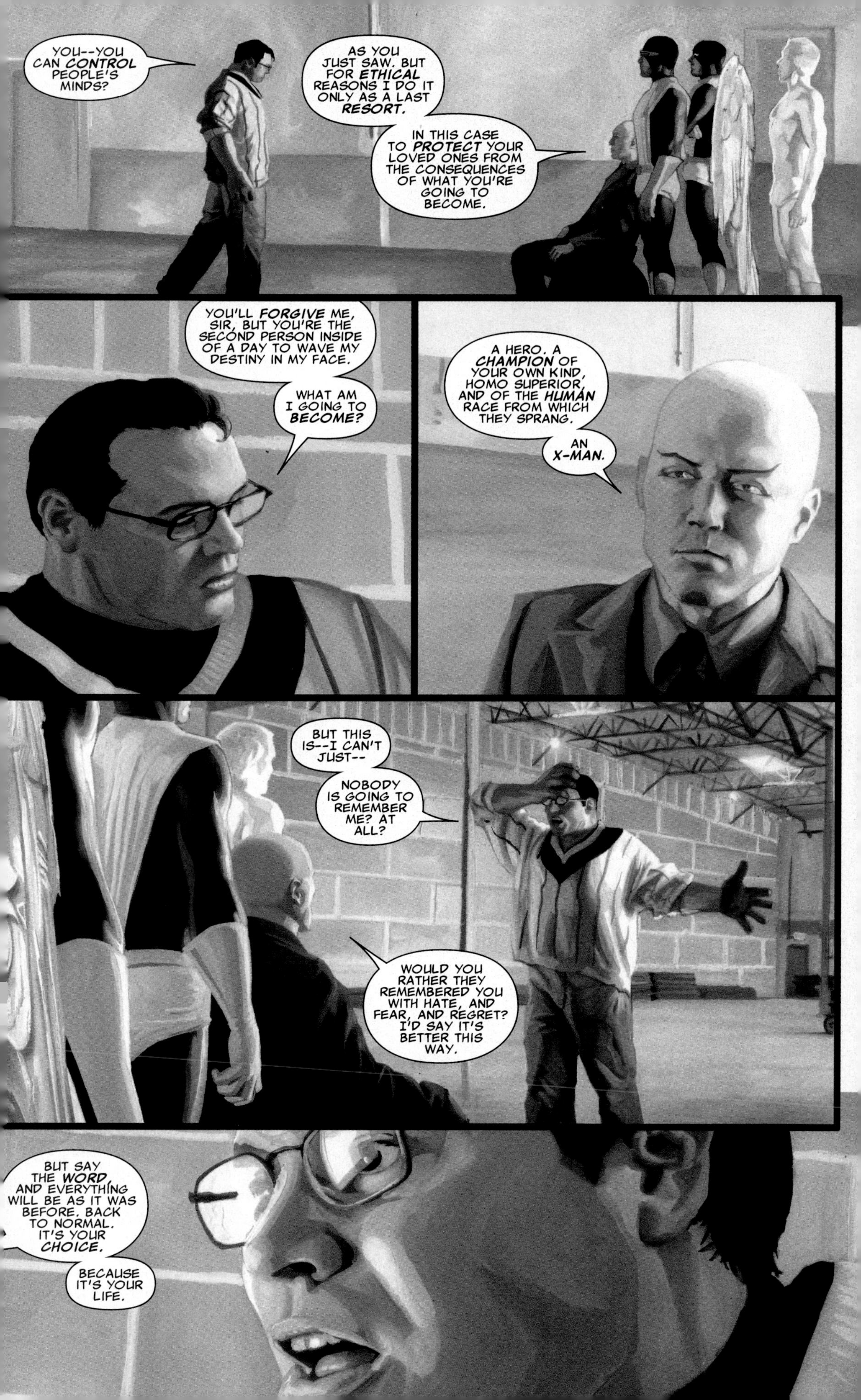
YOU--YOU CAN CONTROL PEOPLE'S MINDS?
AS YOU JUST SAW. BUT FOR ETHICAL REASONS I DO IT ONLY AS A LAST RESORT.
IN THIS CASE TO PROTECT YOUR LOVED ONES FROM THE CONSEQUENCES OF WHAT YOU'RE GOING TO BECOME.
YOU'LL FORGIVE ME, SIR, BUT YOU'RE THE SECOND PERSON INSIDE OF A DAY TO WAVE MY DESTINY IN MY FACE.
WHAT AM I GOING TO BECOME?
A HERO. A CHAMPION OF YOUR OWN KIND, HOMO SUPERIOR, AND OF THE HUMAN RACE FROM WHICH THEY SPRANG.
AN X-MAN.
BUT THIS IS--I CAN'T JUST--
NOBODY IS GOING TO REMEMBER ME? AT ALL?
WOULD YOU RATHER THEY REMEMBERED YOU WITH HATE, AND FEAR, AND REGRET? I'D SAY IT'S BETTER THIS WAY.
BUT SAY THE WORD, AND EVERYTHING WILL BE AS IT WAS BEFORE. BACK TO NORMAL. IT'S YOUR CHOICE.
BECAUSE IT'S YOUR LIFE.

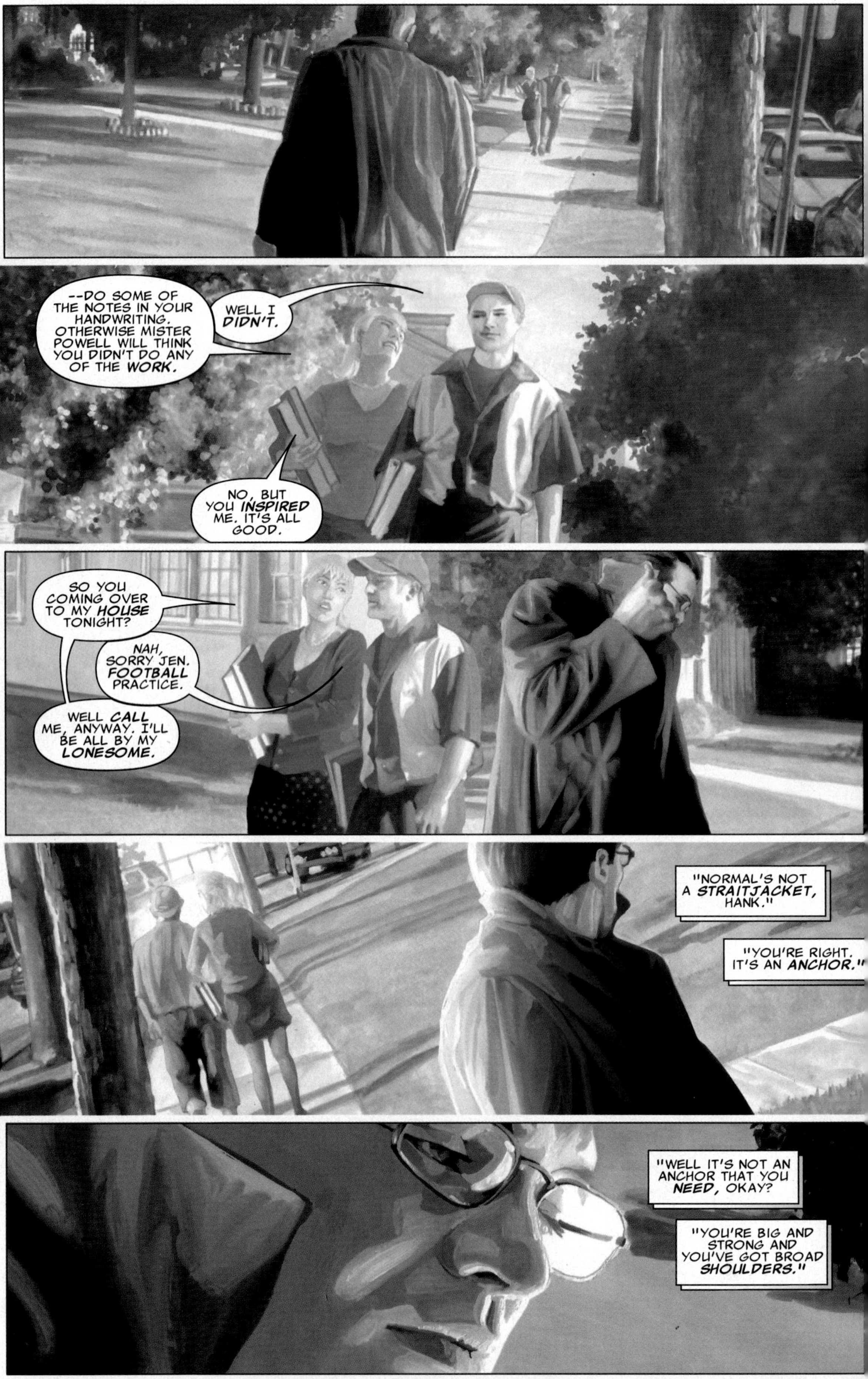
--DO SOME OF THE NOTES IN YOUR HANDWRITING. OTHERWISE MISTER POWELL WILL THINK YOU DIDN'T DO ANY OF THE WORK.
WELL I DIDN'T.
NO, BUT YOU INSPIRED ME. IT'S ALL GOOD.
SO YOU COMING OVER TO MY HOUSE TONIGHT?
NAH, SORRY JEN. FOOTBALL PRACTICE.
WELL CALL ME, ANYWAY. I'LL BE ALL BY MY LONESOME.
"NORMAL'S NOT A STRAITJACKET, HANK."
"YOU'RE RIGHT. IT'S AN ANCHOR."
"WELL IT'S NOT AN ANCHOR THAT YOU NEED, OKAY?
"YOU'RE BIG AND STRONG AND YOU'VE GOT BROAD SHOULDERS."

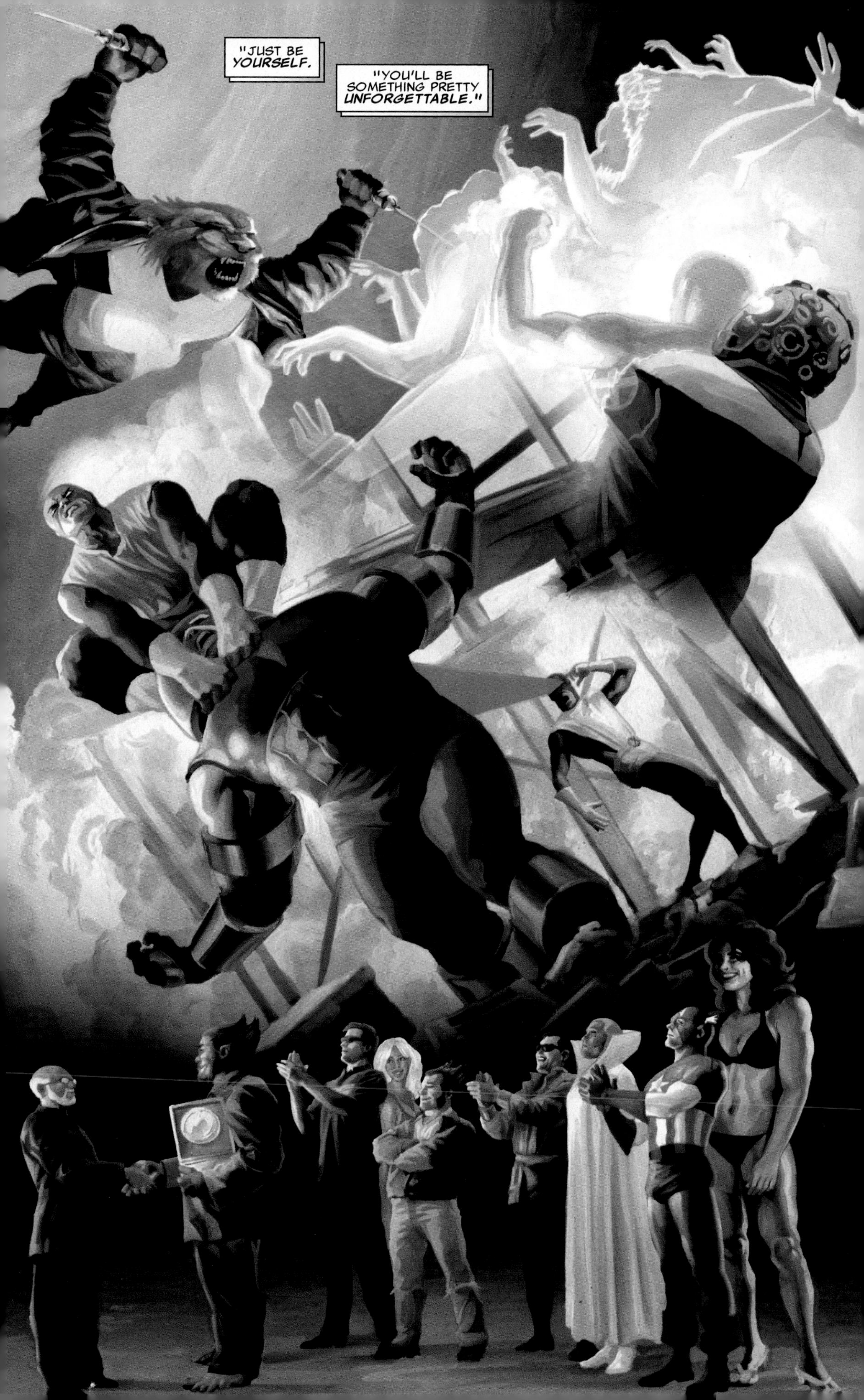
"JUST BE YOURSELF.
"YOU'LL BE SOMETHING PRETTY UNFORGETTABLE."

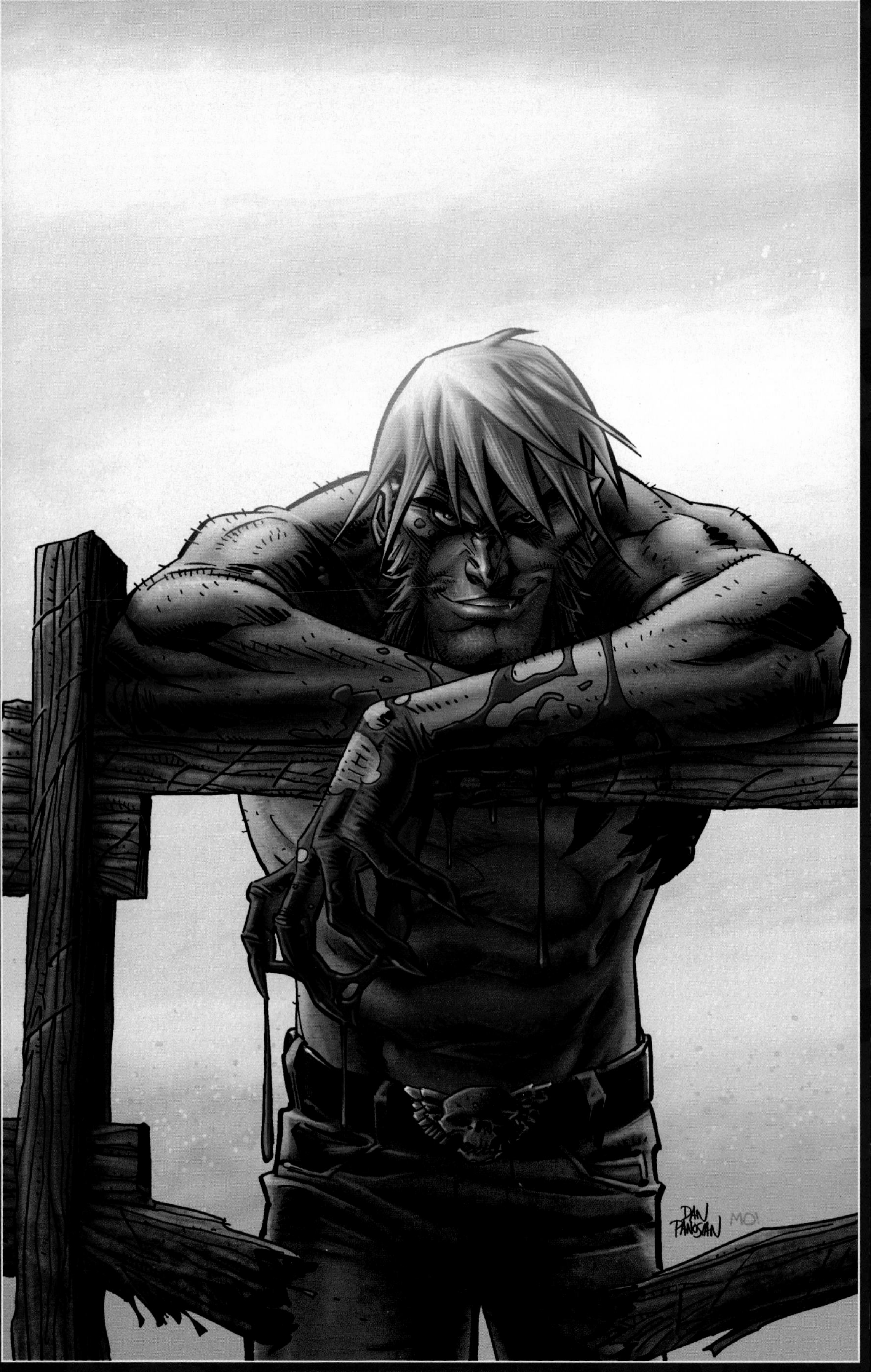
DAN PANOSIAN
MO!

X-MEN ORIGINS: SABRETOOTH

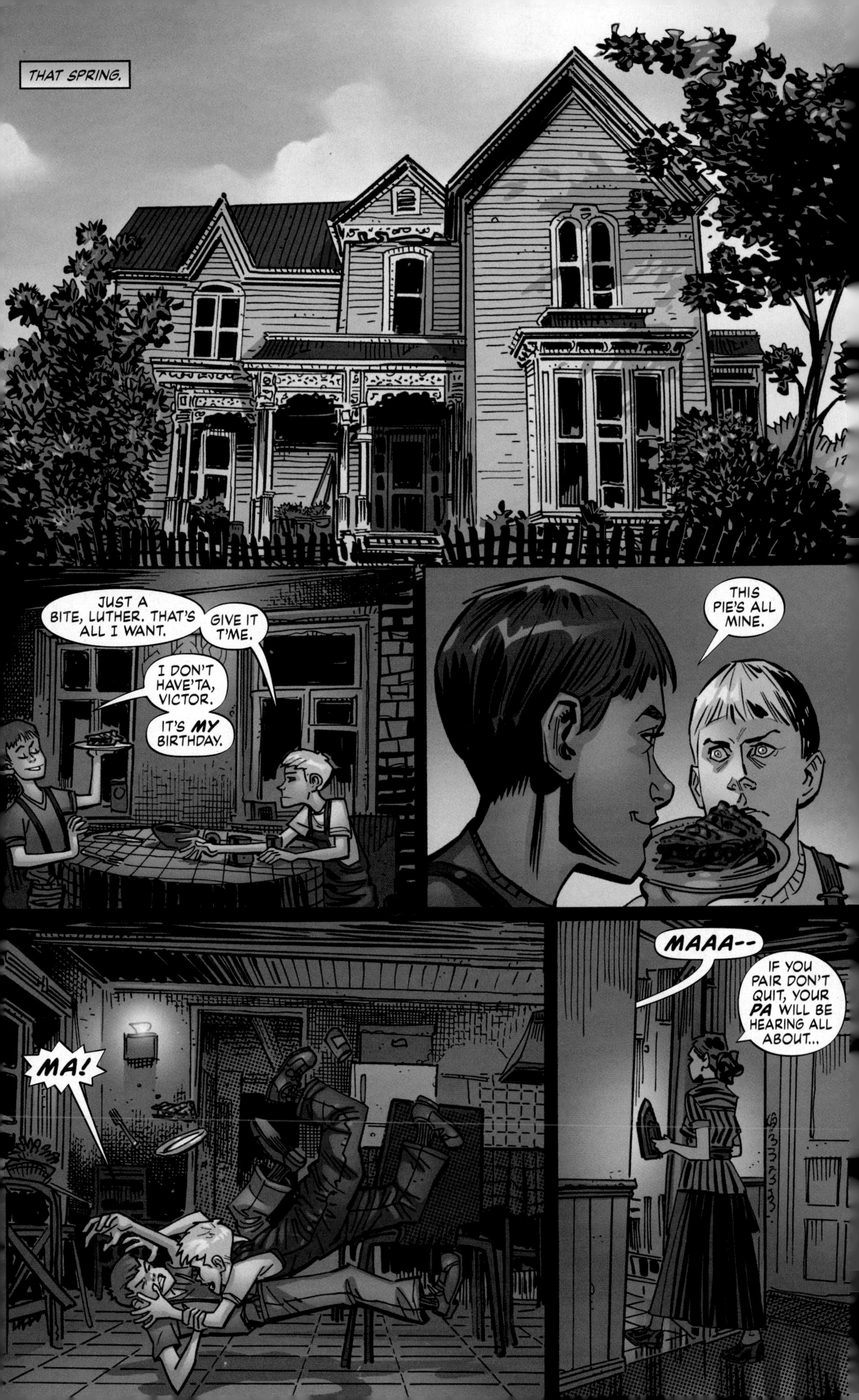

THAT SPRING.
JUST A BITE, LUTHER. THAT'S ALL I WANT.
GIVE IT T'ME.
I DON'T HAVE'TA, VICTOR.
IT'S MY BIRTHDAY.
THIS PIE'S ALL MINE.
MA!
MAAA--
IF YOU PAIR DON'T QUIT, YOUR PA WILL BE HEARING ALL ABOUT...

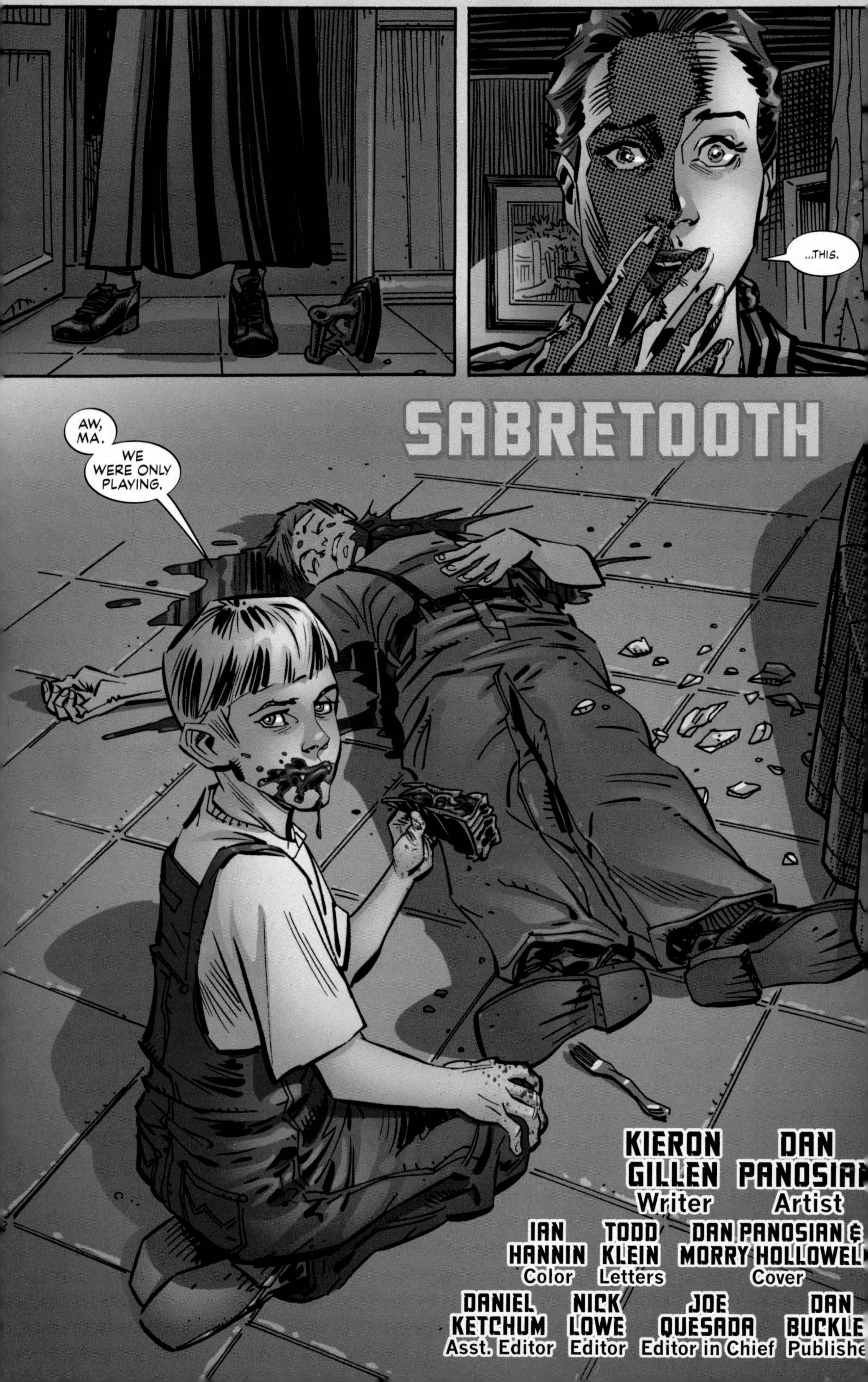
...THIS.
AW, MA.
WE WERE ONLY PLAYING.
SABRETOOTH
KIERON GILLEN Writer
DAN PANOSIAN Artist
IAN HANNIN Color
TODD KLEIN Letters
DAN PANOSIAN & MORRY HOLLOWELL Cover
DANIEL KETCHUM Asst. Editor
NICK LOWE Editor
JOE QUESADA Editor in Chief
DAN BUCKLEY Publisher

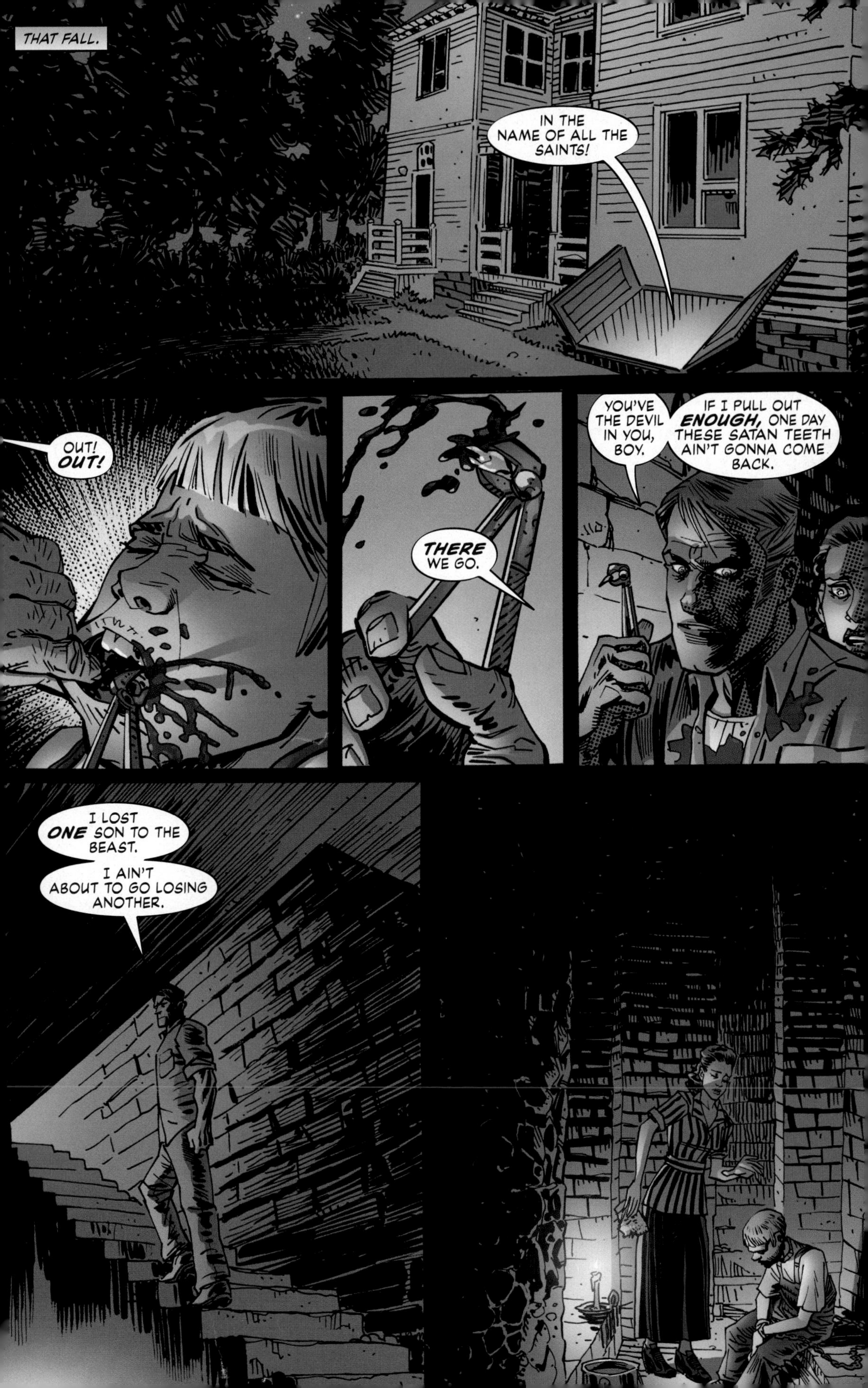
THAT FALL.
IN THE NAME OF ALL THE SAINTS!
OUT! OUT!
THERE WE GO.
YOU'VE THE DEVIL IN YOU, BOY.
IF I PULL OUT ENOUGH, ONE DAY THESE SATAN TEETH AIN'T GONNA COME BACK.
I LOST ONE SON TO THE BEAST.
I AIN'T ABOUT TO GO LOSING ANOTHER.

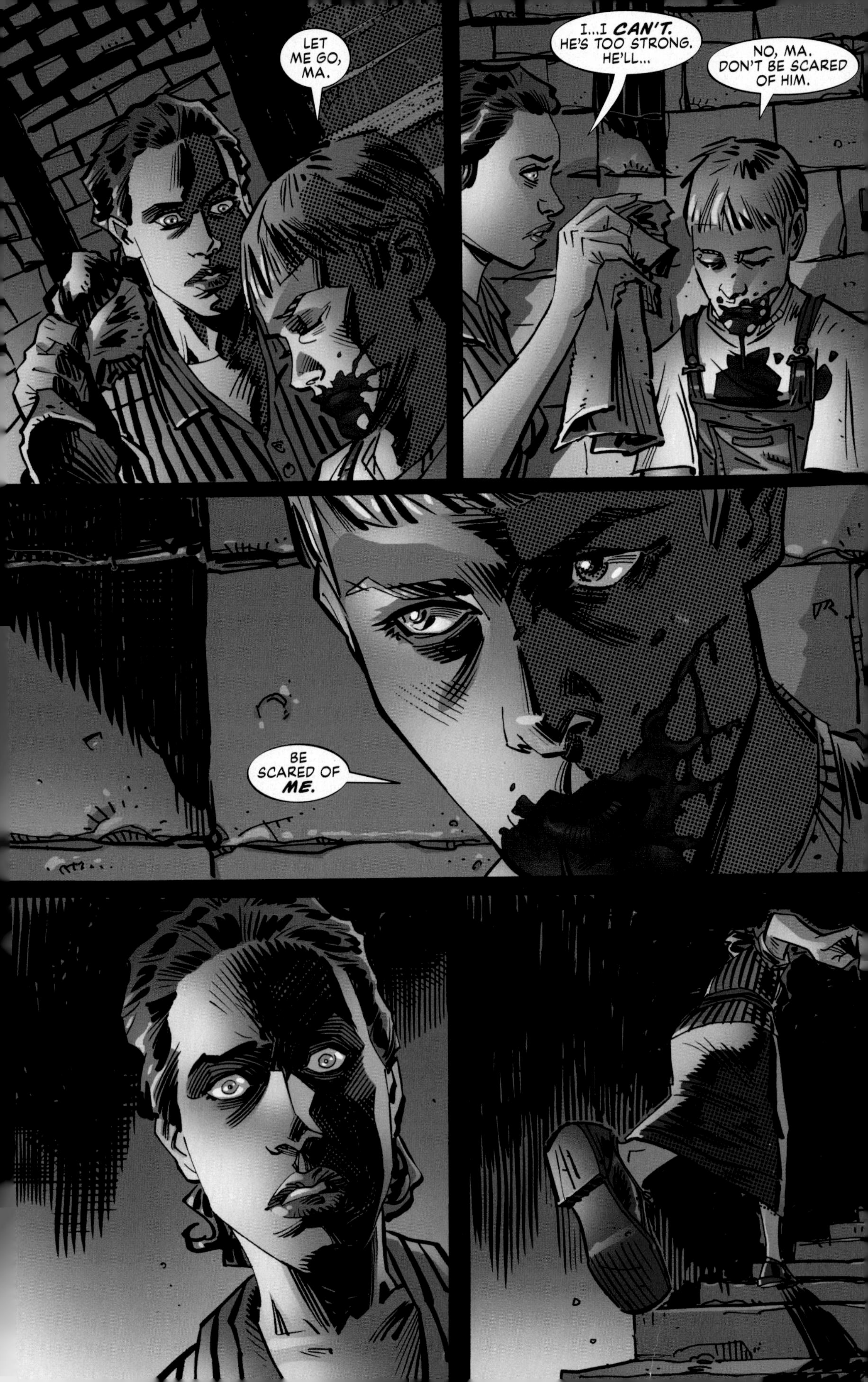
LET ME GO, MA.
I...I **CAN'T.** HE'S TOO STRONG. HE'LL...
NO, MA. DON'T BE SCARED OF HIM.
BE SCARED OF ***ME.***

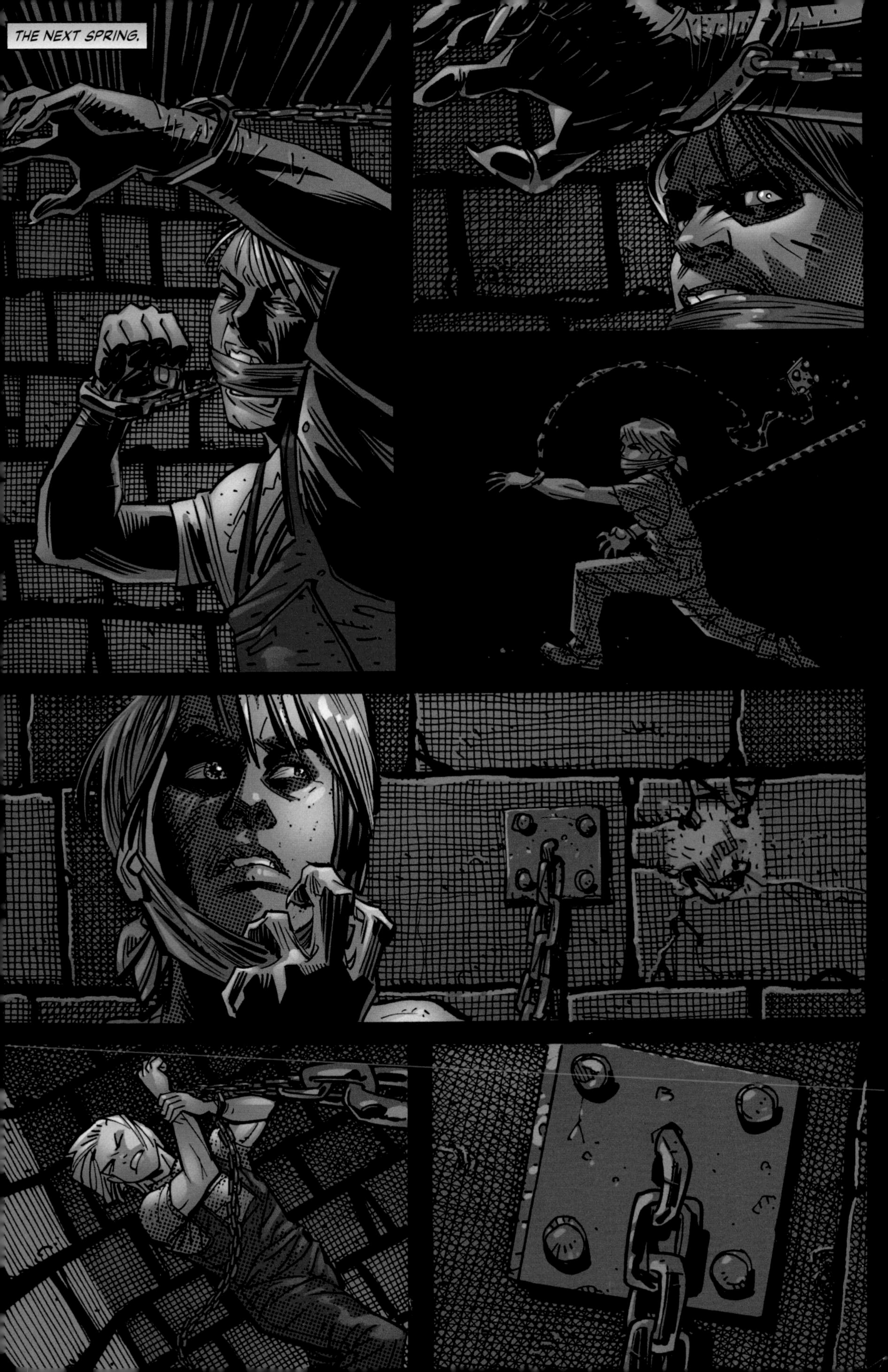
THE NEXT SPRING.

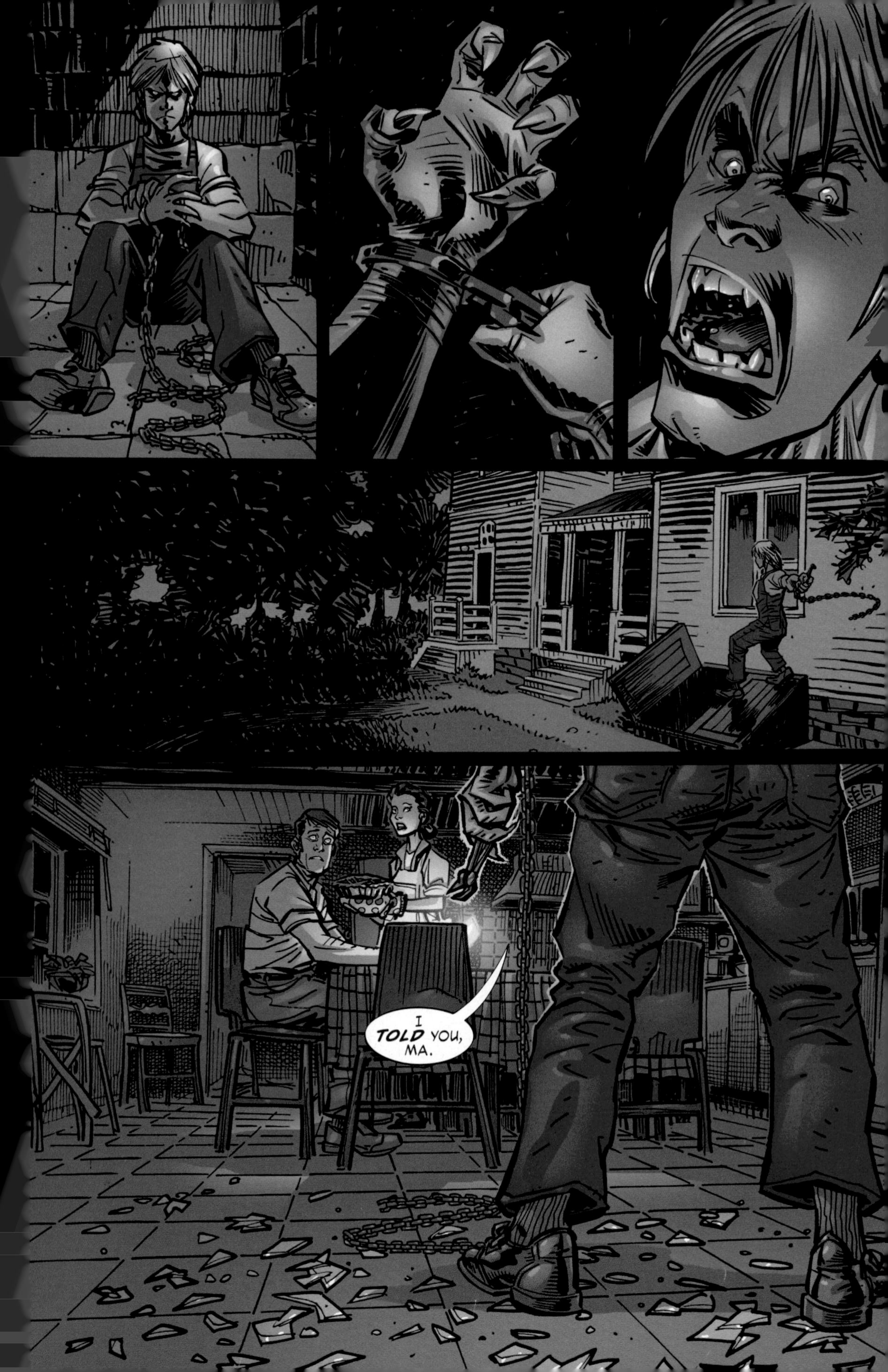
I TOLD YOU, MA.

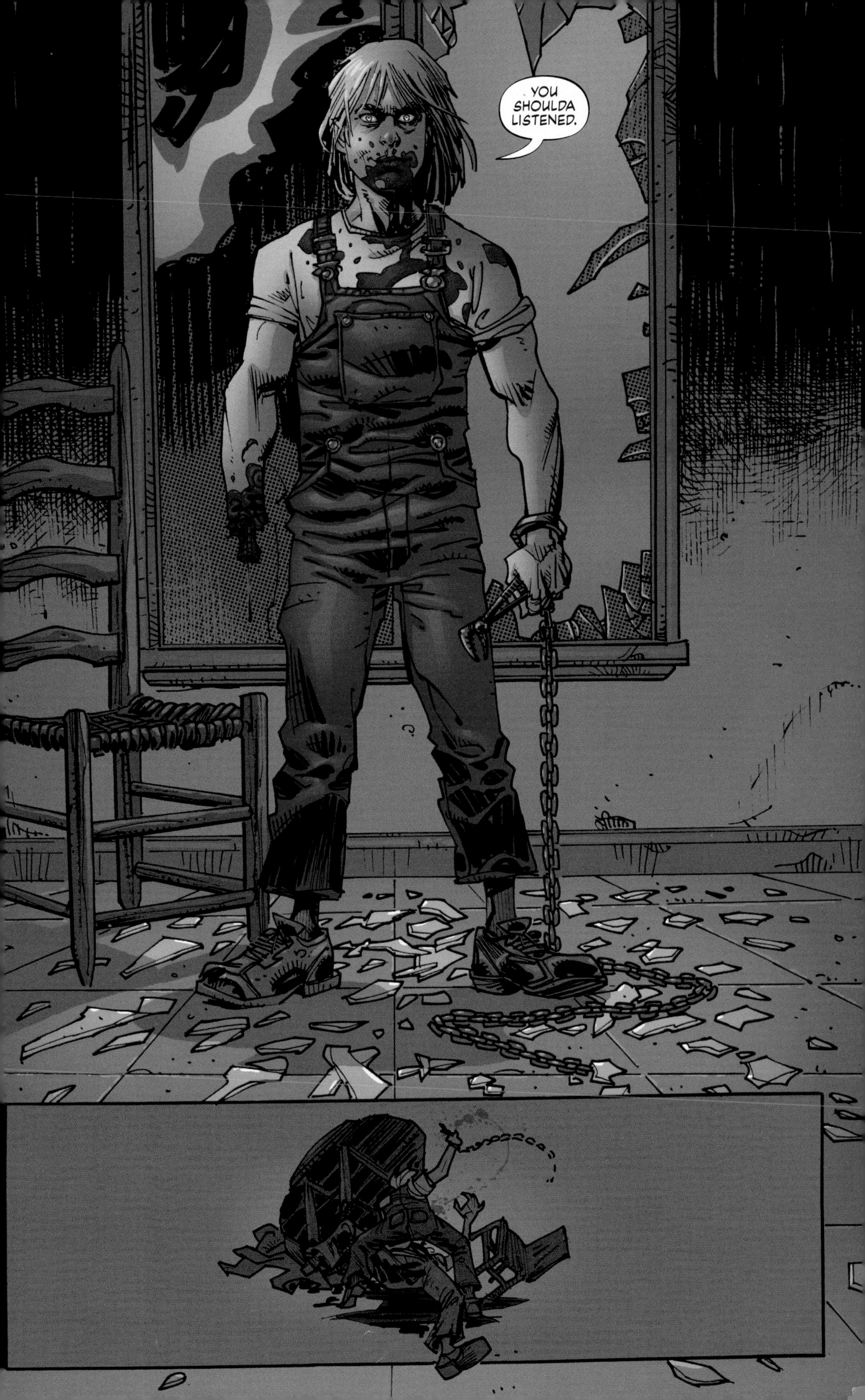
YOU SHOULDA LISTENED.

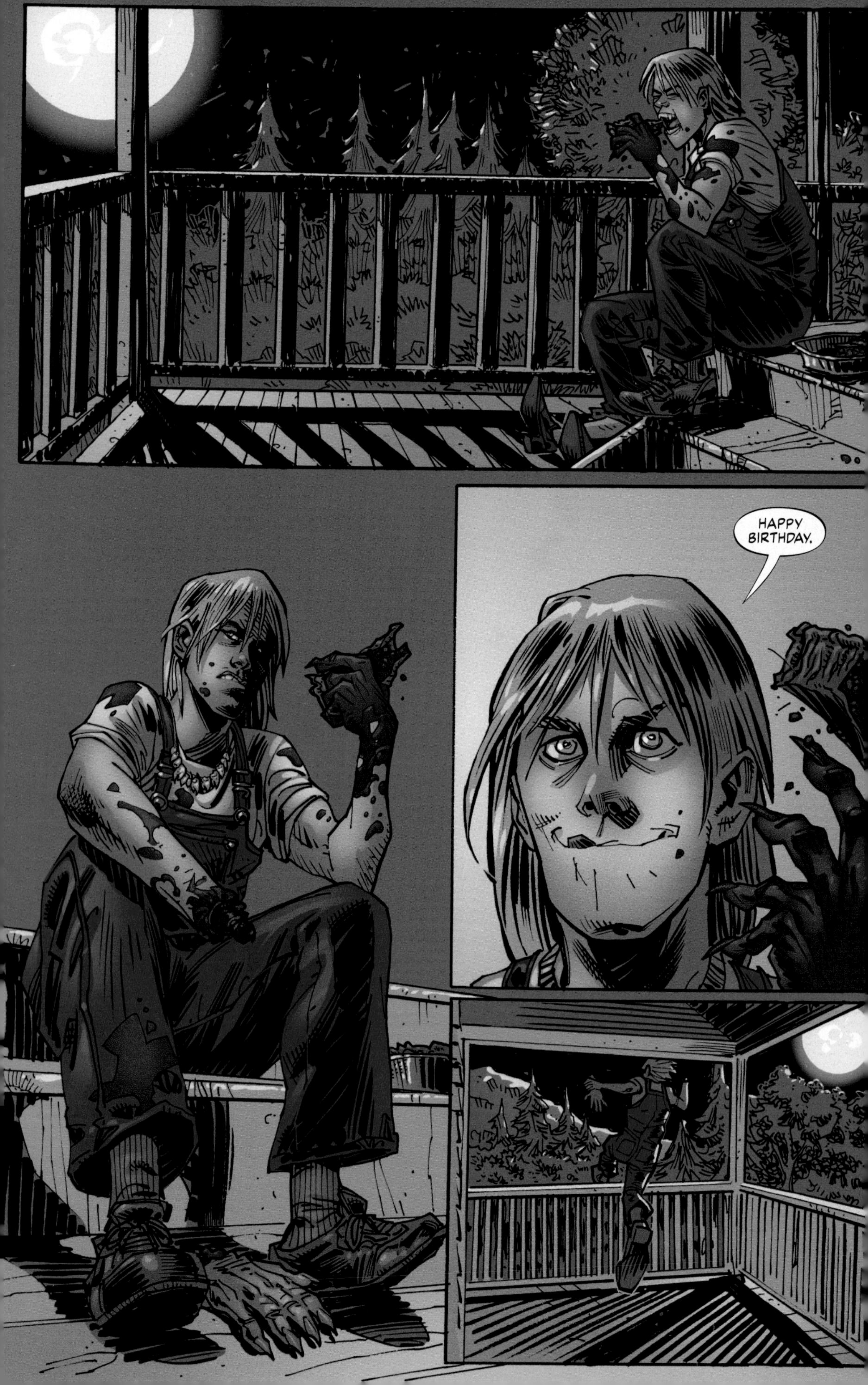
HAPPY BIRTHDAY.

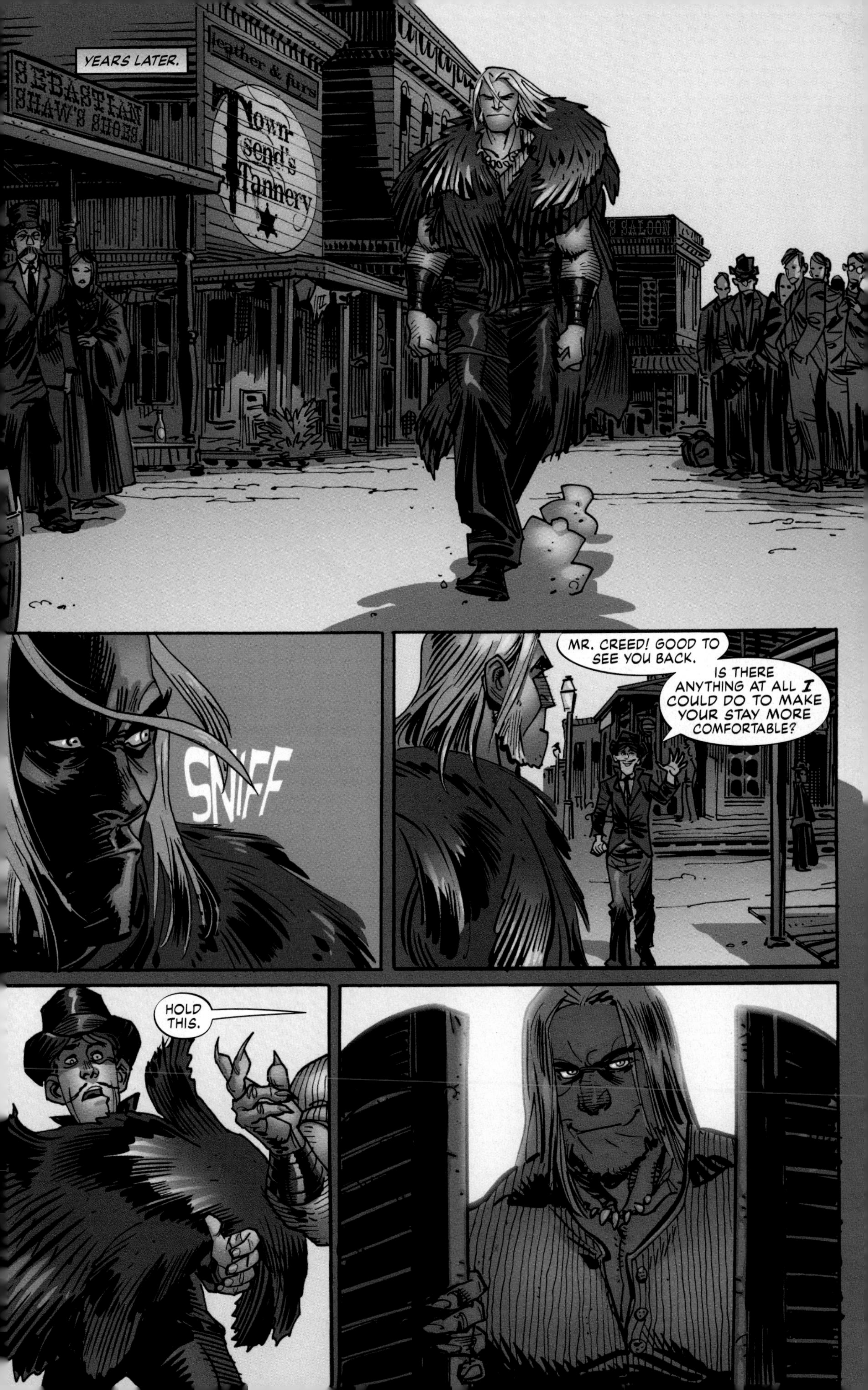
YEARS LATER.
SEBASTIAN SHAW'S SHOES
leather & furs
Townsend's Tannery
SALOON
SNIFF
MR. CREED! GOOD TO SEE YOU BACK.
IS THERE ANYTHING AT ALL I COULD DO TO MAKE YOUR STAY MORE COMFORTABLE?
HOLD THIS.

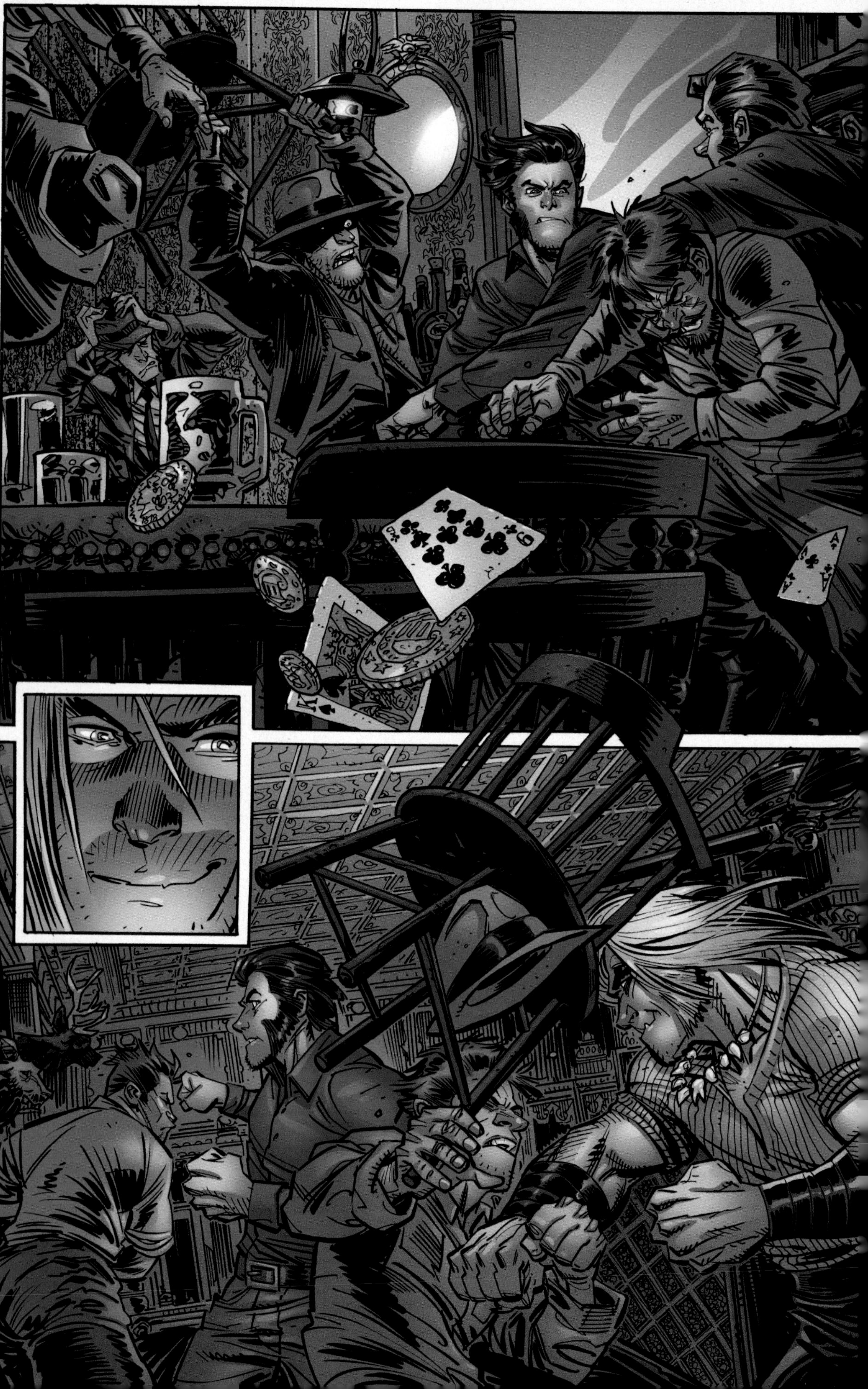

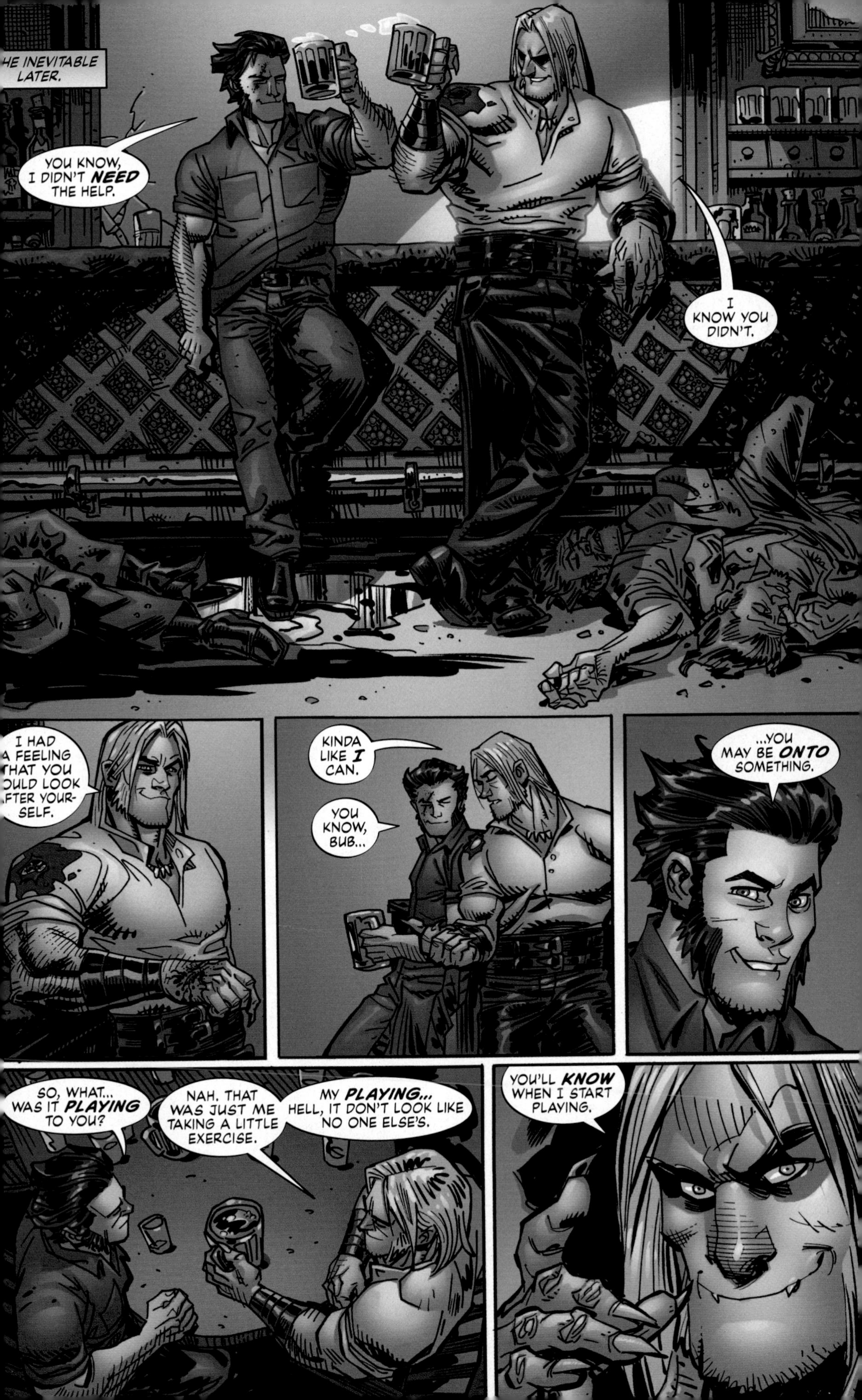
HE INEVITABLE LATER.
YOU KNOW, I DIDN'T NEED THE HELP.
I KNOW YOU DIDN'T.
I HAD A FEELING THAT YOU OULD LOOK FTER YOUR-SELF.
KINDA LIKE I CAN.
YOU KNOW, BUB...
...YOU MAY BE ONTO SOMETHING.
SO, WHAT... WAS IT PLAYING TO YOU?
NAH. THAT WAS JUST ME TAKING A LITTLE EXERCISE.
MY PLAYING... HELL, IT DON'T LOOK LIKE NO ONE ELSE'S.
YOU'LL KNOW WHEN I START PLAYING.

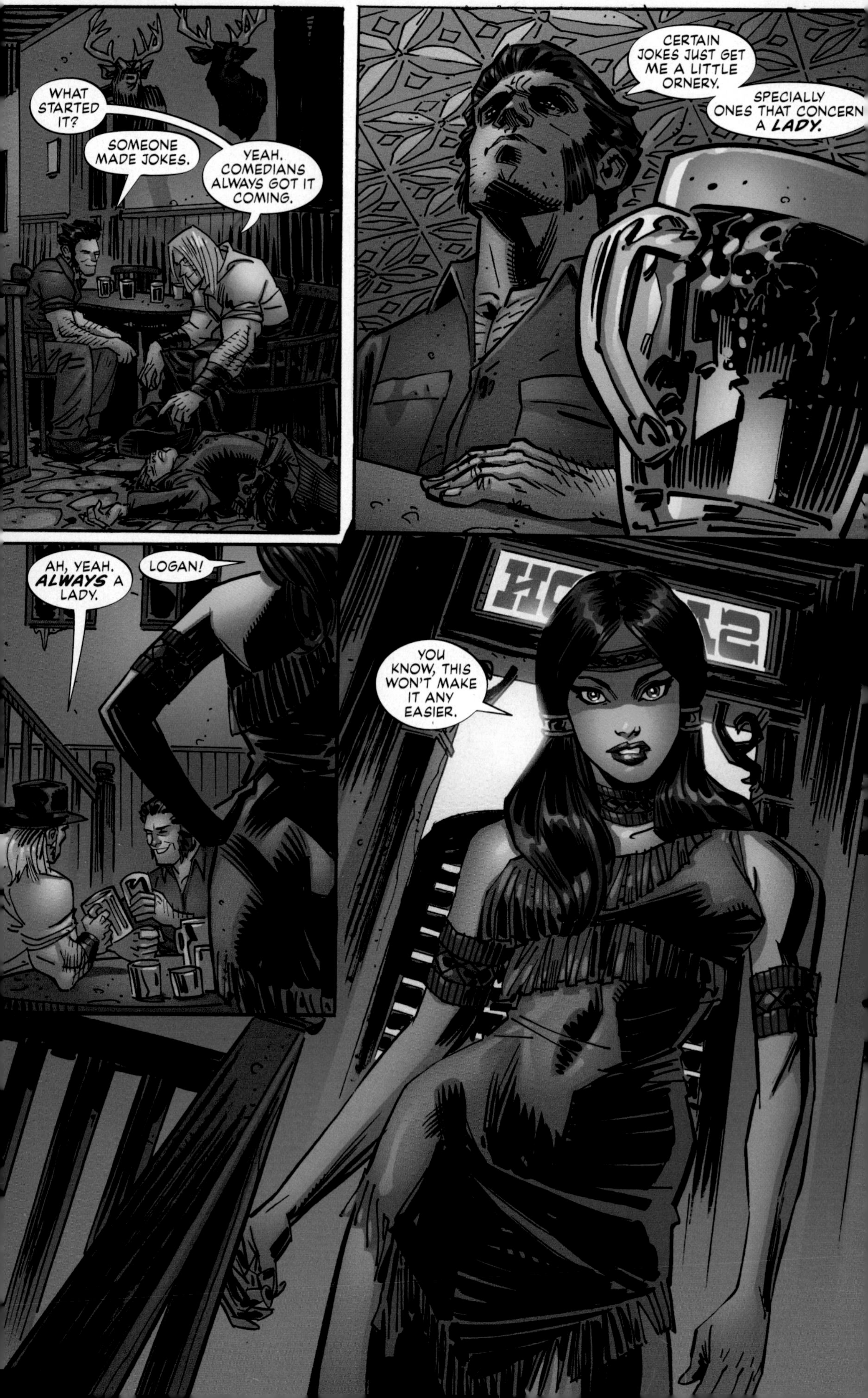
WHAT STARTED IT?
SOMEONE MADE JOKES.
YEAH. COMEDIANS ALWAYS GOT IT COMING.
CERTAIN JOKES JUST GET ME A LITTLE ORNERY.
SPECIALLY ONES THAT CONCERN A **LADY.**
AH, YEAH. ***ALWAYS*** A LADY.
LOGAN!
YOU KNOW, THIS WON'T MAKE IT ANY EASIER.

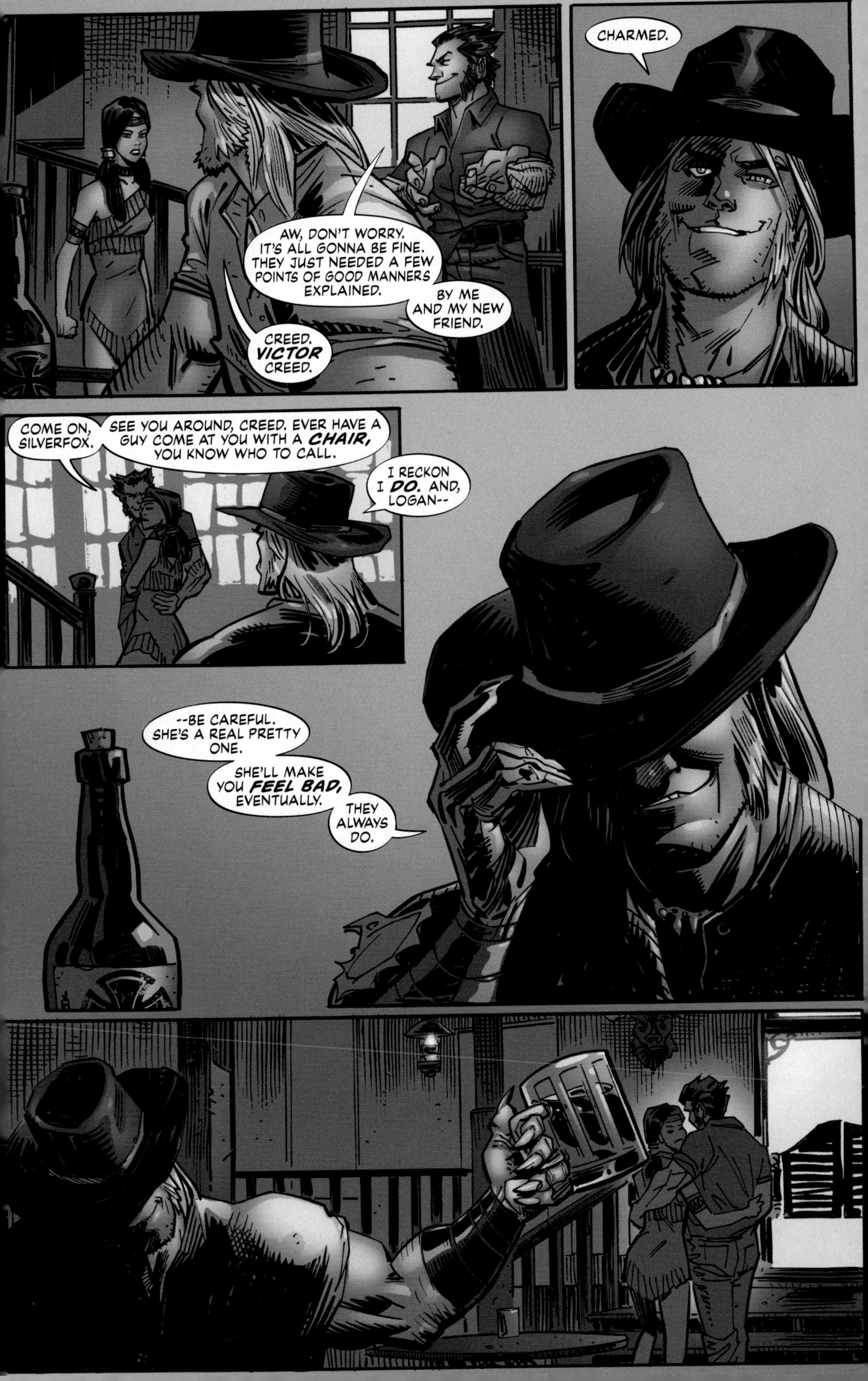
AW, DON'T WORRY. IT'S ALL GONNA BE FINE. THEY JUST NEEDED A FEW POINTS OF GOOD MANNERS EXPLAINED.
BY ME AND MY NEW FRIEND.
CREED. VICTOR CREED.
CHARMED.
COME ON, SILVERFOX.
SEE YOU AROUND, CREED. EVER HAVE A GUY COME AT YOU WITH A CHAIR, YOU KNOW WHO TO CALL.
I RECKON I DO. AND, LOGAN--
--BE CAREFUL. SHE'S A REAL PRETTY ONE.
SHE'LL MAKE YOU FEEL BAD, EVENTUALLY.
THEY ALWAYS DO.

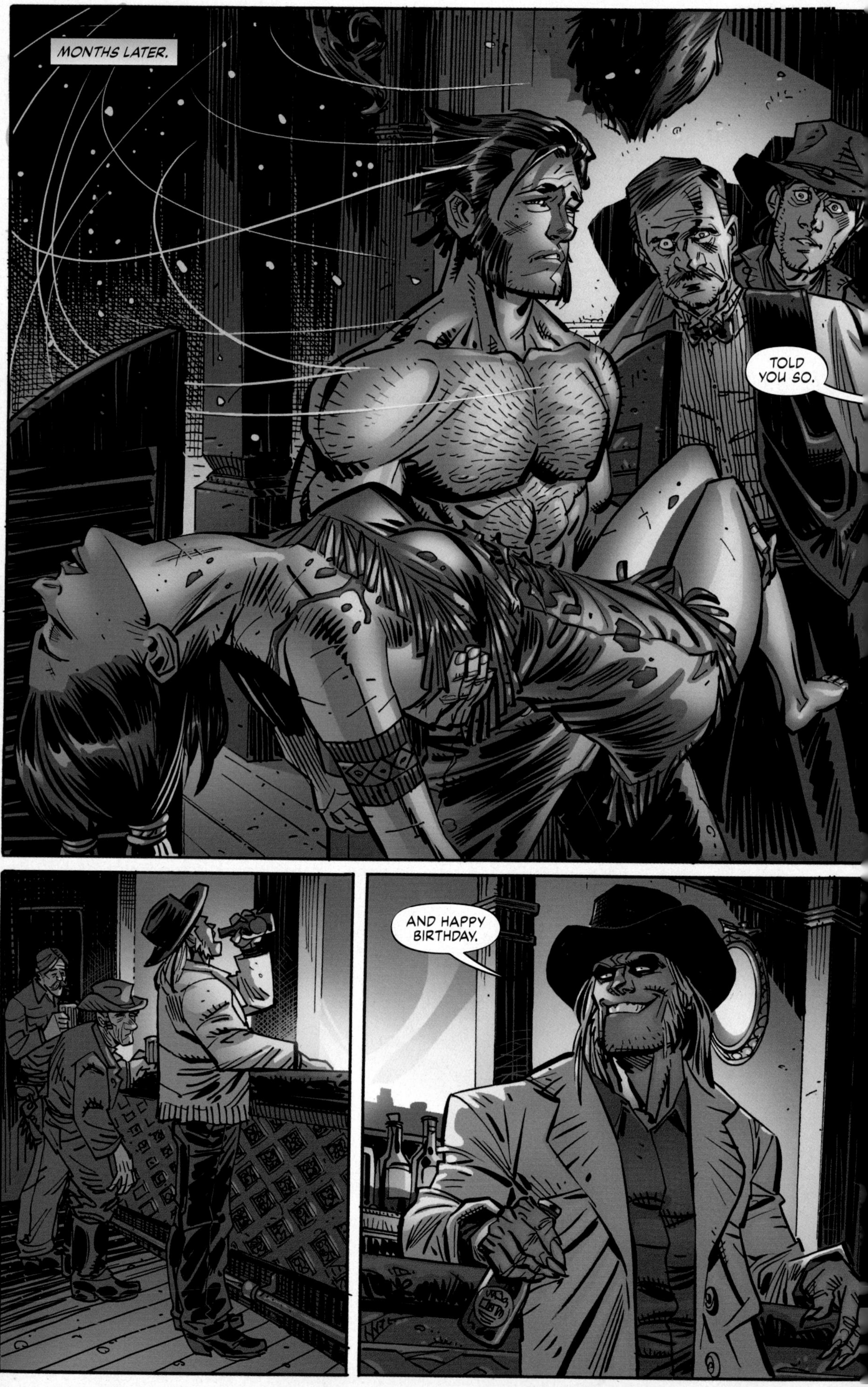
MONTHS LATER.
TOLD YOU SO.
AND HAPPY BIRTHDAY.

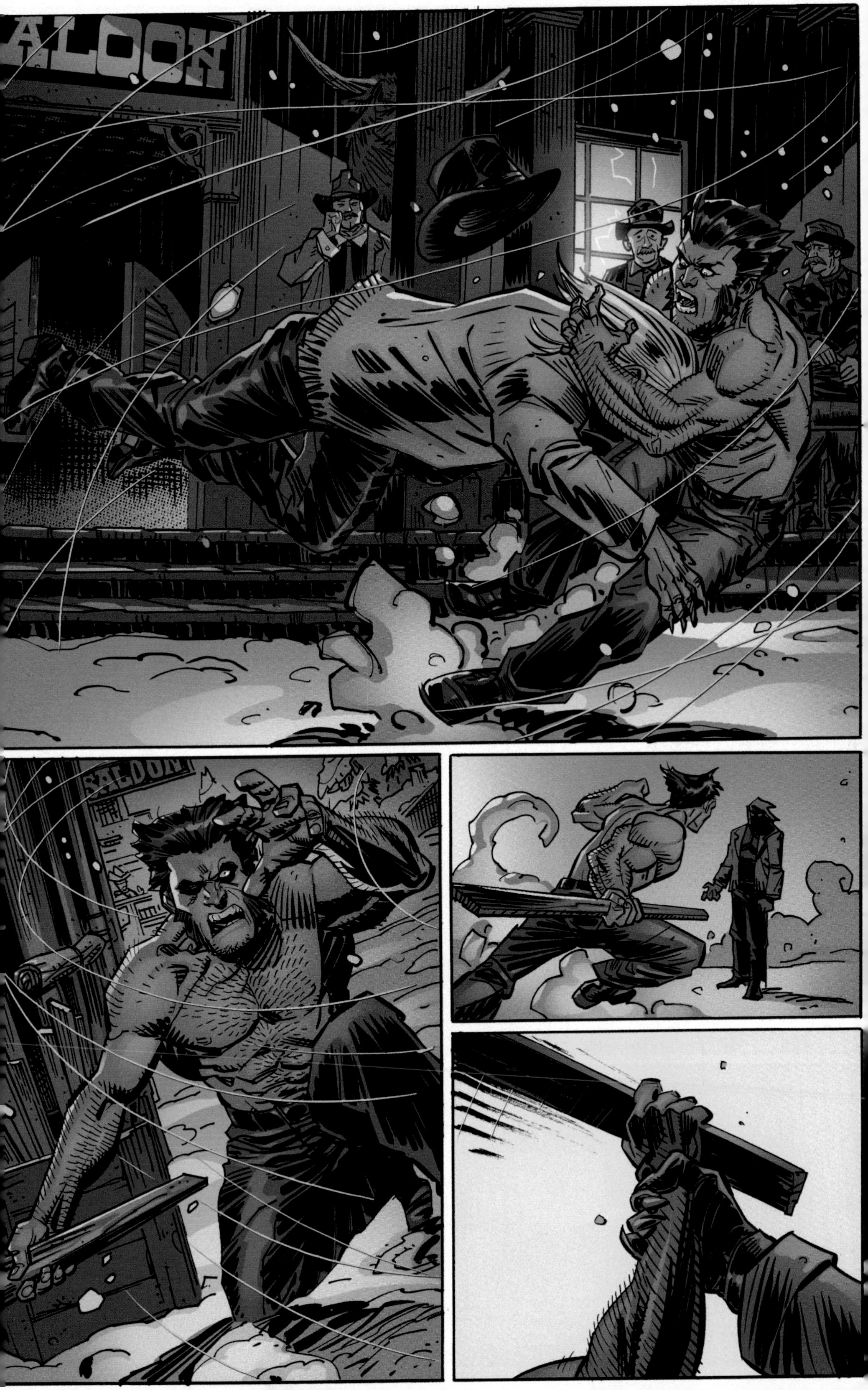
ALOON

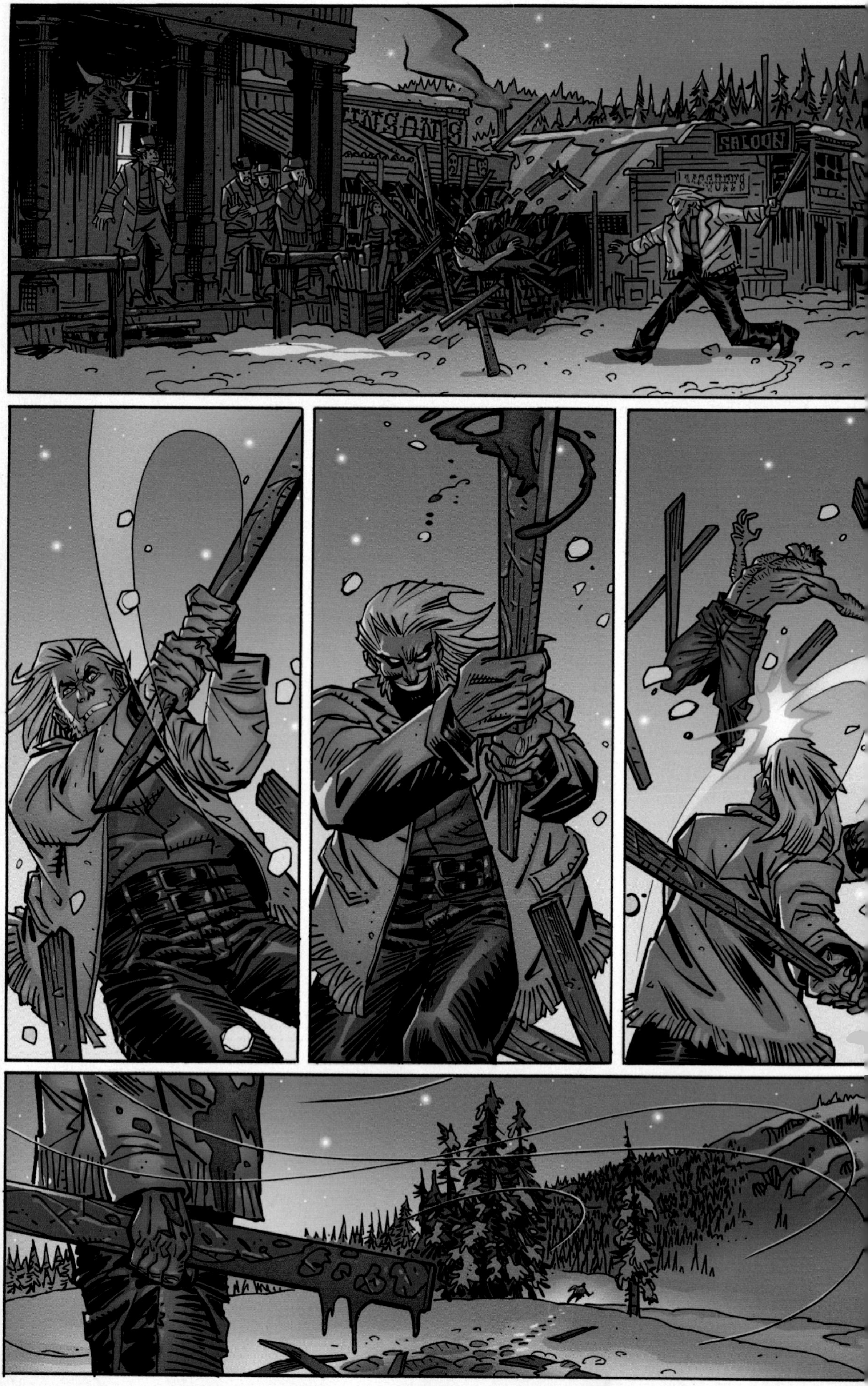
SALOON

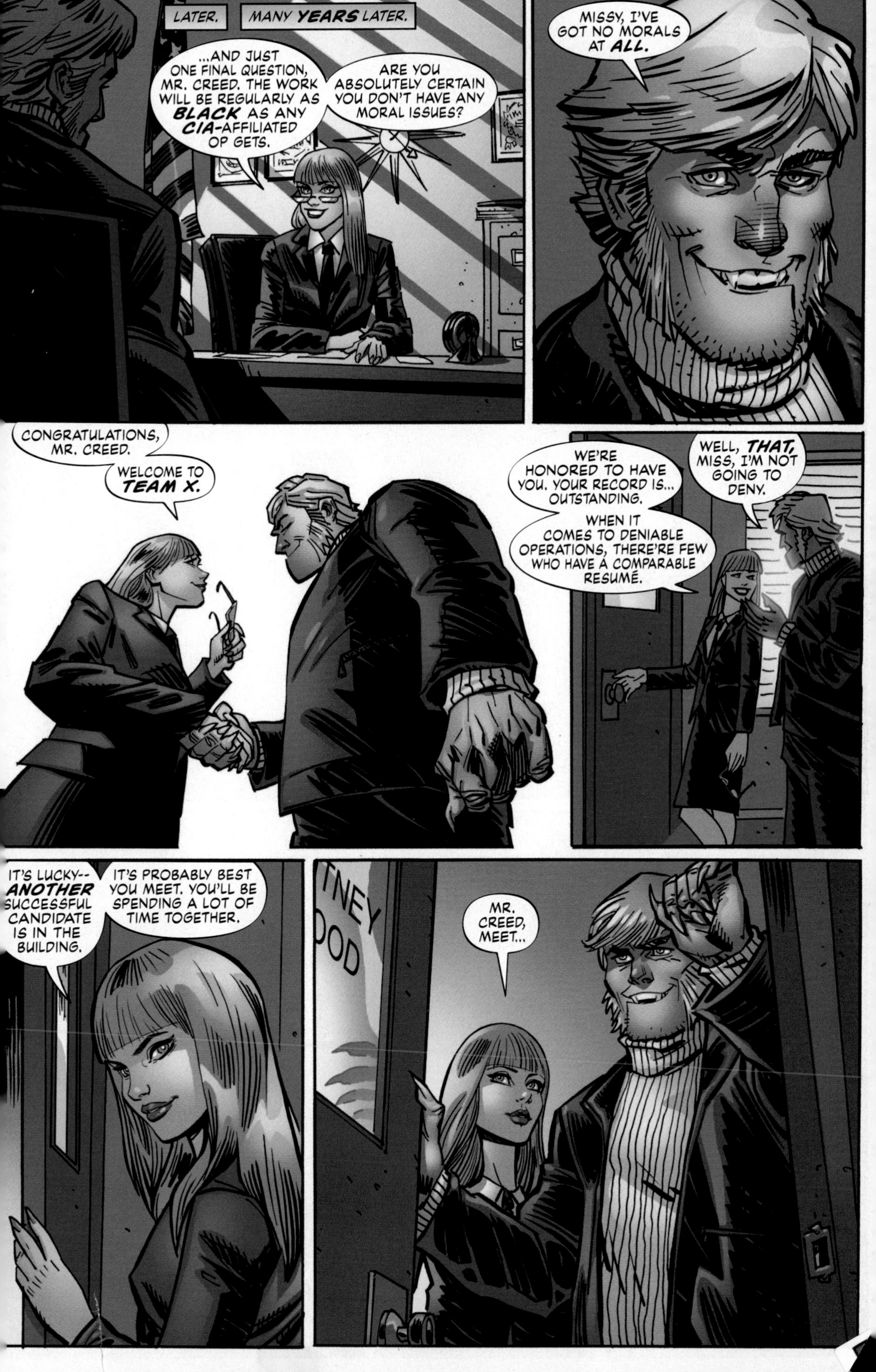
LATER.
MANY YEARS LATER.
...AND JUST ONE FINAL QUESTION, MR. CREED. THE WORK WILL BE REGULARLY AS BLACK AS ANY CIA-AFFILIATED OP GETS.
ARE YOU ABSOLUTELY CERTAIN YOU DON'T HAVE ANY MORAL ISSUES?
MISSY, I'VE GOT NO MORALS AT ALL.
CONGRATULATIONS, MR. CREED.
WELCOME TO TEAM X.
WE'RE HONORED TO HAVE YOU. YOUR RECORD IS... OUTSTANDING.
WHEN IT COMES TO DENIABLE OPERATIONS, THERE'RE FEW WHO HAVE A COMPARABLE RESUMÉ.
WELL, THAT, MISS, I'M NOT GOING TO DENY.
IT'S LUCKY-- ANOTHER SUCCESSFUL CANDIDATE IS IN THE BUILDING.
IT'S PROBABLY BEST YOU MEET. YOU'LL BE SPENDING A LOT OF TIME TOGETHER.
MR. CREED, MEET...

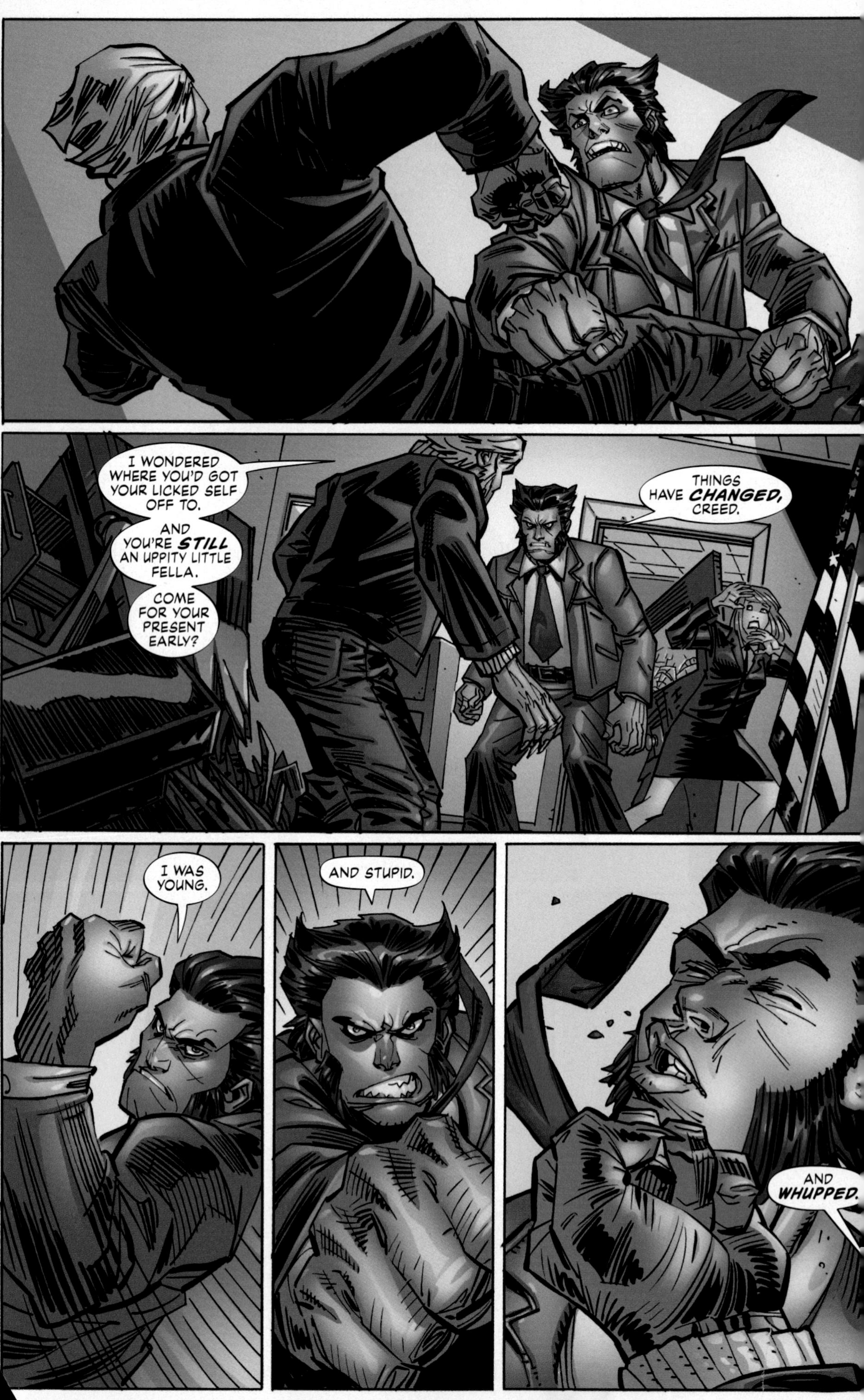
I WONDERED WHERE YOU'D GOT YOUR LICKED SELF OFF TO.
AND YOU'RE ***STILL*** AN UPPITY LITTLE FELLA.
COME FOR YOUR PRESENT EARLY?
THINGS HAVE ***CHANGED,*** CREED.
I WAS YOUNG.
AND STUPID.
AND ***WHUPPED.***

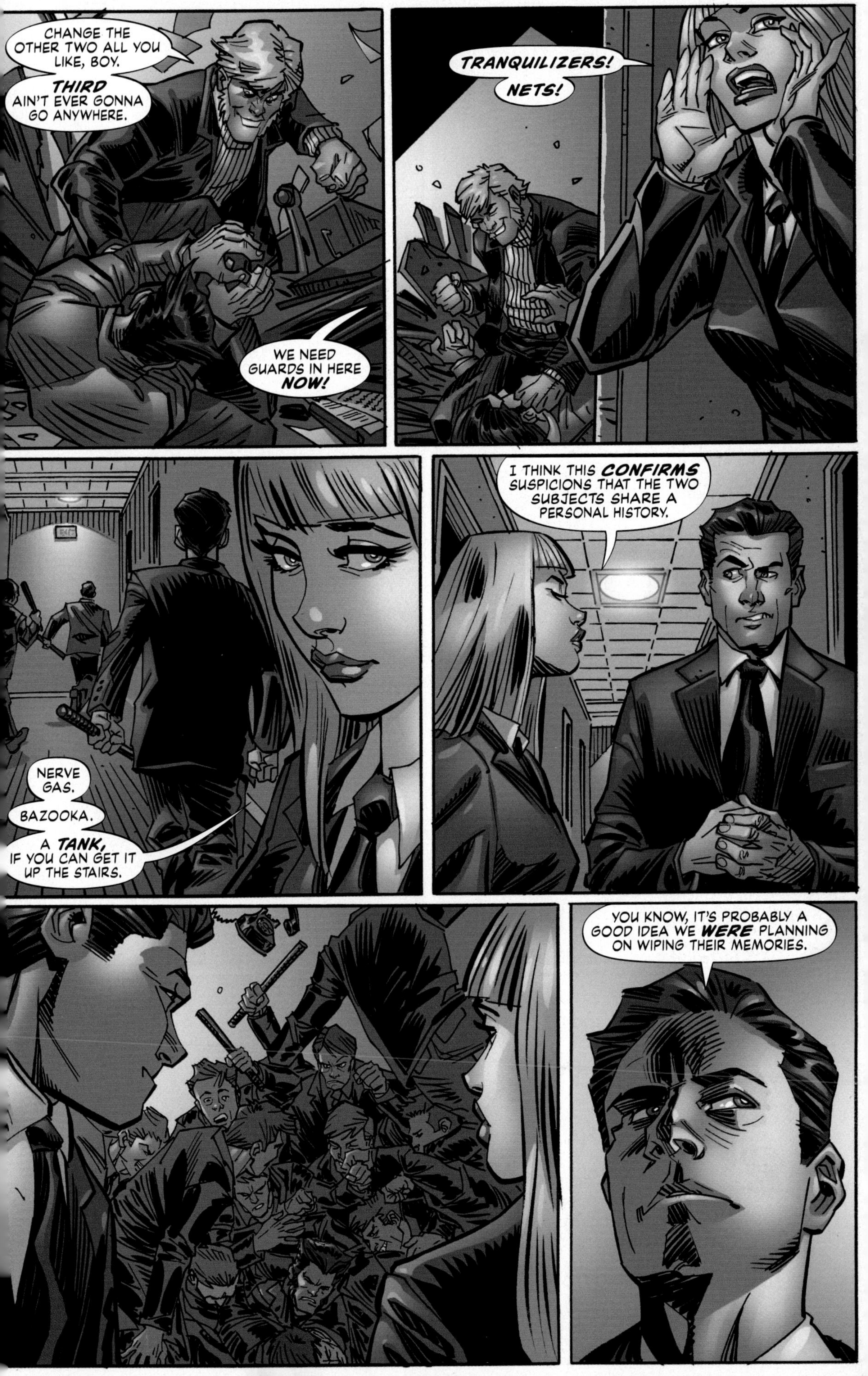

CHANGE THE OTHER TWO ALL YOU LIKE, BOY.
THIRD AIN'T EVER GONNA GO ANYWHERE.
WE NEED GUARDS IN HERE NOW!
TRANQUILIZERS!
NETS!
NERVE GAS.
BAZOOKA.
A TANK, IF YOU CAN GET IT UP THE STAIRS.
I THINK THIS CONFIRMS SUSPICIONS THAT THE TWO SUBJECTS SHARE A PERSONAL HISTORY.
YOU KNOW, IT'S PROBABLY A GOOD IDEA WE WERE PLANNING ON WIPING THEIR MEMORIES.

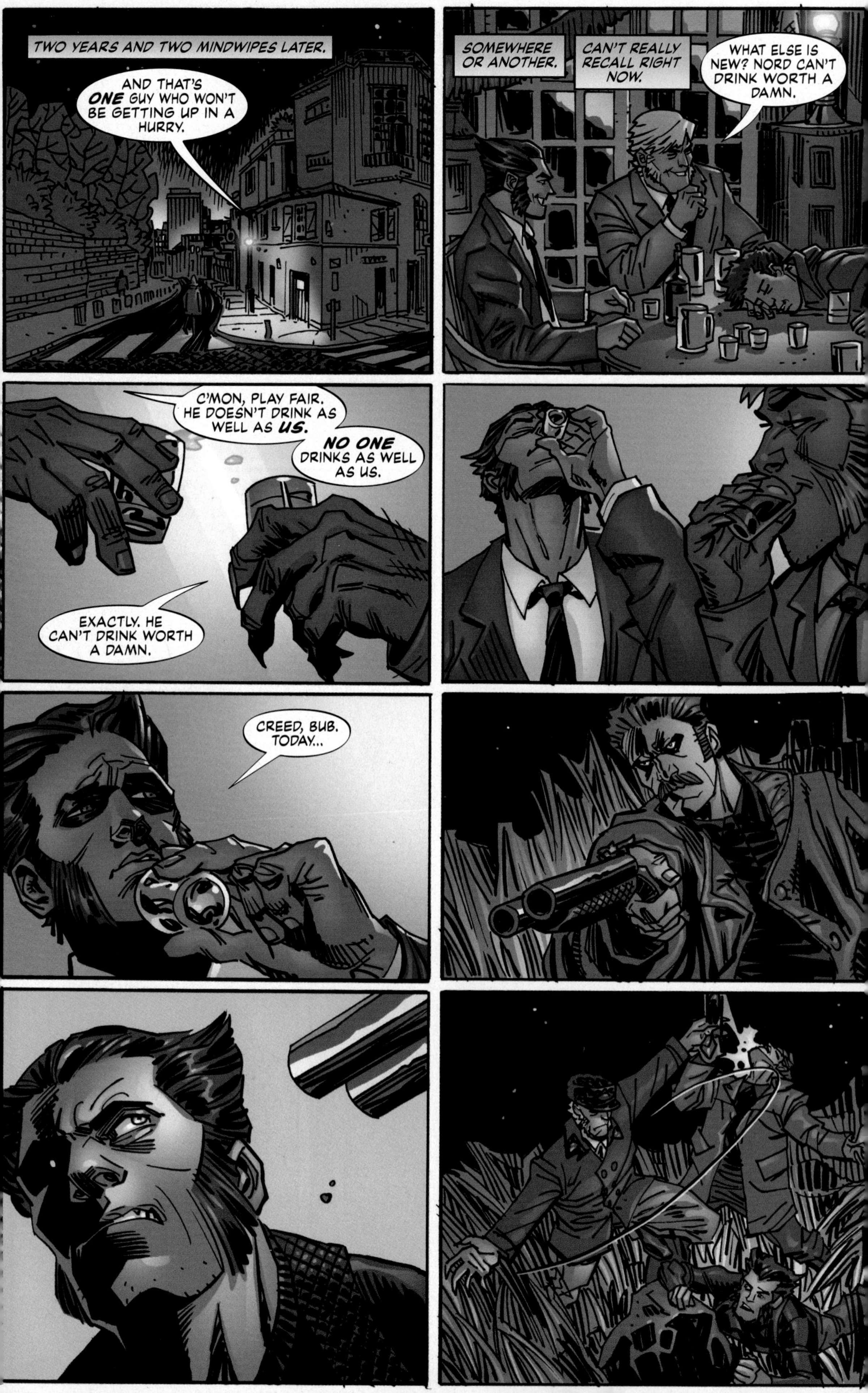
TWO YEARS AND TWO MINDWIPES LATER.
AND THAT'S ONE GUY WHO WON'T BE GETTING UP IN A HURRY.
SOMEWHERE OR ANOTHER.
CAN'T REALLY RECALL RIGHT NOW.
WHAT ELSE IS NEW? NORD CAN'T DRINK WORTH A DAMN.
C'MON, PLAY FAIR. HE DOESN'T DRINK AS WELL AS US.
NO ONE DRINKS AS WELL AS US.
EXACTLY. HE CAN'T DRINK WORTH A DAMN.
CREED, BUB. TODAY...

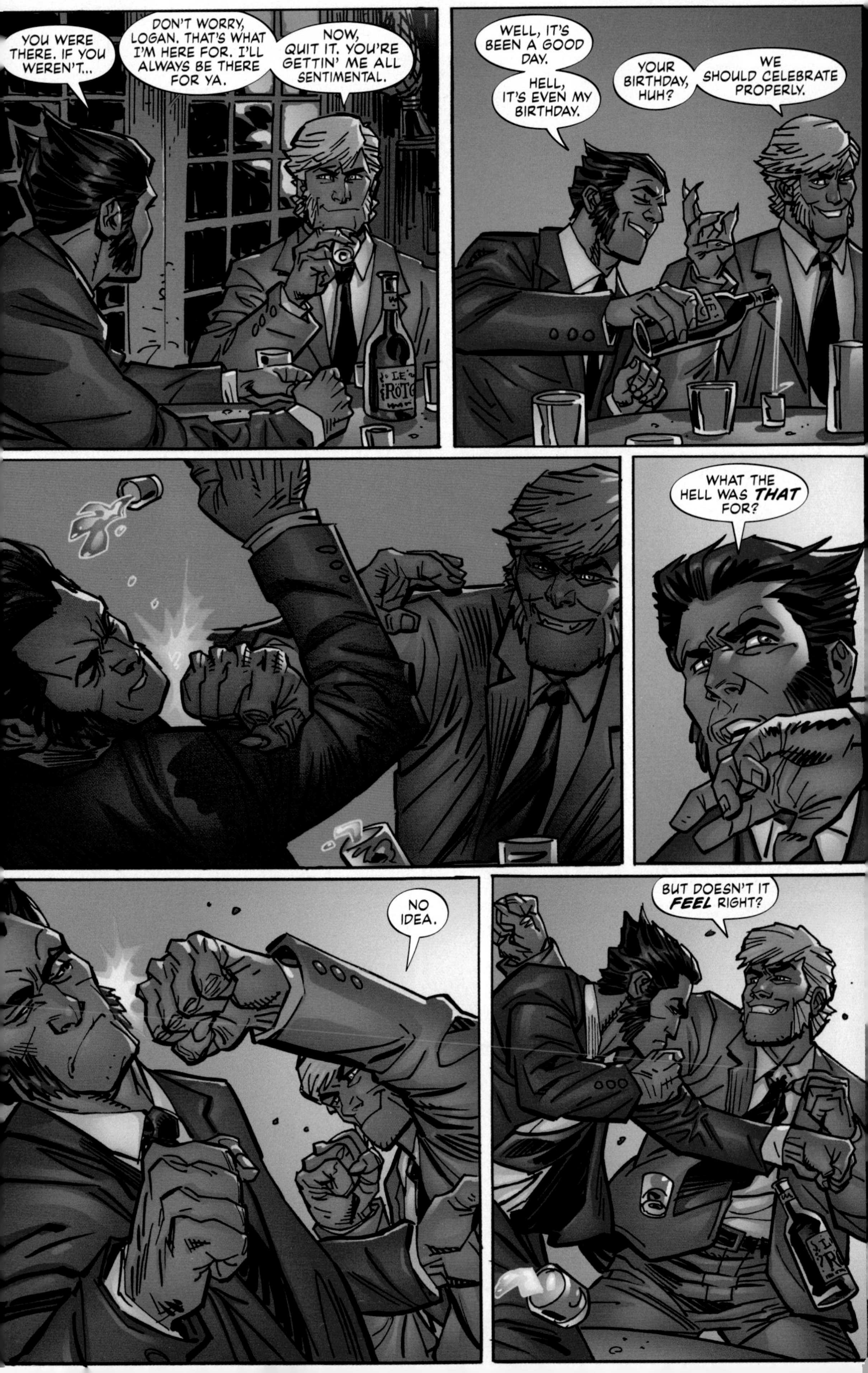
YOU WERE THERE. IF YOU WEREN'T...
DON'T WORRY, LOGAN. THAT'S WHAT I'M HERE FOR. I'LL ALWAYS BE THERE FOR YA.
NOW, QUIT IT. YOU'RE GETTIN' ME ALL SENTIMENTAL.
WELL, IT'S BEEN A GOOD DAY.
HELL, IT'S EVEN MY BIRTHDAY.
YOUR BIRTHDAY, HUH?
WE SHOULD CELEBRATE PROPERLY.
WHAT THE HELL WAS **THAT** FOR?
NO IDEA.
BUT DOESN'T IT **FEEL** RIGHT?

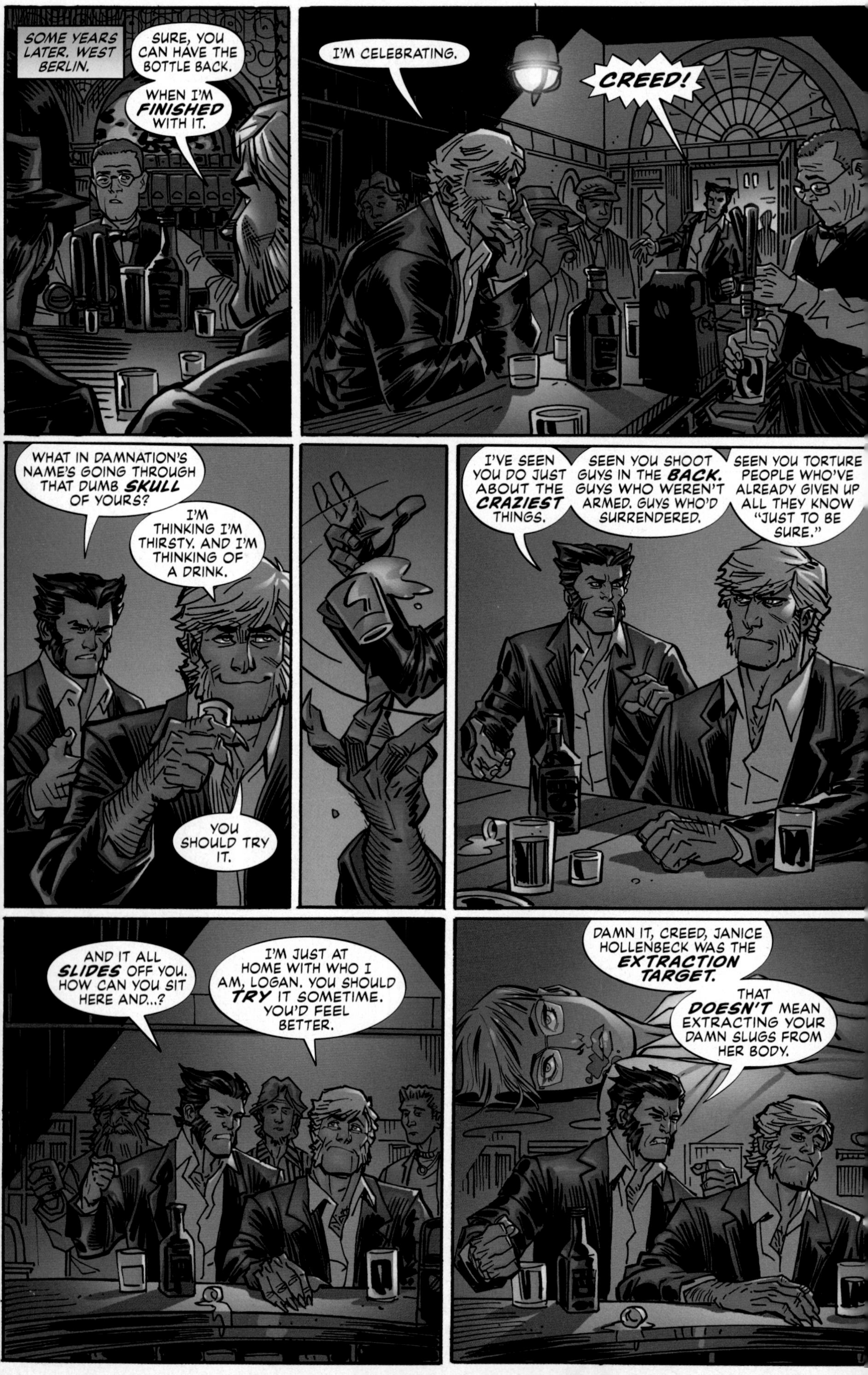
SOME YEARS LATER. WEST BERLIN.
SURE, YOU CAN HAVE THE BOTTLE BACK.
WHEN I'M FINISHED WITH IT.
I'M CELEBRATING.
CREED!
WHAT IN DAMNATION'S NAME'S GOING THROUGH THAT DUMB SKULL OF YOURS?
I'M THINKING I'M THIRSTY. AND I'M THINKING OF A DRINK.
YOU SHOULD TRY IT.
I'VE SEEN YOU DO JUST ABOUT THE CRAZIEST THINGS.
SEEN YOU SHOOT GUYS IN THE BACK. GUYS WHO WEREN'T ARMED. GUYS WHO'D SURRENDERED.
SEEN YOU TORTURE PEOPLE WHO'VE ALREADY GIVEN UP ALL THEY KNOW "JUST TO BE SURE."
AND IT ALL SLIDES OFF YOU. HOW CAN YOU SIT HERE AND...?
I'M JUST AT HOME WITH WHO I AM, LOGAN. YOU SHOULD TRY IT SOMETIME. YOU'D FEEL BETTER.
DAMN IT, CREED, JANICE HOLLENBECK WAS THE EXTRACTION TARGET.
THAT DOESN'T MEAN EXTRACTING YOUR DAMN SLUGS FROM HER BODY.

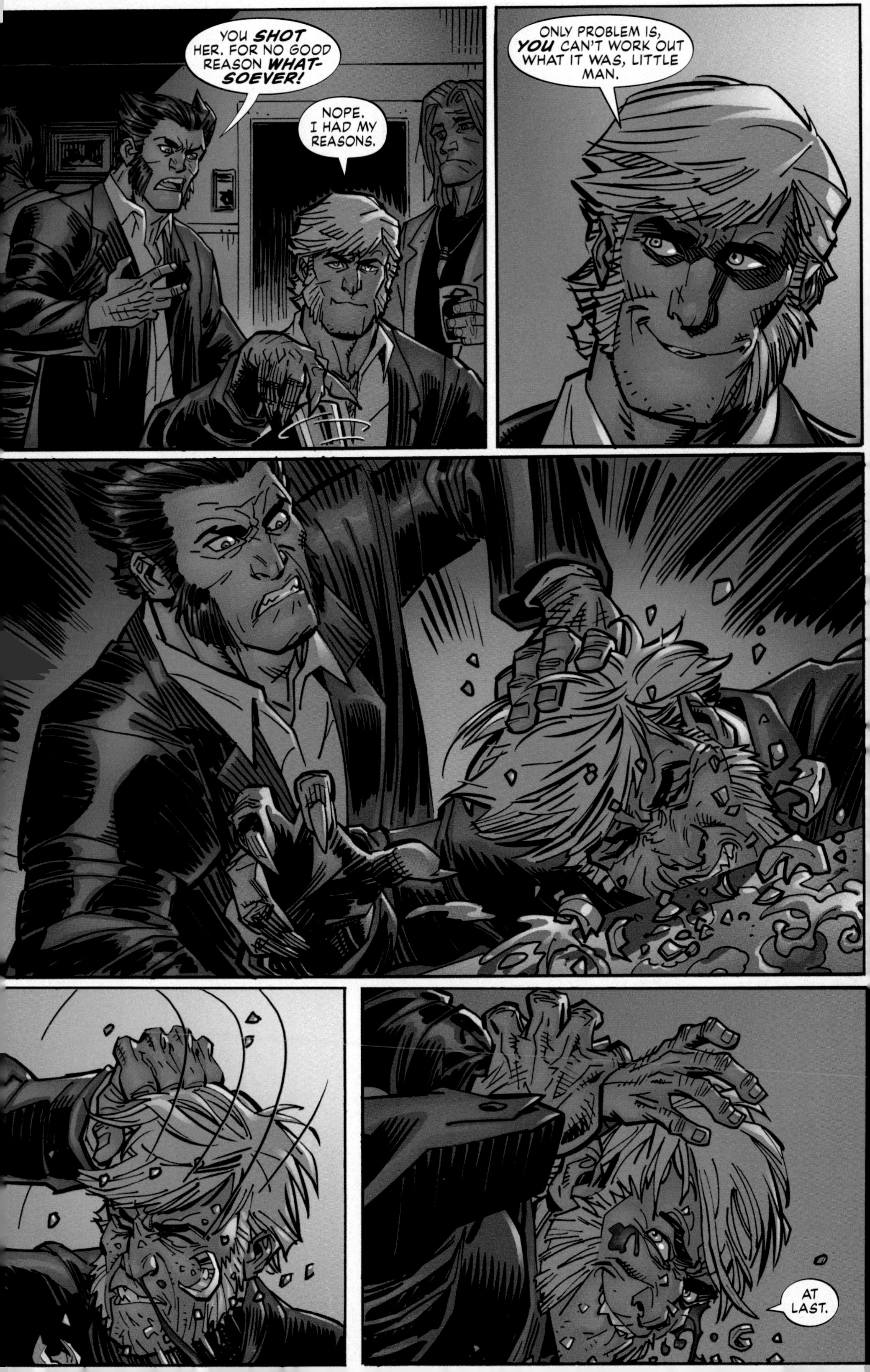
YOU SHOT HER. FOR NO GOOD REASON WHAT-SOEVER!
NOPE. I HAD MY REASONS.
ONLY PROBLEM IS, YOU CAN'T WORK OUT WHAT IT WAS, LITTLE MAN.
AT LAST.

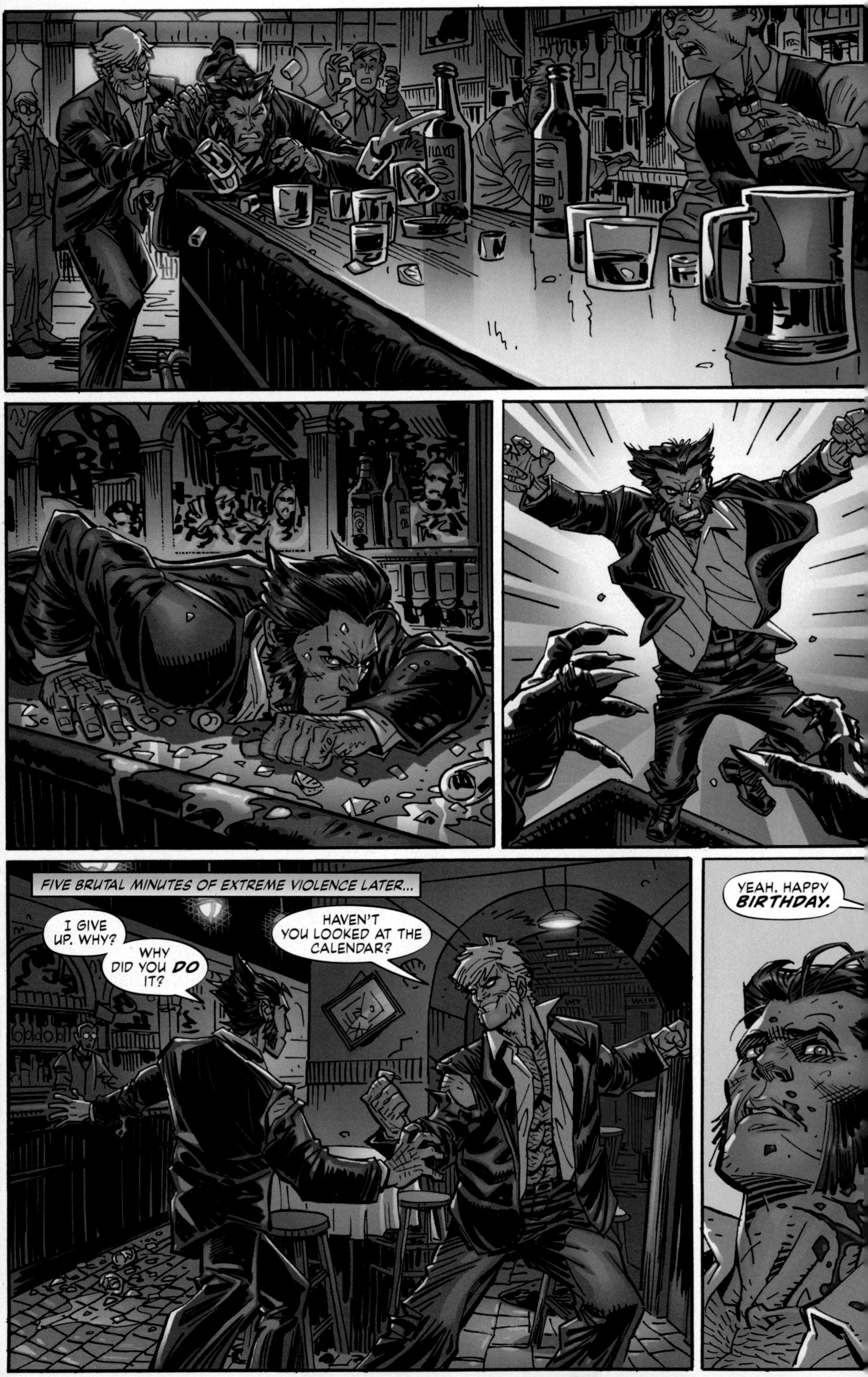
FIVE BRUTAL MINUTES OF EXTREME VIOLENCE LATER...
I GIVE UP. WHY?
WHY DID YOU **DO** IT?
HAVEN'T YOU LOOKED AT THE CALENDAR?
YEAH. HAPPY **BIRTHDAY.**

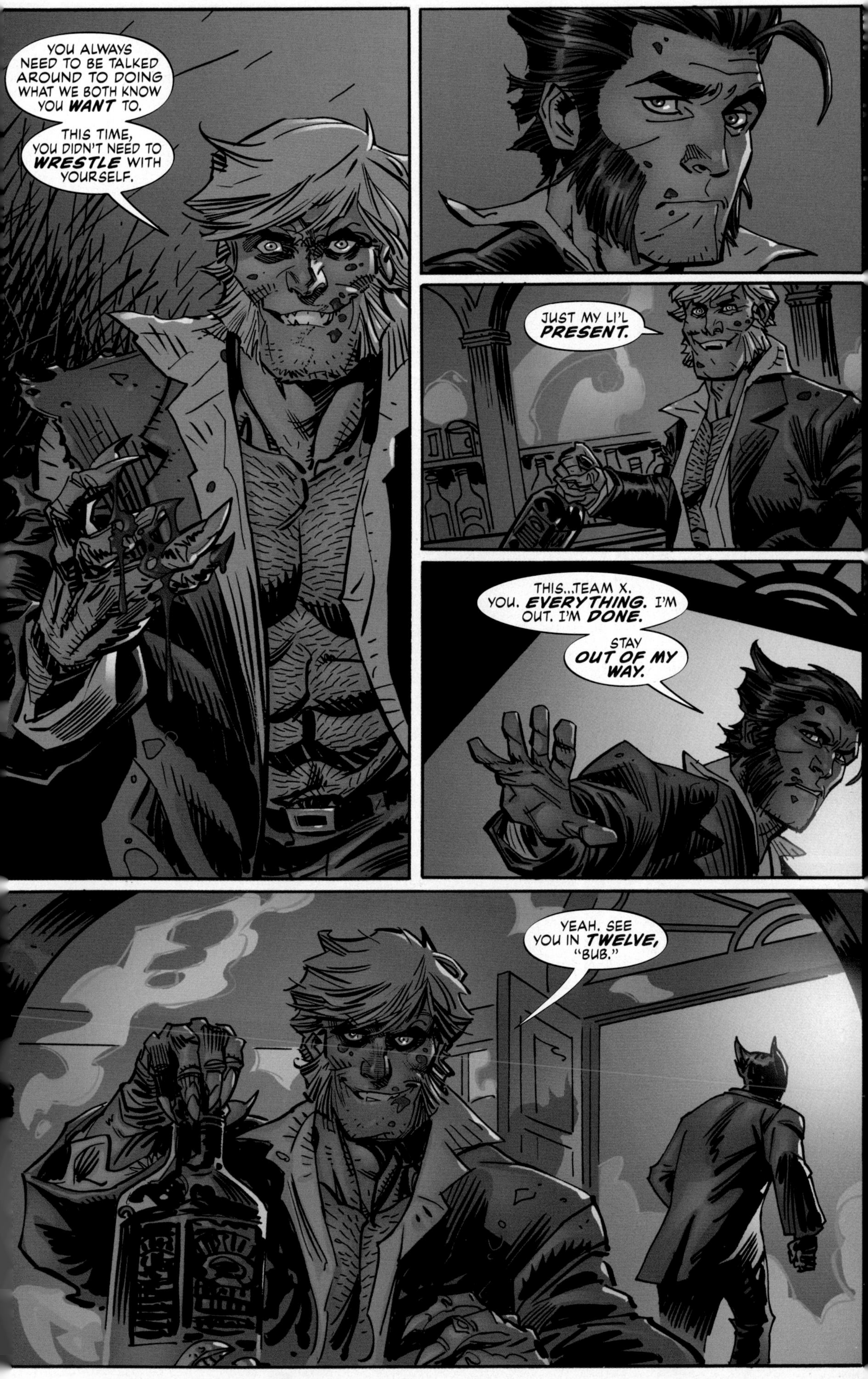
YOU ALWAYS NEED TO BE TALKED AROUND TO DOING WHAT WE BOTH KNOW YOU **WANT** TO.
THIS TIME, YOU DIDN'T NEED TO **WRESTLE** WITH YOURSELF.
JUST MY LI'L **PRESENT.**
THIS...TEAM X. YOU. **EVERYTHING.** I'M OUT. I'M **DONE.**
STAY **OUT OF MY WAY.**
YEAH. SEE YOU IN **TWELVE,** "BUB."

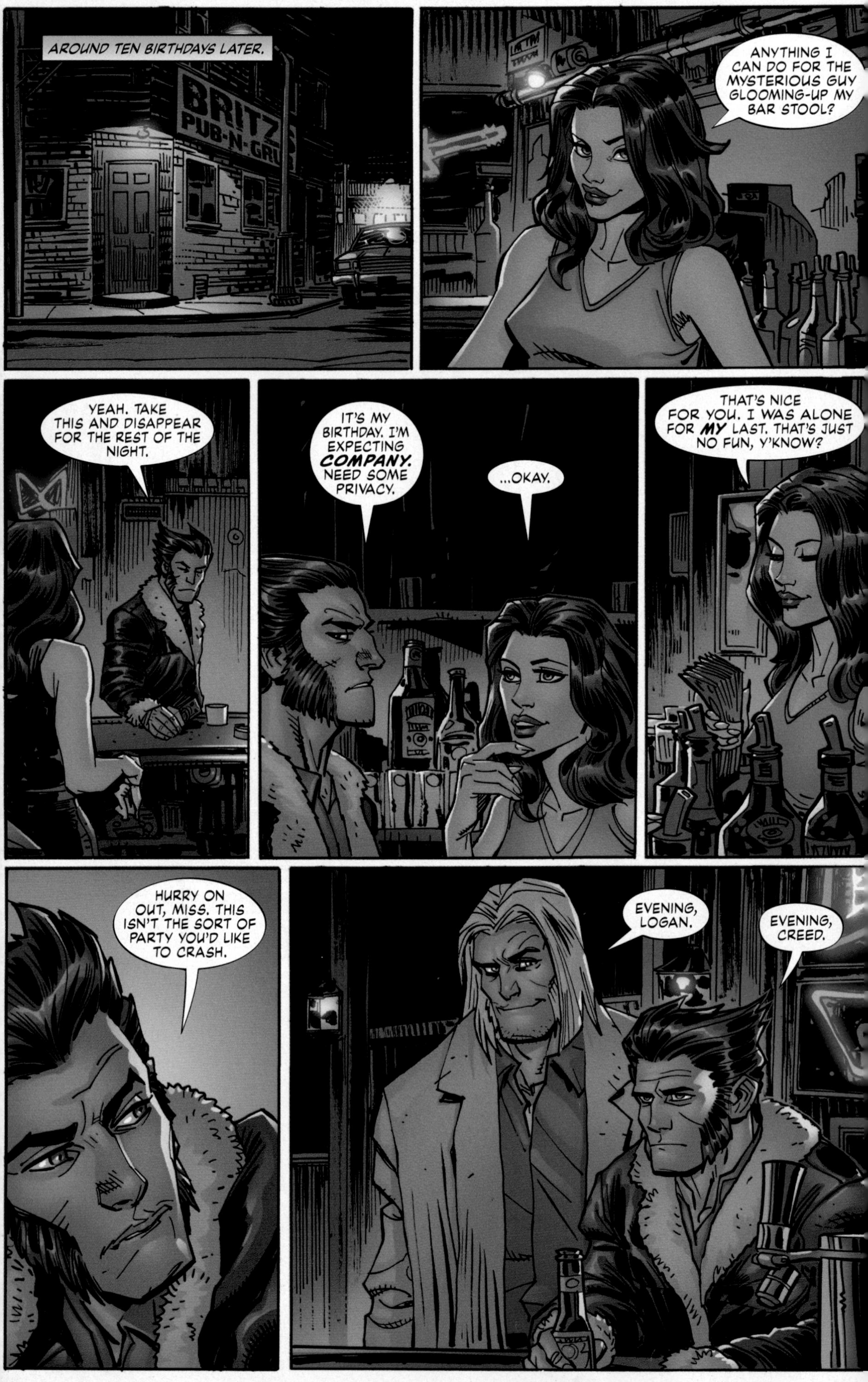
AROUND TEN BIRTHDAYS LATER.
BRITZ PUB-N-GRU
ANYTHING I CAN DO FOR THE MYSTERIOUS GUY GLOOMING-UP MY BAR STOOL?
YEAH. TAKE THIS AND DISAPPEAR FOR THE REST OF THE NIGHT.
IT'S MY BIRTHDAY. I'M EXPECTING COMPANY. NEED SOME PRIVACY.
...OKAY.
THAT'S NICE FOR YOU. I WAS ALONE FOR MY LAST. THAT'S JUST NO FUN, Y'KNOW?
HURRY ON OUT, MISS. THIS ISN'T THE SORT OF PARTY YOU'D LIKE TO CRASH.
EVENING, LOGAN.
EVENING, CREED.

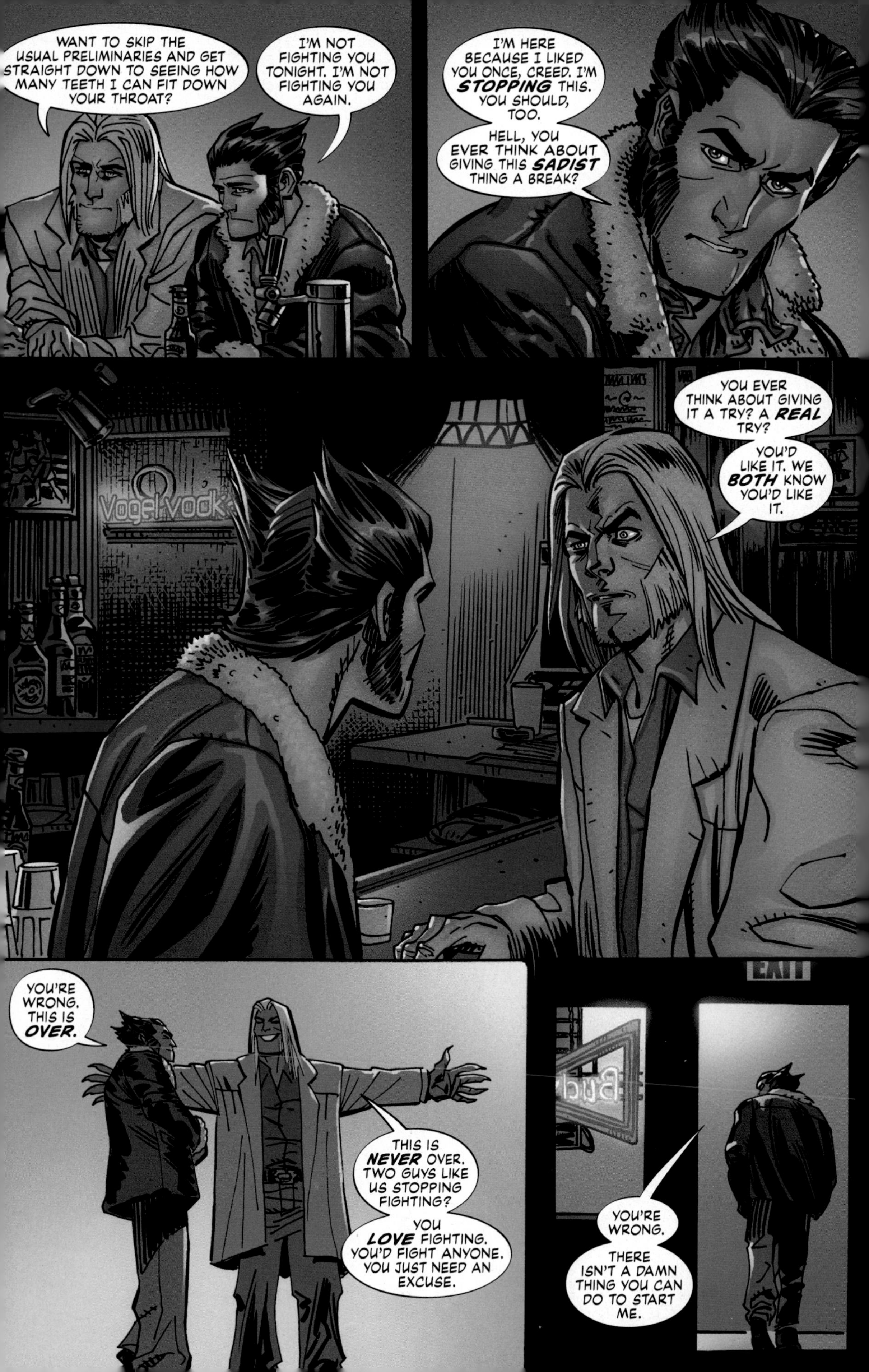
WANT TO SKIP THE USUAL PRELIMINARIES AND GET STRAIGHT DOWN TO SEEING HOW MANY TEETH I CAN FIT DOWN YOUR THROAT?
I'M NOT FIGHTING YOU TONIGHT. I'M NOT FIGHTING YOU AGAIN.
I'M HERE BECAUSE I LIKED YOU ONCE, CREED. I'M STOPPING THIS. YOU SHOULD, TOO.
HELL, YOU EVER THINK ABOUT GIVING THIS SADIST THING A BREAK?
Vogelvodka
YOU EVER THINK ABOUT GIVING IT A TRY? A REAL TRY?
YOU'D LIKE IT. WE BOTH KNOW YOU'D LIKE IT.
YOU'RE WRONG. THIS IS OVER.
THIS IS NEVER OVER. TWO GUYS LIKE US STOPPING FIGHTING?
YOU LOVE FIGHTING. YOU'D FIGHT ANYONE. YOU JUST NEED AN EXCUSE.
EXIT
YOU'RE WRONG.
THERE ISN'T A DAMN THING YOU CAN DO TO START ME.

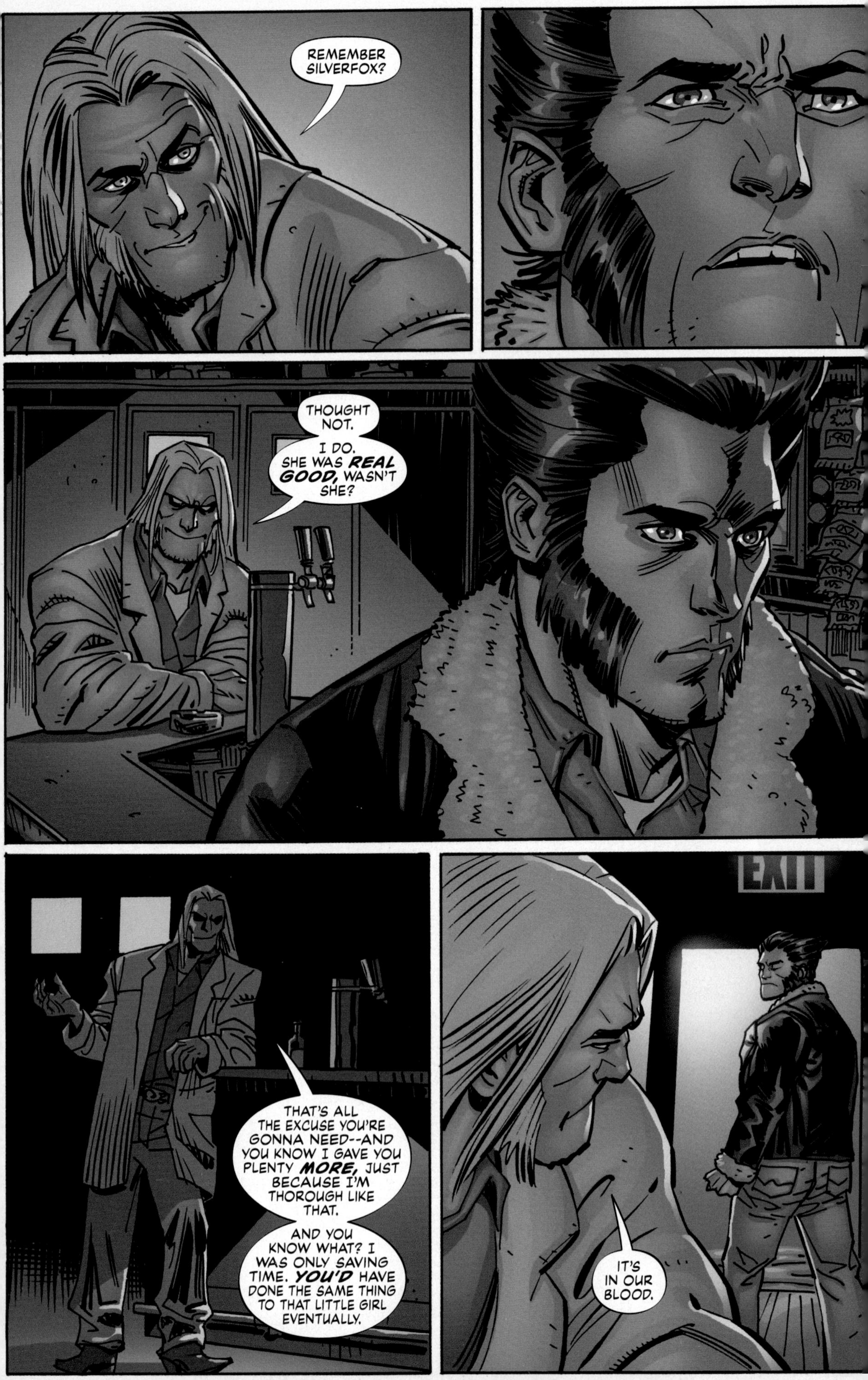
REMEMBER SILVERFOX?
THOUGHT NOT.
I DO. SHE WAS **REAL GOOD,** WASN'T SHE?
THAT'S ALL THE EXCUSE YOU'RE GONNA NEED--AND YOU KNOW I GAVE YOU PLENTY **MORE,** JUST BECAUSE I'M THOROUGH LIKE THAT.
AND YOU KNOW WHAT? I WAS ONLY SAVING TIME. **YOU'D** HAVE DONE THE SAME THING TO THAT LITTLE GIRL EVENTUALLY.
EXIT
IT'S IN OUR BLOOD.

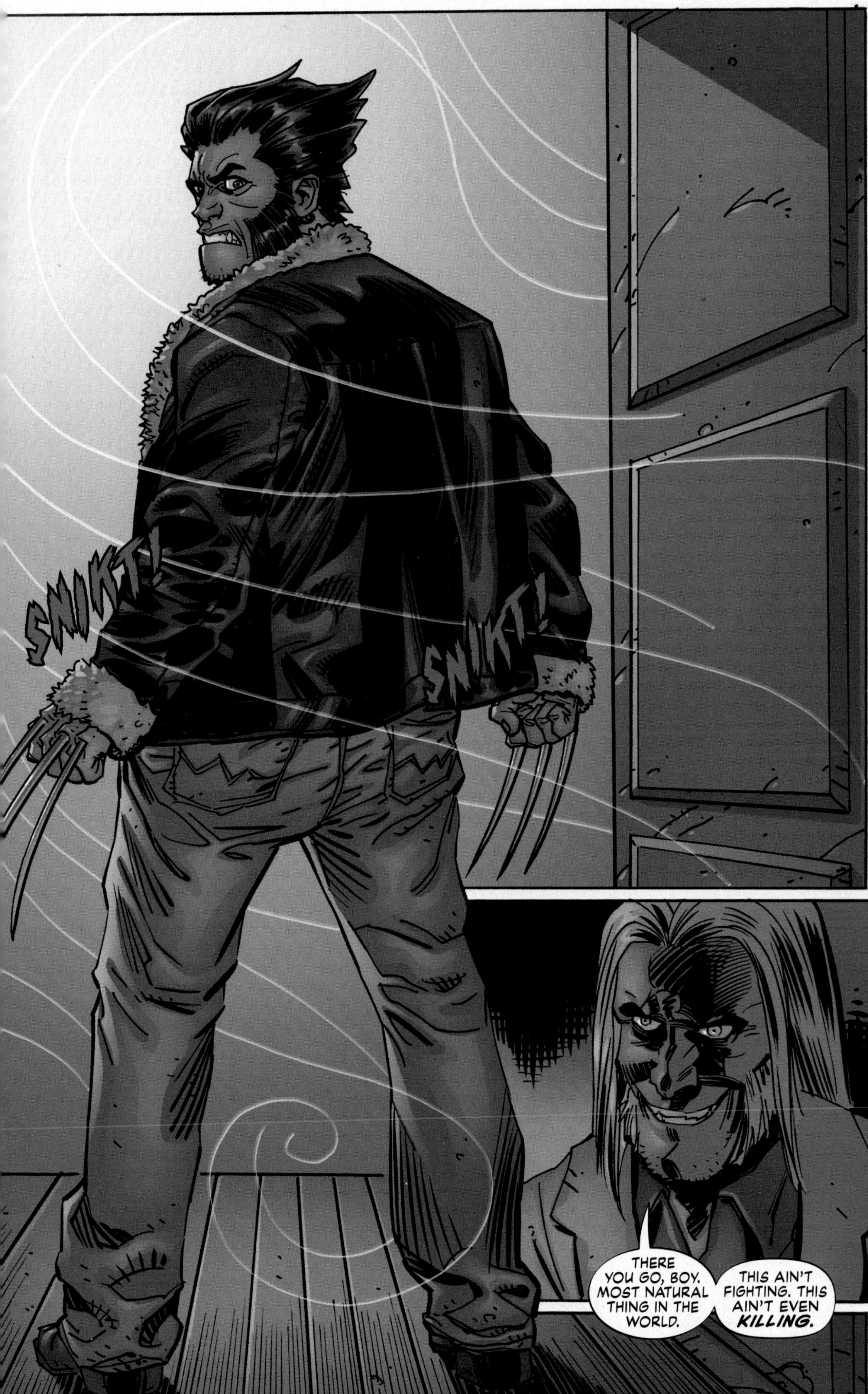
SNIKT!
SNIKT!
THERE YOU GO, BOY. MOST NATURAL THING IN THE WORLD.
THIS AIN'T FIGHTING. THIS AIN'T EVEN *KILLING.*

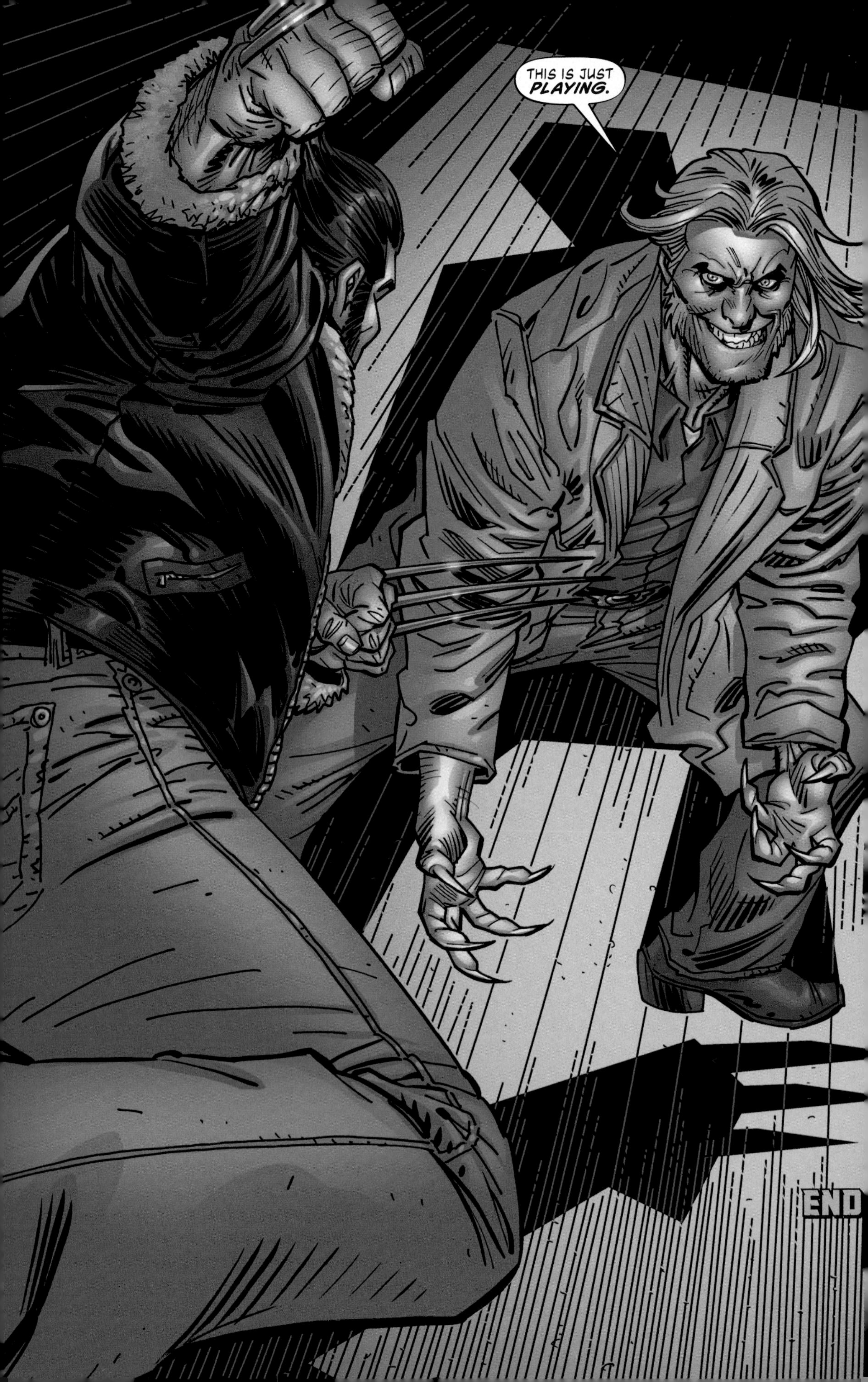
THIS IS JUST *PLAYING.*
END

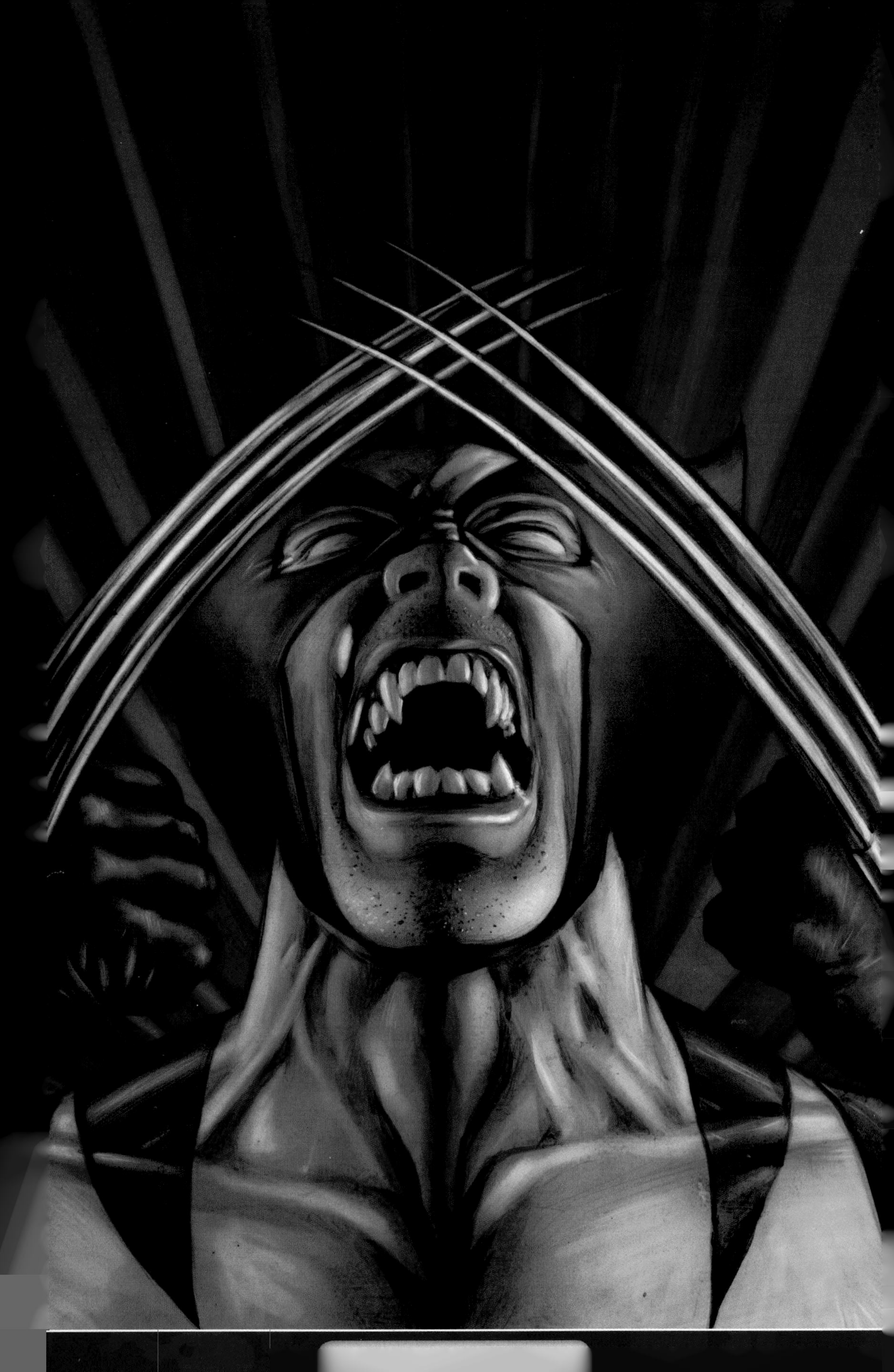

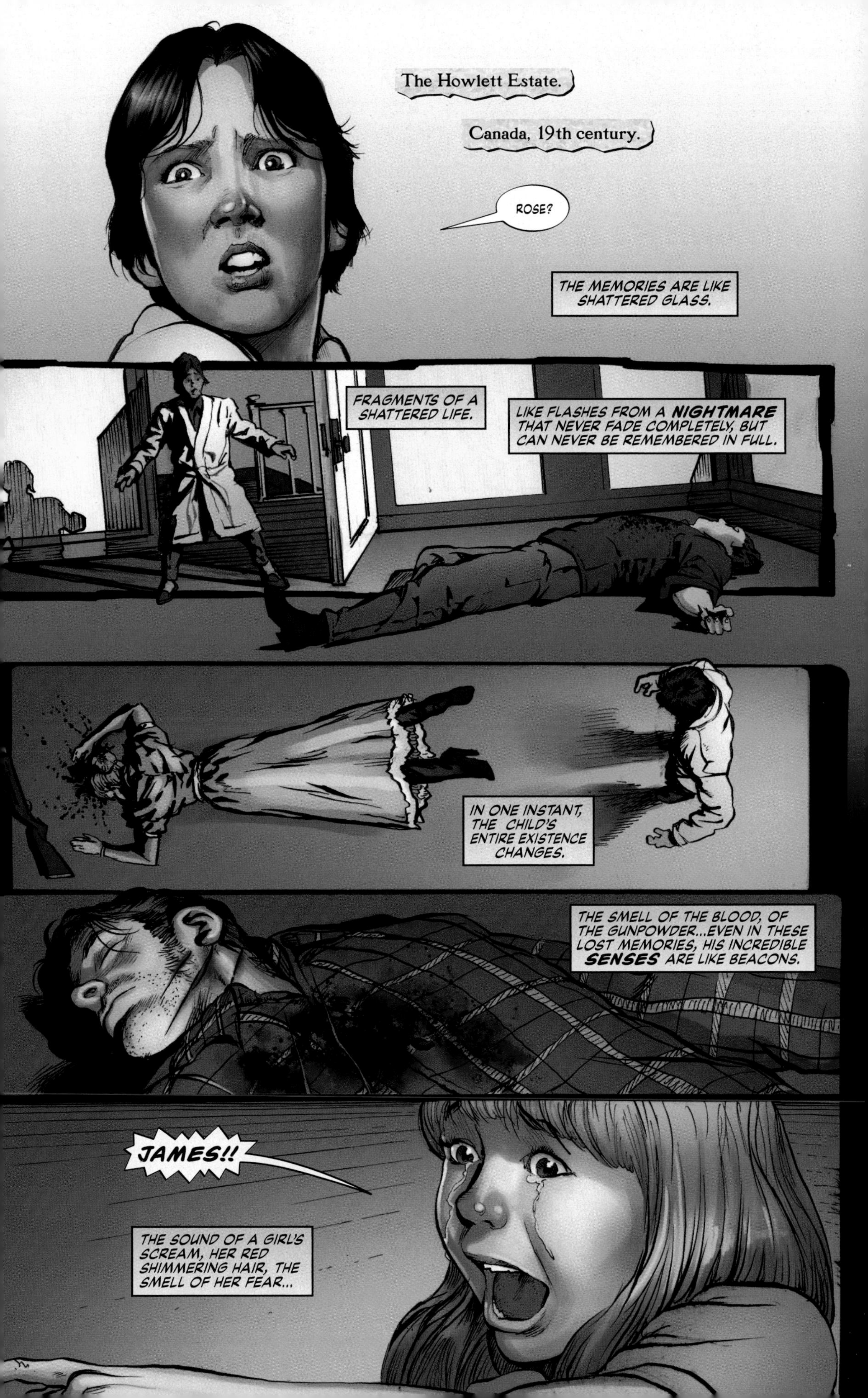
The Howlett Estate.
Canada, 19th century.
ROSE?
THE MEMORIES ARE LIKE SHATTERED GLASS.
FRAGMENTS OF A SHATTERED LIFE.
LIKE FLASHES FROM A NIGHTMARE THAT NEVER FADE COMPLETELY, BUT CAN NEVER BE REMEMBERED IN FULL.
IN ONE INSTANT, THE CHILD'S ENTIRE EXISTENCE CHANGES.
THE SMELL OF THE BLOOD, OF THE GUNPOWDER...EVEN IN THESE LOST MEMORIES, HIS INCREDIBLE SENSES ARE LIKE BEACONS.
JAMES!!
THE SOUND OF A GIRL'S SCREAM, HER RED SHIMMERING HAIR, THE SMELL OF HER FEAR...

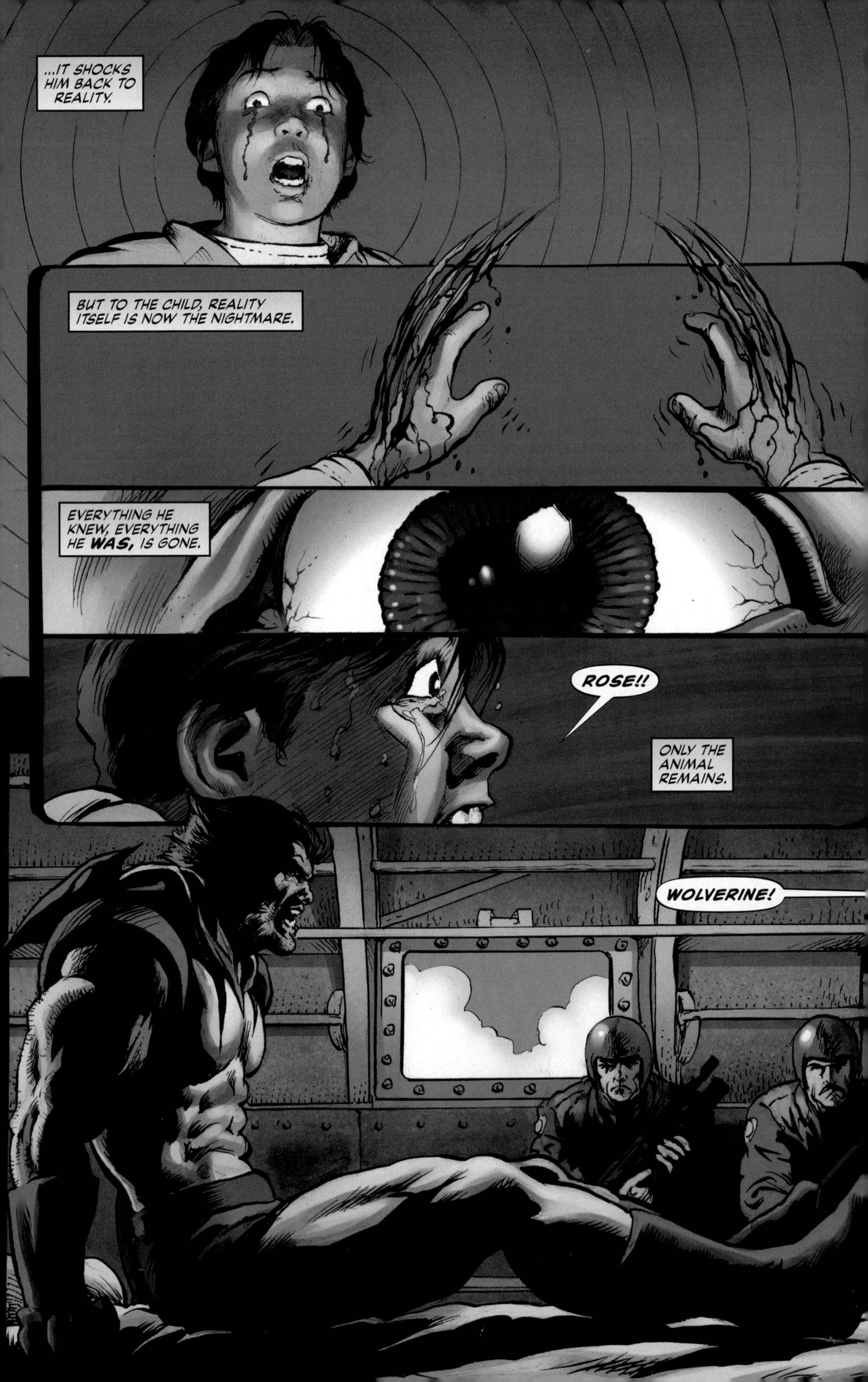
...IT SHOCKS HIM BACK TO REALITY.
BUT TO THE CHILD, REALITY ITSELF IS NOW THE NIGHTMARE.
EVERYTHING HE KNEW, EVERYTHING HE **WAS,** IS GONE.
ROSE!!
ONLY THE ANIMAL REMAINS.
WOLVERINE!

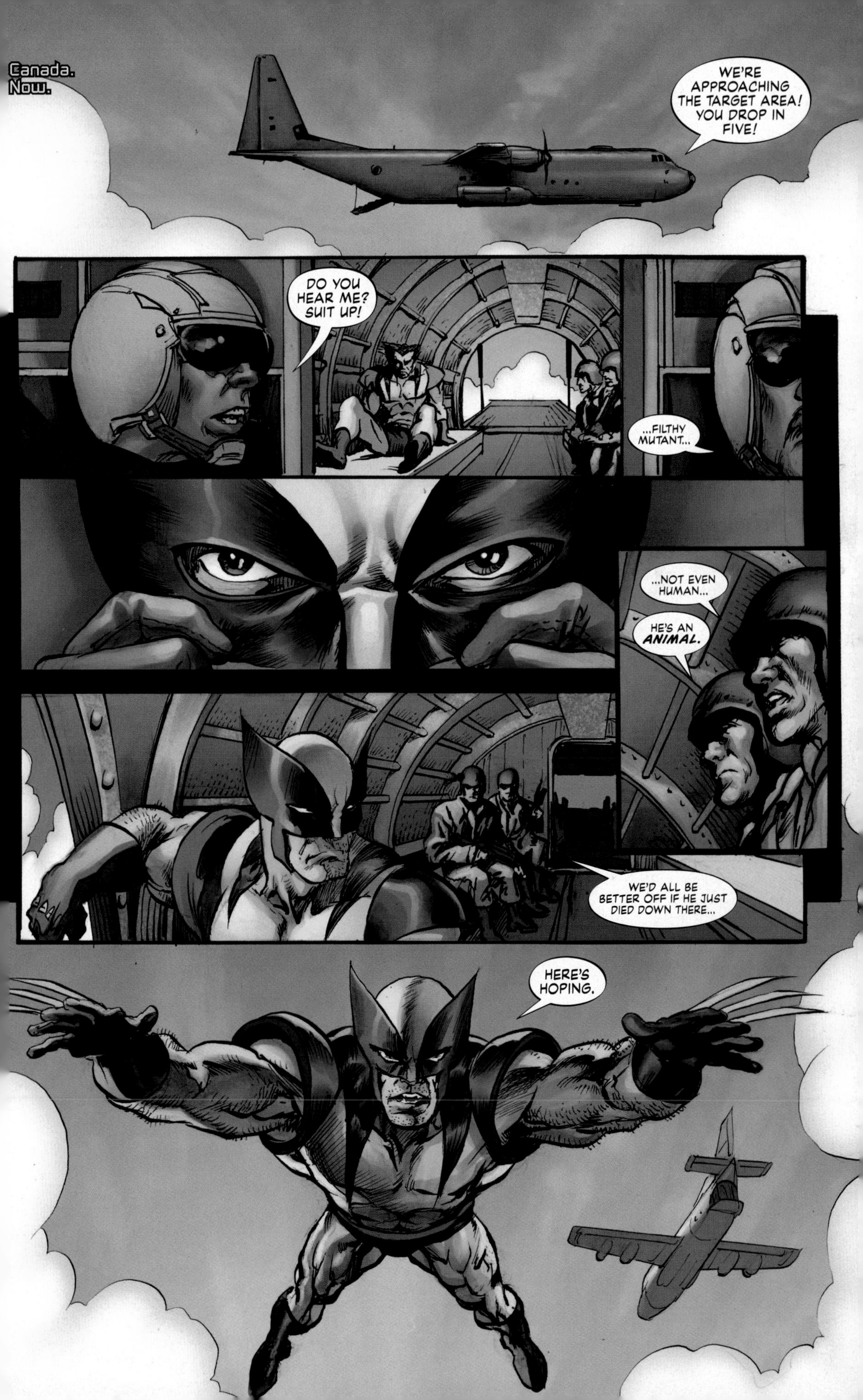

Canada. Now.
WE'RE APPROACHING THE TARGET AREA! YOU DROP IN FIVE!
DO YOU HEAR ME? SUIT UP!
...FILTHY MUTANT...
...NOT EVEN HUMAN...
HE'S AN ANIMAL.
WE'D ALL BE BETTER OFF IF HE JUST DIED DOWN THERE...
HERE'S HOPING.

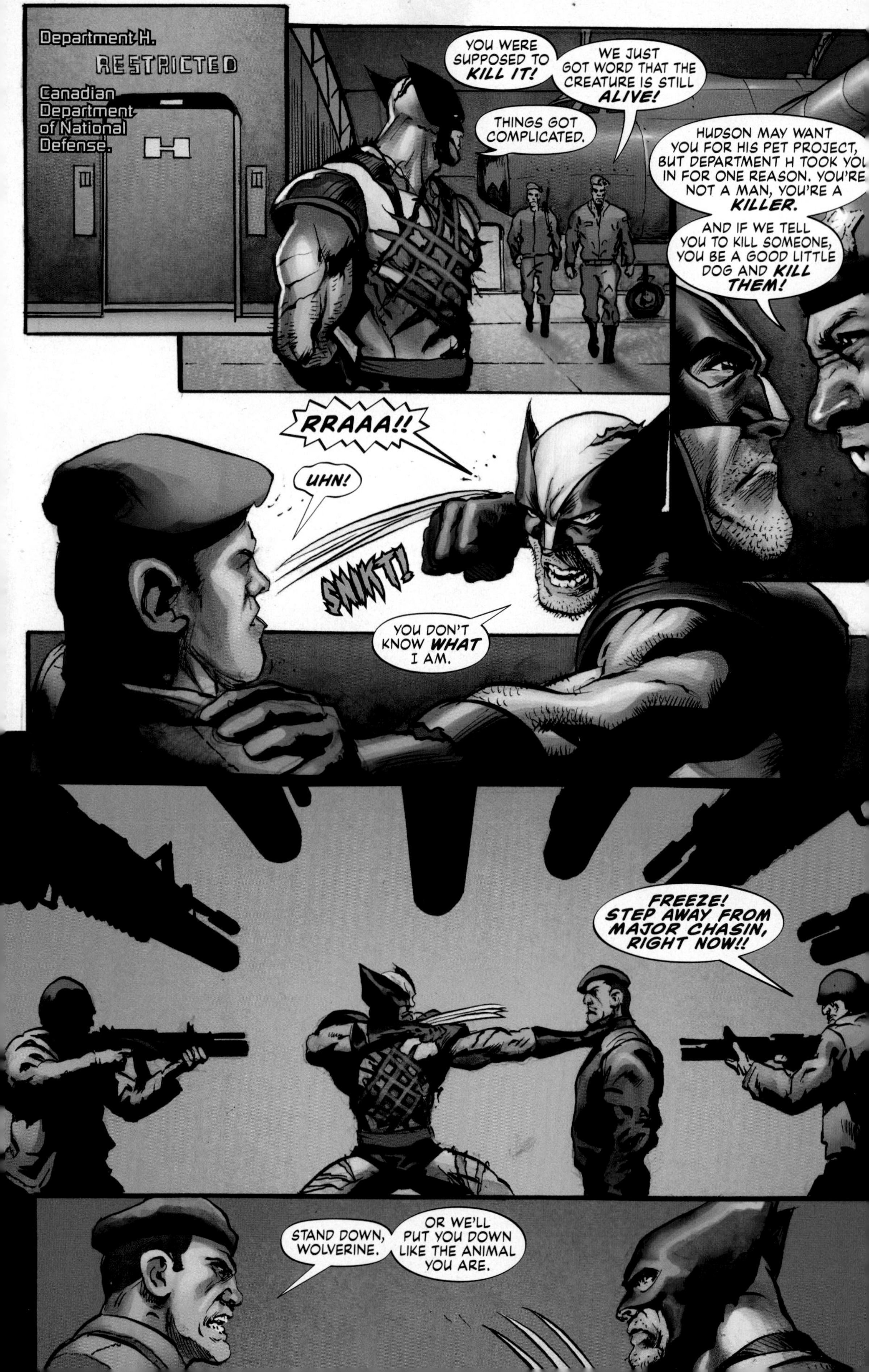

Department H.
RESTRICTED
Canadian Department of National Defense.
YOU WERE SUPPOSED TO KILL IT!
WE JUST GOT WORD THAT THE CREATURE IS STILL ALIVE!
THINGS GOT COMPLICATED.
HUDSON MAY WANT YOU FOR HIS PET PROJECT, BUT DEPARTMENT H TOOK YOU IN FOR ONE REASON. YOU'RE NOT A MAN, YOU'RE A KILLER.
AND IF WE TELL YOU TO KILL SOMEONE, YOU BE A GOOD LITTLE DOG AND KILL THEM!
RRAAA!!
UHN!
SNIKT!
YOU DON'T KNOW WHAT I AM.
FREEZE! STEP AWAY FROM MAJOR CHASIN, RIGHT NOW!!
STAND DOWN, WOLVERINE.
OR WE'LL PUT YOU DOWN LIKE THE ANIMAL YOU ARE.

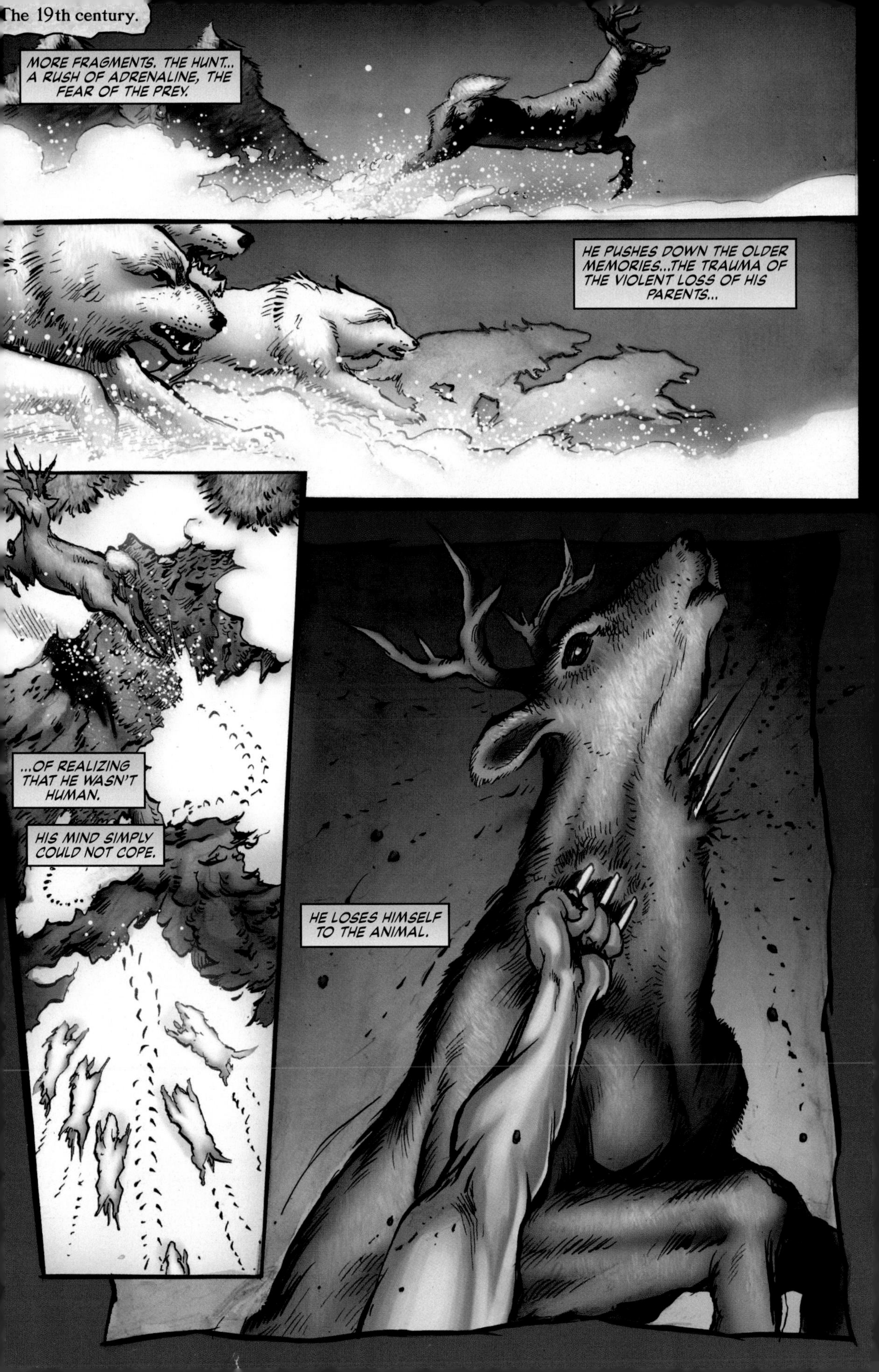
The 19th century.
MORE FRAGMENTS. THE HUNT... A RUSH OF ADRENALINE, THE FEAR OF THE PREY.
HE PUSHES DOWN THE OLDER MEMORIES...THE TRAUMA OF THE VIOLENT LOSS OF HIS PARENTS...
...OF REALIZING THAT HE WASN'T HUMAN.
HIS MIND SIMPLY COULD NOT COPE.
HE LOSES HIMSELF TO THE ANIMAL.

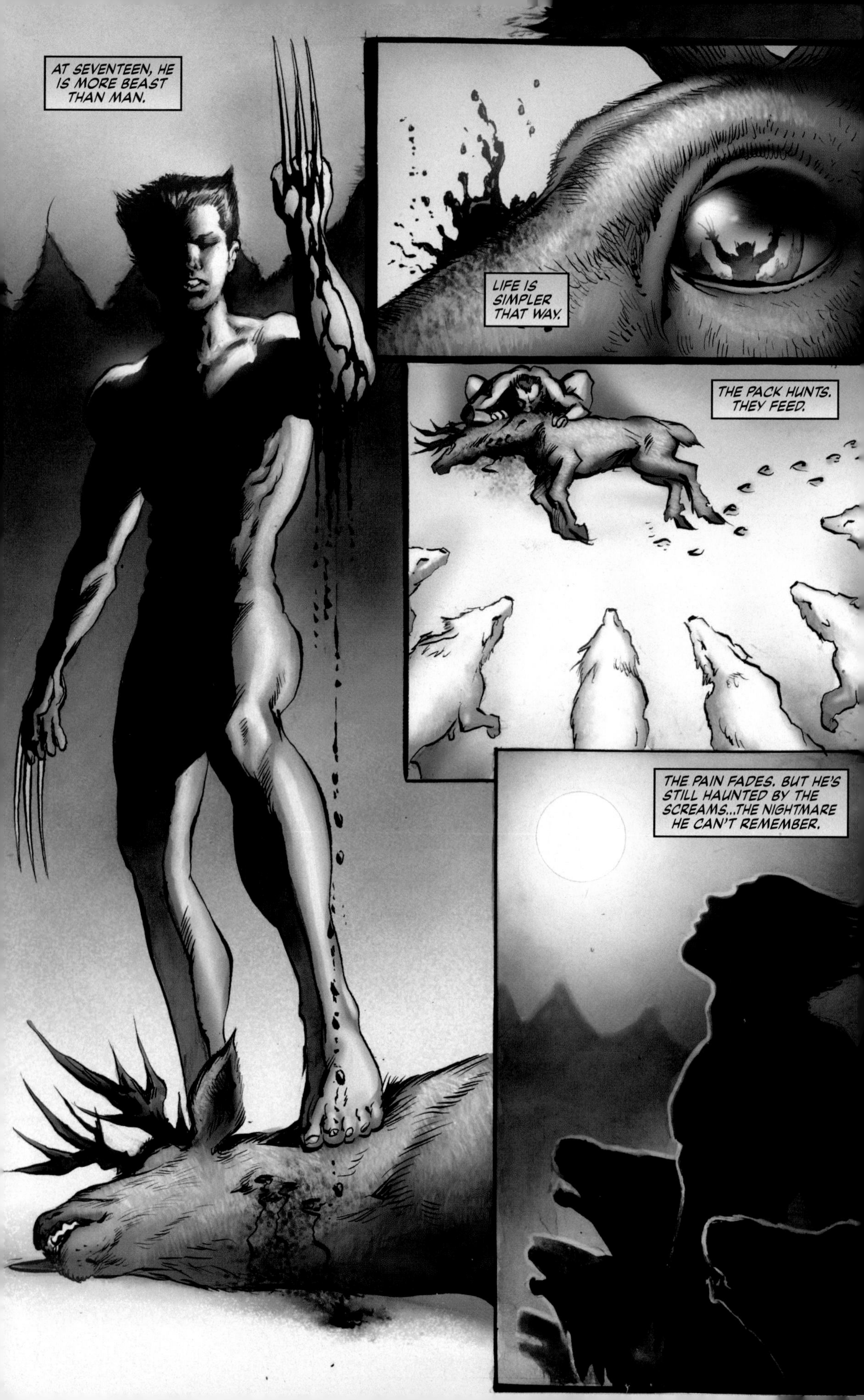
AT SEVENTEEN, HE IS MORE BEAST THAN MAN.
LIFE IS SIMPLER THAT WAY.
THE PACK HUNTS. THEY FEED.
THE PAIN FADES. BUT HE'S STILL HAUNTED BY THE SCREAMS...THE NIGHTMARE HE CAN'T REMEMBER.

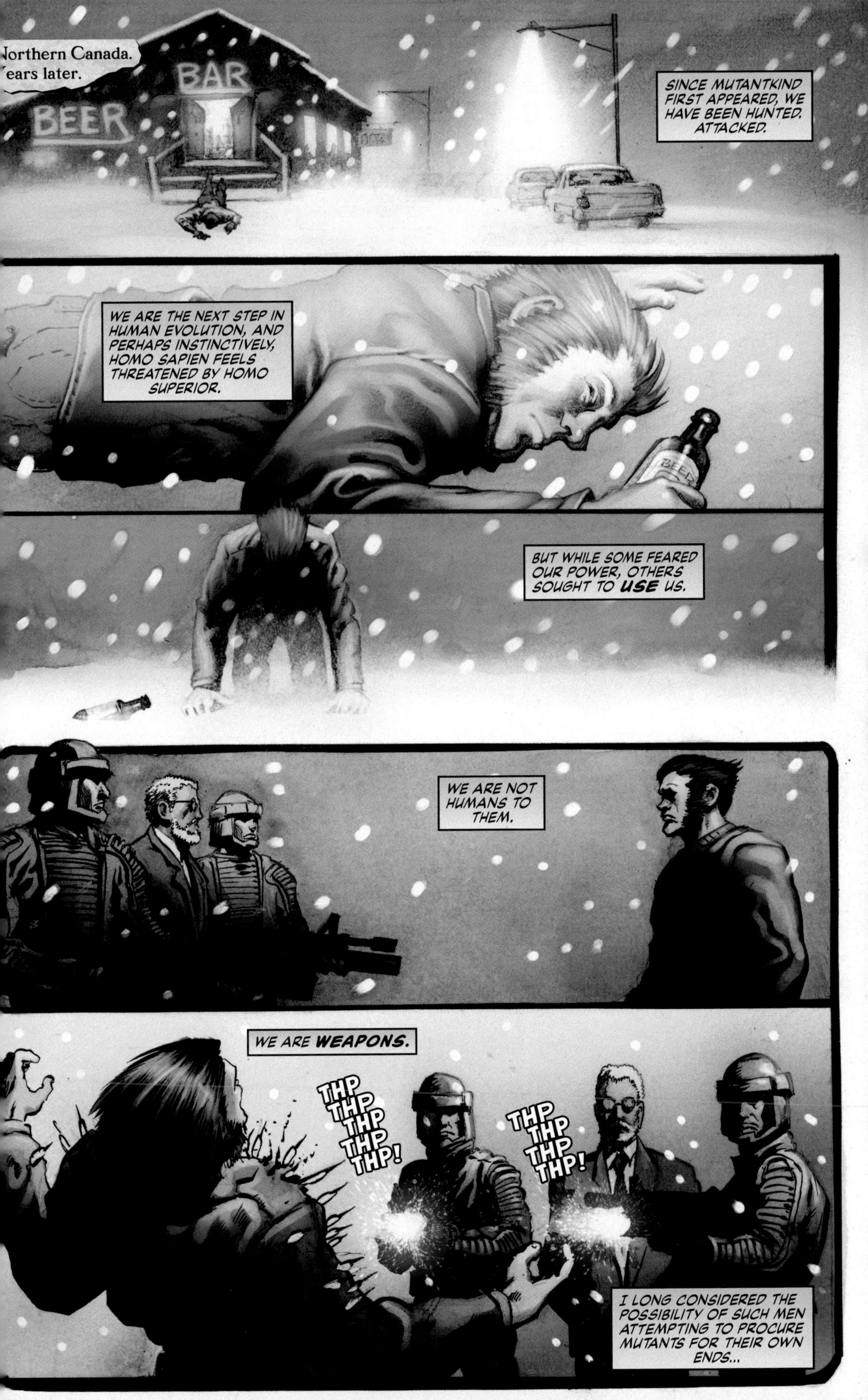
Northern Canada.
Years later.
BAR
BEER
SINCE MUTANTKIND FIRST APPEARED, WE HAVE BEEN HUNTED. ATTACKED.
WE ARE THE NEXT STEP IN HUMAN EVOLUTION, AND PERHAPS INSTINCTIVELY, HOMO SAPIEN FEELS THREATENED BY HOMO SUPERIOR.
BEER
BUT WHILE SOME FEARED OUR POWER, OTHERS SOUGHT TO USE US.
WE ARE NOT HUMANS TO THEM.
WE ARE WEAPONS.
THP THP THP THP THP!
THP THP THP THP!
I LONG CONSIDERED THE POSSIBILITY OF SUCH MEN ATTEMPTING TO PROCURE MUTANTS FOR THEIR OWN ENDS...

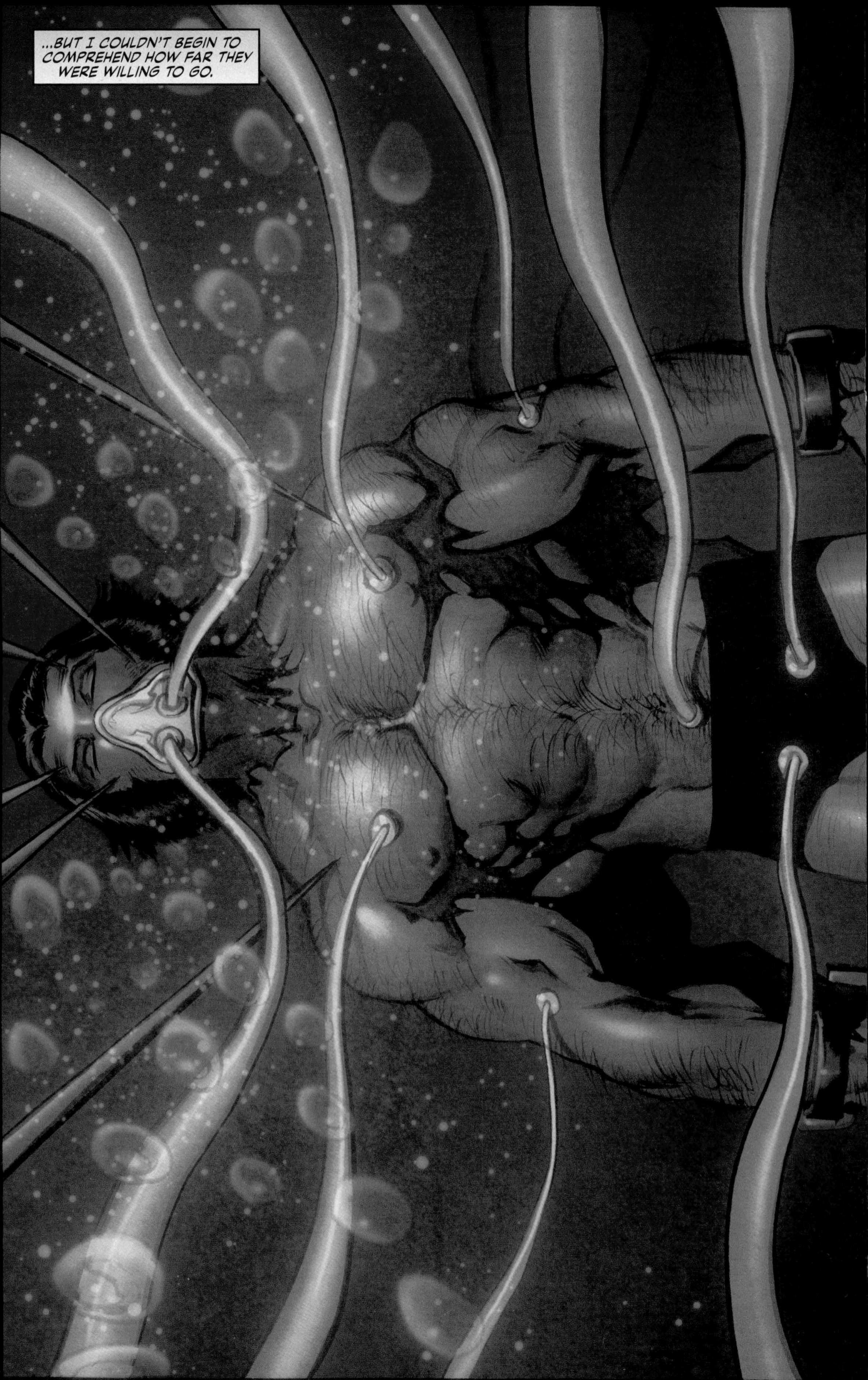
...BUT I COULDN'T BEGIN TO COMPREHEND HOW FAR THEY WERE WILLING TO GO.

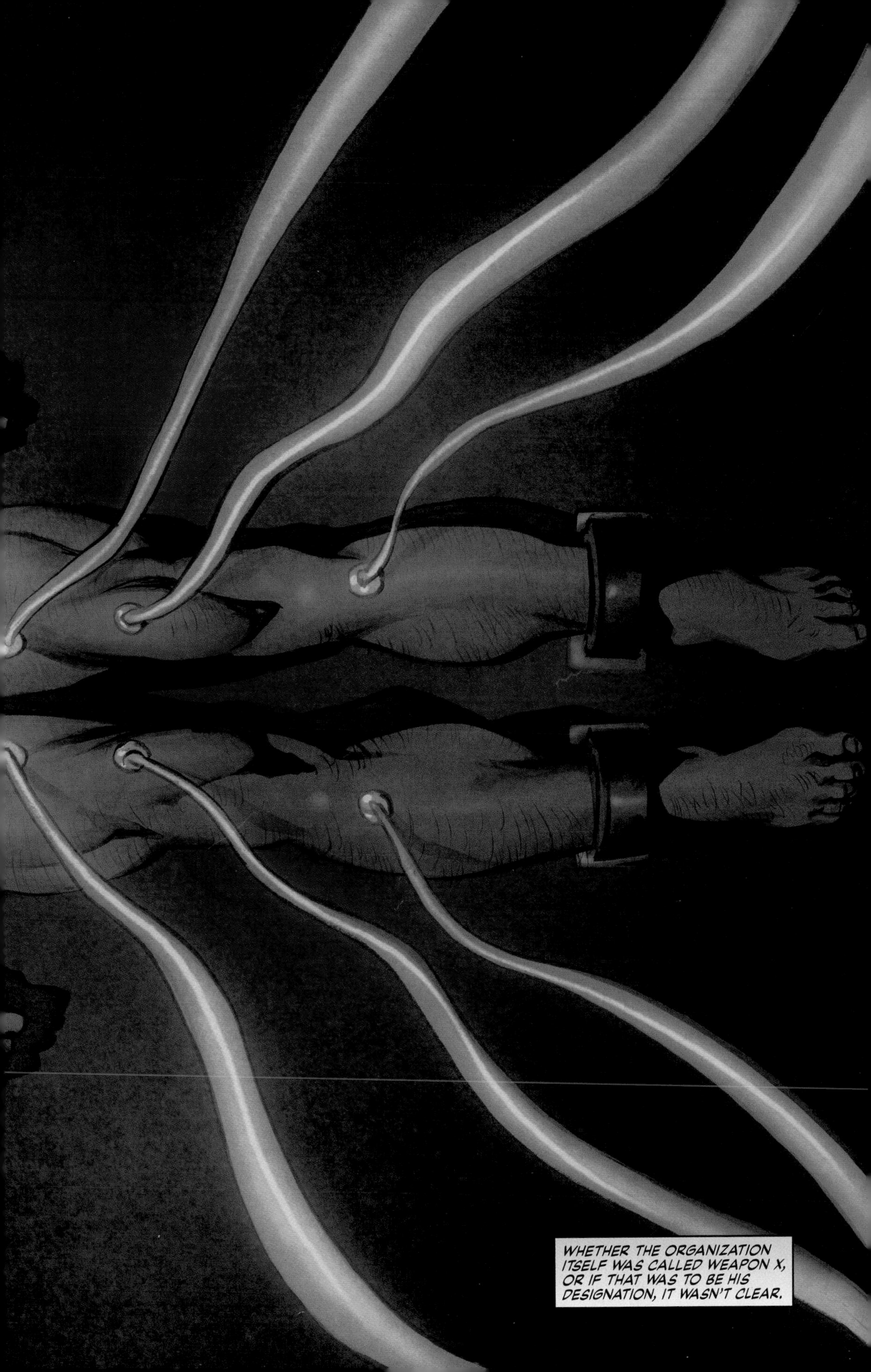
WHETHER THE ORGANIZATION ITSELF WAS CALLED WEAPON X, OR IF THAT WAS TO BE HIS DESIGNATION, IT WASN'T CLEAR.

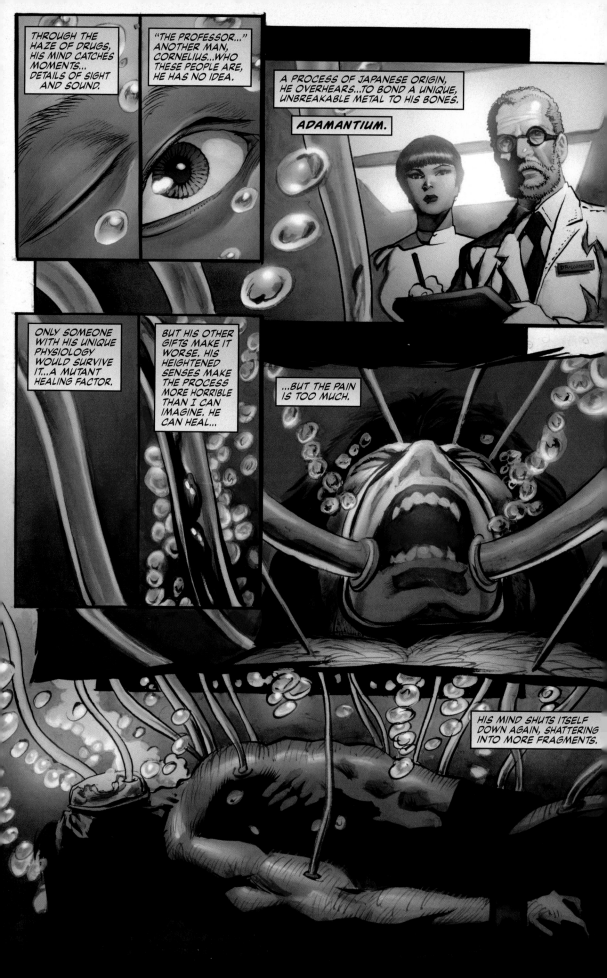

THROUGH THE HAZE OF DRUGS, HIS MIND CATCHES MOMENTS... DETAILS OF SIGHT AND SOUND.

"THE PROFESSOR..." ANOTHER MAN, CORNELIUS...WHO THESE PEOPLE ARE, HE HAS NO IDEA.

A PROCESS OF JAPANESE ORIGIN, HE OVERHEARS...TO BOND A UNIQUE, UNBREAKABLE METAL TO HIS BONES.

ADAMANTIUM.

ONLY SOMEONE WITH HIS UNIQUE PHYSIOLOGY WOULD SURVIVE IT...A MUTANT HEALING FACTOR.

BUT HIS OTHER GIFTS MAKE IT WORSE. HIS HEIGHTENED SENSES MAKE THE PROCESS MORE HORRIBLE THAN I CAN IMAGINE. HE CAN HEAL...

...BUT THE PAIN IS TOO MUCH.

HIS MIND SHUTS ITSELF DOWN AGAIN, SHATTERING INTO MORE FRAGMENTS.

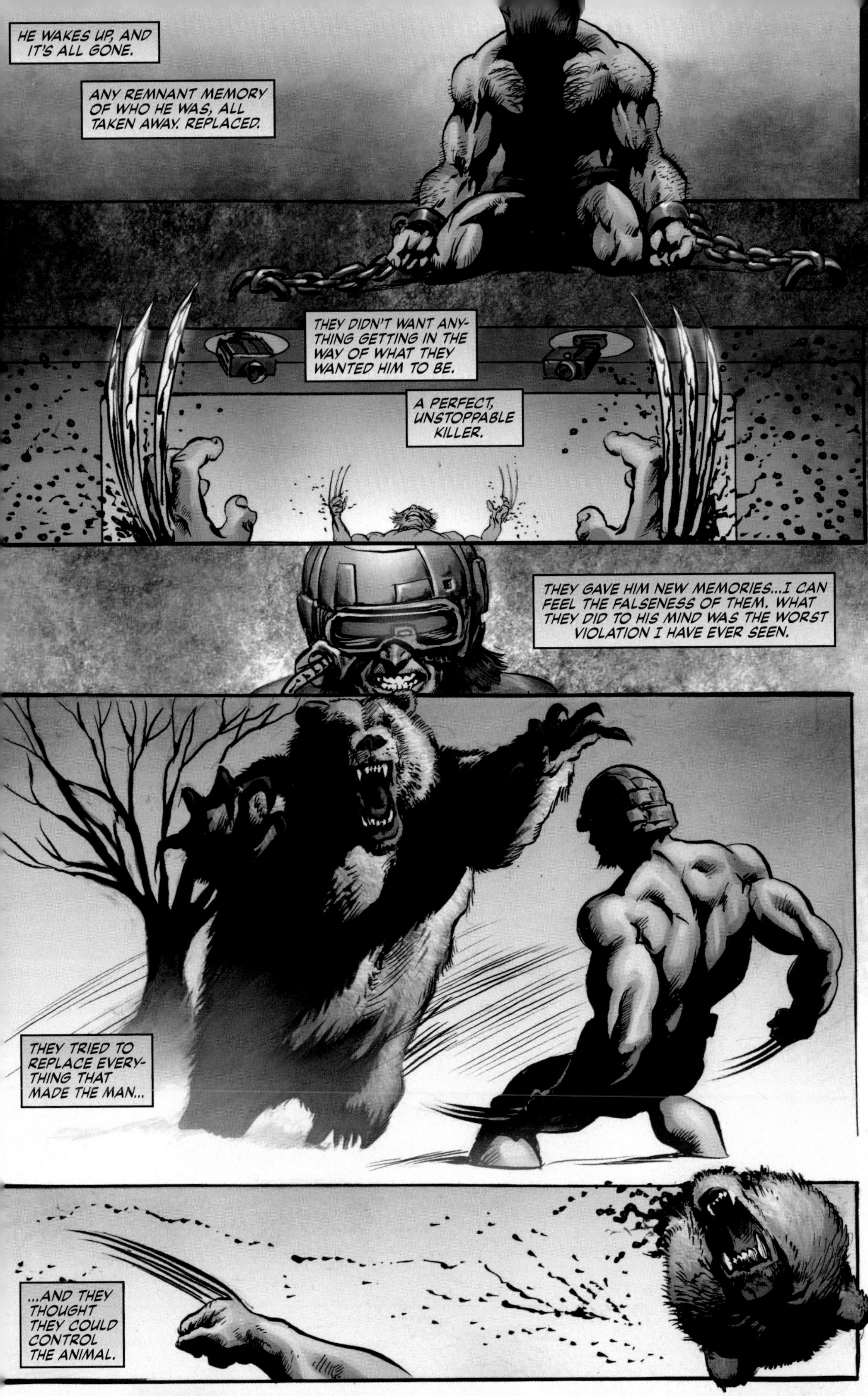
HE WAKES UP, AND IT'S ALL GONE.
ANY REMNANT MEMORY OF WHO HE WAS, ALL TAKEN AWAY. REPLACED.
THEY DIDN'T WANT ANY-THING GETTING IN THE WAY OF WHAT THEY WANTED HIM TO BE.
A PERFECT, UNSTOPPABLE KILLER.
THEY GAVE HIM NEW MEMORIES...I CAN FEEL THE FALSENESS OF THEM. WHAT THEY DID TO HIS MIND WAS THE WORST VIOLATION I HAVE EVER SEEN.
THEY TRIED TO REPLACE EVERY-THING THAT MADE THE MAN...
...AND THEY THOUGHT THEY COULD CONTROL THE ANIMAL.

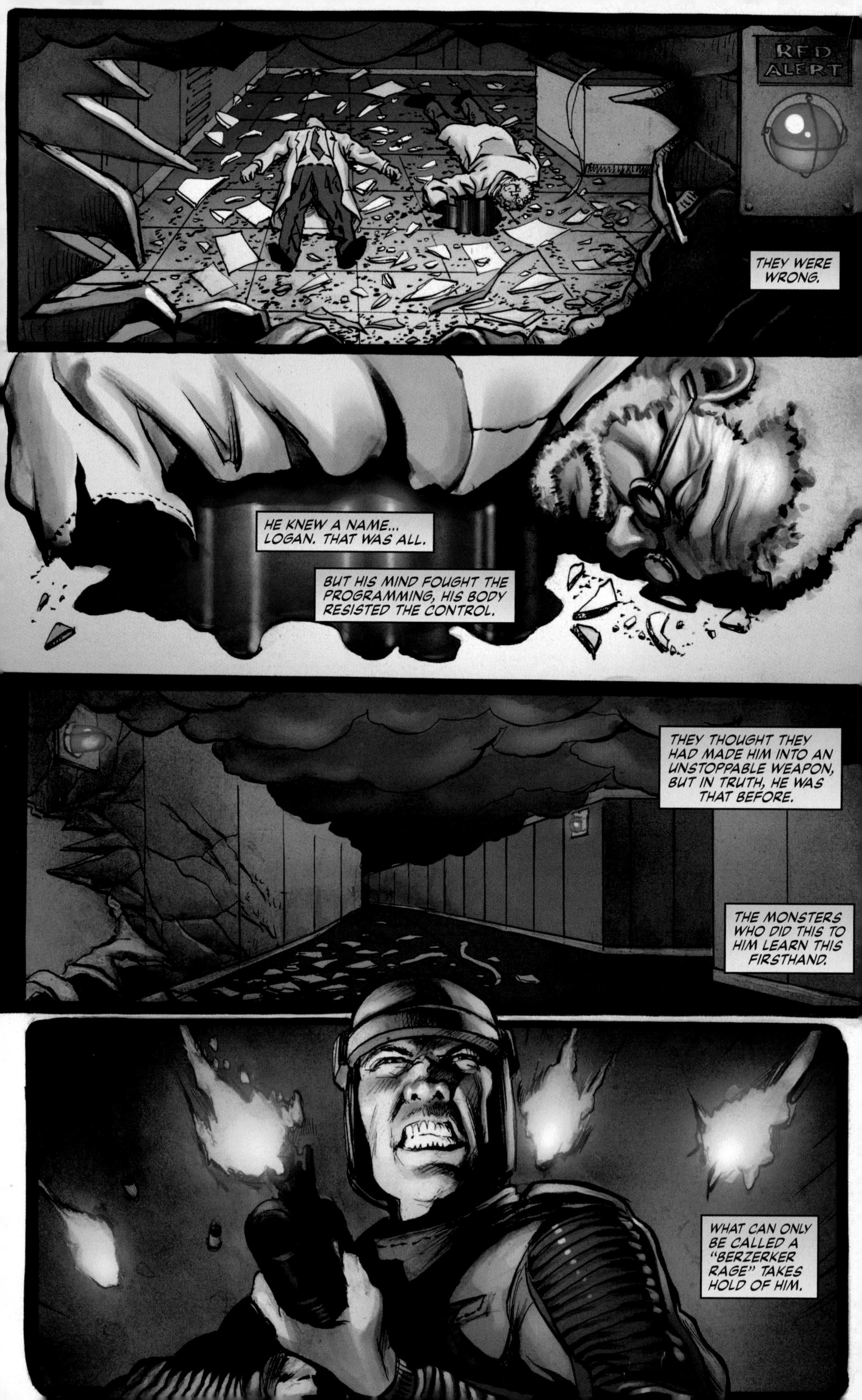
RED ALERT
THEY WERE WRONG.
HE KNEW A NAME... LOGAN. THAT WAS ALL.
BUT HIS MIND FOUGHT THE PROGRAMMING, HIS BODY RESISTED THE CONTROL.
THEY THOUGHT THEY HAD MADE HIM INTO AN UNSTOPPABLE WEAPON, BUT IN TRUTH, HE WAS THAT BEFORE.
THE MONSTERS WHO DID THIS TO HIM LEARN THIS FIRSTHAND.
WHAT CAN ONLY BE CALLED A "BERZERKER RAGE" TAKES HOLD OF HIM.

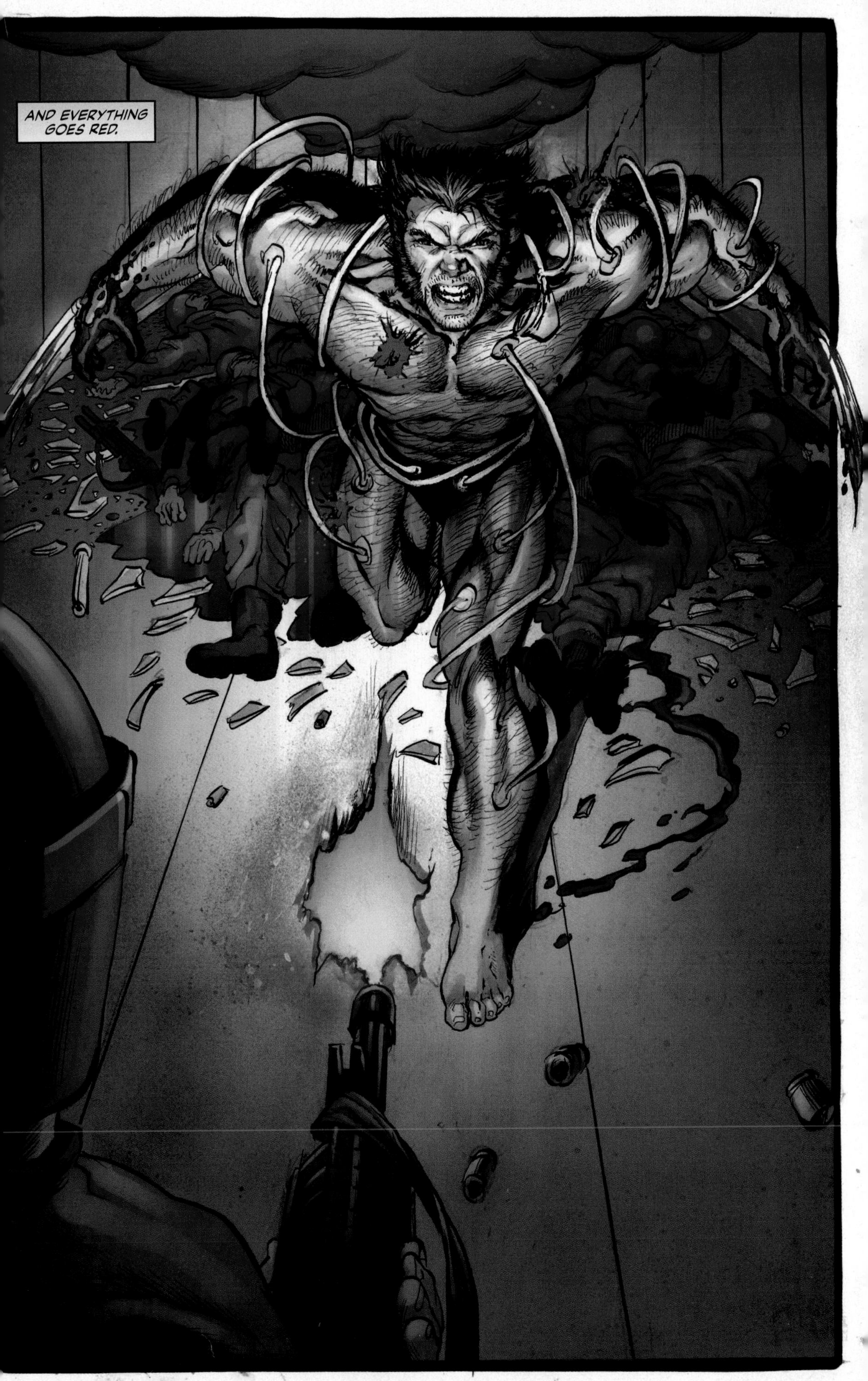
AND EVERYTHING GOES RED.

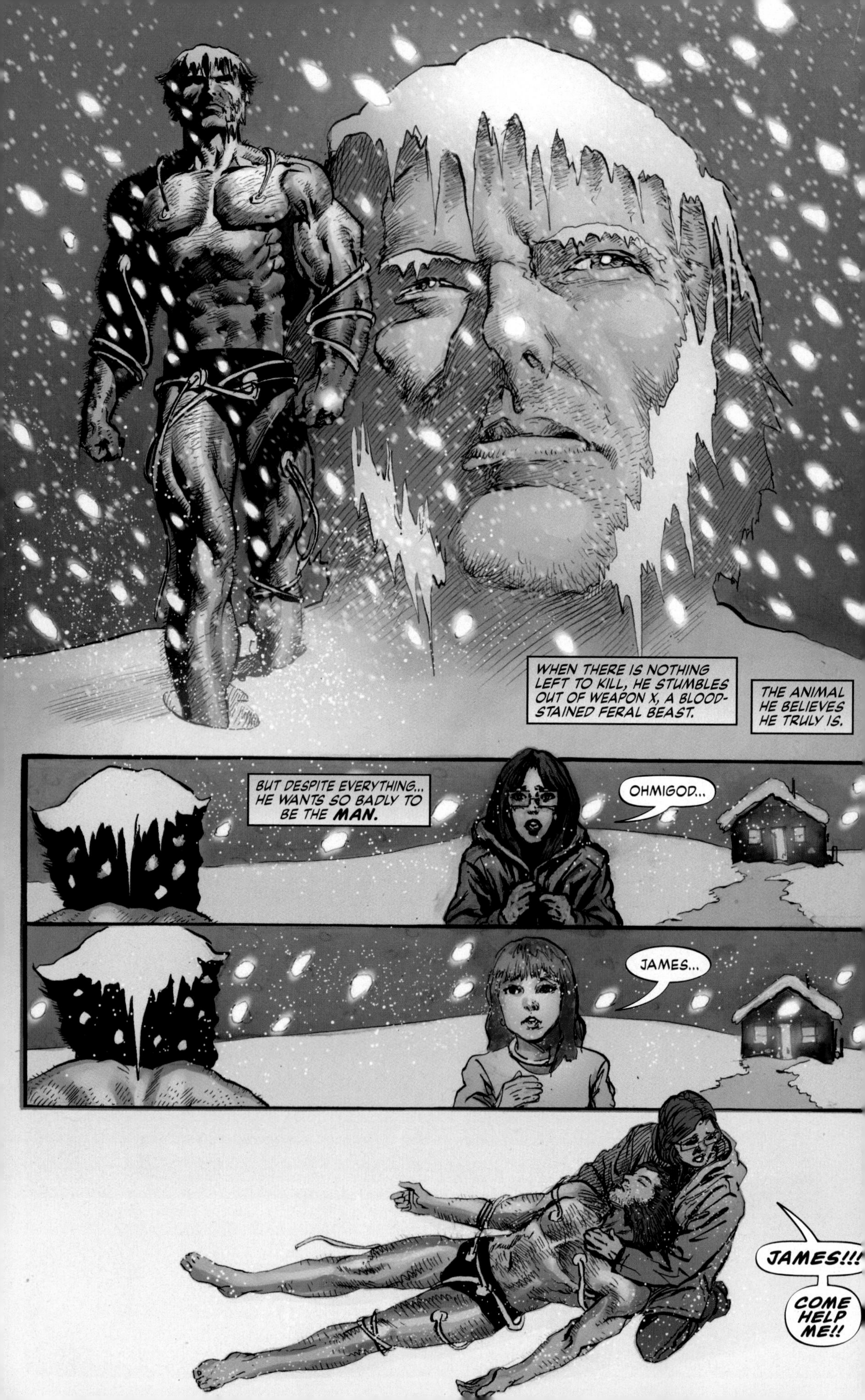
WHEN THERE IS NOTHING LEFT TO KILL, HE STUMBLES OUT OF WEAPON X, A BLOOD-STAINED FERAL BEAST.
THE ANIMAL HE BELIEVES HE TRULY IS.
BUT DESPITE EVERYTHING... HE WANTS SO BADLY TO BE THE MAN.
OHMIGOD...
JAMES...
JAMES!!!
COME HELP ME!!

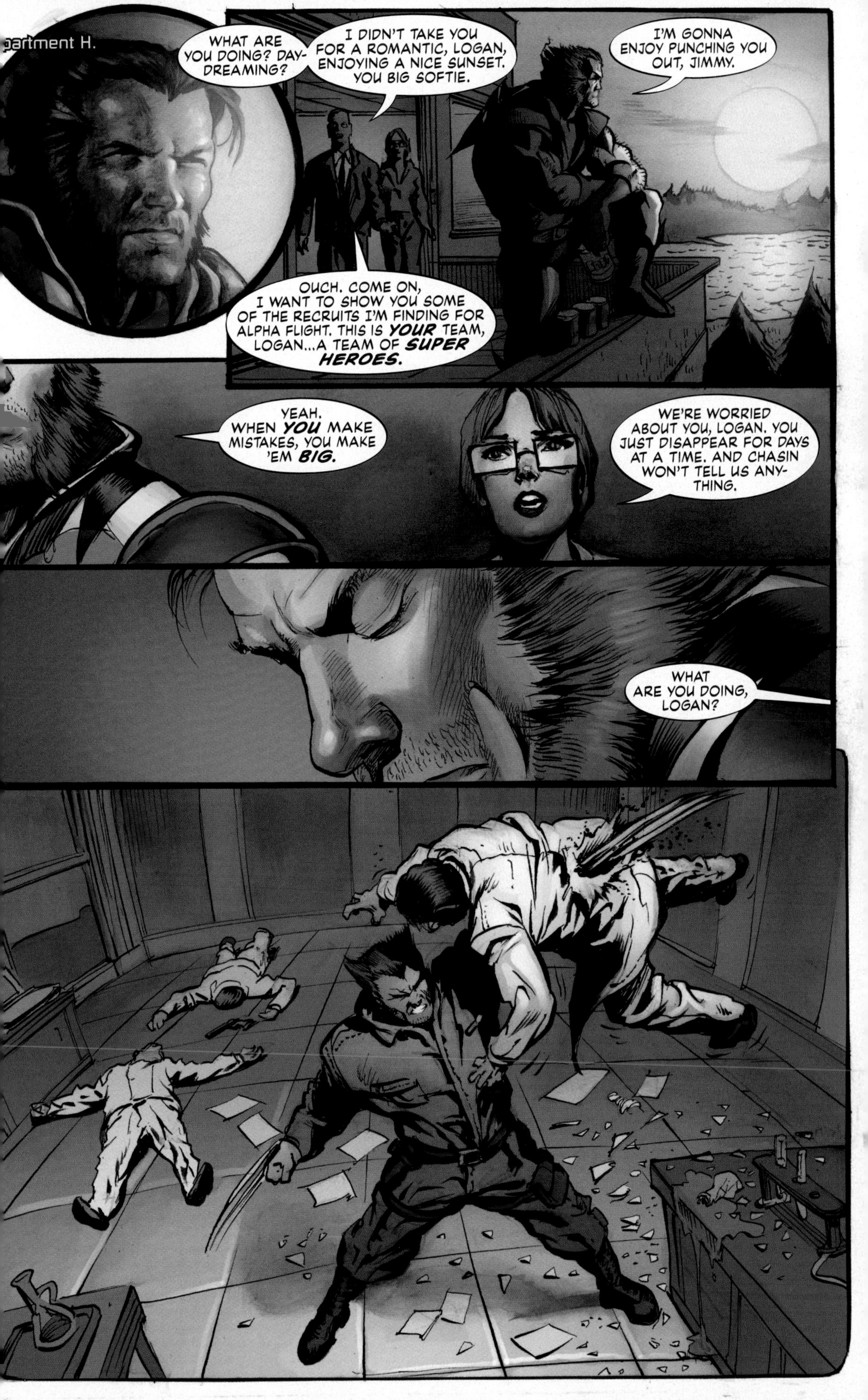

...partment H.
WHAT ARE YOU DOING? DAY-DREAMING?
I DIDN'T TAKE YOU FOR A ROMANTIC, LOGAN, ENJOYING A NICE SUNSET. YOU BIG SOFTIE.
I'M GONNA ENJOY PUNCHING YOU OUT, JIMMY.
OUCH. COME ON, I WANT TO SHOW YOU SOME OF THE RECRUITS I'M FINDING FOR ALPHA FLIGHT. THIS IS YOUR TEAM, LOGAN...A TEAM OF SUPER HEROES.
YEAH. WHEN YOU MAKE MISTAKES, YOU MAKE 'EM BIG.
WE'RE WORRIED ABOUT YOU, LOGAN. YOU JUST DISAPPEAR FOR DAYS AT A TIME. AND CHASIN WON'T TELL US ANY-THING.
WHAT ARE YOU DOING, LOGAN?

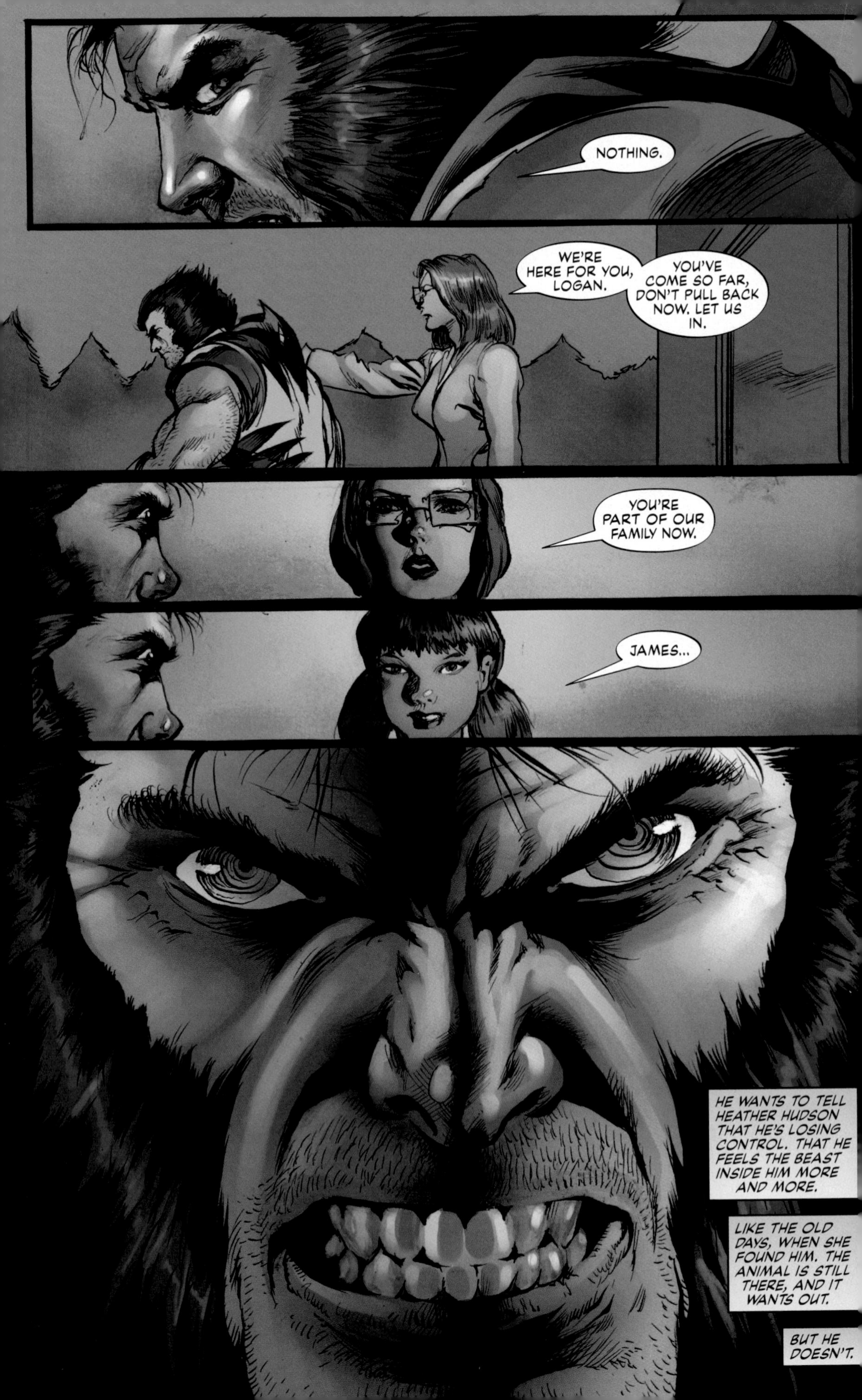
NOTHING.
WE'RE HERE FOR YOU, LOGAN.
YOU'VE COME SO FAR, DON'T PULL BACK NOW. LET US IN.
YOU'RE PART OF OUR FAMILY NOW.
JAMES...
HE WANTS TO TELL HEATHER HUDSON THAT HE'S LOSING CONTROL. THAT HE FEELS THE BEAST INSIDE HIM MORE AND MORE.
LIKE THE OLD DAYS, WHEN SHE FOUND HIM. THE ANIMAL IS STILL THERE, AND IT WANTS OUT.
BUT HE DOESN'T.

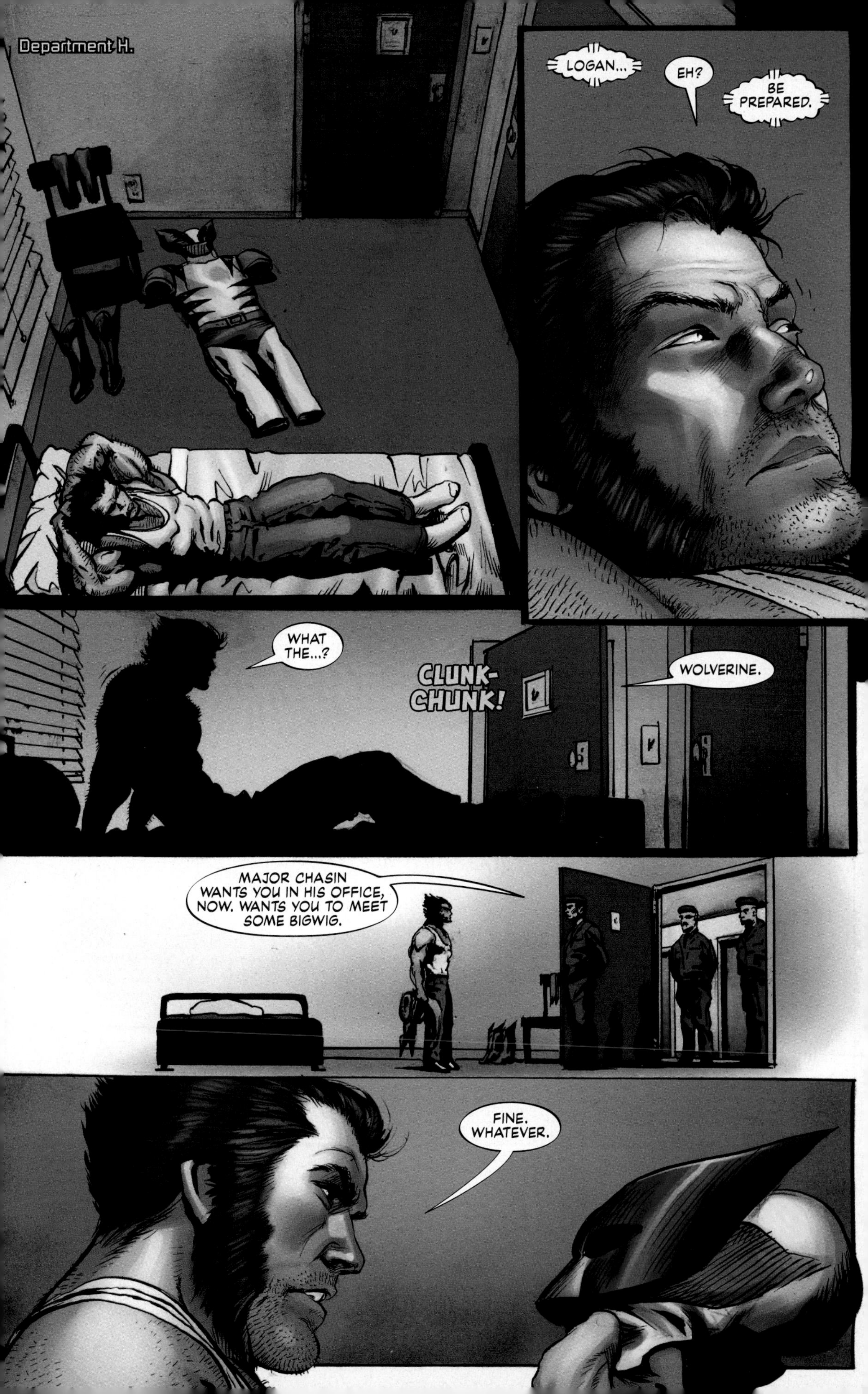
Department H.
LOGAN...
EH?
BE PREPARED.
WHAT THE...?
CLUNK-CHUNK!
WOLVERINE.
MAJOR CHASIN WANTS YOU IN HIS OFFICE, NOW. WANTS YOU TO MEET SOME BIGWIG.
FINE. WHATEVER.

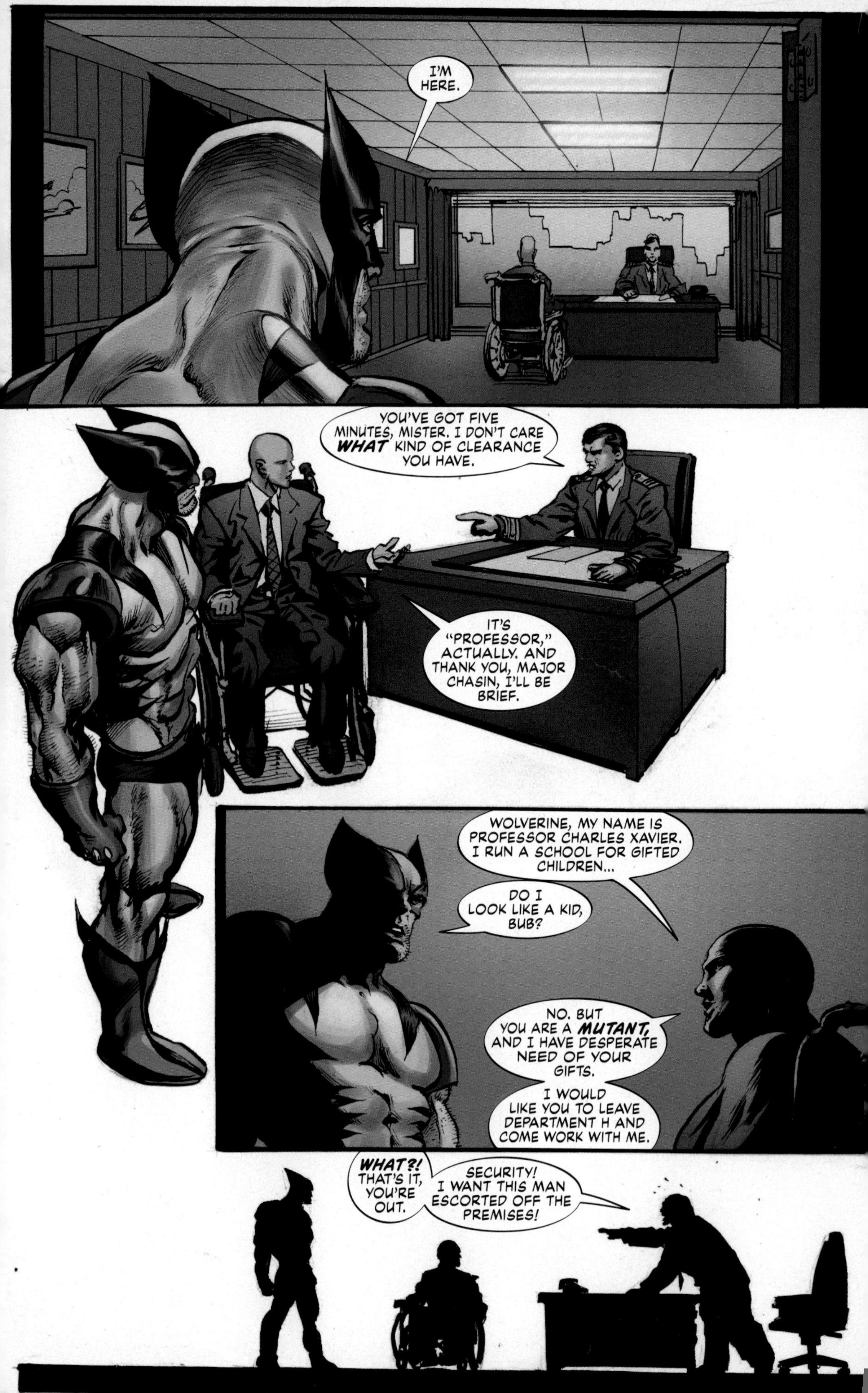
I'M HERE.
YOU'VE GOT FIVE MINUTES, MISTER. I DON'T CARE **WHAT** KIND OF CLEARANCE YOU HAVE.
IT'S "PROFESSOR," ACTUALLY. AND THANK YOU, MAJOR CHASIN, I'LL BE BRIEF.
WOLVERINE, MY NAME IS PROFESSOR CHARLES XAVIER. I RUN A SCHOOL FOR GIFTED CHILDREN...
DO I LOOK LIKE A KID, BUB?
NO. BUT YOU ARE A **MUTANT,** AND I HAVE DESPERATE NEED OF YOUR GIFTS.
I WOULD LIKE YOU TO LEAVE DEPARTMENT H AND COME WORK WITH ME.
**WHAT?!** THAT'S IT, YOU'RE OUT.
SECURITY! I WANT THIS MAN ESCORTED OFF THE PREMISES!

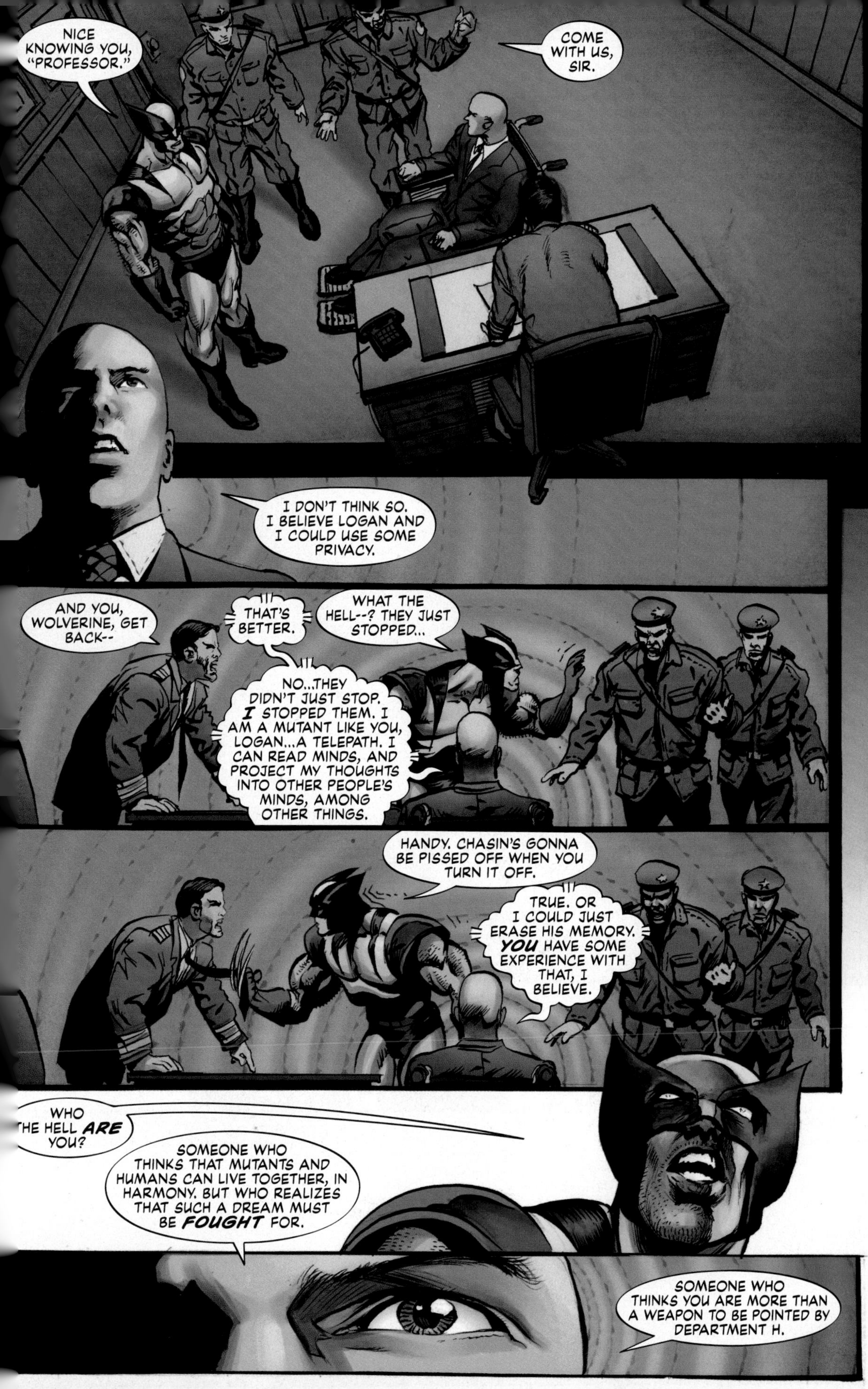
NICE KNOWING YOU, "PROFESSOR."
COME WITH US, SIR.
I DON'T THINK SO. I BELIEVE LOGAN AND I COULD USE SOME PRIVACY.
AND YOU, WOLVERINE, GET BACK--
THAT'S BETTER.
WHAT THE HELL--? THEY JUST STOPPED...
NO...THEY DIDN'T JUST STOP. I STOPPED THEM. I AM A MUTANT LIKE YOU, LOGAN...A TELEPATH. I CAN READ MINDS, AND PROJECT MY THOUGHTS INTO OTHER PEOPLE'S MINDS, AMONG OTHER THINGS.
HANDY. CHASIN'S GONNA BE PISSED OFF WHEN YOU TURN IT OFF.
TRUE. OR I COULD JUST ERASE HIS MEMORY. YOU HAVE SOME EXPERIENCE WITH THAT, I BELIEVE.
WHO THE HELL ARE YOU?
SOMEONE WHO THINKS THAT MUTANTS AND HUMANS CAN LIVE TOGETHER, IN HARMONY. BUT WHO REALIZES THAT SUCH A DREAM MUST BE FOUGHT FOR.
SOMEONE WHO THINKS YOU ARE MORE THAN A WEAPON TO BE POINTED BY DEPARTMENT H.

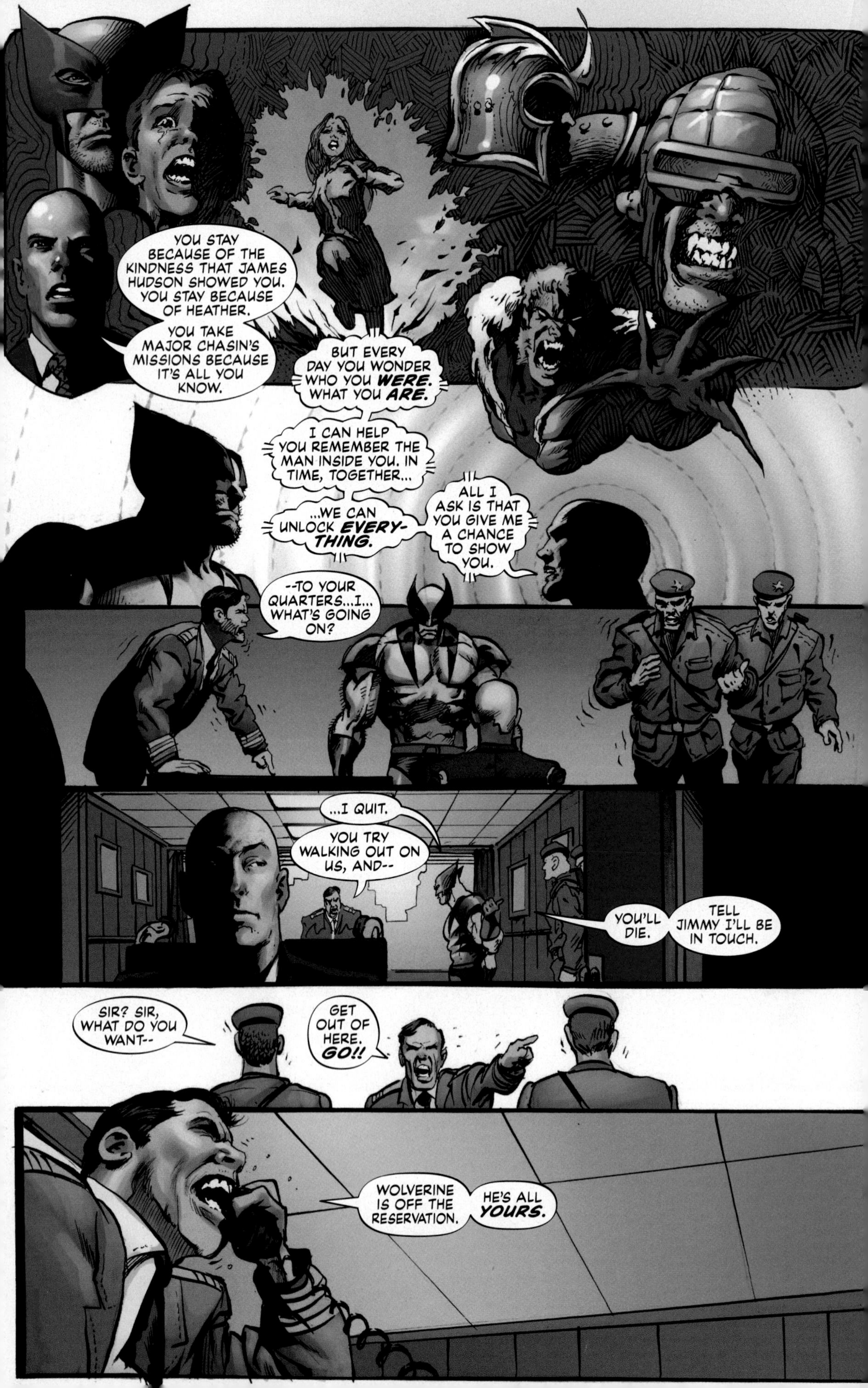
YOU STAY BECAUSE OF THE KINDNESS THAT JAMES HUDSON SHOWED YOU. YOU STAY BECAUSE OF HEATHER.
YOU TAKE MAJOR CHASIN'S MISSIONS BECAUSE IT'S ALL YOU KNOW.
BUT EVERY DAY YOU WONDER WHO YOU WERE. WHAT YOU ARE.
I CAN HELP YOU REMEMBER THE MAN INSIDE YOU. IN TIME, TOGETHER...
...WE CAN UNLOCK EVERYTHING.
ALL I ASK IS THAT YOU GIVE ME A CHANCE TO SHOW YOU.
--TO YOUR QUARTERS...I... WHAT'S GOING ON?
...I QUIT.
YOU TRY WALKING OUT ON US, AND--
YOU'LL DIE.
TELL JIMMY I'LL BE IN TOUCH.
SIR? SIR, WHAT DO YOU WANT--
GET OUT OF HERE. GO!!
WOLVERINE IS OFF THE RESERVATION.
HE'S ALL YOURS.

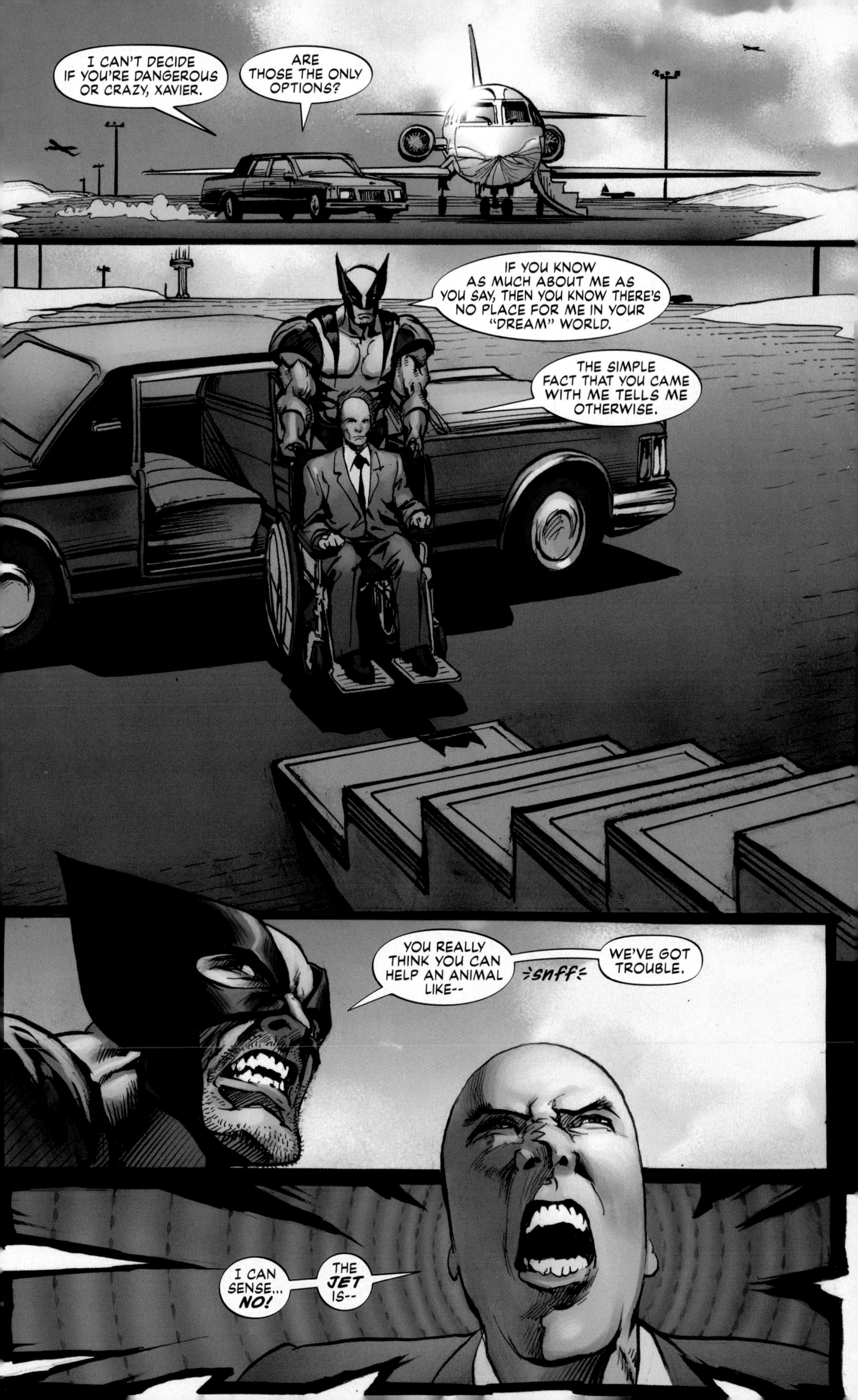
I CAN'T DECIDE IF YOU'RE DANGEROUS OR CRAZY, XAVIER.
ARE THOSE THE ONLY OPTIONS?
IF YOU KNOW AS MUCH ABOUT ME AS YOU SAY, THEN YOU KNOW THERE'S NO PLACE FOR ME IN YOUR "DREAM" WORLD.
THE SIMPLE FACT THAT YOU CAME WITH ME TELLS ME OTHERWISE.
YOU REALLY THINK YOU CAN HELP AN ANIMAL LIKE--
snff
WE'VE GOT TROUBLE.
I CAN SENSE... NO!
THE JET IS--

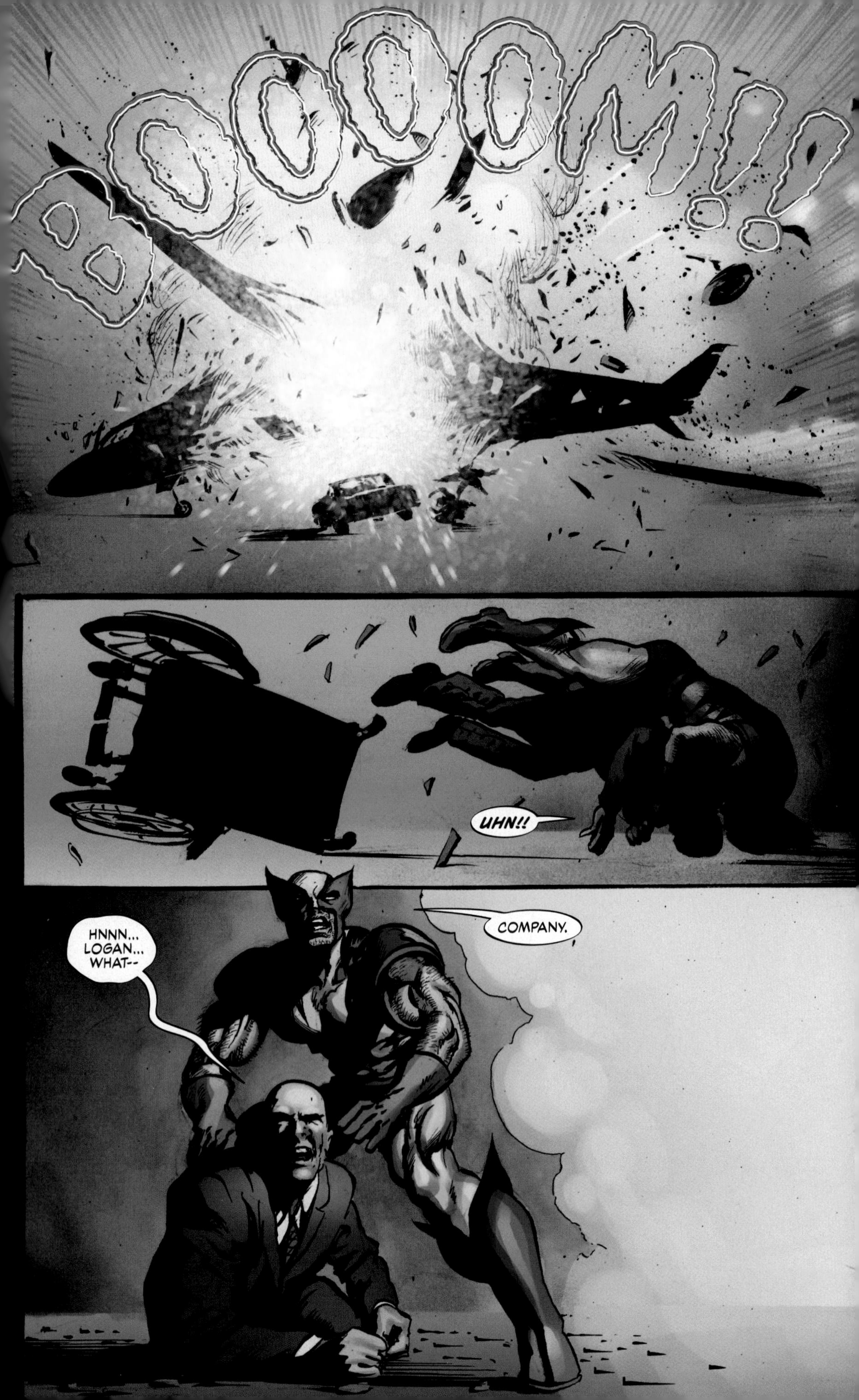
BOOOOOM!!
UHN!!
HNNN... LOGAN... WHAT--
COMPANY.

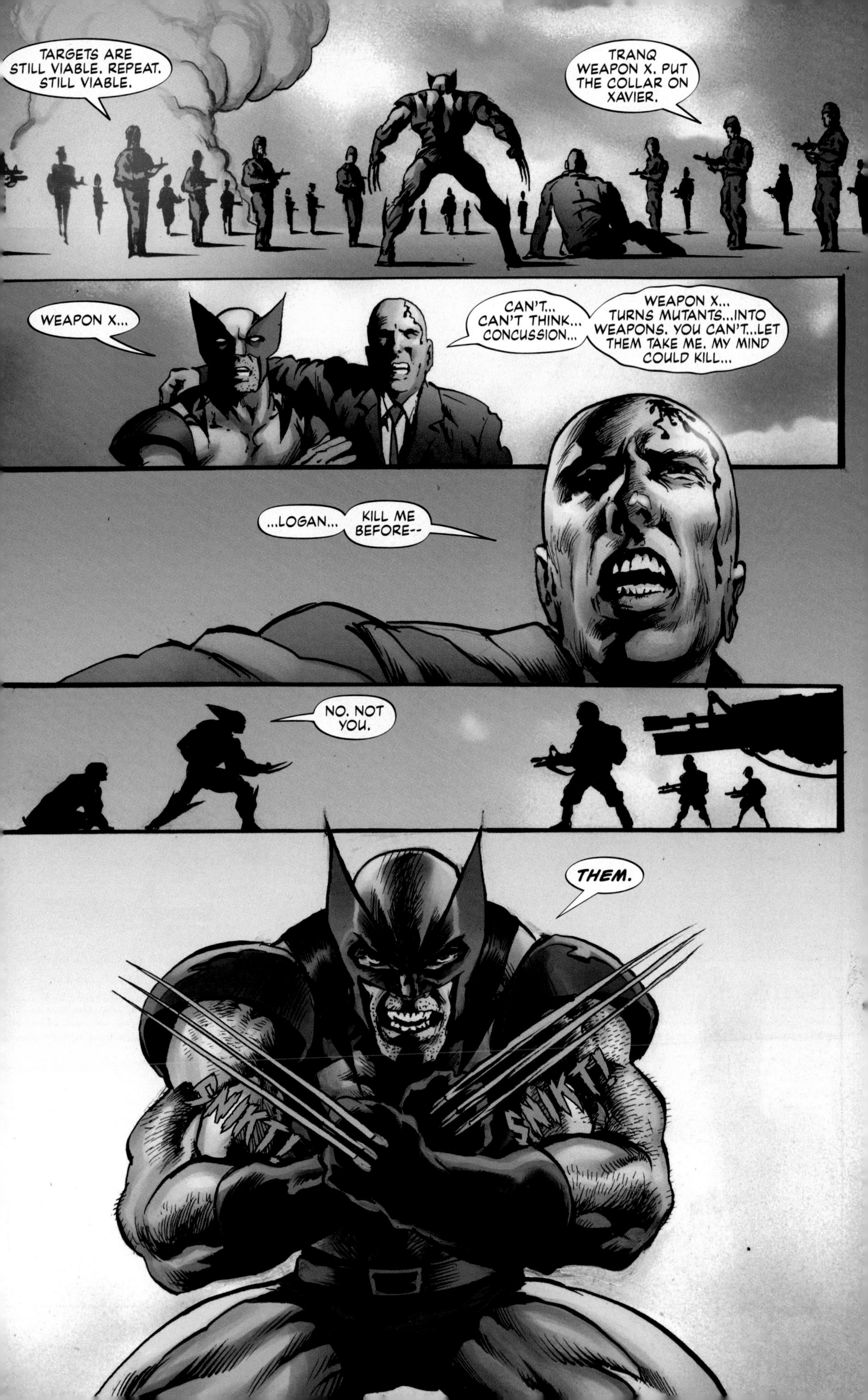
TARGETS ARE STILL VIABLE. REPEAT. STILL VIABLE.
TRANQ WEAPON X. PUT THE COLLAR ON XAVIER.
WEAPON X...
CAN'T... CAN'T THINK... CONCUSSION...
WEAPON X... TURNS MUTANTS...INTO WEAPONS. YOU CAN'T...LET THEM TAKE ME. MY MIND COULD KILL...
...LOGAN...
KILL ME BEFORE--
NO. NOT YOU.
THEM.
SNIKT!
SNIKT!

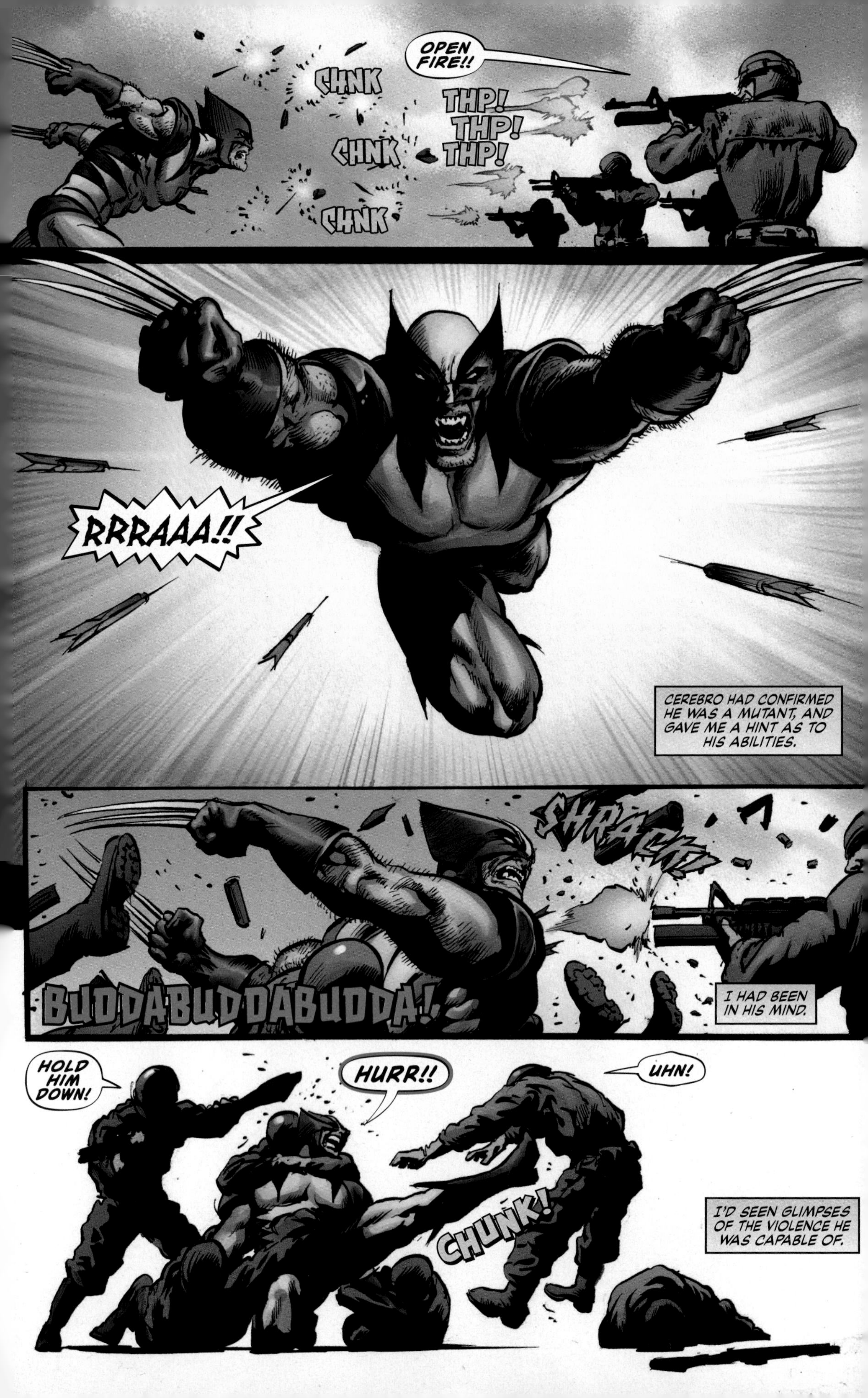
OPEN FIRE!!
CHNK
CHNK
CHNK
THP!
THP!
THP!
RRRAAA!!
CEREBRO HAD CONFIRMED HE WAS A MUTANT, AND GAVE ME A HINT AS TO HIS ABILITIES.
SHRACK!!
BUDDABUDDABUDDA!!
I HAD BEEN IN HIS MIND.
HOLD HIM DOWN!
HURR!!
UHN!
CHUNK!
I'D SEEN GLIMPSES OF THE VIOLENCE HE WAS CAPABLE OF.

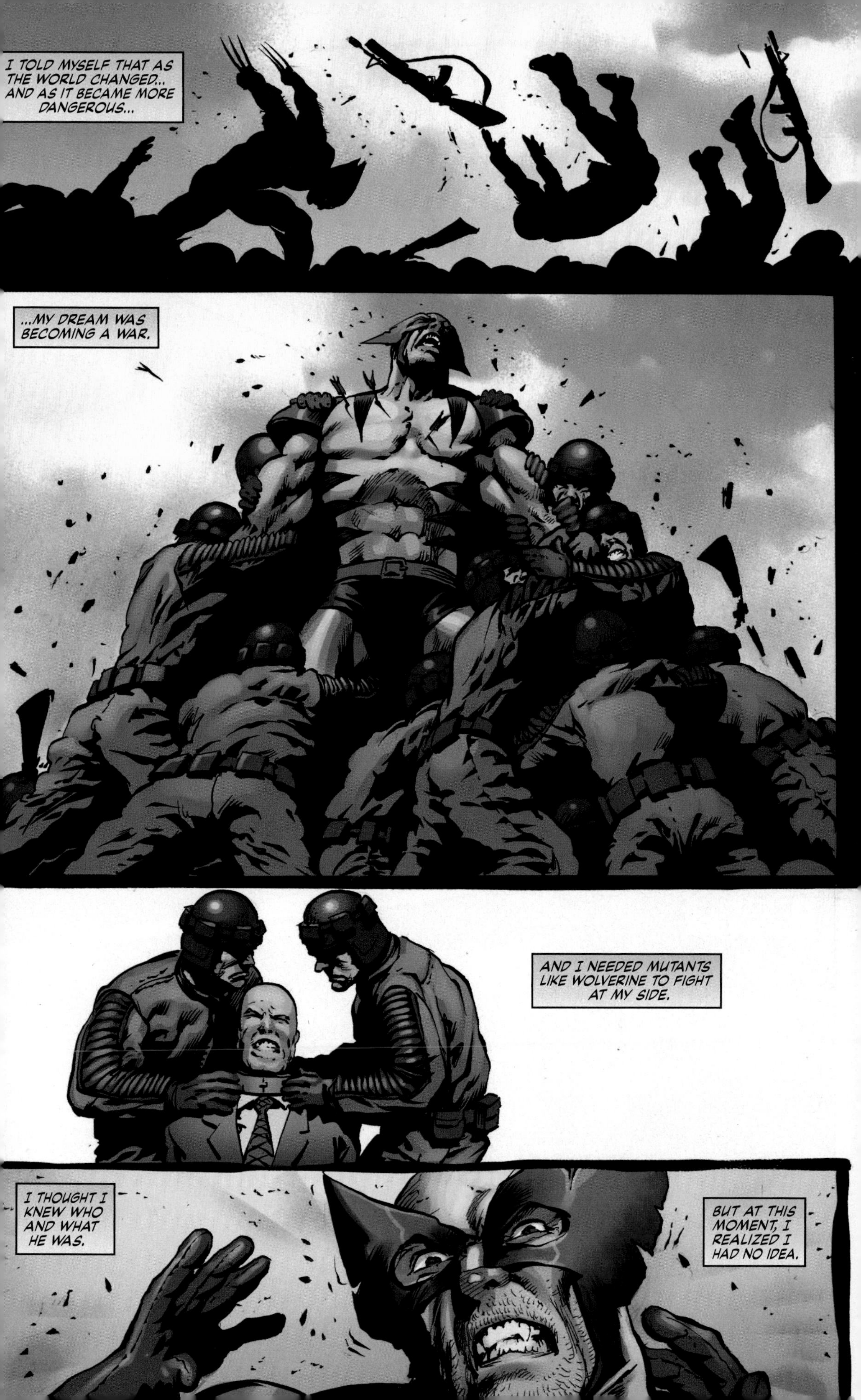
I TOLD MYSELF THAT AS THE WORLD CHANGED... AND AS IT BECAME MORE DANGEROUS...
...MY DREAM WAS BECOMING A WAR.
AND I NEEDED MUTANTS LIKE WOLVERINE TO FIGHT AT MY SIDE.
I THOUGHT I KNEW WHO AND WHAT HE WAS.
BUT AT THIS MOMENT, I REALIZED I HAD NO IDEA.

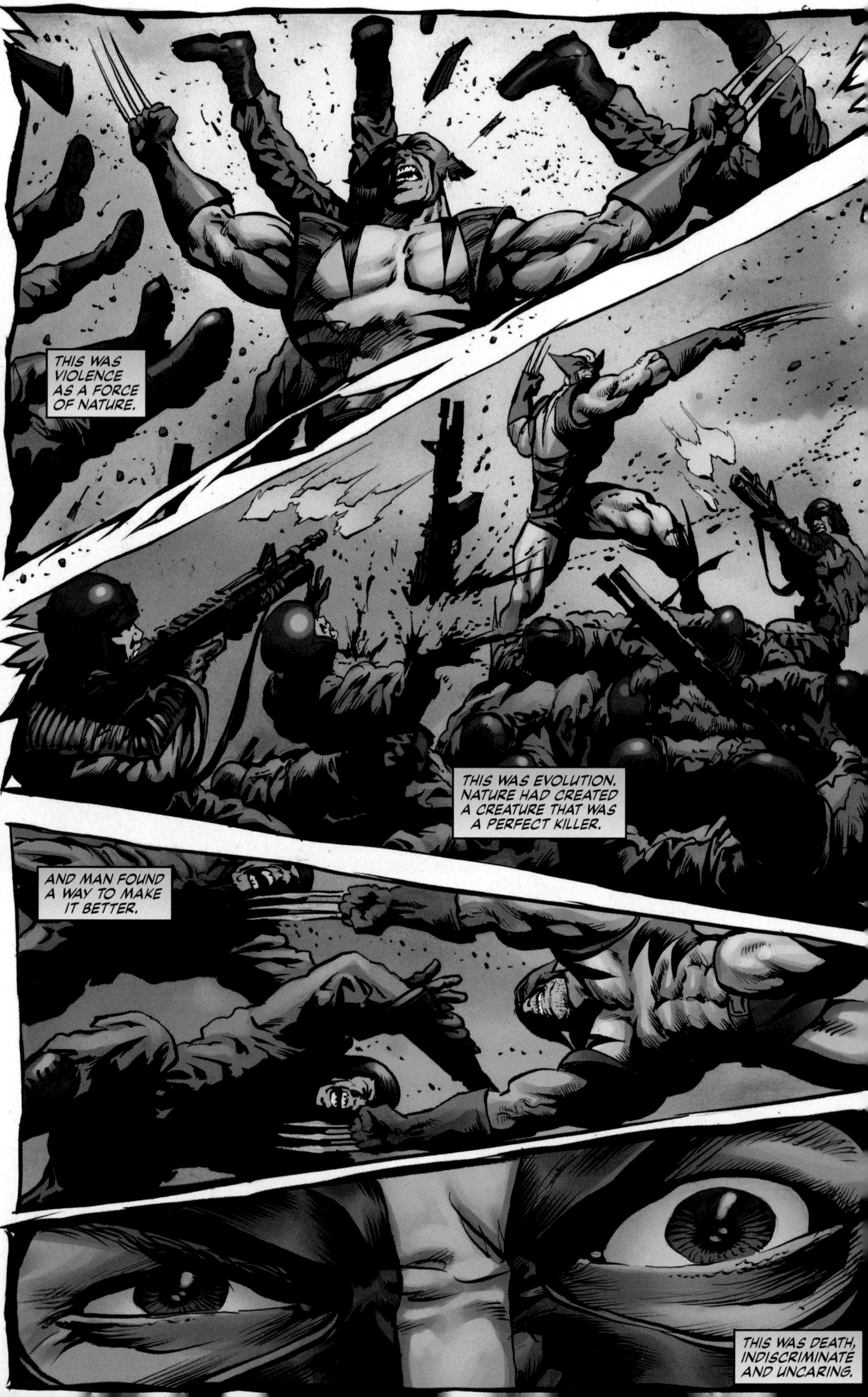
THIS WAS VIOLENCE AS A FORCE OF NATURE.
THIS WAS EVOLUTION. NATURE HAD CREATED A CREATURE THAT WAS A PERFECT KILLER.
AND MAN FOUND A WAY TO MAKE IT BETTER.
THIS WAS DEATH, INDISCRIMINATE AND UNCARING.

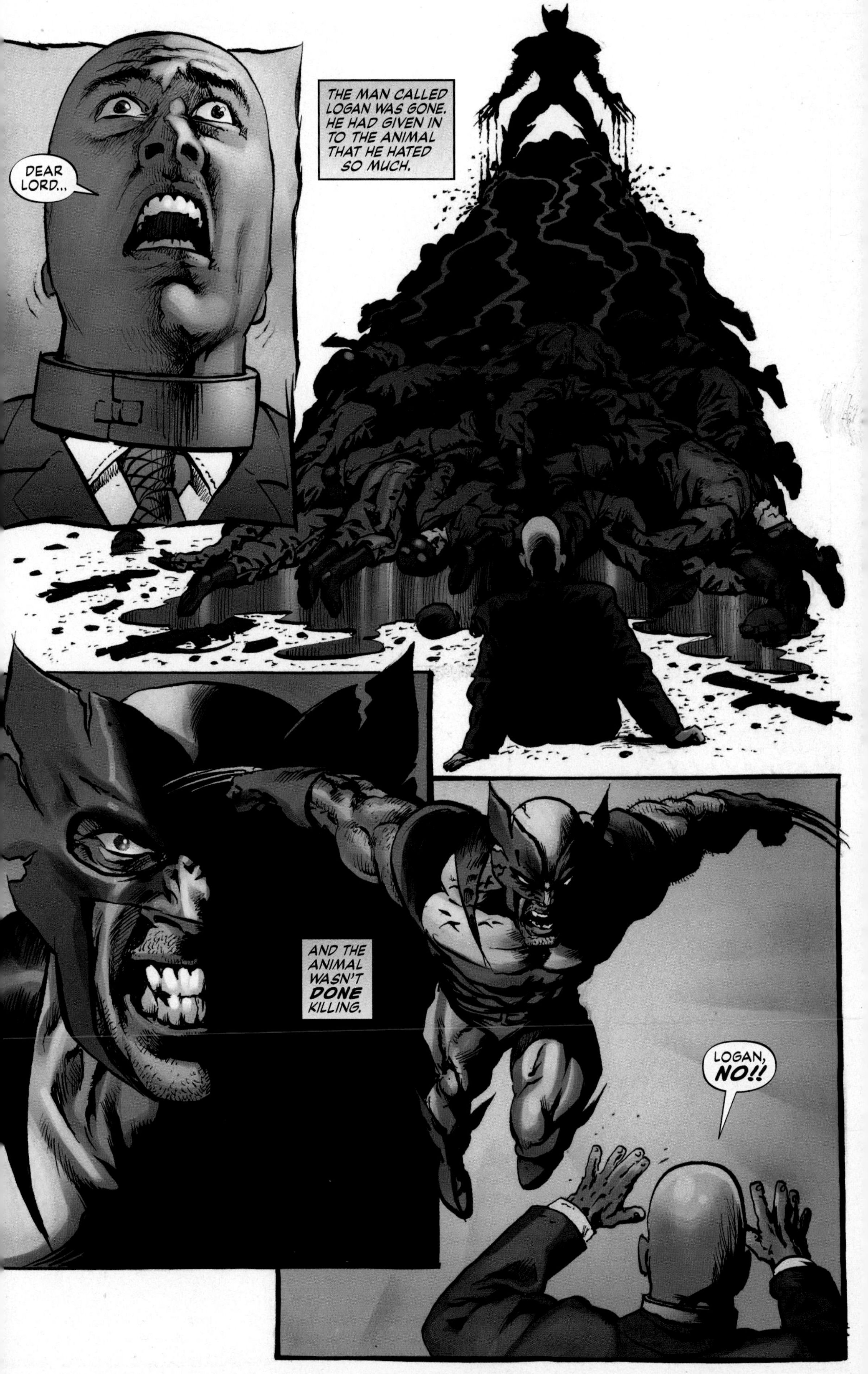
DEAR LORD...
THE MAN CALLED LOGAN WAS GONE. HE HAD GIVEN IN TO THE ANIMAL THAT HE HATED SO MUCH.
AND THE ANIMAL WASN'T **DONE** KILLING.
LOGAN, **NO!!**

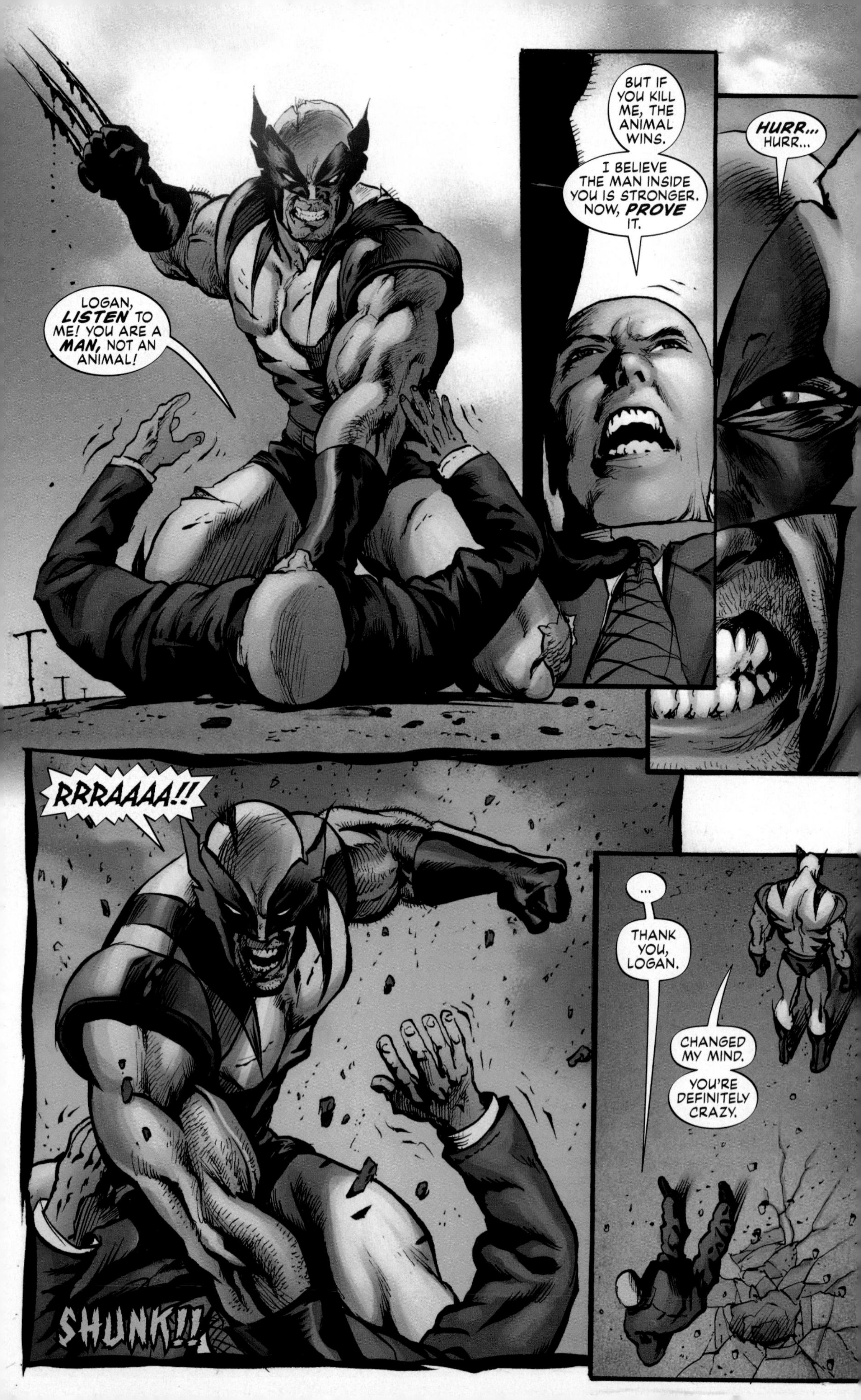
LOGAN, LISTEN TO ME! YOU ARE A MAN, NOT AN ANIMAL!
BUT IF YOU KILL ME, THE ANIMAL WINS.
I BELIEVE THE MAN INSIDE YOU IS STRONGER. NOW, PROVE IT.
HURR... HURR...
RRRAAAA!!
SHUNK!!
...
THANK YOU, LOGAN.
CHANGED MY MIND.
YOU'RE DEFINITELY CRAZY.

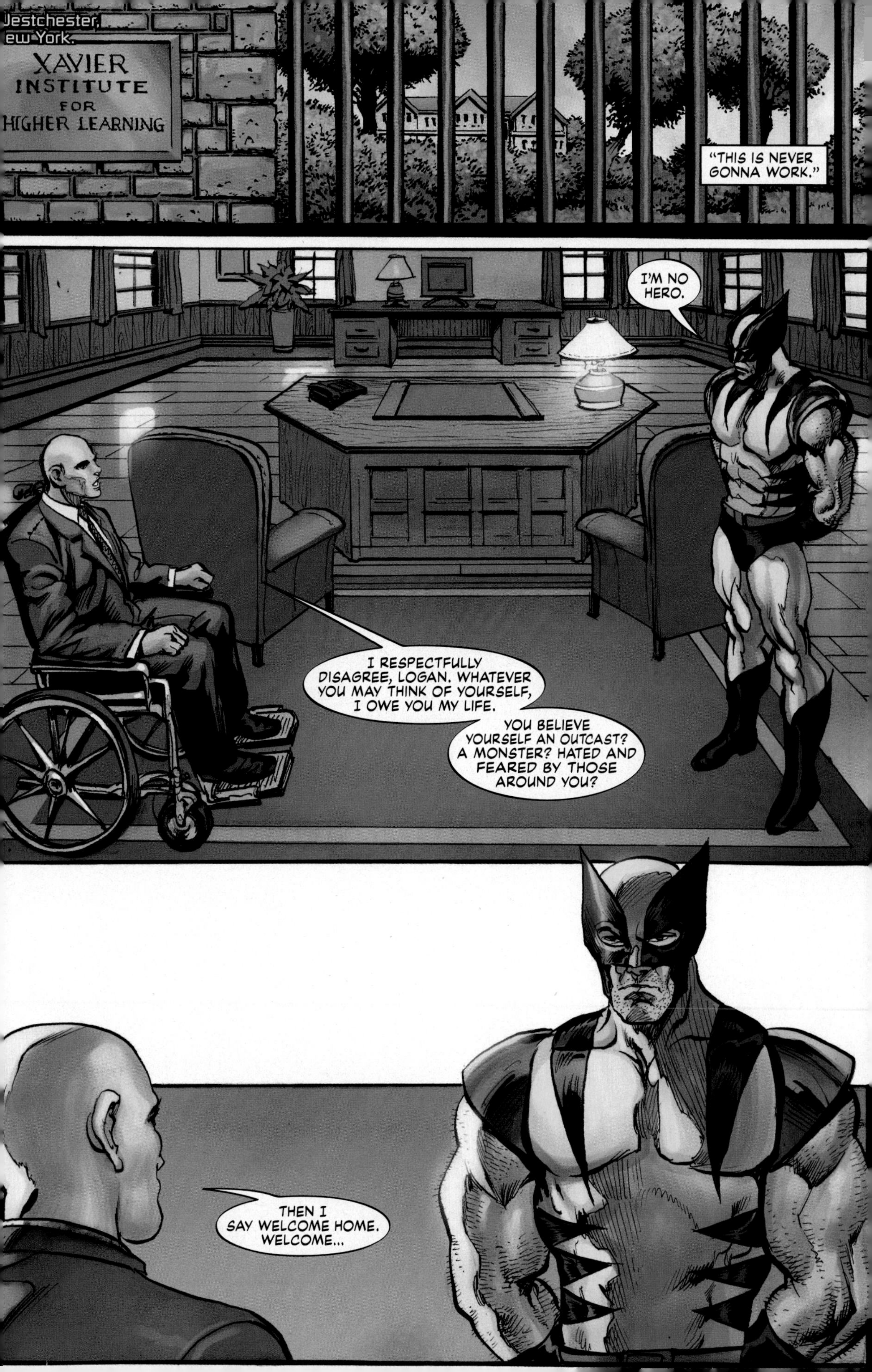

Jestchester,
ew York.
XAVIER INSTITUTE FOR HIGHER LEARNING
"THIS IS NEVER GONNA WORK."
I'M NO HERO.
I RESPECTFULLY DISAGREE, LOGAN. WHATEVER YOU MAY THINK OF YOURSELF, I OWE YOU MY LIFE.
YOU BELIEVE YOURSELF AN OUTCAST? A MONSTER? HATED AND FEARED BY THOSE AROUND YOU?
THEN I SAY WELCOME HOME. WELCOME...

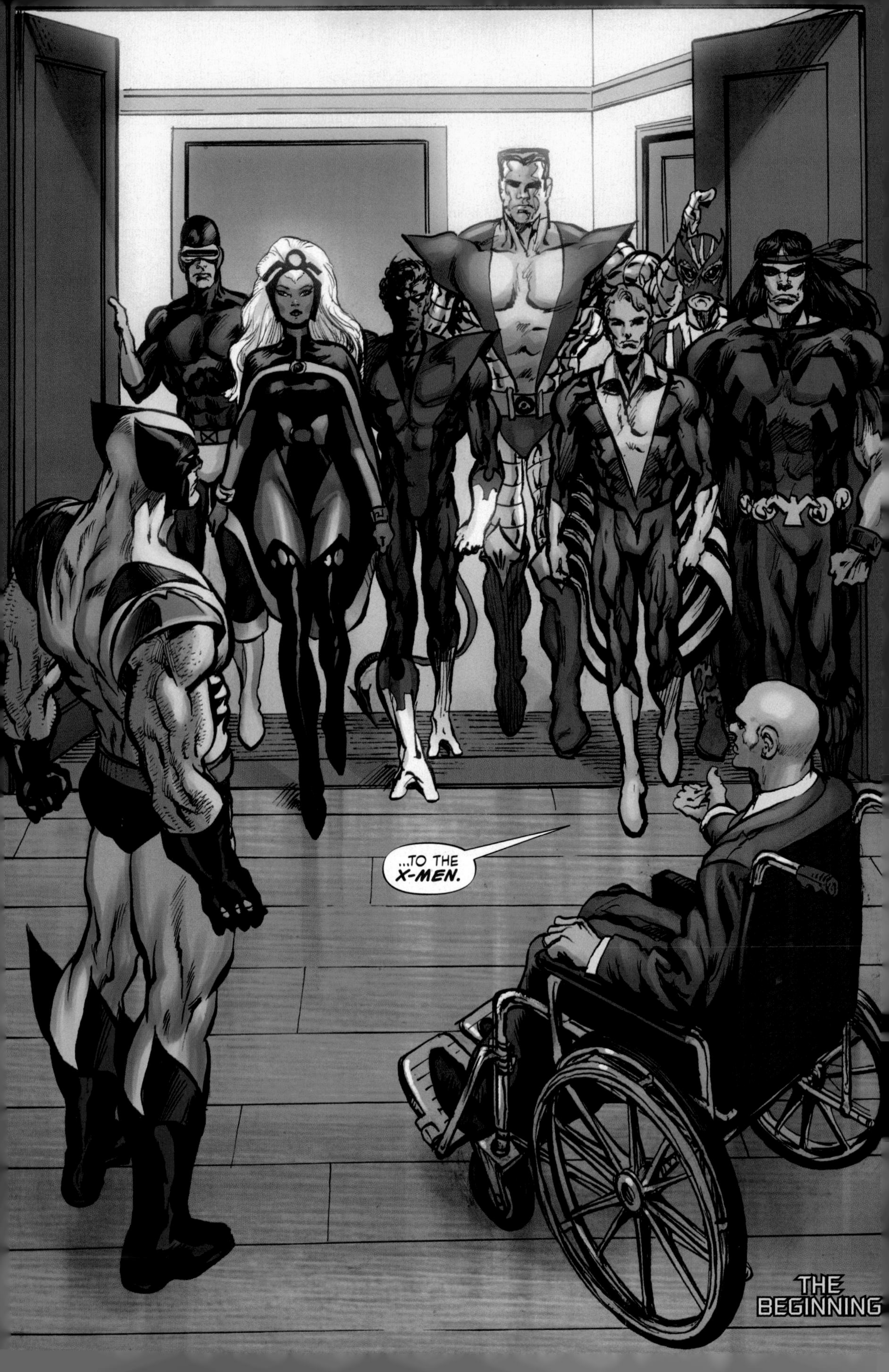
...TO THE X-MEN.
THE BEGINNING

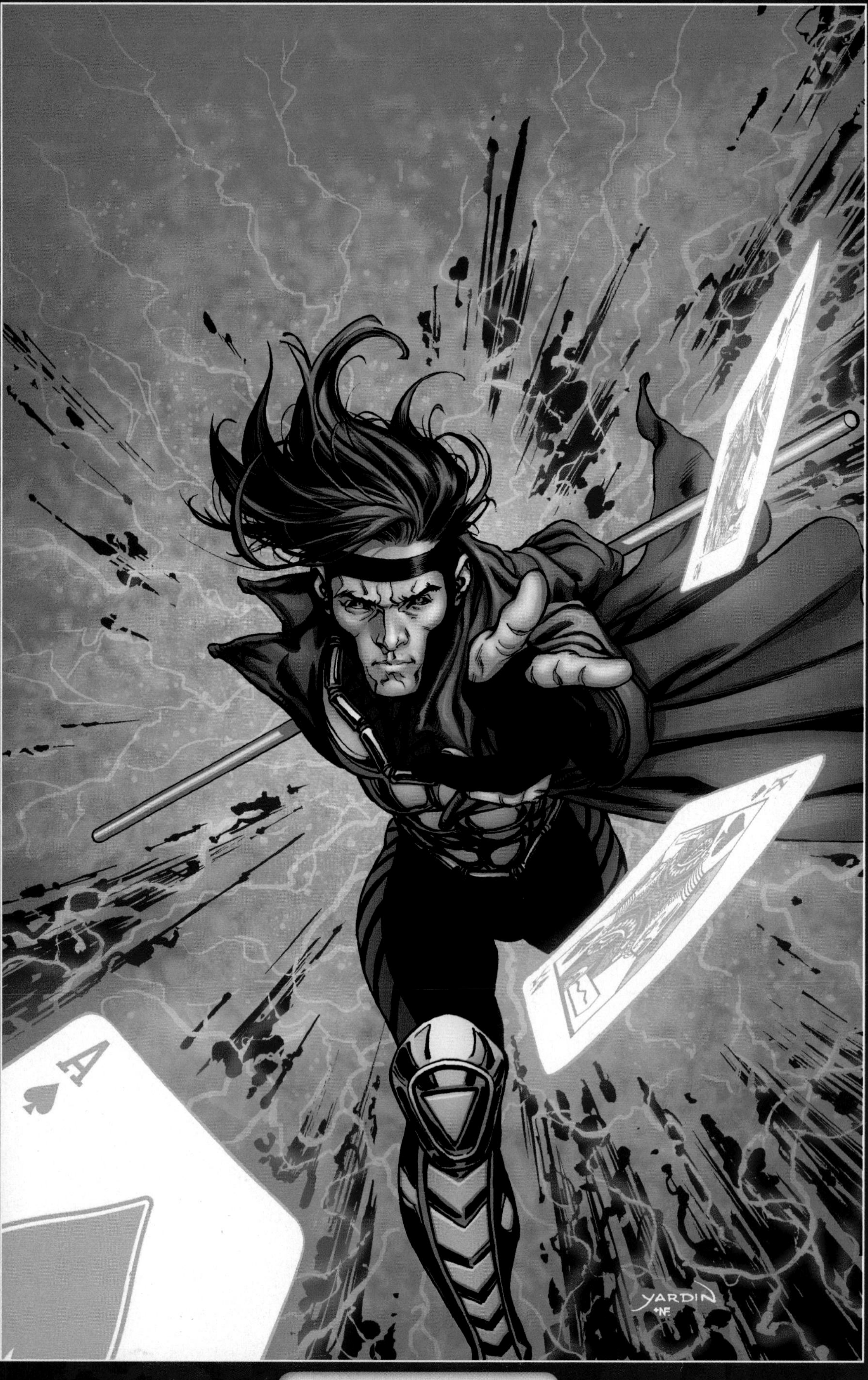
YARDIN
+NF

X-MEN ORIGINS: GAMBIT

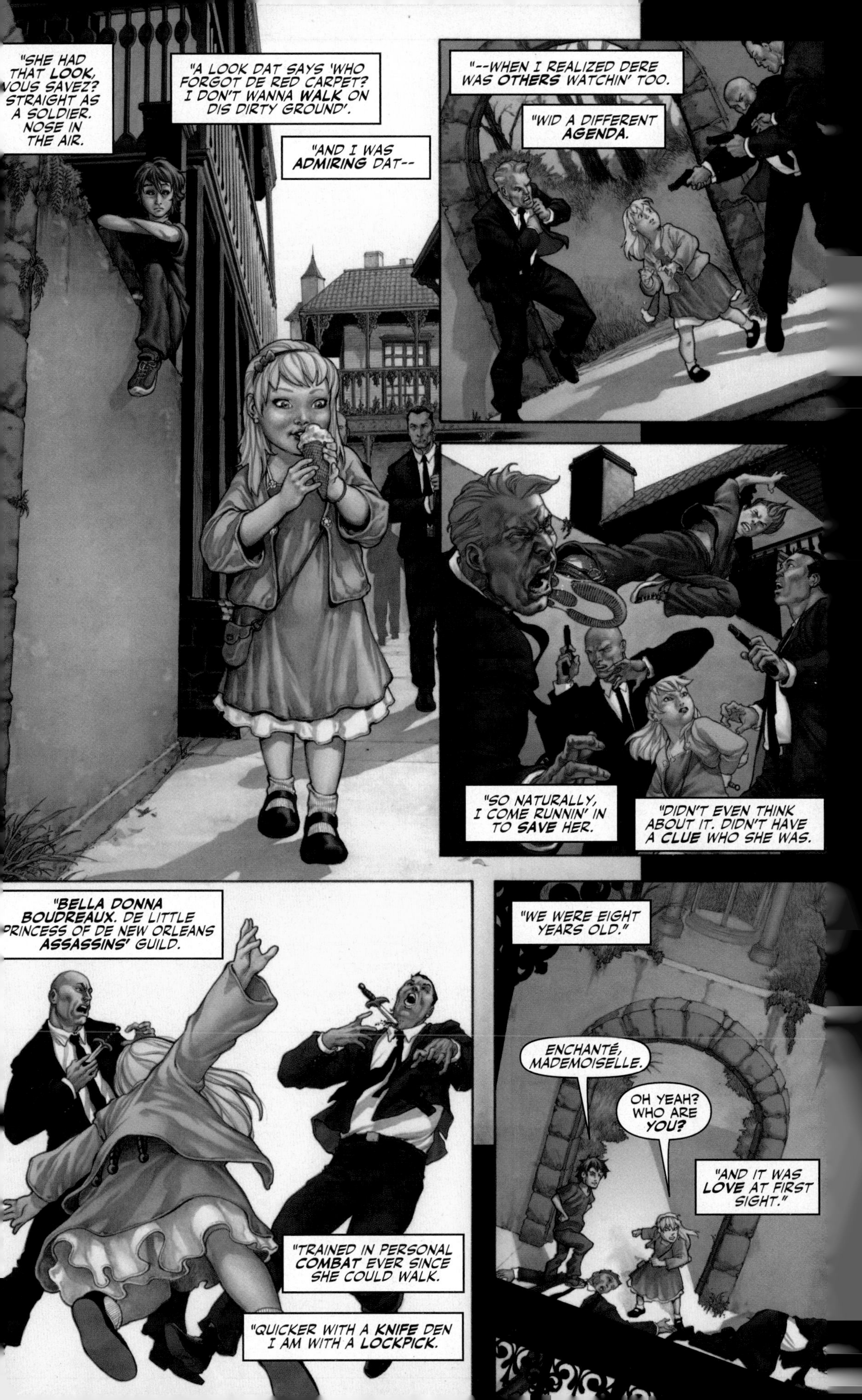
"SHE HAD THAT LOOK, VOUS SAVEZ? STRAIGHT AS A SOLDIER. NOSE IN THE AIR.
"A LOOK DAT SAYS 'WHO FORGOT DE RED CARPET? I DON'T WANNA WALK ON DIS DIRTY GROUND'.
"AND I WAS ADMIRING DAT--
"--WHEN I REALIZED DERE WAS OTHERS WATCHIN' TOO.
"WID A DIFFERENT AGENDA.
"SO NATURALLY, I COME RUNNIN' IN TO SAVE HER.
"DIDN'T EVEN THINK ABOUT IT. DIDN'T HAVE A CLUE WHO SHE WAS.
"BELLA DONNA BOUDREAUX. DE LITTLE PRINCESS OF DE NEW ORLEANS ASSASSINS' GUILD.
"TRAINED IN PERSONAL COMBAT EVER SINCE SHE COULD WALK.
"QUICKER WITH A KNIFE DEN I AM WITH A LOCKPICK.
"WE WERE EIGHT YEARS OLD."
ENCHANTÉ, MADEMOISELLE.
OH YEAH? WHO ARE YOU?
"AND IT WAS LOVE AT FIRST SIGHT."

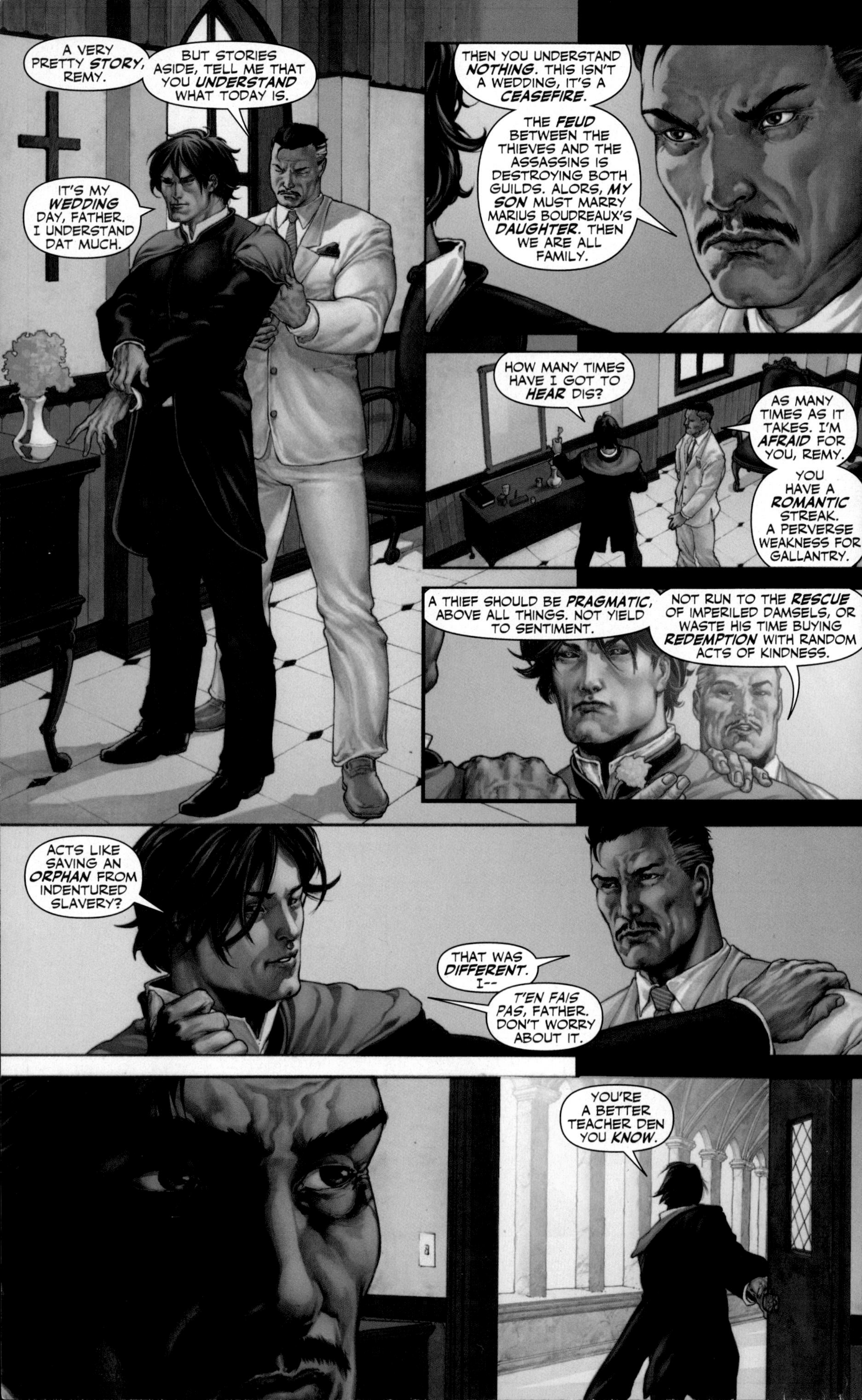
A VERY PRETTY STORY, REMY.
BUT STORIES ASIDE, TELL ME THAT YOU UNDERSTAND WHAT TODAY IS.
IT'S MY WEDDING DAY, FATHER. I UNDERSTAND DAT MUCH.
THEN YOU UNDERSTAND NOTHING. THIS ISN'T A WEDDING, IT'S A CEASEFIRE.
THE FEUD BETWEEN THE THIEVES AND THE ASSASSINS IS DESTROYING BOTH GUILDS. ALORS, MY SON MUST MARRY MARIUS BOUDREAUX'S DAUGHTER. THEN WE ARE ALL FAMILY.
HOW MANY TIMES HAVE I GOT TO HEAR DIS?
AS MANY TIMES AS IT TAKES. I'M AFRAID FOR YOU, REMY.
YOU HAVE A ROMANTIC STREAK. A PERVERSE WEAKNESS FOR GALLANTRY.
A THIEF SHOULD BE PRAGMATIC, ABOVE ALL THINGS. NOT YIELD TO SENTIMENT.
NOT RUN TO THE RESCUE OF IMPERILED DAMSELS, OR WASTE HIS TIME BUYING REDEMPTION WITH RANDOM ACTS OF KINDNESS.
ACTS LIKE SAVING AN ORPHAN FROM INDENTURED SLAVERY?
THAT WAS DIFFERENT. I--
T'EN FAIS PAS, FATHER. DON'T WORRY ABOUT IT.
YOU'RE A BETTER TEACHER DEN YOU KNOW.

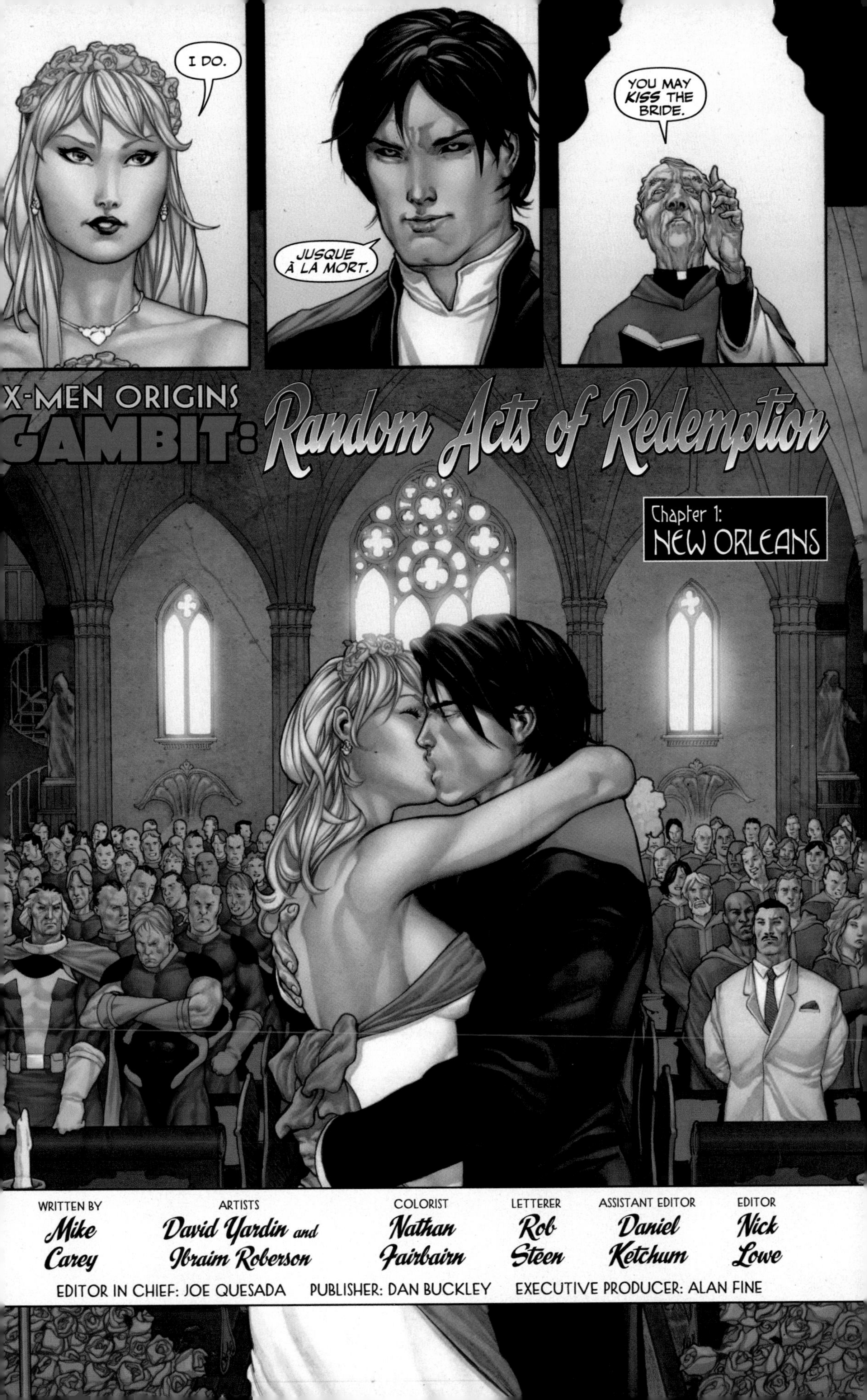
I DO.
JUSQUE À LA MORT.
YOU MAY KISS THE BRIDE.
X-MEN ORIGINS
GAMBIT: Random Acts of Redemption
Chapter 1: NEW ORLEANS
WRITTEN BY Mike Carey
ARTISTS David Yardin and Ibraim Roberson
COLORIST Nathan Fairbairn
LETTERER Rob Steen
ASSISTANT EDITOR Daniel Ketchum
EDITOR Nick Lowe
EDITOR IN CHIEF: JOE QUESADA PUBLISHER: DAN BUCKLEY EXECUTIVE PRODUCER: ALAN FINE

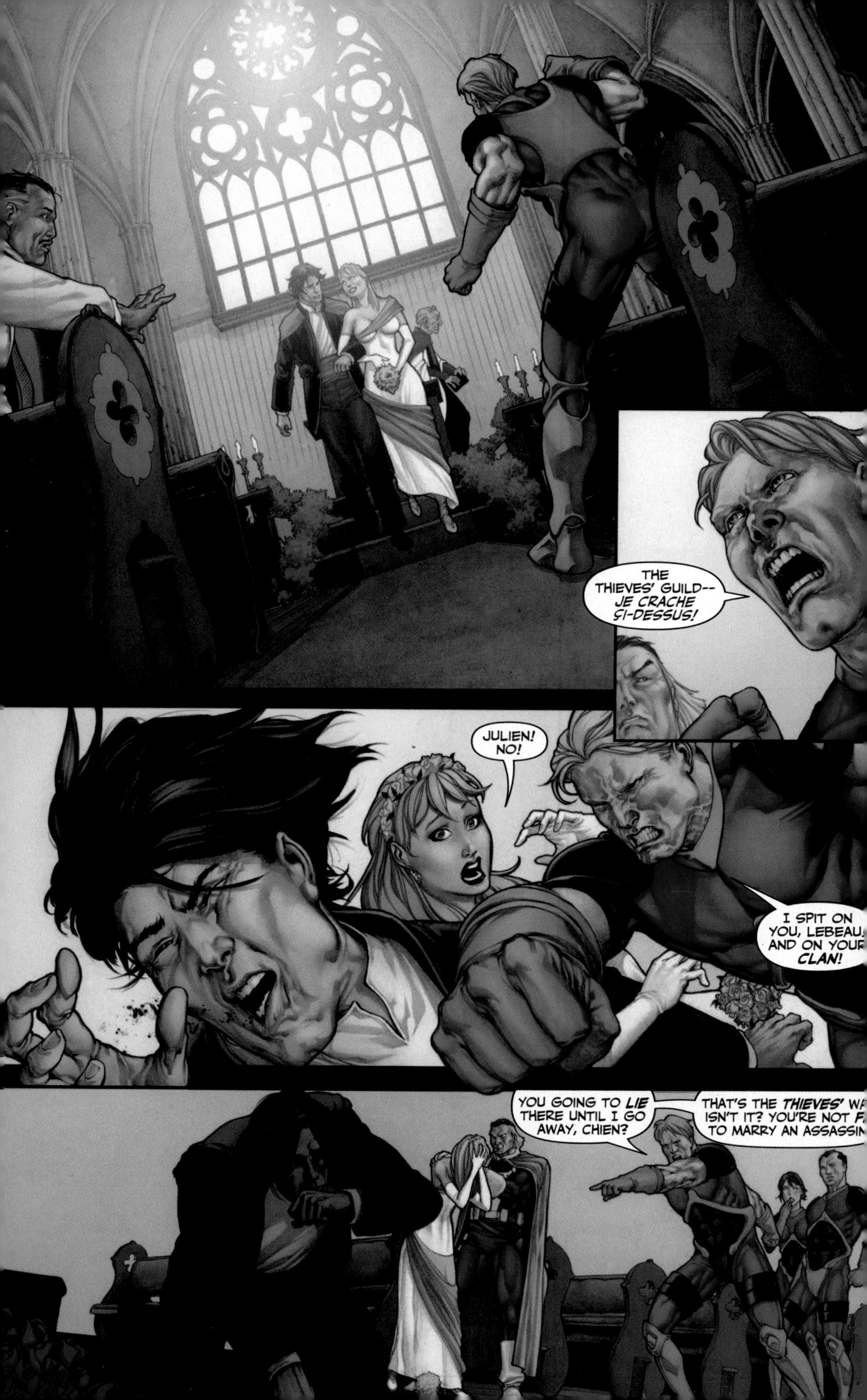
THE THIEVES' GUILD-- JE CRACHE ÇI-DESSUS!
JULIEN! NO!
I SPIT ON YOU, LEBEAU. AND ON YOUR CLAN!
YOU GOING TO LIE THERE UNTIL I GO AWAY, CHIEN?

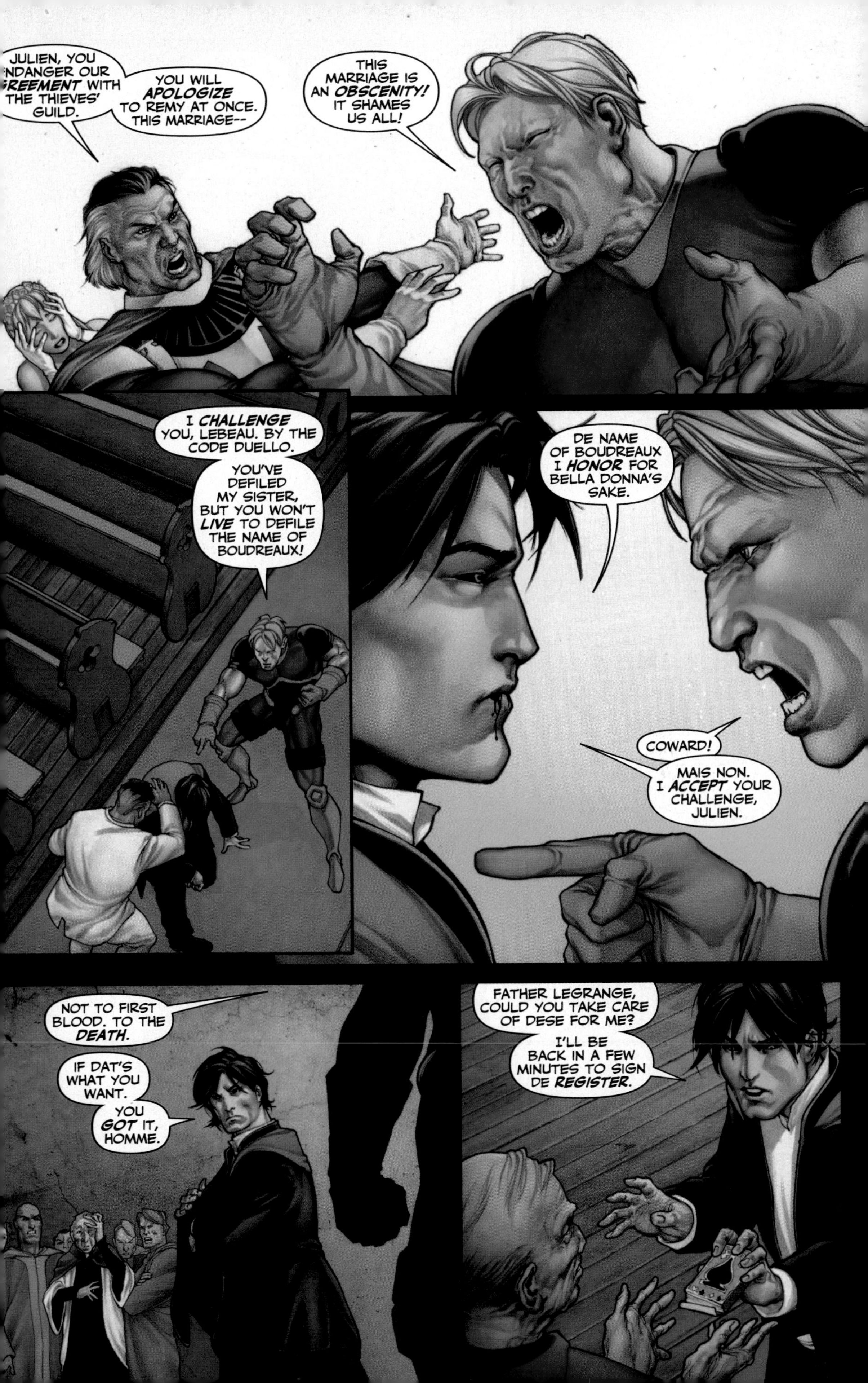
JULIEN, YOU ENDANGER OUR AGREEMENT WITH THE THIEVES' GUILD.
YOU WILL APOLOGIZE TO REMY AT ONCE. THIS MARRIAGE--
THIS MARRIAGE IS AN OBSCENITY! IT SHAMES US ALL!
I CHALLENGE YOU, LEBEAU. BY THE CODE DUELLO.
YOU'VE DEFILED MY SISTER, BUT YOU WON'T LIVE TO DEFILE THE NAME OF BOUDREAUX!
DE NAME OF BOUDREAUX I HONOR FOR BELLA DONNA'S SAKE.
COWARD!
MAIS NON. I ACCEPT YOUR CHALLENGE, JULIEN.
NOT TO FIRST BLOOD. TO THE DEATH.
IF DAT'S WHAT YOU WANT.
YOU GOT IT, HOMME.
FATHER LEGRANGE, COULD YOU TAKE CARE OF DESE FOR ME?
I'LL BE BACK IN A FEW MINUTES TO SIGN DE REGISTER.

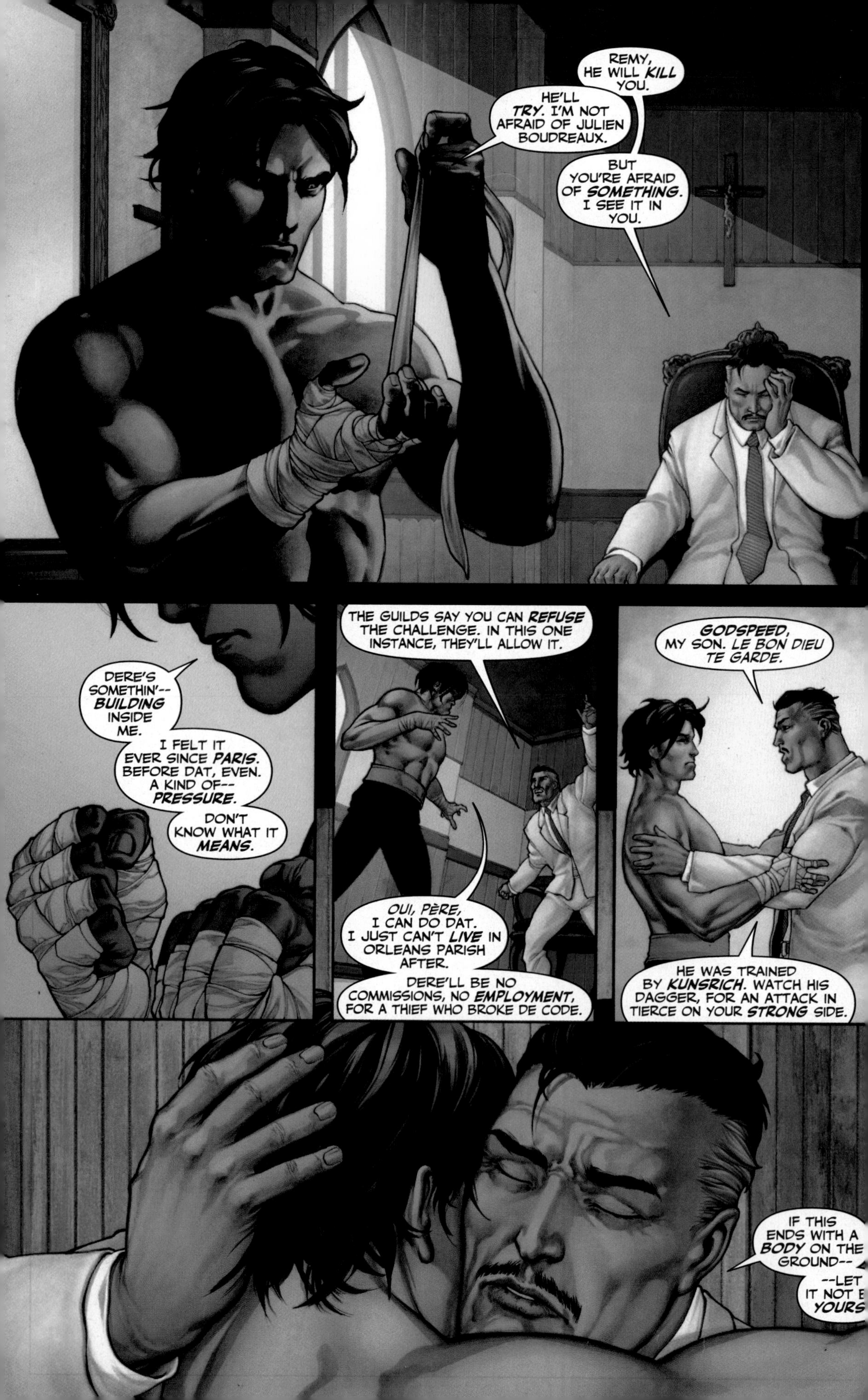
REMY, HE WILL KILL YOU.
HE'LL TRY. I'M NOT AFRAID OF JULIEN BOUDREAUX.
BUT YOU'RE AFRAID OF SOMETHING. I SEE IT IN YOU.
DERE'S SOMETHIN'-- BUILDING INSIDE ME.
I FELT IT EVER SINCE PARIS. BEFORE DAT, EVEN. A KIND OF-- PRESSURE.
DON'T KNOW WHAT IT MEANS.
THE GUILDS SAY YOU CAN REFUSE THE CHALLENGE. IN THIS ONE INSTANCE, THEY'LL ALLOW IT.
OUI, PÈRE, I CAN DO DAT. I JUST CAN'T LIVE IN ORLEANS PARISH AFTER.
DERE'LL BE NO COMMISSIONS, NO EMPLOYMENT, FOR A THIEF WHO BROKE DE CODE.
GODSPEED, MY SON. LE BON DIEU TE GARDE.
HE WAS TRAINED BY KUNSRICH. WATCH HIS DAGGER, FOR AN ATTACK IN TIERCE ON YOUR STRONG SIDE.
IF THIS ENDS WITH A BODY ON THE GROUND--
--LET IT NOT

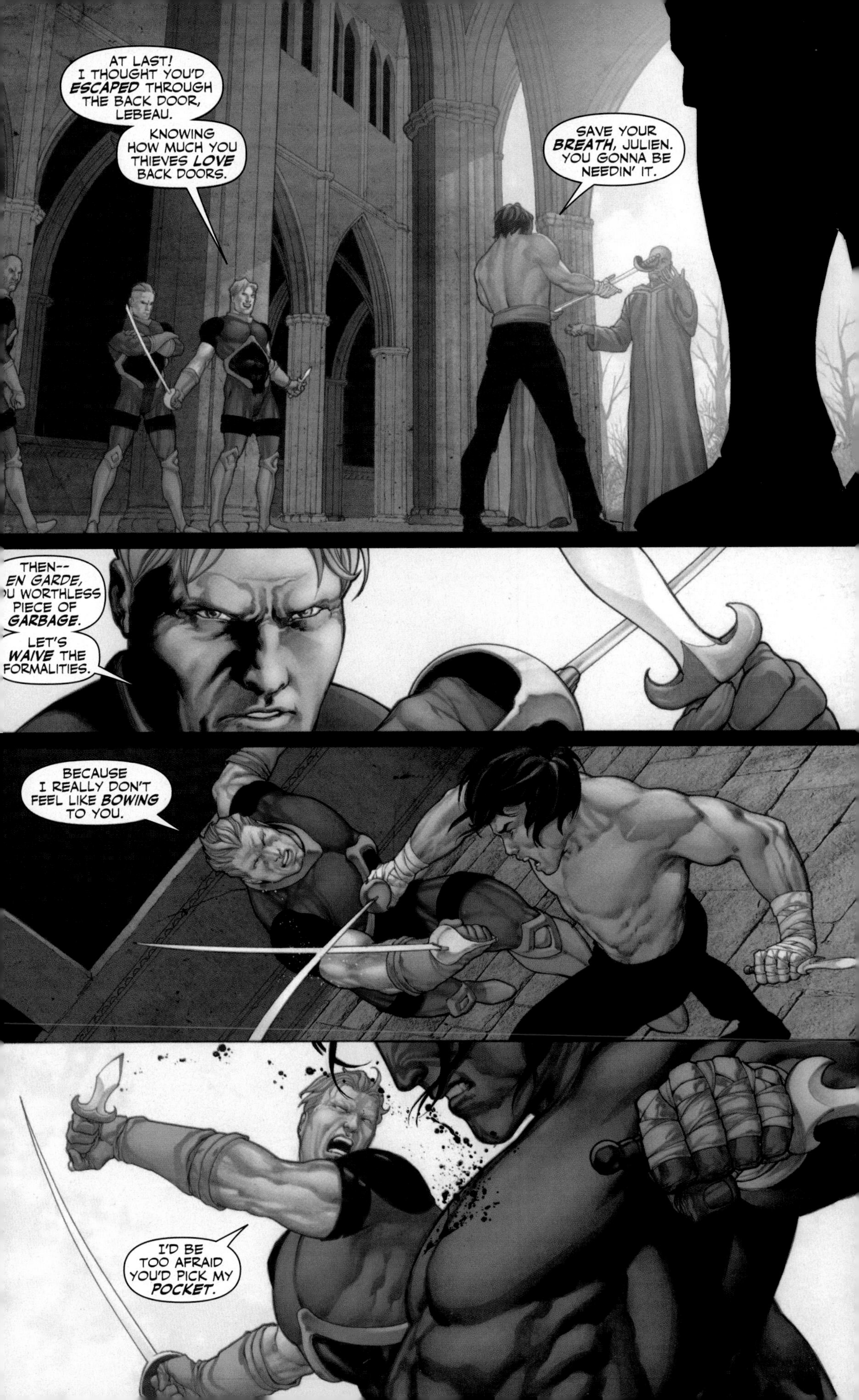

AT LAST! I THOUGHT YOU'D *ESCAPED* THROUGH THE BACK DOOR, LEBEAU.
KNOWING HOW MUCH YOU THIEVES *LOVE* BACK DOORS.
SAVE YOUR *BREATH*, JULIEN. YOU GONNA BE NEEDIN' IT.
THEN-- *EN GARDE*, YOU WORTHLESS PIECE OF *GARBAGE*.
LET'S *WAIVE* THE FORMALITIES.
BECAUSE I REALLY DON'T FEEL LIKE *BOWING* TO YOU.
I'D BE TOO AFRAID YOU'D PICK MY *POCKET*.

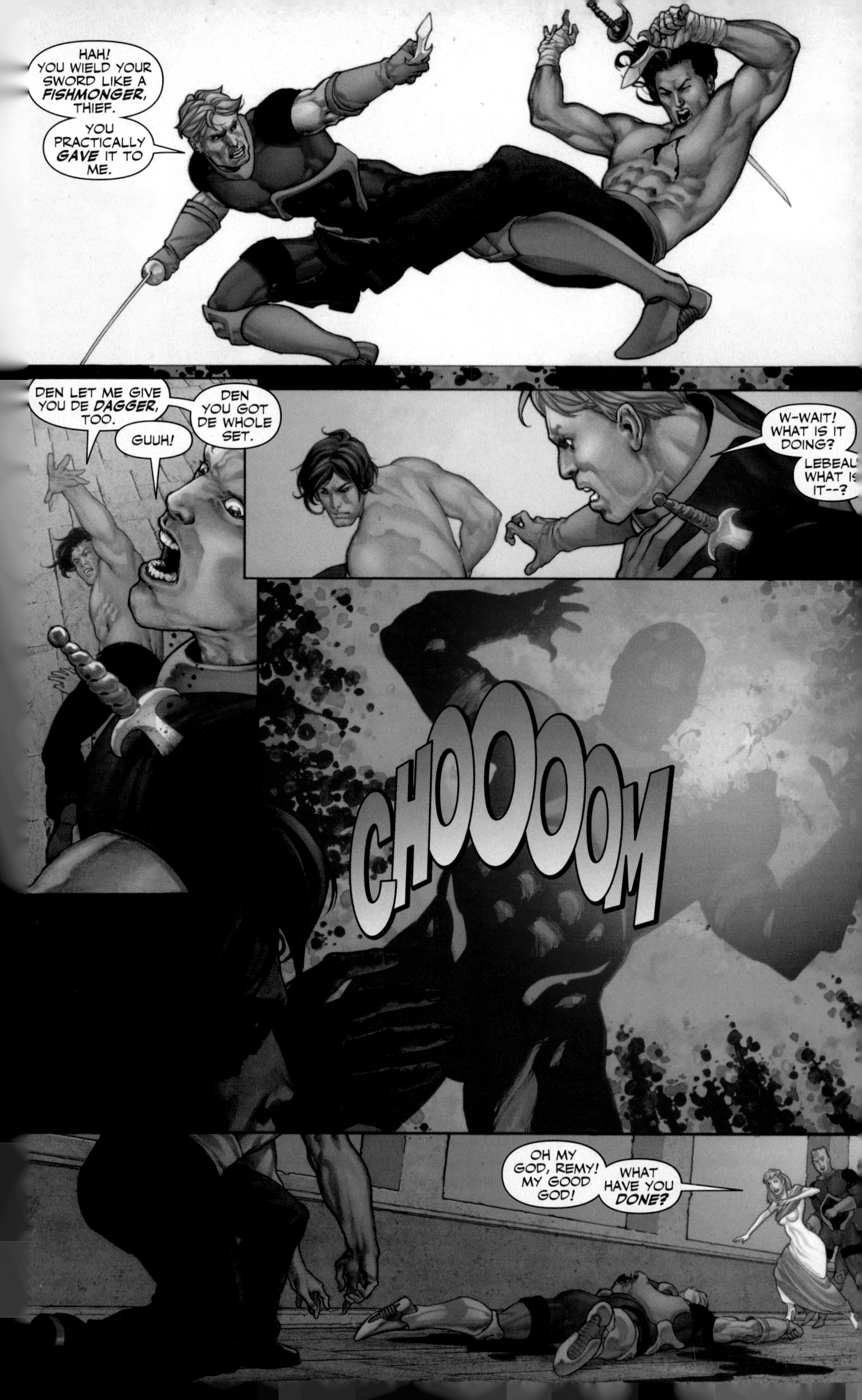
HAH! YOU WIELD YOUR SWORD LIKE A *FISHMONGER*, THIEF.
YOU PRACTICALLY *GAVE* IT TO ME.
DEN LET ME GIVE YOU DE *DAGGER*, TOO.
GUUH!
DEN YOU GOT DE WHOLE SET.
W-WAIT! WHAT IS IT DOING?
LEBEAU WHAT IS IT--?
CHOOOOM
OH MY GOD, REMY! MY GOOD GOD!
WHAT HAVE YOU *DONE?*

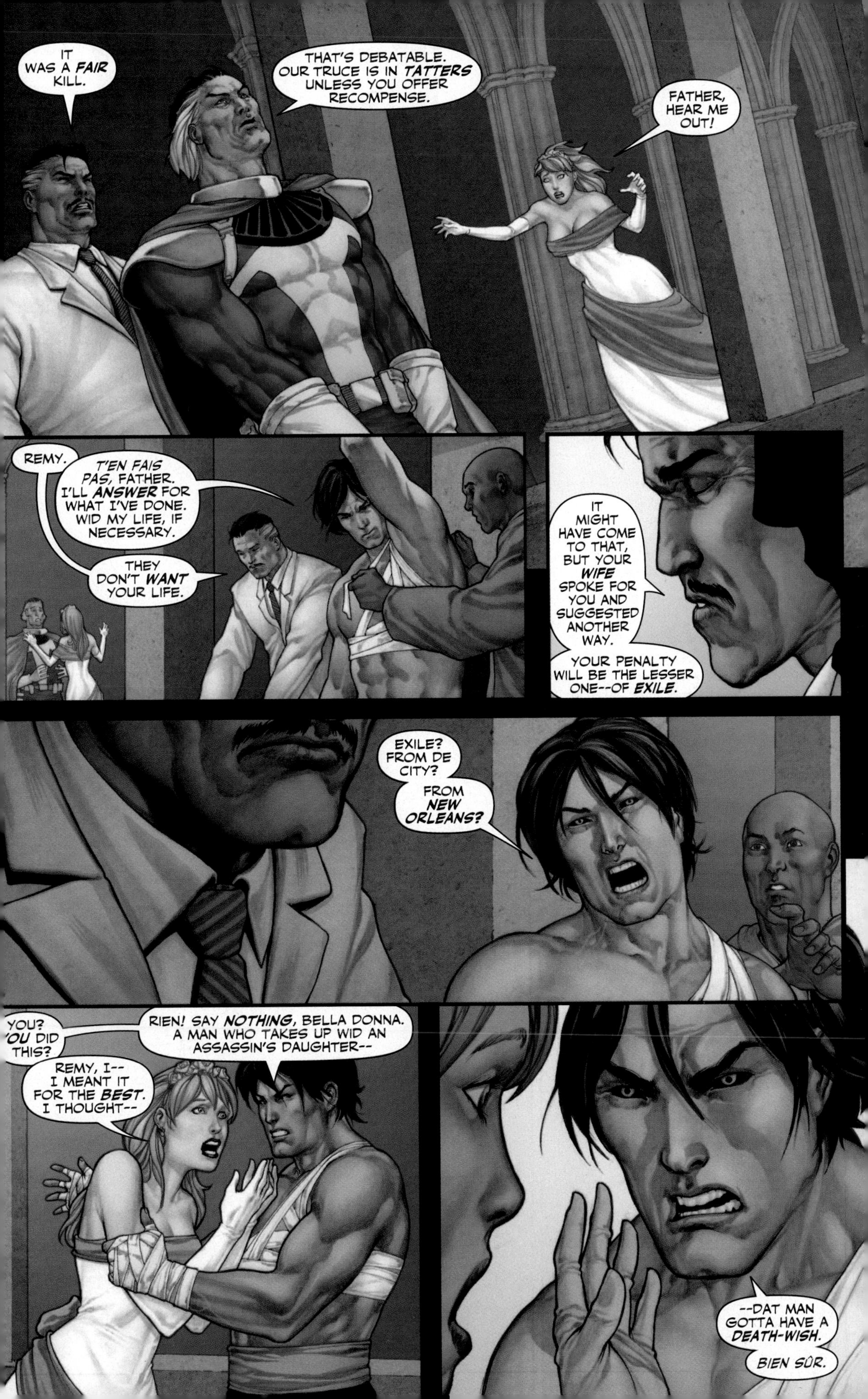
IT WAS A FAIR KILL.
THAT'S DEBATABLE. OUR TRUCE IS IN TATTERS UNLESS YOU OFFER RECOMPENSE.
FATHER, HEAR ME OUT!
REMY.
T'EN FAIS PAS, FATHER. I'LL ANSWER FOR WHAT I'VE DONE. WID MY LIFE, IF NECESSARY.
THEY DON'T WANT YOUR LIFE.
IT MIGHT HAVE COME TO THAT, BUT YOUR WIFE SPOKE FOR YOU AND SUGGESTED ANOTHER WAY.
YOUR PENALTY WILL BE THE LESSER ONE--OF EXILE.
EXILE? FROM DE CITY?
FROM NEW ORLEANS?
YOU? YOU DID THIS?
RIEN! SAY NOTHING, BELLA DONNA. A MAN WHO TAKES UP WID AN ASSASSIN'S DAUGHTER--
REMY, I-- I MEANT IT FOR THE BEST. I THOUGHT--
--DAT MAN GOTTA HAVE A DEATH-WISH.
BIEN SÛR.

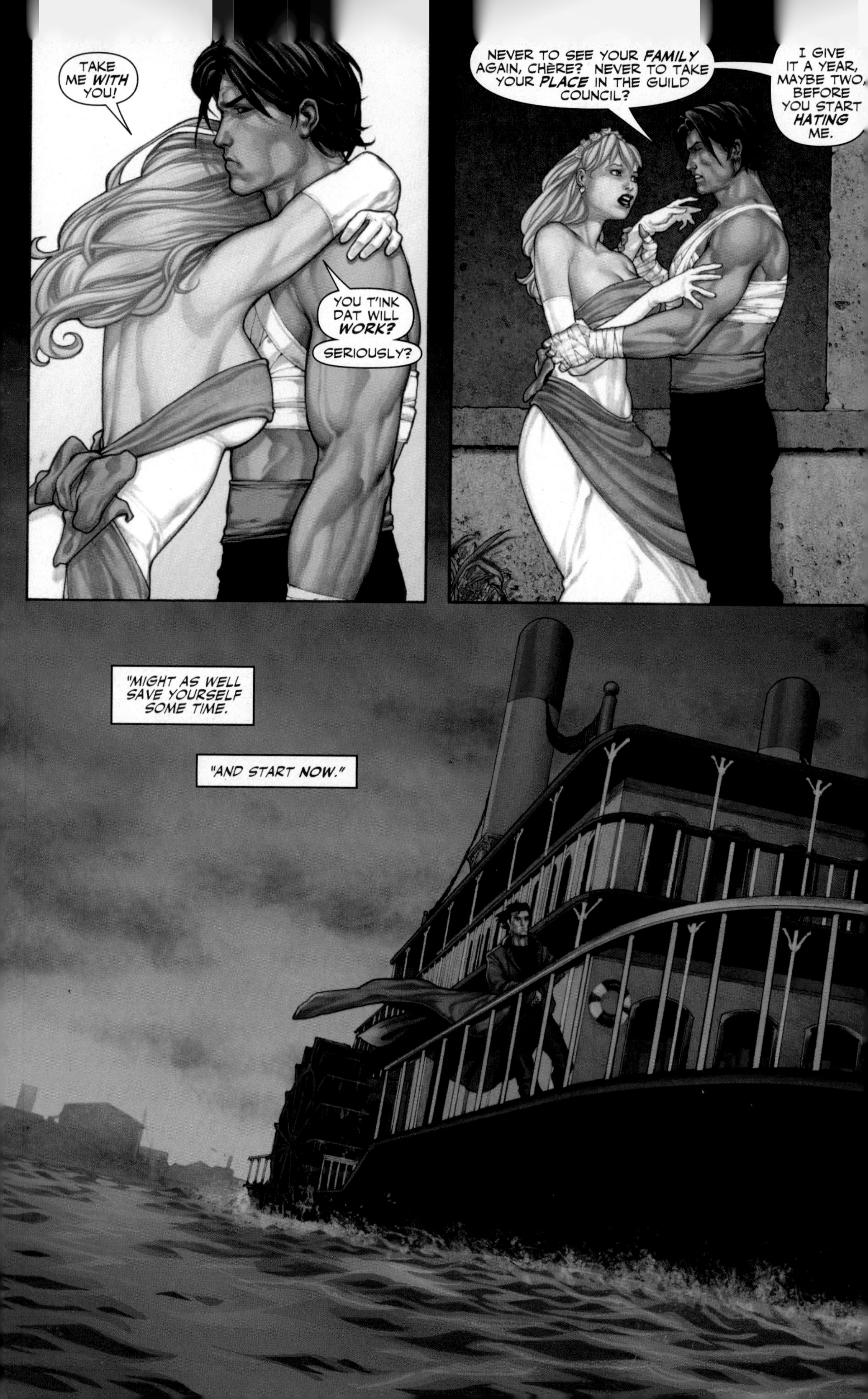
TAKE ME WITH YOU!
YOU T'INK DAT WILL WORK?
SERIOUSLY?
NEVER TO SEE YOUR FAMILY AGAIN, CHÈRE? NEVER TO TAKE YOUR PLACE IN THE GUILD COUNCIL?
I GIVE IT A YEAR, MAYBE TWO, BEFORE YOU START HATING ME.
"MIGHT AS WELL SAVE YOURSELF SOME TIME.
"AND START NOW."

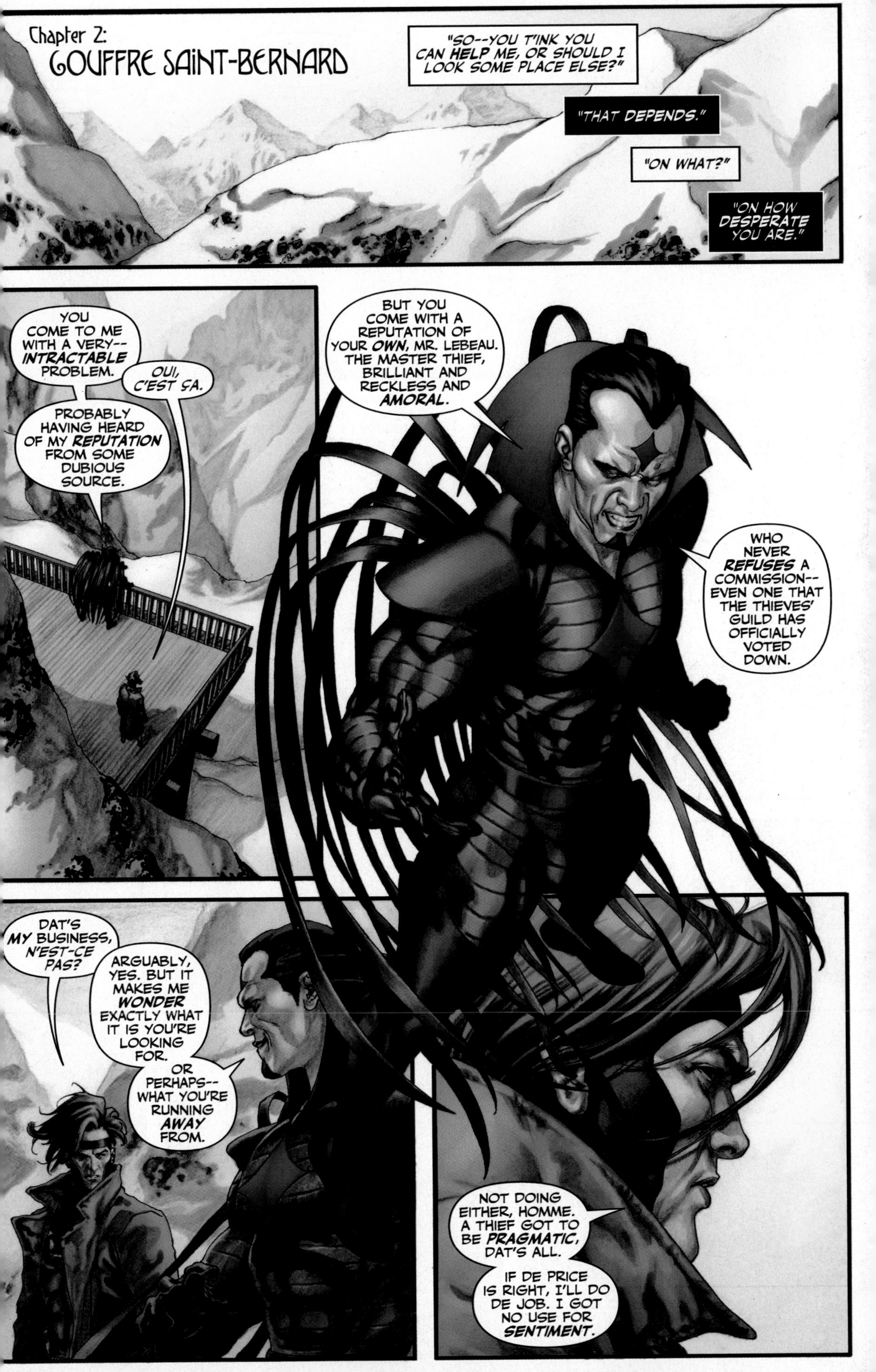
Chapter 2:
GOUFFRE SAINT-BERNARD
"SO--YOU T'INK YOU CAN HELP ME, OR SHOULD I LOOK SOME PLACE ELSE?"
"THAT DEPENDS."
"ON WHAT?"
"ON HOW DESPERATE YOU ARE."
YOU COME TO ME WITH A VERY--INTRACTABLE PROBLEM.
OUI, C'EST ÇA.
PROBABLY HAVING HEARD OF MY REPUTATION FROM SOME DUBIOUS SOURCE.
BUT YOU COME WITH A REPUTATION OF YOUR OWN, MR. LEBEAU. THE MASTER THIEF, BRILLIANT AND RECKLESS AND AMORAL.
WHO NEVER REFUSES A COMMISSION--EVEN ONE THAT THE THIEVES' GUILD HAS OFFICIALLY VOTED DOWN.
DAT'S MY BUSINESS, N'EST-CE PAS?
ARGUABLY, YES. BUT IT MAKES ME WONDER EXACTLY WHAT IT IS YOU'RE LOOKING FOR.
OR PERHAPS--WHAT YOU'RE RUNNING AWAY FROM.
NOT DOING EITHER, HOMME. A THIEF GOT TO BE PRAGMATIC, DAT'S ALL.
IF DE PRICE IS RIGHT, I'LL DO DE JOB. I GOT NO USE FOR SENTIMENT.

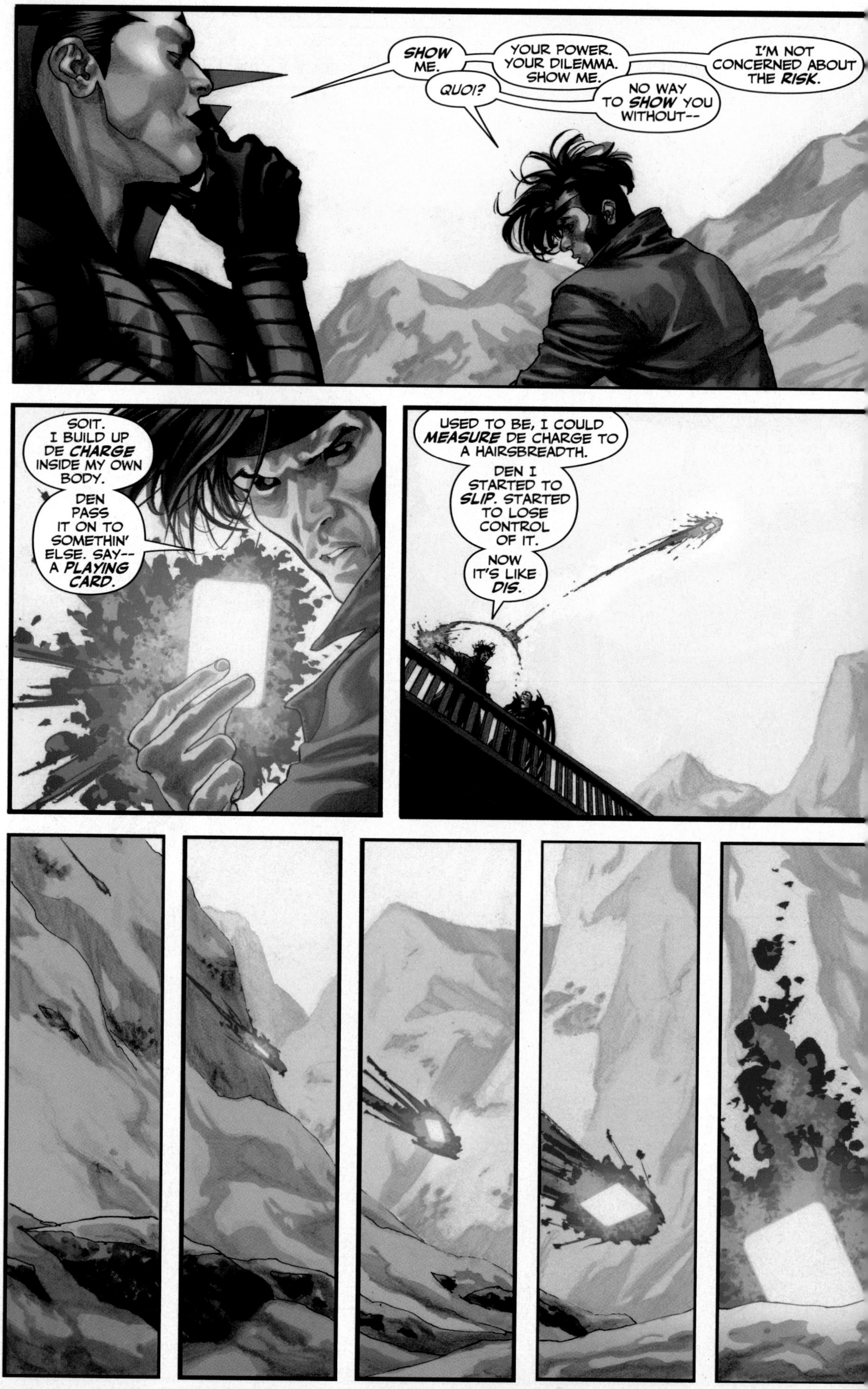
SHOW ME.
QUOI?
YOUR POWER. YOUR DILEMMA. SHOW ME.
NO WAY TO SHOW YOU WITHOUT--
I'M NOT CONCERNED ABOUT THE RISK.
SOIT. I BUILD UP DE CHARGE INSIDE MY OWN BODY.
DEN PASS IT ON TO SOMETHIN' ELSE. SAY-- A PLAYING CARD.
USED TO BE, I COULD MEASURE DE CHARGE TO A HAIRSBREADTH.
DEN I STARTED TO SLIP. STARTED TO LOSE CONTROL OF IT.
NOW IT'S LIKE DIS.

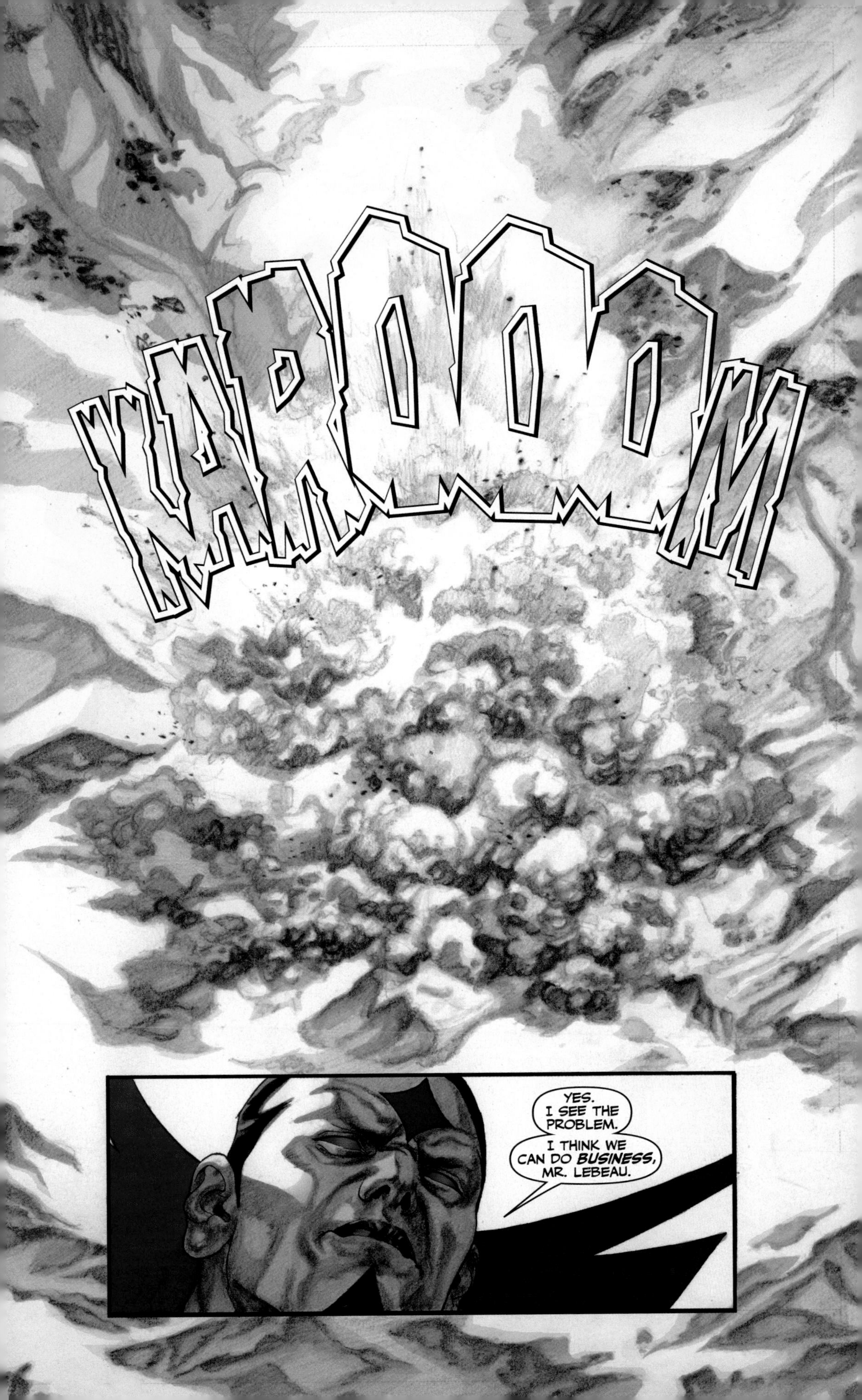
KAROOOOM
YES. I SEE THE PROBLEM.
I THINK WE CAN DO BUSINESS, MR. LEBEAU.

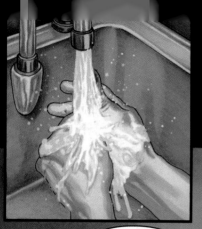

YOU EVER HEAR OF *ANAESTHETIC*, ESSEX?

IT HAS ITS *USES*. BUT I NEED YOU AWAKE AND AWARE FOR THIS.

CEREBRAL *FEEDBACK* WILL ENABLE ME TO LOCATE THE PART OF YOUR BRAIN THAT CONTROLS YOUR *POWER*.

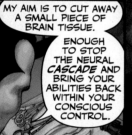

MY AIM IS TO CUT AWAY A SMALL PIECE OF BRAIN TISSUE.

ENOUGH TO STOP THE NEURAL *CASCADE* AND BRING YOUR ABILITIES BACK WITHIN YOUR CONSCIOUS CONTROL.

AND I'LL--I'LL STILL BE *ME*, WHEN YOU'VE FINISHED?

DERE'LL BE NO *DAMAGE*?

OF COURSE NOT. I NEED YOU *INTACT*, LEBEAU--

--SO THAT YOU CAN KEEP *YOUR* SIDE OF THE BARGAIN.

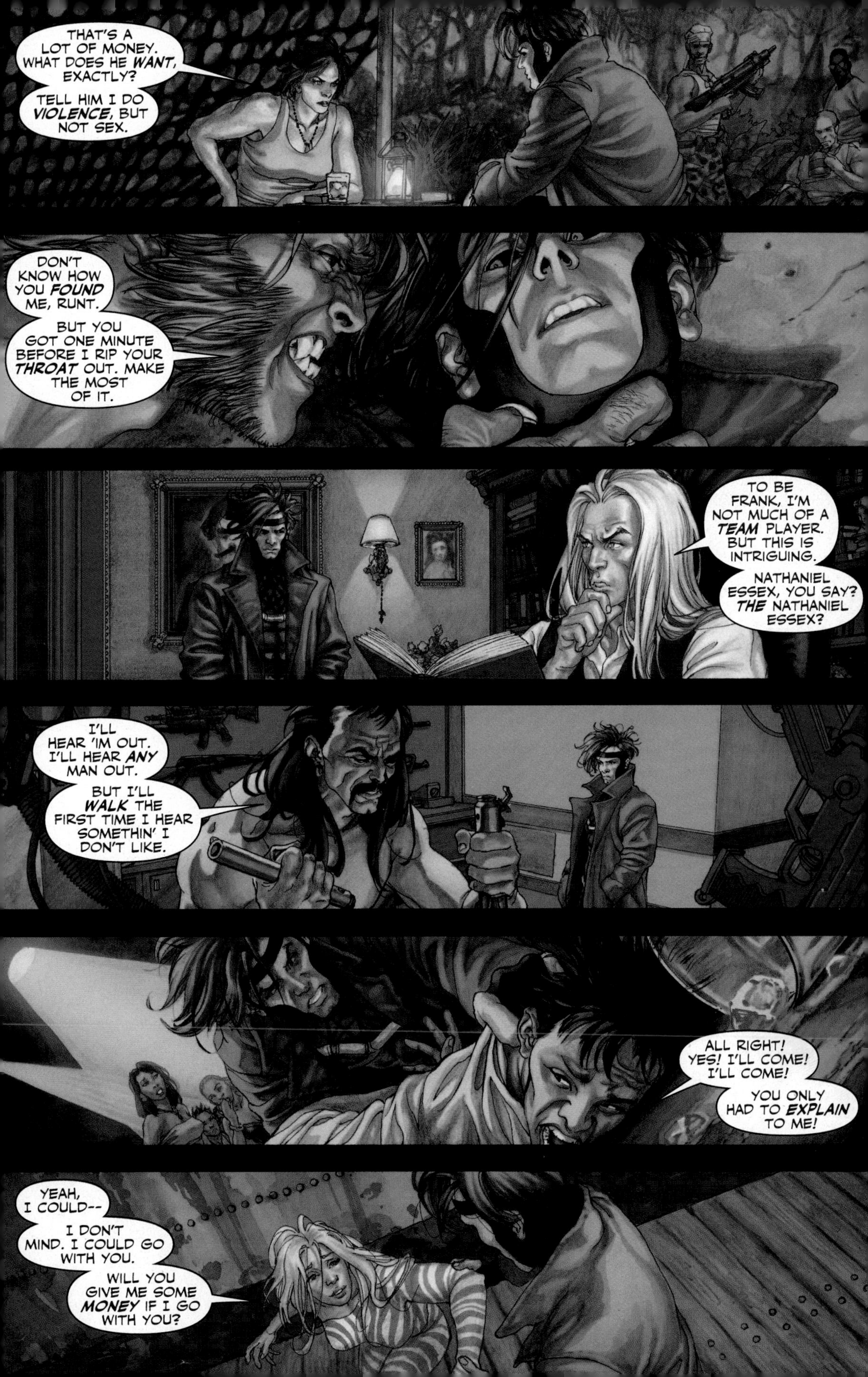
THAT'S A LOT OF MONEY. WHAT DOES HE WANT, EXACTLY?
TELL HIM I DO VIOLENCE, BUT NOT SEX.
DON'T KNOW HOW YOU FOUND ME, RUNT.
BUT YOU GOT ONE MINUTE BEFORE I RIP YOUR THROAT OUT. MAKE THE MOST OF IT.
TO BE FRANK, I'M NOT MUCH OF A TEAM PLAYER. BUT THIS IS INTRIGUING.
NATHANIEL ESSEX, YOU SAY? THE NATHANIEL ESSEX?
I'LL HEAR 'IM OUT. I'LL HEAR ANY MAN OUT.
BUT I'LL WALK THE FIRST TIME I HEAR SOMETHIN' I DON'T LIKE.
ALL RIGHT! YES! I'LL COME! I'LL COME!
YOU ONLY HAD TO EXPLAIN TO ME!
YEAH, I COULD--
I DON'T MIND. I COULD GO WITH YOU.
WILL YOU GIVE ME SOME MONEY IF I GO WITH YOU?

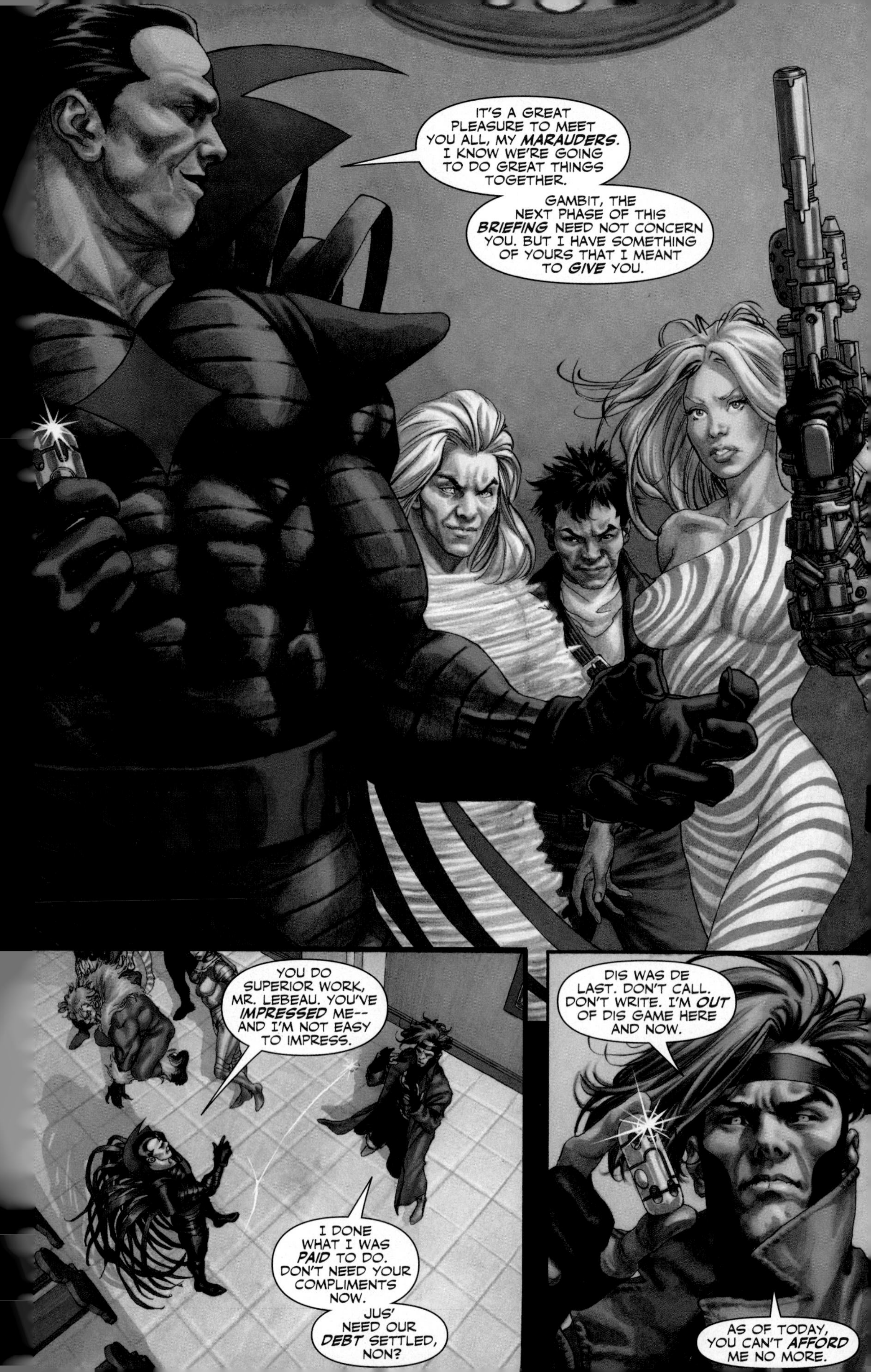
IT'S A GREAT PLEASURE TO MEET YOU ALL, MY MARAUDERS. I KNOW WE'RE GOING TO DO GREAT THINGS TOGETHER.
GAMBIT, THE NEXT PHASE OF THIS BRIEFING NEED NOT CONCERN YOU. BUT I HAVE SOMETHING OF YOURS THAT I MEANT TO GIVE YOU.
YOU DO SUPERIOR WORK, MR. LEBEAU. YOU'VE IMPRESSED ME-- AND I'M NOT EASY TO IMPRESS.
I DONE WHAT I WAS PAID TO DO. DON'T NEED YOUR COMPLIMENTS NOW.
JUS' NEED OUR DEBT SETTLED, NON?
DIS WAS DE LAST. DON'T CALL. DON'T WRITE. I'M OUT OF DIS GAME HERE AND NOW.
AS OF TODAY, YOU CAN'T AFFORD ME NO MORE.

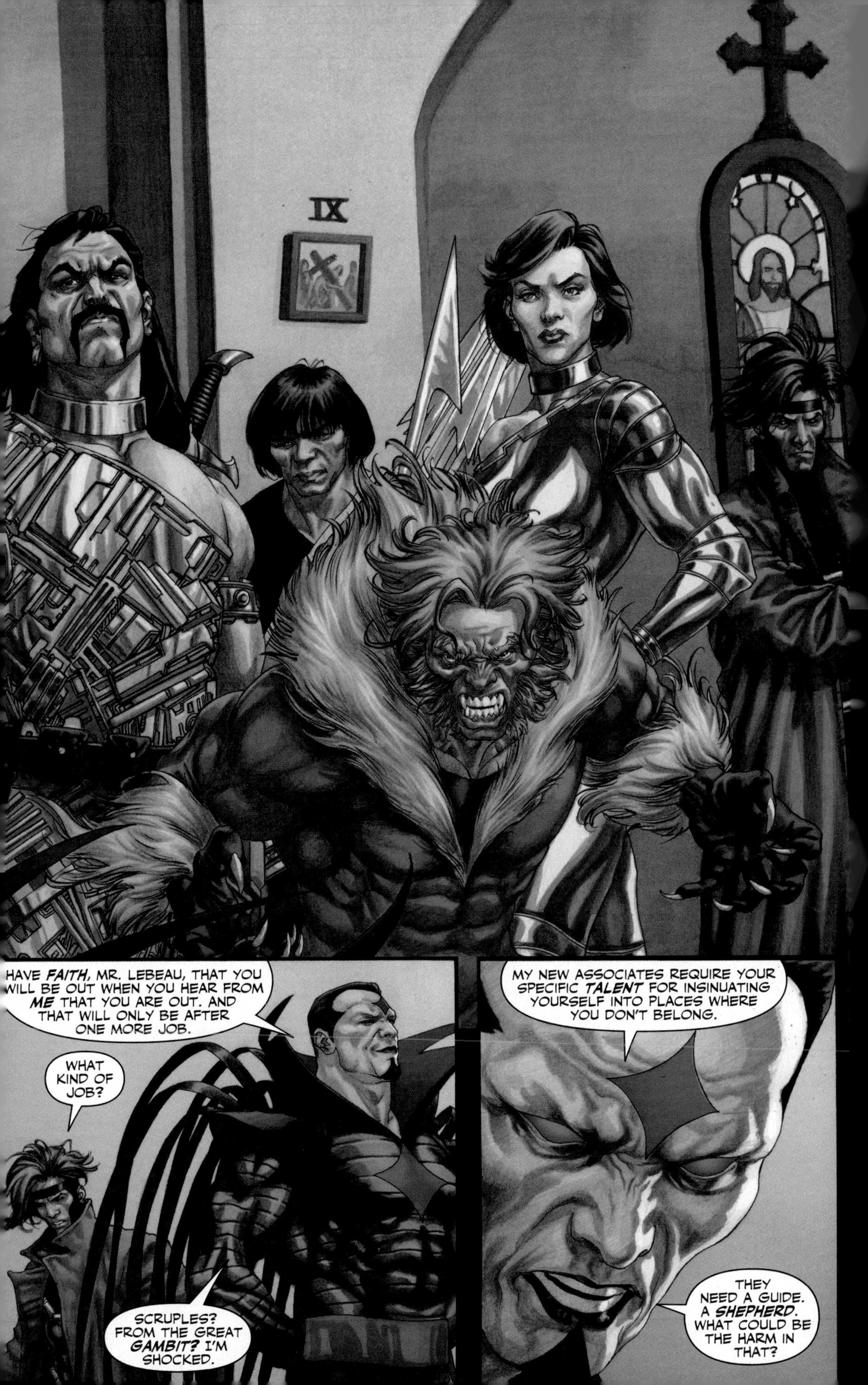
HAVE FAITH, MR. LEBEAU, THAT YOU WILL BE OUT WHEN YOU HEAR FROM ME THAT YOU ARE OUT. AND THAT WILL ONLY BE AFTER ONE MORE JOB.
WHAT KIND OF JOB?
SCRUPLES? FROM THE GREAT GAMBIT? I'M SHOCKED.
MY NEW ASSOCIATES REQUIRE YOUR SPECIFIC TALENT FOR INSINUATING YOURSELF INTO PLACES WHERE YOU DON'T BELONG.
THEY NEED A GUIDE. A SHEPHERD. WHAT COULD BE THE HARM IN THAT?

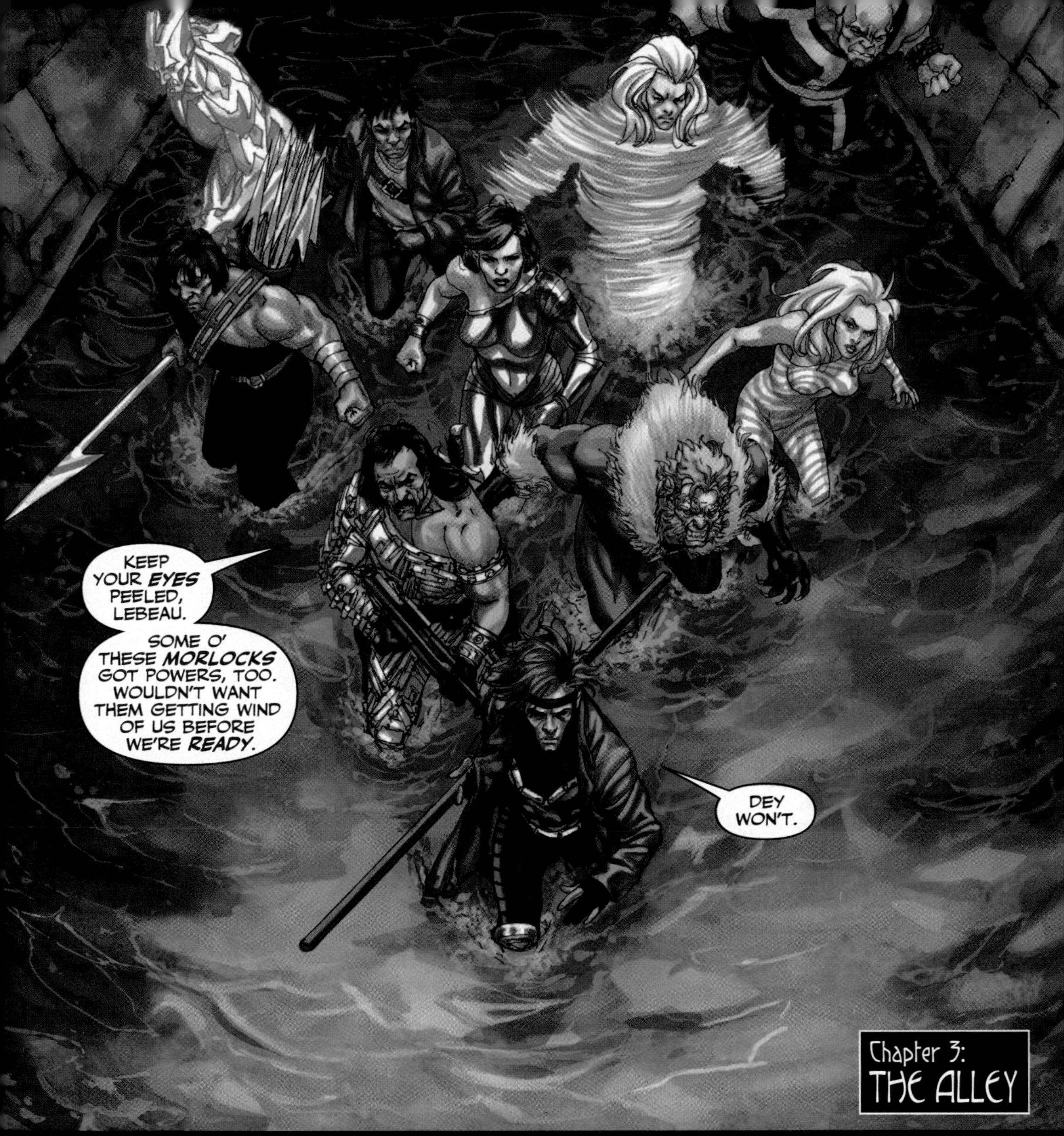
KEEP YOUR EYES PEELED, LEBEAU.
SOME O' THESE MORLOCKS GOT POWERS, TOO. WOULDN'T WANT THEM GETTING WIND OF US BEFORE WE'RE READY.
DEY WON'T.
Chapter 3: THE ALLEY

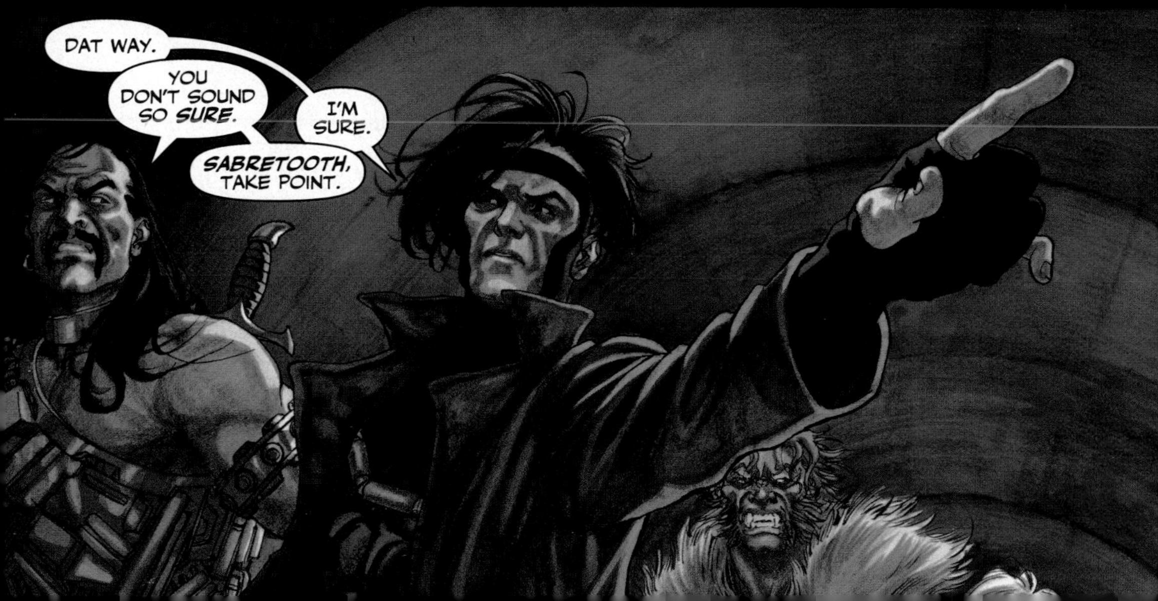
DAT WAY.
YOU DON'T SOUND SO SURE.
I'M SURE.
SABRETOOTH, TAKE POINT.

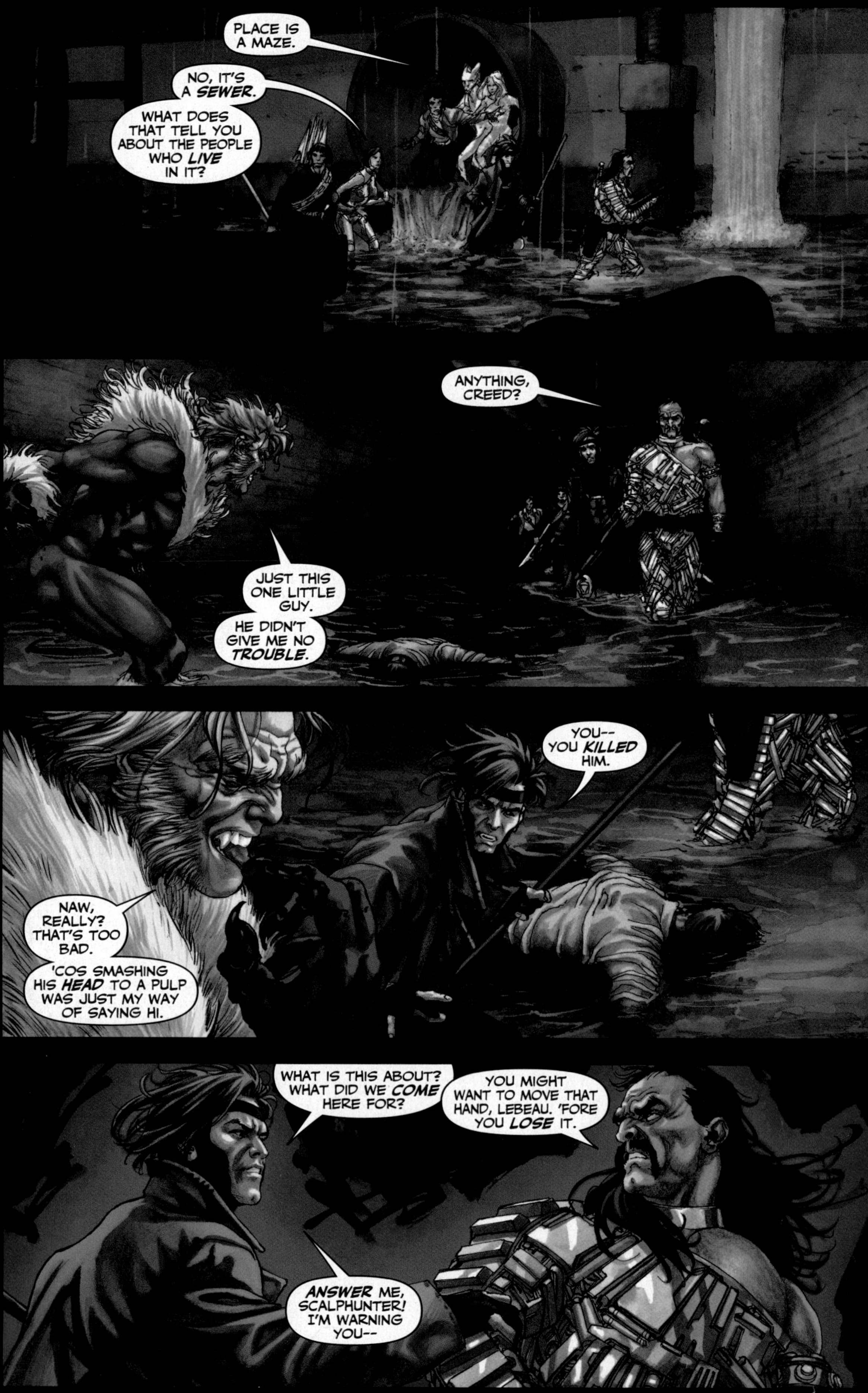
PLACE IS A MAZE.
NO, IT'S A SEWER.
WHAT DOES THAT TELL YOU ABOUT THE PEOPLE WHO LIVE IN IT?
ANYTHING, CREED?
JUST THIS ONE LITTLE GUY.
HE DIDN'T GIVE ME NO TROUBLE.
YOU-- YOU KILLED HIM.
NAW, REALLY? THAT'S TOO BAD.
'COS SMASHING HIS HEAD TO A PULP WAS JUST MY WAY OF SAYING HI.
WHAT IS THIS ABOUT? WHAT DID WE COME HERE FOR?
YOU MIGHT WANT TO MOVE THAT HAND, LEBEAU. 'FORE YOU LOSE IT.
ANSWER ME, SCALPHUNTER! I'M WARNING YOU--

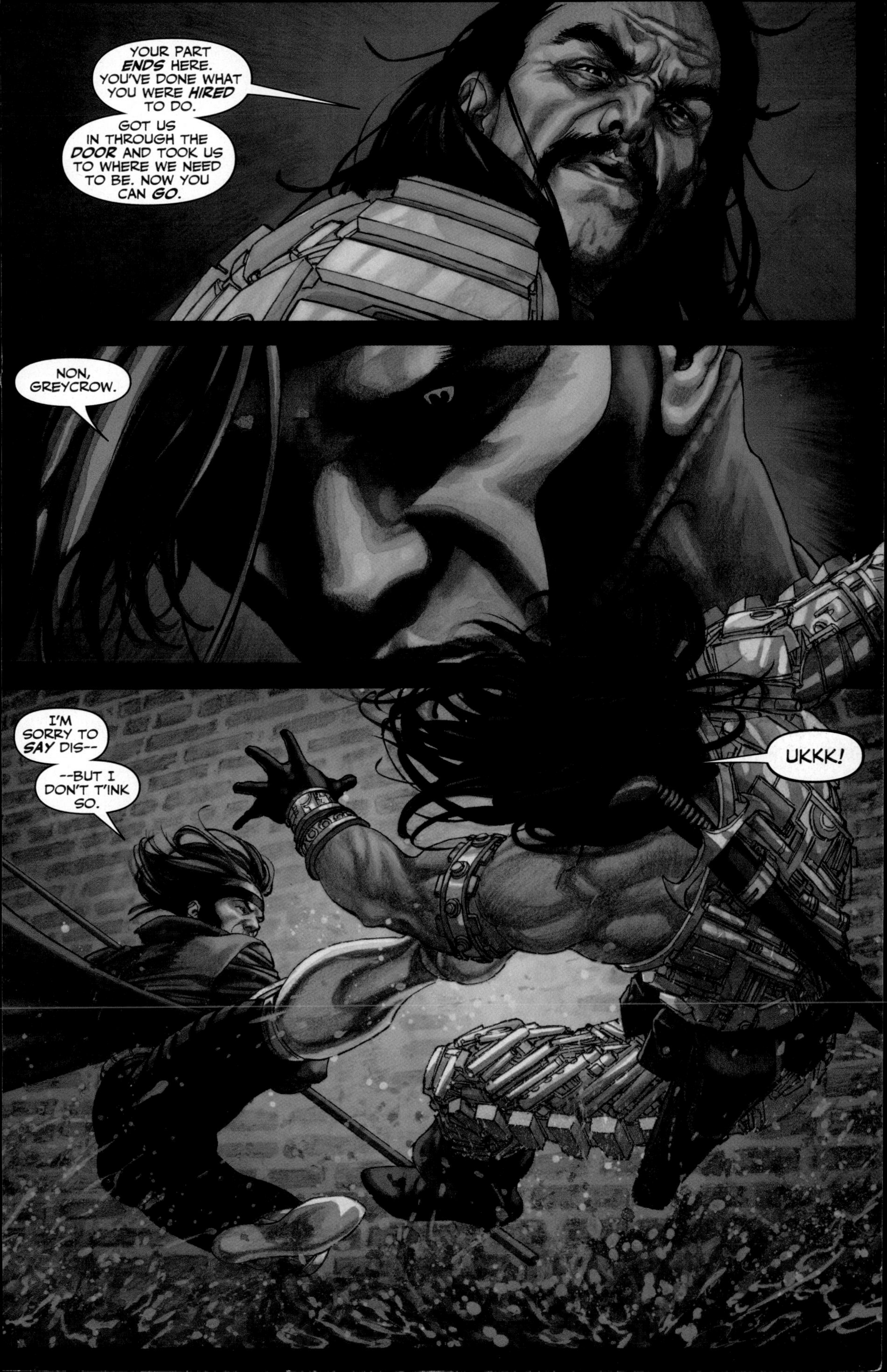
YOUR PART ENDS HERE. YOU'VE DONE WHAT YOU WERE HIRED TO DO.
GOT US IN THROUGH THE DOOR AND TOOK US TO WHERE WE NEED TO BE. NOW YOU CAN GO.
NON, GREYCROW.
I'M SORRY TO SAY DIS--
--BUT I DON'T T'INK SO.
UKKK!

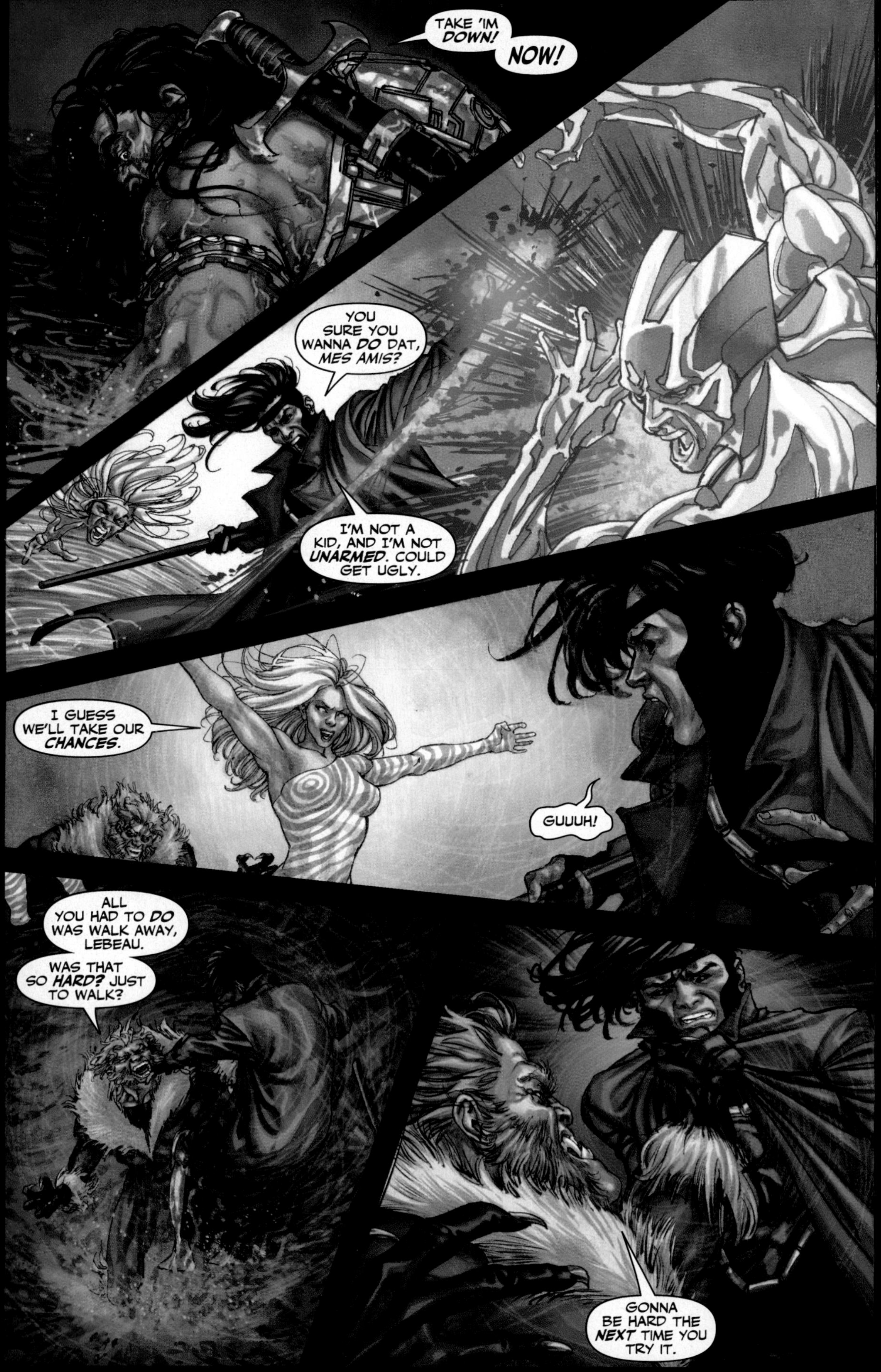
TAKE 'IM DOWN! NOW!
YOU SURE YOU WANNA DO DAT, MES AMIS?
I'M NOT A KID, AND I'M NOT UNARMED. COULD GET UGLY.
I GUESS WE'LL TAKE OUR CHANCES.
GUUUH!
ALL YOU HAD TO DO WAS WALK AWAY, LEBEAU.
WAS THAT SO HARD? JUST TO WALK?
GONNA BE HARD THE NEXT TIME YOU TRY IT.

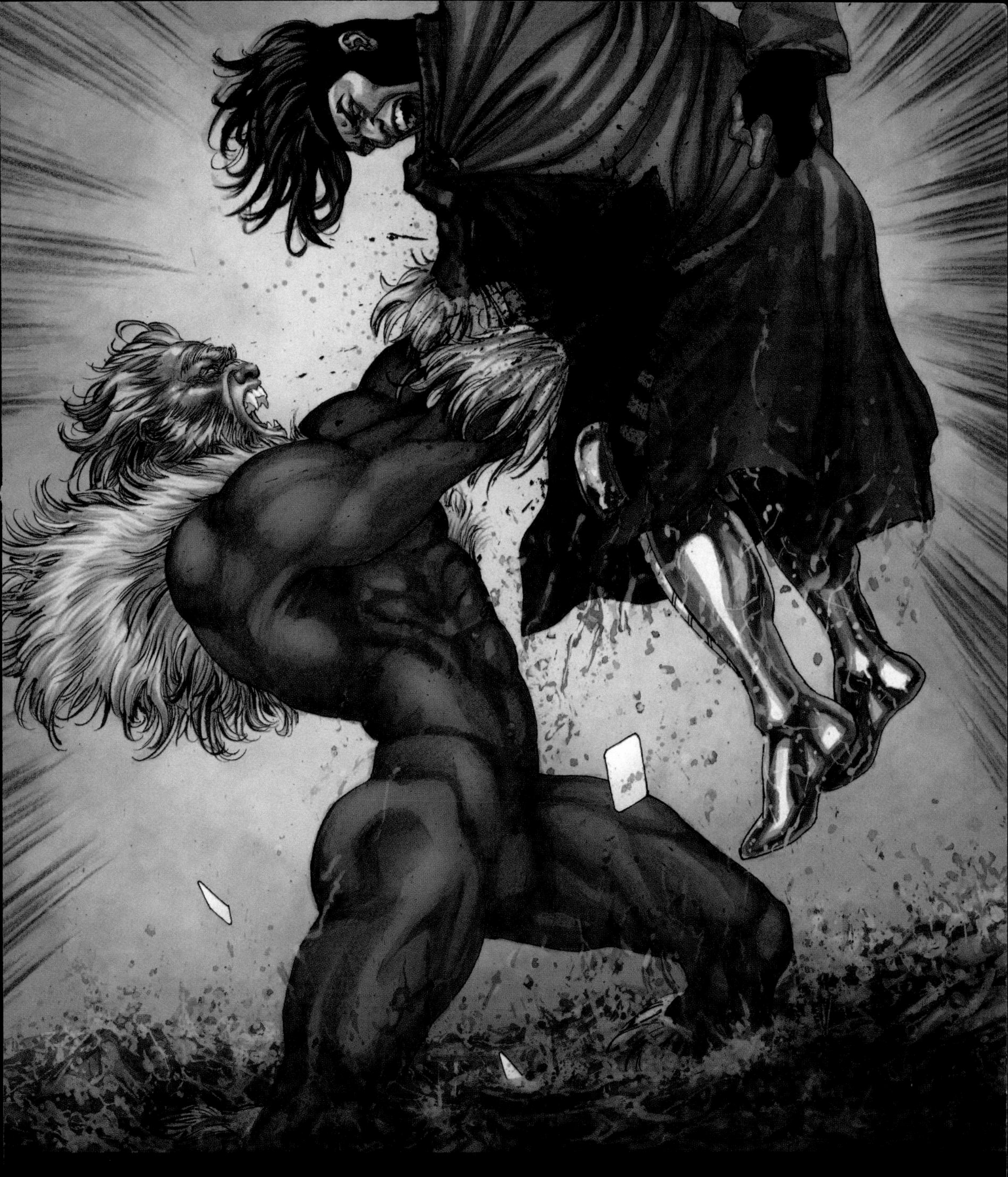

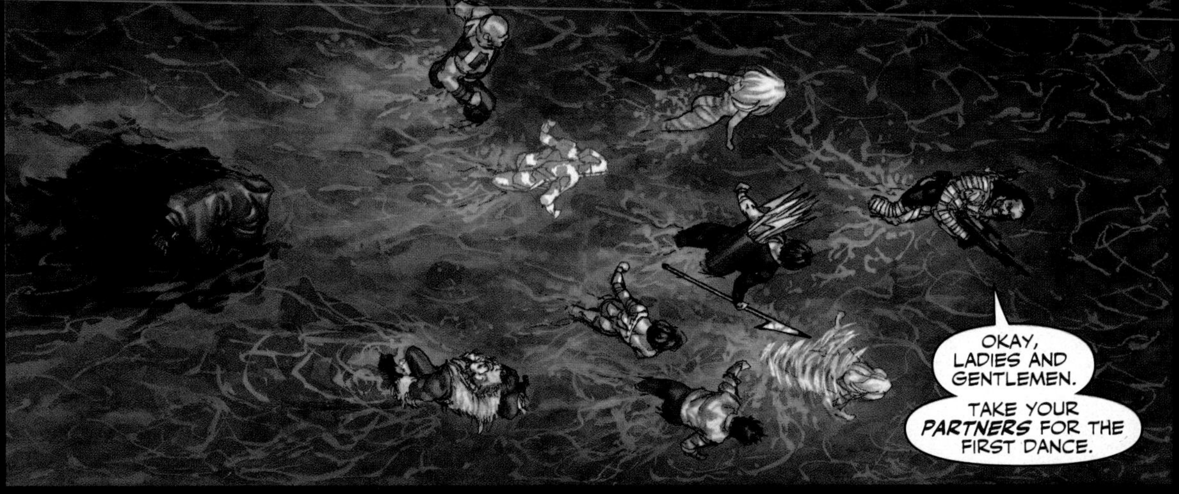
OKAY, LADIES AND GENTLEMEN.
TAKE YOUR PARTNERS FOR THE FIRST DANCE.

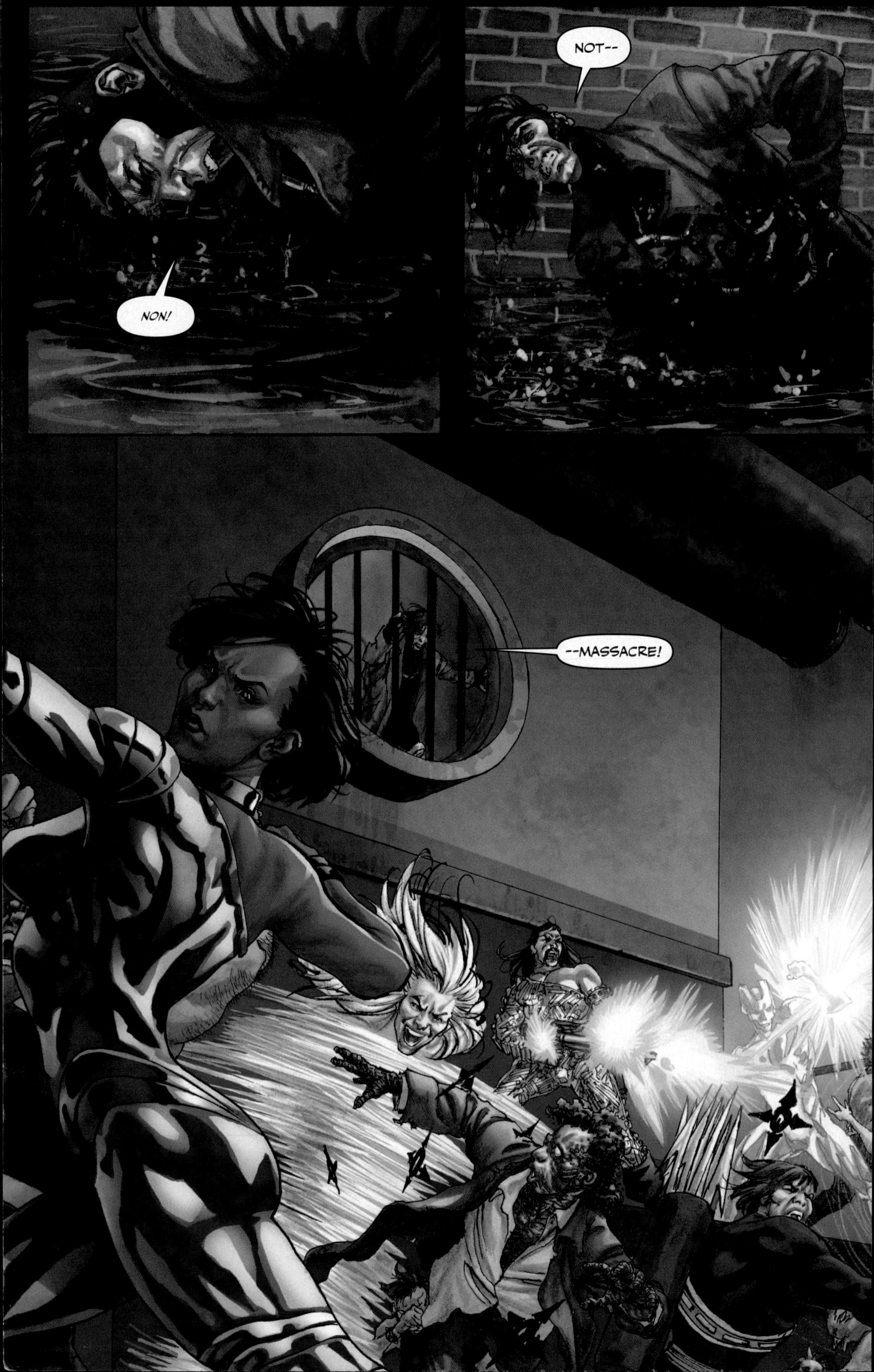
NON!
NOT--
--MASSACRE!

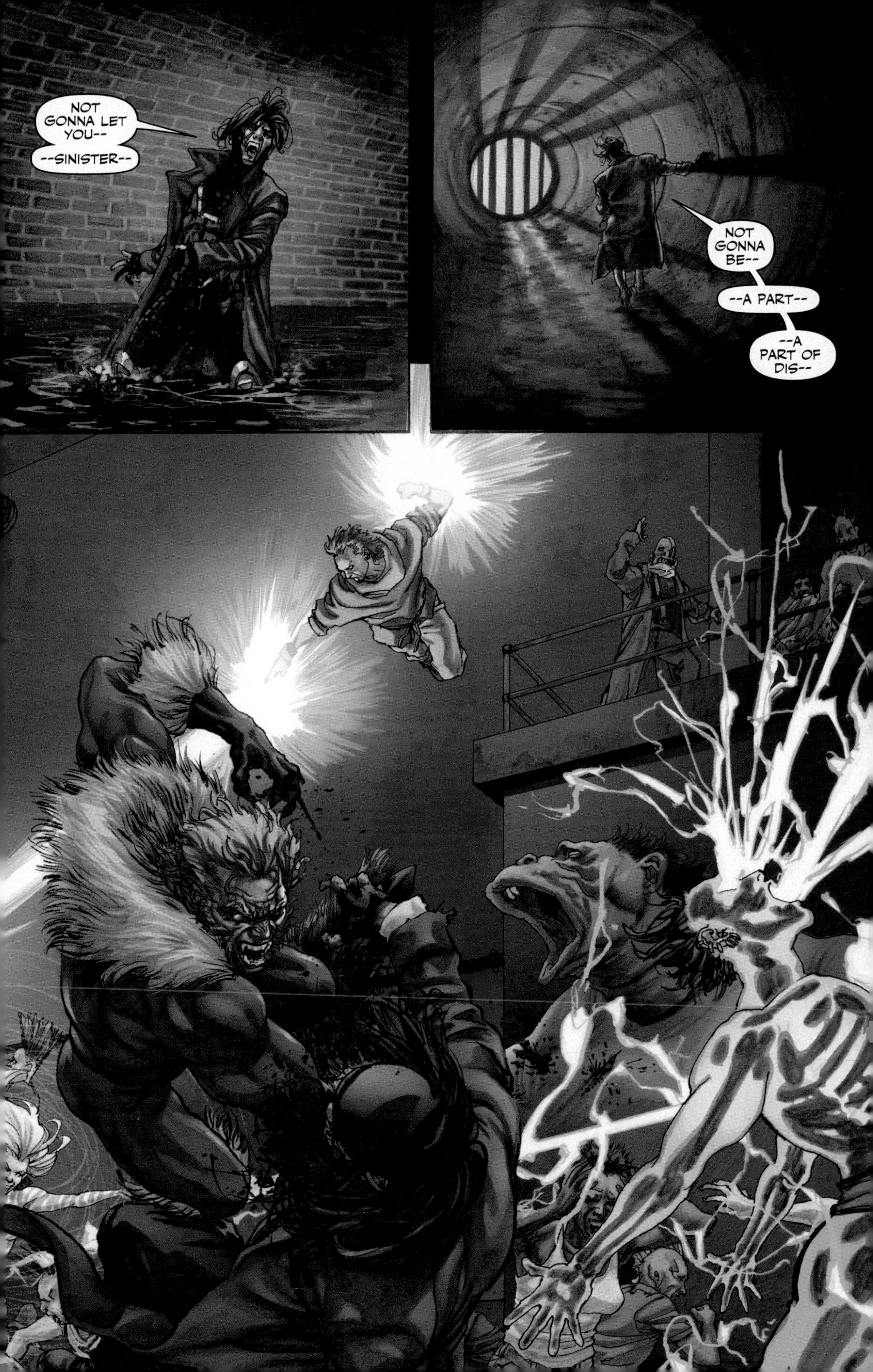
NOT GONNA LET YOU--
--SINISTER--
NOT GONNA BE--
--A PART--
--A PART OF DIS--

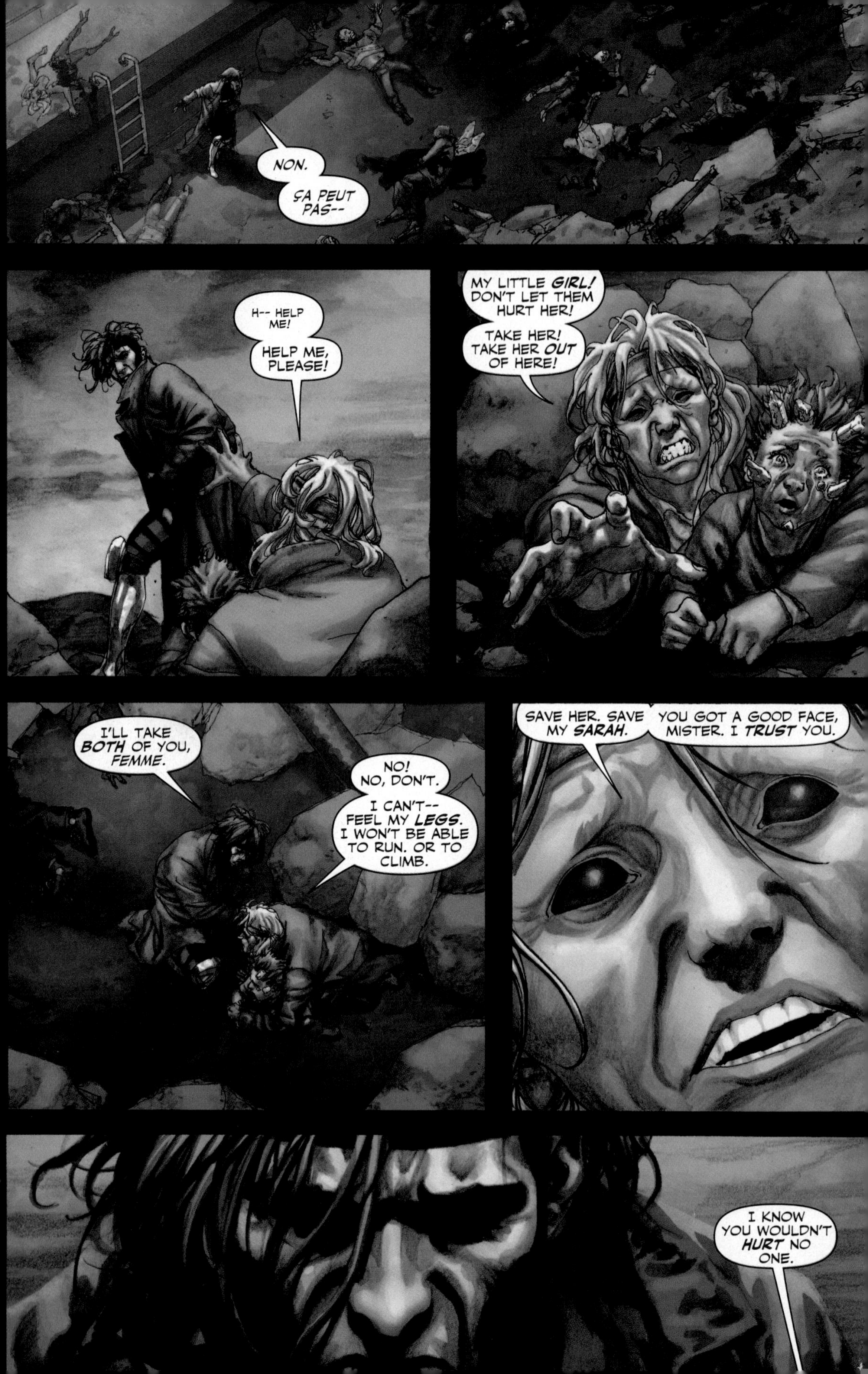
NON.
ÇA PEUT PAS--
H-- HELP ME!
HELP ME, PLEASE!
MY LITTLE GIRL! DON'T LET THEM HURT HER!
TAKE HER! TAKE HER OUT OF HERE!
I'LL TAKE BOTH OF YOU, FEMME.
NO! NO, DON'T.
I CAN'T-- FEEL MY LEGS. I WON'T BE ABLE TO RUN. OR TO CLIMB.
SAVE HER. SAVE MY SARAH.
YOU GOT A GOOD FACE, MISTER. I TRUST YOU.
I KNOW YOU WOULDN'T HURT NO ONE.

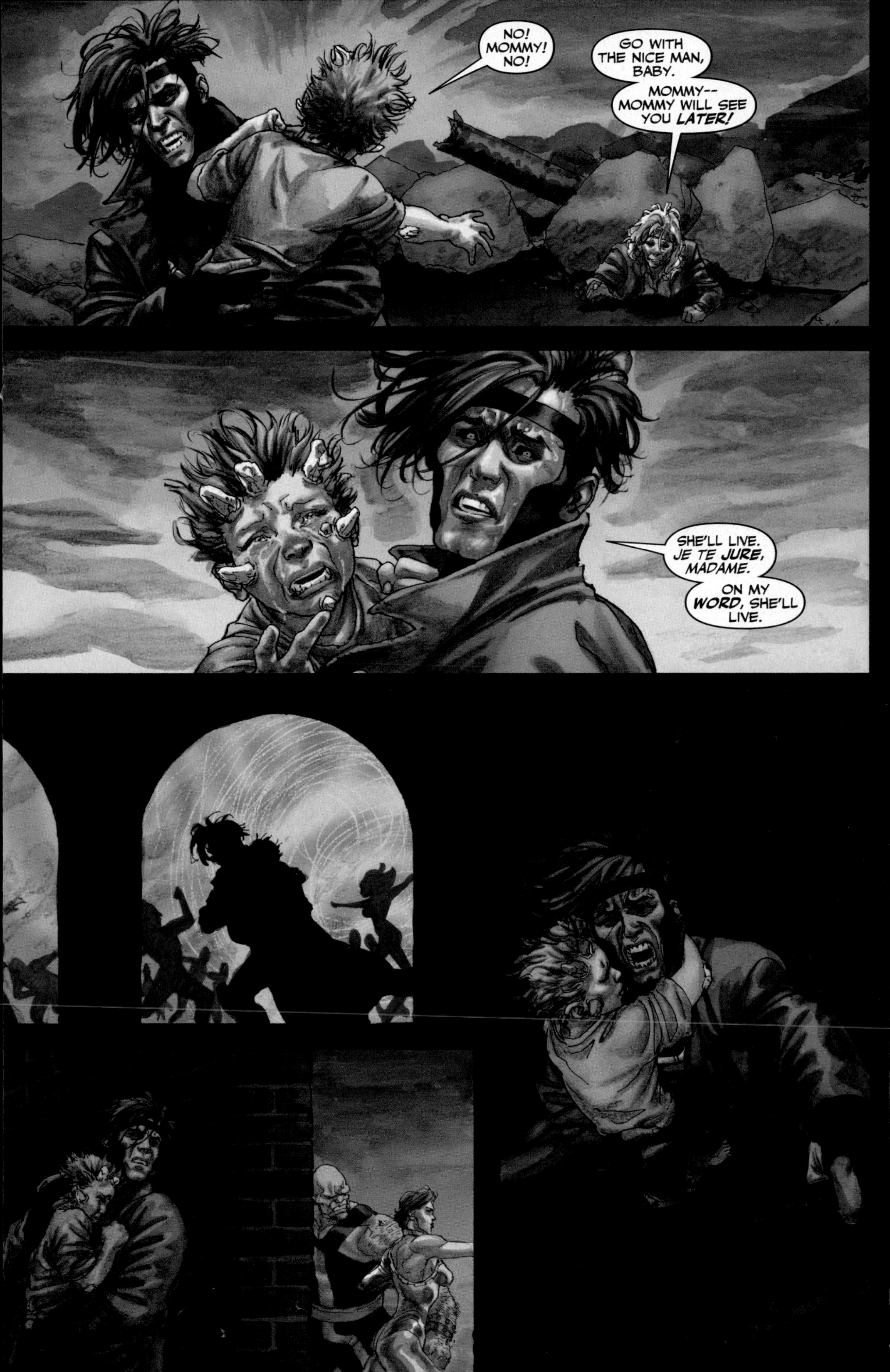
NO! MOMMY! NO!
GO WITH THE NICE MAN, BABY.
MOMMY-- MOMMY WILL SEE YOU LATER!
SHE'LL LIVE. JE TE JURE, MADAME.
ON MY WORD, SHE'LL LIVE.

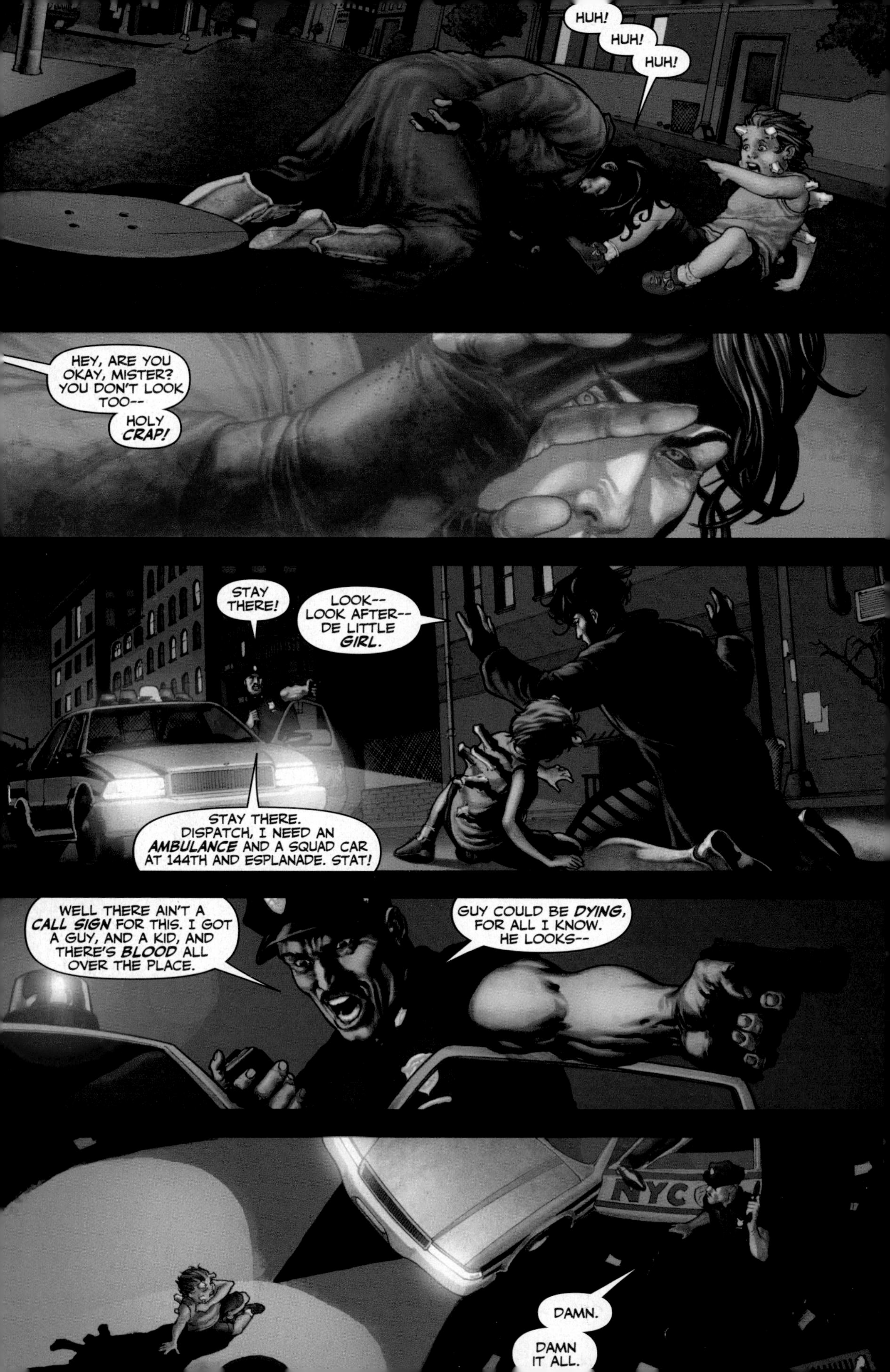
HUH!
HUH!
HUH!
HEY, ARE YOU OKAY, MISTER? YOU DON'T LOOK TOO--
HOLY CRAP!
STAY THERE!
LOOK-- LOOK AFTER-- DE LITTLE GIRL.
STAY THERE. DISPATCH, I NEED AN AMBULANCE AND A SQUAD CAR AT 144TH AND ESPLANADE. STAT!
WELL THERE AIN'T A CALL SIGN FOR THIS. I GOT A GUY, AND A KID, AND THERE'S BLOOD ALL OVER THE PLACE.
GUY COULD BE DYING, FOR ALL I KNOW. HE LOOKS--
NYC
DAMN.
DAMN IT ALL.

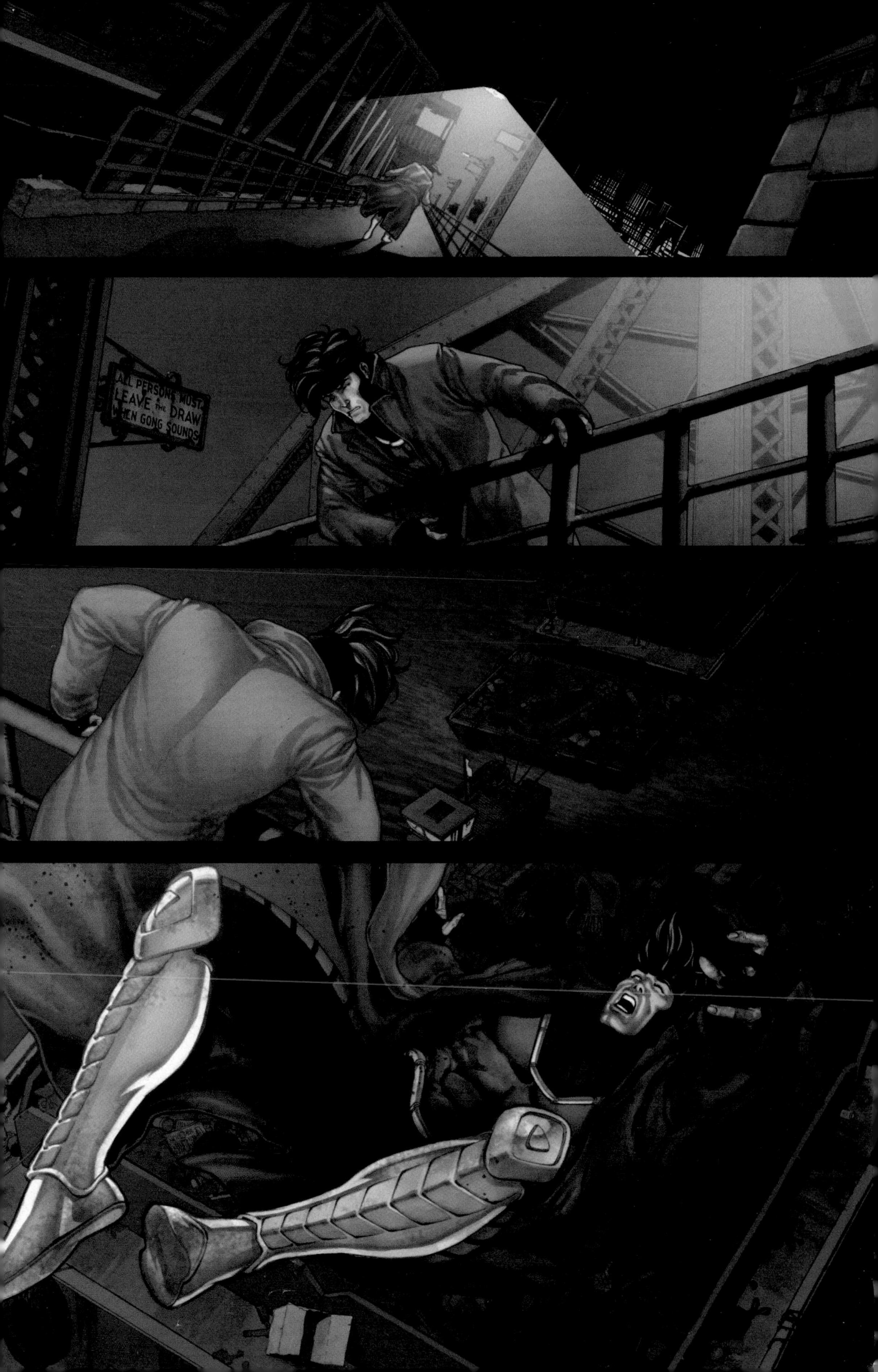
ALL PERSONS MUST
LEAVE THE DRAW
WHEN GONG SOUNDS

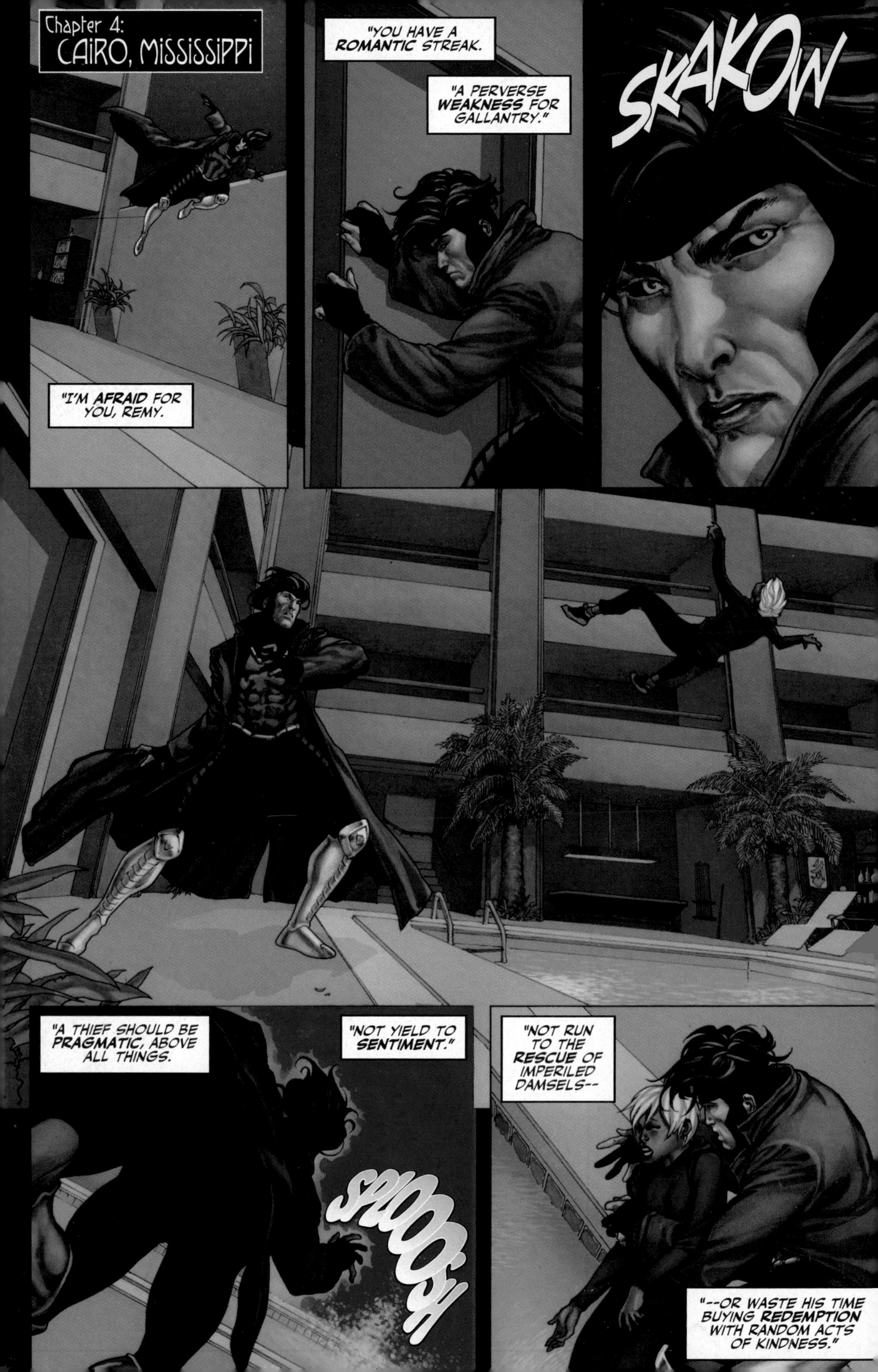
Chapter 4:
CAIRO, MISSISSIPPI
"I'M AFRAID FOR YOU, REMY.
"YOU HAVE A ROMANTIC STREAK.
"A PERVERSE WEAKNESS FOR GALLANTRY."
SKAKOW
"A THIEF SHOULD BE PRAGMATIC, ABOVE ALL THINGS.
"NOT YIELD TO SENTIMENT."
SPLOOOSH
"NOT RUN TO THE RESCUE OF IMPERILED DAMSELS--
"--OR WASTE HIS TIME BUYING REDEMPTION WITH RANDOM ACTS OF KINDNESS."

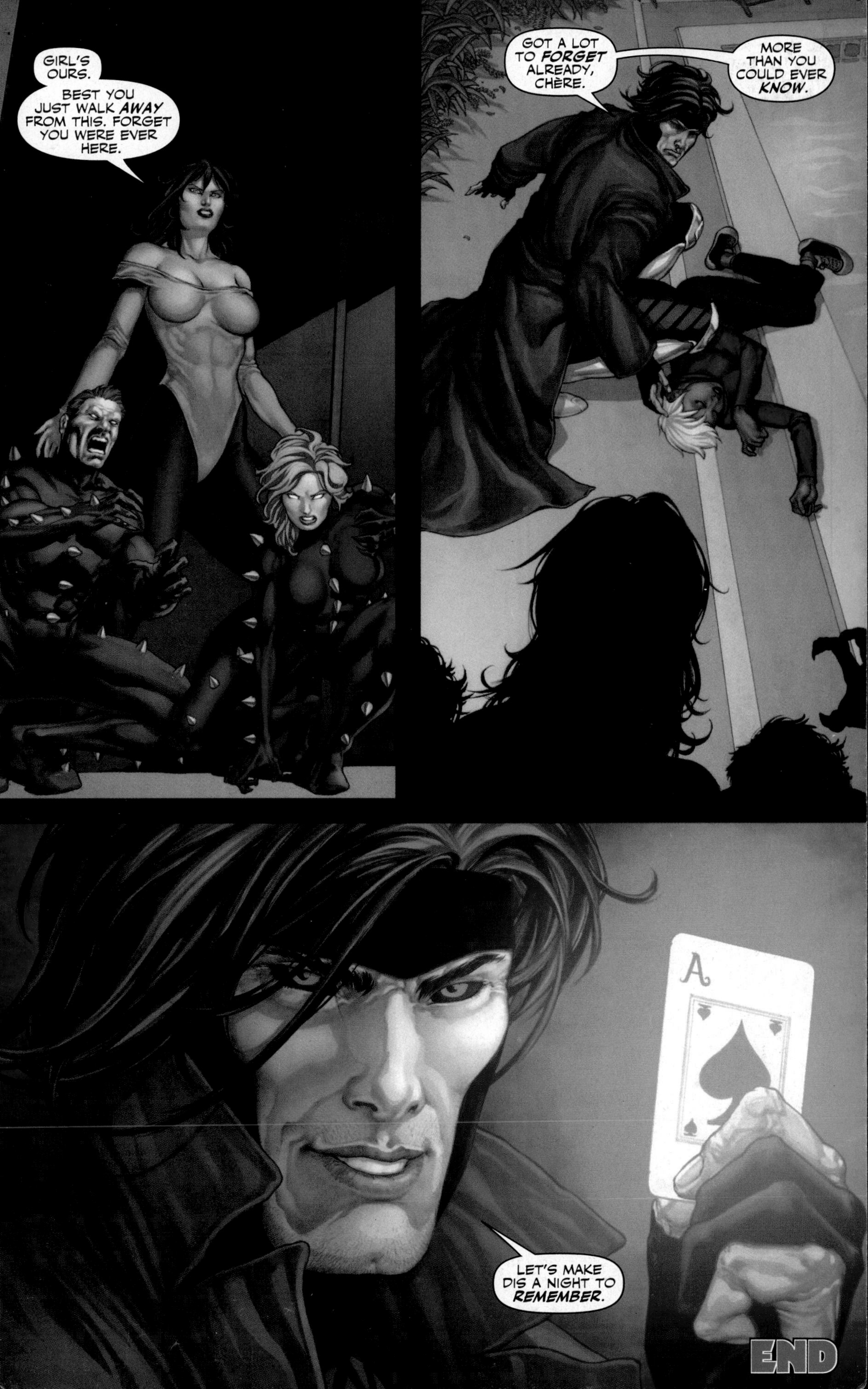
GIRL'S OURS.
BEST YOU JUST WALK AWAY FROM THIS. FORGET YOU WERE EVER HERE.
GOT A LOT TO FORGET ALREADY, CHÈRE.
MORE THAN YOU COULD EVER KNOW.
LET'S MAKE DIS A NIGHT TO REMEMBER.
END